A HISTORY OF
THE WORLD
WITH THE WOMEN
PUT BACK IN

KERSTIN LÜCKER AND UTE DAENSCHEL

TRANSLATED BY RUTH AHMEDZAI KEMP AND JESSICA WEST

The
History
Press

Supported using public funding by
ARTS COUNCIL
ENGLAND

This book has been selected to receive financial assistance from English PEN's 'PEN Translates' programme, supported by Arts Council England. English PEN exists to promote literature and our understanding of it, to uphold writers' freedoms around the world, to campaign against the persecution and imprisonment of writers for stating their views, and to promote the friendly co-operation of writers and the free exchange of ideas. www.englishpen.org

The translation of this work was supported by a grant given by the Goethe-Institut London.

Originally published in German as *Weltgeschichte für junge Leserinnen* by Kein & Aber AG Zürich – Berlin, 2017

This English language edition first published by The History Press, 2019

The History Press
97 St George's Place, Cheltenham
Gloucestershire, GL50 3QB
www.thehistorypress.co.uk

British Library Cataloguing in Publication Data.
A catalogue record for this book is available from the British Library.

ISBN 978 0 7509 8909 1

Typesetting and origination by The History Press
Printed in Turkey by Imak

CONTENTS

CONTENTS

PREFACE

This book was originally intended for young readers. Over time, the focus has changed. More and more adults showed an interest, and it became clear that the book was no longer just addressing younger readers but everyone – male and female, young and old. It has been gratifying that the book has attracted so much interest. However, our adult readers may notice that, in addressing our original target audience, we placed less focus on two key issues that are central to understanding the relationship between men and women: violence and sexuality.

He who holds unchecked power can treat others as he wishes. He can use violence and torture. He can make mistakes and even commit crimes, and then place the blame on others. Very often throughout history, women have not only suffered violence, but have also been blamed for being victims. Many times, they have been accused of goading men into committing violence against them, yet nobody has thought to ask themselves why a woman would choose to do this of her own free will.

Over the course of history, people have accepted and adapted to tremendous change and innovation, be it space exploration or the inventions of railways, cars, planes and smartphones. But the idea that everyone benefits from equal rights for men and women, and from a society based on the dignity and equality of all its members? This is a concept that has taken a very long time to gain acceptance – even though it's been around for several thousand years.

Over the centuries, history has seen unimaginable atrocities and violence against all genders. And yet violence against women has a special quality: it is an injustice that, for a very long time, wasn't seen as wrong. For years, many countries' laws stated that men were entitled to beat their wives.

It could seem like we're downplaying the suffering involved if we simply write that, throughout history, women have had to serve men, be silent and obedient, and put up with all kinds of injustices being committed against them. And yet we didn't want that to be our sole focus; there are other aspects to world history too. We didn't want to limit ourselves to horrific descriptions of horrific situations. Because although history is full of violence, it is also full of occasions where people have successfully overcome violence and embraced values such as equality and the dignity of all people.

'... History, real solemn history, I cannot be interested in. Can you?'

[...]

'I read it a little as a duty, but it tells me nothing that does not either vex or weary me. The quarrels of popes and kings, with wars or pestilences, in every page; the men all so good for nothing, and hardly any women at all — it is very tiresome: and yet I often think it odd that it should be so dull, for a great deal of it must be invention.'

Jane Austen, *Northanger Abbey*

Charlotte Corday

Harriet Tubman

Christine de Pizan

Margaret Hamilton

La Malinche

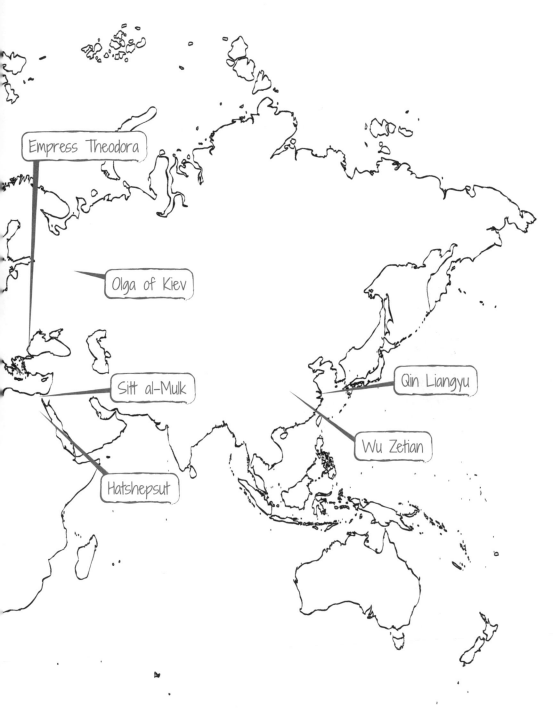

Empress Theodora

Olga of Kiev

Sitt al-Mulk

Qin Liangyu

Wu Zetian

Hatshepsut

HATSHEPSUT

EIGHTEENTH-DYNASTY EGYPT

The daughter of kings, the wife of kings, the sister of kings and a king herself. Alongside her nephew Thutmose III, Hatshepsut focused her reign on trade, exploration and creating remarkable buildings that still stand today.

SITT AL-MULK

ELEVENTH-CENTURY AFRICA

The de facto caliph who saved a city. Sitt al-Mulk took the throne after her younger brother mysteriously vanished, and tore down his bizarre laws – laws that banned women from leaving their homes or laughing in the street.

EMPRESS THEODORA

SIXTH-CENTURY BYZANTINE EMPIRE

The circus performer who ruled an empire. Theodora ruled side by side with her husband Justin, reshaping the Eastern Roman Empire in their image and creating some of the first laws to protect and aid women.

OLGA OF KIEV

TENTH-CENTURY RUSSIA

The vengeful royal widow who brought Christianity to Russia. Left as regent after her husband was killed by a rival tribe, Olga destroyed the tribe – and then sent envoys to the outside world to learn about Christianity.

CHRISTINE DE PIZAN

FIFTEENTH-CENTURY FRANCE

The woman who wrote 'I, Christine', and told the world about her anger. A widow at 25, Christine de Pizan took up her pen to earn a living; in doing so, she challenged the conventions and opinions of medieval France.

CHARLOTTE CORDAY

EIGHTEENTH-CENTURY FRANCE

The revolutionary who murdered to save France. Horrified by the Reign of Terror, Charlotte Corday thought she could save the ideals of revolution by killing journalist Jean Paul Marat – instead, it led to a push for women to stay out of politics.

WU ZETIAN

SEVENTH-CENTURY CHINA

The mother of emperors who took the throne herself. Empress Wu was a woman of contradictions; she ruled with uncompromising violence, but with great foresight that brought prosperity to China.

QIN LIANGYU

SEVENTEENTH-CENTURY CHINA

The general who never lost a battle. After her husband died, Qin Liangyu took up her spear and took over his army, defending Ming-dynasty China against invaders and rebels.

LA MALINCHE

SIXTEENTH-CENTURY MEXICO

The slave who conquered the new world. A noble-woman who had been sold to the Mayans and then gifted to the conquistadors, La Malinche was a translator for Hernán Cortés who helped the Spanish conquer Mexico.

MARGARET HAMILTON

TWENTIETH-CENTURY AMERICA

The software engineer who saved the moon landing. Margaret Hamilton wrote 'Forget it', a code to help Apollo 11's computers prioritise its decisions – without it, it's doubtful that anyone would have landed on the moon.

HARRIET TUBMAN

NINETEENTH-CENTURY AMERICA

The runaway slave who wanted to stop people suffering like she had. Harriet Tubman escaped to Canada via the Underground Railroad, and then almost immediately turned around and began to work on it herself, becoming one of the most famous anti-abolitionists.

IN THE BEGINNING

When we tell the story of our planet, we can't avoid phrases like 'maybe', 'probably' and 'it is thought'.

Around 4.6 billion years ago, it is thought, the Earth formed from a swirling mass of dust and debris orbiting a young, yellow star. Probably. And in the beginning, the Earth was desolate and empty. Maybe. Then, very gradually, over the course of millions of years, minute single-cell organisms evolved into ever more complex life-forms, until eventually there were gigantic dinosaurs roaming the Earth. It is thought. And somewhere in the world, somewhere in the mists of time, an ape stood up on two legs. Possibly.

But maybe it didn't happen like this at all. Perhaps the world and its inhabitants developed along these lines but not precisely like this. When we talk about history (the events of the past) and before that prehistory (the events of the far distant past), phrases like 'probably' and 'it is thought' crop up a lot, simply because there's so much we can't tell for sure. Many things that we think of as being fact are not proven to be definitely true, but are the stories that scientists and natural historians have developed to explain the evidence that we have.

Though there might be guesswork involved, our conclusions are usually based on sound reasoning. The past has left a trail, and clues about what really happened can be found all around us. Some of these clues can seem quite ordinary. Take a stone with knife-sharp edges: did somebody sharpen it like that deliberately or did it just break off a cliff?

Other signs that seem easy to understand at first, such as newspapers, letters and chronicles of the year's events, can be much more complex when looked at closely. When looking at this sort of evidence, we must consider whether the description has been influenced by a particular motive or point of view. Did somebody pay the writer to present them

Around 13.8 billion years ago: The universe is formed in the Big Bang. Probably.

Around 4.6 billion years ago: Planet Earth is formed from a swirling mass of dust and debris. Maybe.

as a hero? Was the book meant as a parable, rather than a realistic account of real-life events? Was a letter written to tarnish someone's reputation, for no reason other than that the writer didn't like them? Suddenly, nothing's as clear-cut any more.

Before any theories or conclusions can be made, thousands of pieces of evidence have to be collected and carefully analysed. Only then can we reach a conclusion or come up with a theory. These theories are then reviewed, revised, and may even be rejected altogether, regardless of how convincing they seemed at first.

When we write history, we have to cut our way through this tangled web. Historians must decide which witnesses to trust and how to interpret the evidence. Only then can we form an opinion. No one can ever discover 'the truth', but we may find new ways of looking at the things we *do* know. By painstakingly piecing together the jigsaw puzzle of history, we can transform that 'maybe' into a 'probably'.

A puzzle with lots of missing pieces

Historians never stop working on this puzzle, even though they know they'll never get their hands on all the pieces. No matter how exciting or frustrating this job might be, they're spurred on by the hope that, one day, they'll find enough pieces to build a more complete picture of the past. Unfortunately, it just so happens that the missing pieces are often the ones that could tell us more about the lives of women.

There are various reasons for this. When telling the history of the world, we focus on the extraordinary, on the events that changed the world. We focus on wars, the founding of states, new religions and inventions – and most of the people who have been responsible for these events have been men. Women, on the other hand, were responsible for looking after the home, the kitchen and the children throughout much of history. For a long time, this was more or less the case all over the world, so men have had more opportunities to become famous and to make their mark on history.

But this isn't the whole story. Time and time again, women have pushed beyond the boundaries of their conventional role; they've done what they felt was right and used their own individual talents to do it. They've been rulers and warriors, philosophers and writers, composers and artists, and have shown the world exactly what they can do – when given the chance. There are more important women in history than you might think. Often, though, we just don't know enough about them. This is because people thought it was wrong for women to do amazing things. It went against their idea of how the world worked. It was men who went out and did extraordinary things; women stayed at home.

For this reason, the men who recorded the events of their era simply disregarded the contribution of women. This started as far back as Ancient Egypt, where the name of the female pharaoh Hatshepsut was chiselled out of the pyramids after her death. Back then, it wasn't unusual for a jealous Egyptian ruler to remove the names of his predecessors from the historic record – but in the case of Hatshepsut, it wasn't her existence as a woman that was erased. It was the fact that she had been 'king'. Some suggest this happened because her successors believed that a woman ruler was a violation of the world order.

Similarly, in Mongolia, a historian discovered a thirteenth-century parchment where the section on women's history had simply been ripped out. Furthermore, in almost 1,000 years of Roman history, relatively few women are mentioned at all. Whether this was because women were removed from the record later on or because women had fewer opportunities to shine in this warrior society (the more likely scenario!), we know nowhere near enough about the lives of Roman women, and remarkably little of what we do know is noteworthy.

Throughout history, women who dared to intervene or voice an opinion were often portrayed in a negative light. Such women are regularly described as crafty, ruthless, dishonest and wicked. All over the world, chroniclers of history seem to have shared a similar goal: using all the resources at their disposal, they seemed determined to prove that women interfering in politics brings only disaster.

Unfortunately, these attempts to erase women from history have been very successful. Often the only thing we know about female writers is that they were famous. Their writings have disappeared while the works of their male counterparts have been preserved and republished over and over again. There's correspondence where the only letters surviving are the ones sent by the man: the woman's letters were either deliberately destroyed or lost through carelessness. Throughout history, forgetfulness has shrouded the lives of women and their work like a veil. Over the past few decades, though, the world's historians have started searching for the traces left behind by these women, so that we now know more about them today than we did 100 or even 50 years ago. Through the work of these historians, the veil that obscured our view of these women for so long is gradually being lifted.

In this book, when we attempt to put together the pieces of this 'world history puzzle', we won't leave out the many men who have made important contributions to history. If we did, the picture we'd end up with would be just as one-sided and incomplete as the one we have now. We don't want to rewrite the past, so rather than trying to solve the puzzle with entirely new pieces, we're going to try to find the missing pieces for the picture we already have.

The history of the world that we tell here has its roots in a version of history that was taught in school textbooks for a long time. That traditional narrative is now viewed critically, and for good reason. It's no accident that, for us in Europe, 'world history' has traditionally begun in Mesopotamia and Ancient Egypt and that treasures from these two regions are kept in the museums of London, Paris and Berlin. This shows just how powerful the Europeans were until very recently. They decided how the history of the world should be told, and to demonstrate how central they were to that history, they simply helped themselves to the treasures they wanted from elsewhere in the world.

Our history of the world is inevitably very European in focus. Why, we could also ask ourselves, does Africa play such a minor role and why do we know so little about such a massive continent? It's no coincidence that Europe's museums still haven't returned precious artworks to Egypt, Greece or any of the other countries they were taken from, despite criticism from all sides. This might perhaps be the greater injustice than being side-lined from world history. But this doesn't mean the old narrative of world history is invalid. We need to explore it in order to understand how these injustices happened in the first place. But we also need to take a critical view and remember that the traditional narrative is just one of many ways of telling history. This particular way was thought up by Europeans and it views the world from a Eurocentric perspective.

In this book, we won't *just* be talking about women; putting the women back in doesn't mean we have to push the men out. Neither will we be able to talk about *all* the strong, clever, brave women in history, even if they were great leaders, philosophers and artists (often in the face of great adversity). To focus exclusively on women would result in a different book, a 'History of the World's Women'. That would be interesting, but it would be a specialised, niche perspective on history. Our aim instead is to put the women back into a global history that concerns all of us.

PREHISTORY

Lucy

The Earth is around 4.6 billion years old. We don't know for certain how the continents, mountains and forests, and the rivers, lakes and oceans, came into being or how life began, but we do have a few theories.

According to one of these theories, there was a beginning, and during this beginning, the universe and all its planets were created. We call this the Big Bang – even though nothing actually exploded. The name 'Big Bang' instead describes a time when the solar system and planets were completely different to what they are today. This beginning may have happened a very long time ago – billions of years ago, in fact – when our universe, made up of matter, space and time, was concentrated in just one small, dense point called a 'singularity'. The universe then started to expand. Billions of years later, water appeared on Earth, possibly from comets, and slowly life began to develop. From simple self-replicating molecules, a growing diversity of life evolved in the oceans and on the land.

Around 200,000 years ago: The first *Homo sapiens* evolve.

There are many opinions about how and when the age of modern humans (*Homo sapiens*) began. Some scientists believe that these two-legged hunters, thinkers and fire-makers have been around for 2 or 3 million years. Others think that the first people who could really be compared to *Homo sapiens*, us modern humans, only evolved as recently as 200,000 years ago. The difference between these two figures is huge, but either way, the numbers are pretty mind-blowing. In fact, the history we actually know something about is relatively short – just 5,000 years. A blink of an eye when you think about how long the Earth has been around for!

Human history begins in Africa. Around 5–8 million years ago, there was another species of human living there. The word 'human' describes an ape that, unlike some other primates, walks upright on two legs and has an opposable thumb that can be used with the fingers to pick things up (a bit like tweezers). It's thought that these apes first learned to walk when the forests they inhabited started to thin, meaning they were no longer able to swing from tree to tree.

In 1974, researchers in Africa discovered around fifty bones, clearly from the same skeleton. Most believe the skeleton to be that of a woman who is roughly 3.2 million years old. While analysing the skeleton, the researchers were listening to the Beatles song 'Lucy in the Sky with Diamonds', so they decided to call her Lucy. A few years ago, it was discovered that Lucy may have died after falling from a tree.

Around 3.2 million years ago: The proto-human 'Lucy' walks the Earth.

Between 8 and 2.5 million years ago, hominin brains changed drastically, bringing them one step closer to the ancestors of modern humans. They became more skilled, learned to speak and made plans. At some point, they discovered fire for the first time and used it to warm themselves and cook meat. They fashioned stone tools that made it easier to hunt and prepare food. Later, they used wood to make the very first houses. These were ground-breaking developments! As humans began to make things by hand, this was the start of civilisation and culture – things that are created by humans, as opposed to nature, which exists regardless of humans. One branch, the Neanderthals, evolved in Asia and Europe quite early on, but later went extinct.

Eventually, *Homo sapiens* – Latin for 'wise man' – evolved: a hominin species much more like modern humans. It wasn't until 100,000 years ago or so that humans started to migrate from Africa to other parts of the world, including the Middle East, India, Asia, Australasia and Europe. Lastly, they arrived in America from Siberia via Alaska and continued their journey southward down the continent.

Men hunt, women chat

Around
2.6 million
years ago:
Humans start
making stone
tools. This is the
beginning of the
Stone Age.

For a long time, people imagined that life in the Stone Age was organised more or less the same as it was 50 or 100 years ago. Sure, there wouldn't have been any cities, streets or houses yet, but it was presumed that humans divided labour the way they still did up until a few decades ago. Men provided for the family and women stayed at home by the stove cooking; it's why so many museums and textbooks show pictures of men hunting. The men lie in wait for their prey (large or small, it doesn't matter), kill it and take it home for dinner. The women, meanwhile, are shown gathered round the fire in a cave or a tent, crafting, or stirring a big pot suspended over the flames.

Some people argue that millennia of spending so much time together at the camp has made women chatty, while men would have needed to concentrate on silently stalking their prey, and that this has remained the case ever since. They say that, despite all the advances made over the past millennia, we still behave like prehistoric humans.

But we shouldn't assume anything. Nobody can prove that life 50,000 or 100,000 years ago was organised along the same lines as today. Archaeological finds can only tell us so much.

Prehistoric vases showing figures in long robes have also been found. These robes are triangular and look just like skirts. There was no doubt about it, people thought: the figures on the vase must be women. Later, though, the same robes were found on painted figures who definitely had beards. It turned out that the skirted figures were, in fact, men. Archaeologists started to take a closer look and discovered more and more objects that didn't quite fit the 'men hunt and women chat' pattern. For example, some women were found buried with weapons and tools, while some men were buried with beads and distaffs for spinning thread. Could it be that women were able to carry weapons – and use them? And that there were men who made their living from making textiles, even though we tend to see spinning and weaving as typically female activities?

The great mother

Aside from vases and other items found in graves, many other archaeological finds help us form a picture of the Stone Age. These finds include cave paintings and small figures made from limestone, mammoth ivory, clay (back then, people had already discovered how to fire clay to make ceramics). One of these figurines is a limestone statue of a curvaceous woman, measuring just 11 centimetres tall. Archaeologists named it 'the Venus of Willendorf', after the small town in Austria where it was found. When the first of these small figures was discovered, they were named 'Venus figurines' after the Roman goddess of love. Today some archaeologists prefer to call them 'female statuettes' as the name 'Venus' is a little misleading: the figurines don't actually have an awful lot in common with the Roman goddess at all.

What puzzled the researchers, though, was that similar statuettes had been found all over Europe, from France to Russia – even as far as Siberia. They quickly came to the conclusion that the figurines were representations of goddesses and a sign of common religious beliefs among the people who lived in the vast expanse between France and Siberia. The statuettes' decidedly swollen stomachs could easily be a symbol of pregnancy, they explained later, so it was entirely logical that humans prayed to a female deity when they still lived a very precarious life out in the wild. It was woman who brought forth life from their bodies, just as the Earth brought forth all life and gave humans their food.

People saw a close connection between women and the Earth or nature: in many languages they still are referred to as 'Mother Earth' or 'Mother Nature'. These statuettes, they believed, were depictions of fertility goddesses. But given that the Venus of Willendorf and other similar statues are around 30,000 years old, we will probably never have a definitive explanation. For instance, how do we explain the figurine found at Dolní Věstonice in the Czech Republic, whose facial characteristics match those of a woman found buried nearby? Could this mean that Stone Age humans made images of living people, as well as goddesses?

Around 29,500 years ago: The Venus of Willendorf is made, one of many female statues from the Stone Age.

Whether men hunted, women sat chatting or goddesses gave life, we know very little for sure about the structure of early human society. There's no concrete evidence, and no matter how much we'd like to describe the relationships between men and women, young and old, we can't. An exhibition in a Swiss museum once featured a picture of a young prehistoric girl killing a hare. And why not? Perhaps girls did go hunting 10,000 years ago.

The Neolithic Revolution

Around 5,000 years ago: Humans settle and build the first cities.

At some point in history, hunters and gatherers began to settle. They built permanent homes, cultivated the land and founded villages and towns. Some say this process was the biggest change in the history of humanity. Because it took place during the 'new' Stone Age, or the Neolithic period, it became known as the 'Neolithic Revolution'.

This revolution started almost 20,000 years ago. The biggest change of the Neolithic Revolution was the food people ate: growing crops like wheat, rice and millet rather than foraging for food in the wild meant people could settle in one place. Hunters and gatherers became farmers and herders; their diet of wild fruit and game was supplemented by bread made from the wheat they grew and the meat of the cattle they reared. They could produce larger quantities of food, so they shared tasks across the community and started trading with one another.

Then came the next major step: the discovery of copper, which could be used for making metal tools. These tools were much better than unwieldy stone tools. Copper was followed by metals such as iron and bronze, which gave their names to two archaeological eras, the Iron Age and the Bronze Age.

If you wanted to bake bread and raise cattle you needed land, and at times you would need to defend that land from others. For this you needed weapons and warriors. Some believe the distribution of these tasks also changed the relationship between men and women. Suddenly, one was in charge and the other was left with nothing.

Around 5,000 years ago, larger cities and kingdoms sprang up in some parts of the world, such as North Africa, the Middle East and India. These were highly sophisticated societies and civilisations. We don't know why the first advanced civilisations appeared in these particular regions, while in other parts of the world it took 2,000 years for humans to leave their caves.

In these advanced cities and states, the relationships of power between people became more complex. Work wasn't distributed equally: the building of mighty palaces and temples relied on a small number of master builders, who could calculate and plan, and hundreds of thousands of slaves, who did the heavy labour. This is worth remembering: when we talk about history, we're usually talking about a small handful of powerful individuals and their advisers and assistants. These small groups ruled over most of the population. And at almost all times, life in these societies and their great achievements were built on the shoulders of oppressed, exploited slaves.

The complicated structure of the cities made another invention necessary: writing. Writing was more than just a practical way of dealing with everyday things such as organising the distribution of grain; it also helped people communicate with one another over large distances. 'Send some wool along with the money. It's too expensive here in the city,' an Assyrian businesswoman once wrote to her husband who was away on a merchant trip. The letter was written almost 4,000 years ago.

Around 3100 BC: The Sumerians invent the cuneiform writing script.

Because writing conquers both physical distance and time, we can still read the Assyrian businesswoman's letter today. The written word can survive for centuries, and eventually the world's first historians appeared on the scene – people who consciously documented their experiences for future generations.

SUMERIANS AND BABYLONIANS

Being first is what counts

Being the second or third person on the Moon isn't quite the same as being the first. It's the first person whose name is recorded in the history books; the first is the one we remember.

The first person on the Moon was Neil Armstrong and he was American. The first person ever to go to space was a Russian named Yuri Gagarin, and the first dog in space was Laika, who was also Russian (and female, no less!). As it happens, many of the world's first astronauts were Russian, as was the first female astronaut, Valentina Tereshkova. Her expedition was really something special, as for a long time, few women had had the opportunity to do these kinds of things. It was the men who went to war, became politicians, played football or travelled to space. But why was that and when did it all begin?

When we tell history, we're usually interested in firsts: when and where something happened for the first time. When we tell the history of the world, the events we view as important are the ones that have made the world what it is today. That's why we find the Romans so interesting: they invented laws that are still in use now. Or the Chinese, because their invention of paper and gunpowder changed the world.

Big changes in the way humans lived were almost always connected to new inventions. Astronauts couldn't have travelled into space without the help of complicated, innovative – and astronomically expensive – equipment. For eons, travelling to the Moon seemed like nothing more than a far-fetched dream, and it would take roughly 5,000 years for humanity to make that crazy dream a reality. Valentina Tereshkova, Neil Armstrong and Yuri Gagarin were the first to see our planet from a distance, looking back at the Earth from the Moon.

Today we send satellites into space that can take photos of the minutest of details, such as roads and houses. The view of the Earth from the skies is now something we take for granted.

Of stars and gods

Things were the other way around 5,000 years ago. Humans looked to the heavens and observed the stars: they worked out that the planets appeared in the sky at regular intervals, in exactly the same positions. This got them thinking. As on Earth, events in the heavens seemed to follow a certain order. But if there was order, mustn't there also be someone creating that order? How did the sun rise and set with such fixed regularity from one day to the next? How did the seasons change? Where did life come from and where did it go? What was behind all of this; what brought about this order? In other words, what was it that held the world together?

Humans searched everywhere for an answer. Eventually, they found one that was both simple and complicated at the same time: 'God'. It was God who had created the world and held it all together. But now things got complicated: who or what was this God? Were they living? And were they male or female? Were there lots of similar beings who were all responsible for different things? Not one god but many? Or maybe God was something more abstract, like 'nothingness' or 'eternity'? One thing's for certain, though: since time immemorial, people conceived of gods and spirits who determined their fate. All over the world, people imagined them differently and called them by different names.

Back in prehistory, people believed that the gods lived in nature itself. They believed that a divine being with magical powers lived in every tree and river. When the weather god was angry, he lashed out with thunder and lightning. A raging god of the sea roused the oceans into towering waves. Invisible powers could take their revenge by sending a flood. To keep the gods happy, people made sacrificial offerings to them and communicated with them through song and prayer. Out of these rituals came religions.

But people eventually stopped believing in magical beings that lived in the natural world around them. They began using the fields, rivers and forests for their own benefit and the gods retreated from nature. If the gods had a home anywhere, the sky seemed the most likely bet.

The astrologers

The people of Mesopotamia, a region that roughly corresponds with modern-day Iraq, viewed their kings and queens as immortal beings who lived on as gods after dying. To prepare them for life on the other side, Mesopotamian rulers were lavished with gifts after death – inside Queen Puabi's tomb, for example, archaeologists found a cloak decorated with more than 1,600 beads and a headdress made from around 8 metres of gold ribbon. Of course, a queen couldn't be expected to travel to the world of the gods without a staff of female attendants, so ten slaves were buried with her, as well as a carriage and two oxen with harnesses.

Around 3100 BC: The Sumerians build the world's first city states.

Puabi was the Queen of the Sumerians, who lived in the region that is now Iraq and which the Ancient Greeks called Mesopotamia (literally, 'between two rivers' as it's between the Euphrates and the Tigris). The Sumerians built a sophisticated system of canals, which they used to irrigate large areas of farmland. They founded the cities of Uruk and Ur, where they erected great temples and distributed their harvests. To keep track of their finances, the Sumerians invented cuneiform, a form of writing based on a system of triangles and lines, which was etched into tablets made of soft clay.

To break up the endless cycle of day and night, and to measure the passage of time, the Sumerians invented the seven-day week. They also invented a recipe for beer and whiled away the hours with board games and stories, which were important for creating a link between the past, present and future. In fact, the Sumerians also gave us the world's oldest book, a collection of stories called the *Epic of Gilgamesh*. One of these stories tells of a mighty flood that once devastated the land.

Around 1850 BC: The *Epic of Gilgamesh* is written.

The Sumerians believed that the moon god Nanna watched over Ur and the sky god An (or Anu) watched over Uruk. In each city, they built huge towers in the gods' honour. These towers had a distinctive structure, built in tiers or terraces, with the temple itself placed at the top.

The gods' protection couldn't stop the Sumerian culture from collapsing eventually, but this end was far off.

Until then, a long line of kings reigned successfully over the region. One of these kings, Sargon, married his daughter Enheduanna to the moon god Nanna, making her the high priestess of Ur. This wasn't unusual: rulers all too happily had their daughters ordained high priestesses as a way of strengthening their power. Enheduanna was educated, and one of her tasks as priestess was to write hymns to be sung at the temple in honour of the gods. But Enheduanna was an unusually self-confident young woman. She clearly loved writing and began to write about personal things, such as pain and suffering, human emotions and her relationship with the gods. Although it wasn't the custom at the time, she signed many of her writings in her own name. The phrase 'I was the high priestess; I, Enheduanna' seems to have been as important to her as serving the gods. Perhaps her confidence wasn't entirely misplaced. As it turns out, she would become history's earliest female author – or at least, her writings are the oldest we're still able to read.

Around 2270 BC: The Sumerian high priestess Enheduanna composes religious texts.

Of law and order

After the Sumerians came the Babylonians. They precisely recorded the movements of the stars and gave the constellations the names we still use today, such as 'The Plough', 'The Scales' (Libra), 'The Lion' (Leo) and 'The Archer' (Sagittarius). The Babylonians were convinced that the movements of the planets could be used to tell the future. From this they invented astrology: the belief that events on Earth are affected by events in the heavens – in other words, they thought our fate was influenced by the movement of the stars.

For all their stargazing, the Babylonians didn't neglect more earthly affairs. One of their kings, King Hammurabi, wrote down a legal code

1792 BC: King Hammurabi comes to the throne of the Ancient Babylonian Empire. His laws – the Code of Hammurabi – were carved into stone.

More than 3000 years ago: Assyrian law requires women to wear a veil. This is the oldest evidence we have of men and women being treated differently.

dictating how society should function: 'An eye for an eye, and a tooth for a tooth.' Hammurabi had these laws chiselled in stone and placed in the inner courtyards of the temples, so they could be accessed by anyone at any time. According to one of the laws on women, 'If a "sister of a god" opens a tavern or enters a tavern to drink, this woman shall be burned to death'. A 'sister of a god' may have been a woman with religious duties. Clearly those duties were so important, the women were expected to behave themselves and not waste their time in the pub!

More than 3,000 years ago, the veil, a piece of fabric that courts controversy to this day, made its first appearance in history. According to Assyrian law, women and girls had to cover their faces in public; it was meant to protect them and showed men they were respectable. For slaves and servants, however, wearing the veil was a punishable offence: these women weren't viewed as respectable and their bare heads told men they could be harassed without fear of punishment.

Rather than forbidding men from harassing women, Assyrian law demanded that some women protect themselves while denying others, the 'disrespectable', the same right. For men, there were no such rules. The veil is possibly the oldest visible sign that many societies treated men and women differently – and, almost without exception, women were treated worse.

THE KINGDOM ON THE NILE

The Nile measures time

When we think of history, it's tempting to think of a chronology of events. We might picture it as a timeline of dates running from left to right. But when we come to tell the stories of history, we find things can be more complicated. Important events often take place in lots of different places at once, so we end up having to draw lots of timelines in parallel with one another, with other connecting lines running across them, joining them up in an endless web. But in this book, we don't want to present history as a jumbled web of criss-crossing lines – we want to tell it in words and stories. And that means we're going to have to jump backwards and forwards a bit between places and time.

In several regions of the world, such as Mesopotamia, Egypt, India and China, history got going in several different places, at around about the same time. It always happened by a river: the land along river banks was especially fertile, so people were able to grow crops there, such as wheat and millet. Very soon, they began using the rivers and their tributaries as roads. Goods and heavy objects, such as the stones for houses and palaces, could be transported along them much more easily than over land.

The kingdoms between the Euphrates and Tigris rivers – Sumer, Babylonia and Assyria – ebbed and flowed, but their neighbour Egypt endured for an unimaginably long time. The Egyptian kingdom also had its beginnings more than 5,000 years ago, but unlike most of the others, it survived practically unchanged for more than 3,000 years.

Egypt owed its prosperity to the mighty Nile, a river almost 7,000 kilometres in length. The people of Egypt worshipped it like a god and sang songs to it: 'Hail to you, O Nile, sprung from earth, come to nourish Egypt!'

When the Nile flooded, the earth transformed into a fertile black mud the Egyptians called *kemet* or 'black land'. The land beyond the water's reach was called 'red land' or *desheret*: desert.

For the Egyptians, the Nile offered persuasive evidence that nature was governed by a god-given order. Like clockwork, the river flooded every 365 days. When the Egyptians realised this, they invented a calendar. In this calendar, the 365 days between each flood were divided into twelve moons of thirty days each. This was roughly the time between each full moon. After these twelve months, there were still five days left over. These days were divided between the months and became festivals in honour of the gods responsible for maintaining this orderly structure. With the help of the Moon and the Nile, the Egyptians produced a calendar almost as accurate as the one we use today.

Houses for the afterlife

Around 2700 BC: The first pyramids are built in Egypt.

Perhaps the best way of understanding Ancient Egypt is through its pyramids, mortuary temples and tombs. The Egyptians believed that they didn't stop existing after death; instead they crossed over into the afterlife, and they needed a house to live in once they got there. The Egyptians placed more importance on the afterlife than their fleeting time on Earth, so lots of care was put into furnishing these houses. These were the pyramids.

The rooms inside the tombs were spacious, linked together by long passageways and equipped with large larders for storing food, drink (mostly wine and beer) and a variety of household objects. Other rooms were fitted out with furniture, and those who could afford it took not only clothes, but jewellery, gold and silver on the journey. Every tomb contained *ushabtis*: small figurines made from wood, stone or ceramic that would do all the deceased person's chores in the afterlife.

The Egyptians needed a body in the afterlife, so before the corpse was placed in its sarcophagus, it was embalmed and wrapped in linen cloth. Through this process the body was preserved, producing Egypt's famous mummies. Before the body was preserved, the internal organs were removed and placed in special (canopic) jars. This was because the Egyptians believed that the heart was the source of all human thoughts and feelings. The brain, on the other hand, was considered useless. After death, it was simply removed through the nose and thrown away.

The walls inside the pyramids were decorated with hunting murals and scenes of the pharaoh and his priests conducting rituals in honour of the gods. Others show priestesses at great festivals, singing and dancing. Then, of course, there are the hieroglyphics, which were carved into stone and wet clay. Thanks to Egypt's warm, dry climate and the fact that the tombs were well hidden away, the hieroglyphics have been amazingly well preserved.

These labyrinthine burial chambers offer us a snapshot of life in the past. These everyday objects needed for the afterlife – the jewellery, luxuries, vases and clay pots – all give us a deep insight into how people really lived back then.

This life

Before entering the afterlife, most Egyptians worked as farmers. But Egypt couldn't have gained its reputation as an advanced civilisation if it wasn't for its stonemasons, shipbuilders, joiners, painters and goldsmiths. One of the most well-respected professions in all of Egypt was the scribe. Scribes made long lists of the harvests and goods to be distributed among the people, wrote hymns and prayers to the gods, wrote biographies of the king and recorded the laws that helped everyone live in harmony.

Upon returning from his travels to Egypt, the Greek historian Herodotus told his fellow Greeks about an upside-down world:

5th century BC: The Greek historian Herodotus travels to Egypt and is amazed by what he sees.

Their manners and customs are the reverse of other peoples in almost every way. Egyptian women go to the market to trade, while the men stay at home and weave.

Herodotus was amazed that the streets of Egypt's cities were bustling with women, doing all manner of activities. Egypt's laws gave rights to women that were unknown among other civilisations at the time. Women were allowed to run their own businesses and own and sell land, and when they got married, they could keep everything their parents left them. If a case went to court, women could be called as witnesses just like men and could even represent themselves.

Despite all this, we must remember that everyday life in Egypt was often just the same as in other parts of the world. The men went to work, and the women stayed at home, especially if they were mothers. The Egyptians viewed motherhood as a miracle and childbirth was seen as one of life's key events. There was another reason for this belief: everybody needed offspring who would look after them when they made their own journey to the afterlife.

The realm of the gods

After death, in the peace of the tomb, the gods were especially close. What could be more important than that? The gods permeated every aspect of the world. The Egyptians viewed everything as holy, and all that they saw, felt, tasted and heard had a divine origin. Atum the creator god had created the world from nothingness, the primeval ocean. The harmony of the universe was ensured by *maat*, the divine order. Instead of being permanent and unchanging, the world was defined by change – this meant that *maat* was constantly threatened by *isfet*, chaos.

When the gods appeared on Earth, they took on many different forms. Instead of 'Mother Earth', the Egyptians saw the Earth as a male god called Geb. In this respect, Herodotus's description of Egypt as an upside-down world wasn't too far off the mark. Geb's counterpart was the goddess of the sky, Nut. She was believed to bend over the Earth and swallow the sun in the evenings, pitching the world into darkness, and in the morning, she spat the ball of fire back out. Some gods took the form of animals or were half-human, half-animal, like Thoth, who had the head of an ibis and was the scribe of the gods, or Anubis, who had the head of a dog or jackal and accompanied people to the afterlife. The goddesses Opet, a hippopotamus, and Heket, a frog, helped women in childbirth.

The realm of the kings

The pharaoh was both human and god. His spouse, the Great Royal Wife, was also seen as a divine messenger. The pharaohs were responsible for the divine order; to keep this intact, the royal couple was expected to produce a son as their successor. However, sometimes, the couple was unable to have children, or their children got sick and died prematurely. And sometimes when the king died, his son – the heir to the throne – was just a baby, and a bit too young to be responsible for *maat*, the divine order of the universe.

This is how Queen Hatshepsut came to the throne. As the Great Royal Wife of the deceased king, she ruled as regent on behalf of her nephew, who would be king when he came of age. Hatshepsut has been the subject of much debate, as by the time her nephew Thutmose III was old enough to rule, she had consolidated her power to such an extent that they ruled side by side, as two monarchs. However, because there were two of them, nobody knew what word to use to address 'the king' at official events, so the word 'pharaoh', meaning 'great house' or 'palace', was used instead. In other words, it was through Hatshepsut and Thutmose's unusual form of joint leadership that all of Egypt's kings came to be called 'pharaoh'.

To strengthen her claim, Hatshepsut portrayed herself as both a man and a woman. Some inscriptions read: 'The King of Upper and Lower Egypt that you wanted ... beloved of the gods.' In some portraits she was given male characteristics, in others, female.

Hatshepsut was a successful ruler: she established trade links with Egypt's neighbours, made the country wealthy and constructed awe-inspiring buildings all over the land. The architect Senenmut was one of her closest confidants and tutor to her daughter Neferure, and there are many depictions showing the two together. In Karnak, one of the main temple complexes of the age, she had two enormous obelisks built and a wonderful barque shrine that housed a sailing boat she would need for the journey to the afterlife. Her mortuary temple was something special too, with three terraces that seemed to grow out of the cliff face. This structure sets it apart from the more famous pyramids that, by Hatshepsut's time, had long gone out of fashion. Her mortuary temple is decorated with a large relief depicting scenes from her expedition to the Land of Punt, an ancient kingdom to the south of Egypt. Early in her reign, she and the royal household had travelled to this distant, mysterious land, which supplied Egypt with gold, perfumed resins and incense, cedarwood and lots of other raw materials.

Although Hatshepsut was a good ruler, after her death, the Egyptians argued about whether, by sitting on the throne rather than standing beside it, Hatshepsut had threatened the very order she was meant to protect. For a long time, it was believed that her nephew Thutmose had destroyed many images of her out of hatred. Lately, though, historians have suggested that his aim may have been to make people forget that a woman had been monarch. The images of her that remain intact are mainly those commemorating Hatshepsut as a person rather than as 'the king'.

About 100 years after Hatshepsut's rule, Amenhotep IV became pharaoh. He pushed back against the established order much more strongly than any female ruler of Egypt had ever done. Amenhotep IV did something completely outrageous: instead of upholding *maat* and appeasing the gods, as was his duty, he banned all gods. He asserted that there was only one god, the sun god Aten, and Amenhotep wanted to found his own new religion around this god. He gave himself the title Akhenaten, which means 'the servant of Aten'.

Akhenaten's desire for a new religion may sound harmless, but it was in fact an act of violence. He sent stonemasons all over Egypt to chisel the names of the gods from all the temples and obelisks. For many Egyptians, this was the malicious destruction of all that was holy and gave their lives meaning; they protested, but Akhenaten was unfazed and went on to develop a new alphabet and build a new capital dedicated solely to the worship of Aten.

Why Akhenaten chose to wage war against such a successful way of life and destroy its colourful pantheon of gods in favour of one single god remains a mystery.

This wasn't the only mystery surrounding the self-proclaimed sun king. His rule might have been dismissed as nothing more than a mad episode in history if it hadn't been for his charismatic wife. Her name was Nefertiti, which translates to 'the beautiful one has come'. She stayed close to her husband's side and was proclaimed the daughter of Aten. In this new cult, she had an important role, as it was through her alone that people could access the sun god. Akhenaten and Nefertiti were a radiant couple and some pictures even give the impression that Nefertiti herself is on the throne, with Akhenaten by her side, the position traditionally taken by the pharaoh's wife.

However, it seems that Nefertiti died suddenly. She may have died after falling from a carriage, as the mummy some presume to be Nefertiti has serious injuries to its face and chest. Others say that the injured mummy isn't Nefertiti at all, so we don't know when and how she died. Recently another archaeologist has claimed to have found her tomb somewhere else.

To this day, it's still unclear whether Nefertiti did indeed die a sudden death or whether she simply disappeared, which adds to the general aura of mystery around her. One thing is certain, though: with her disappearance, the magic surrounding the royal couple disappeared too.

Akhenaten had tried to use violence to introduce a religion focused on one god. However, his son Tutankhamen brought back the old gods, and with them, stability. The new pharaohs left Akhenaten's city and his palace returned to dust under the Egyptian sun. The Egyptian empire itself would survive another 2,000 years.

Egypt's neighbours: the kingdom of Kush

Most of Egypt's resources, especially gold and slaves, came from Nubia, a region in the south where the Blue Nile and White Nile merged together into one colossal river. The local people, the Nubians, looked different to the Egyptians and had darker skin. Eventually, a Nubian prince successfully founded a state that was independent from Egypt. This kingdom was known as Kush; here the ruler could

From around 8 BC to around AD 350: The kingdom of Kush emerges south of Egypt.

now build his own temples, palaces and tombs. The Kushites worshipped the Egyptian gods but had their own alphabet, which has been deciphered but remains untranslated to this day. They also built pyramids at a time when they were no longer being built in Egypt. The Kushite city of Meroë is located in modern-day Sudan and is home to the largest group of pyramids anywhere in the world.

During the Kushite era the city of Meroë became the new seat of government. Over the years that followed, the reins of power were handed down to a succession of Kushite queens. Some ruled alone, but even the married ones were extremely influential; they were both mothers and warriors, and may even have taken on the role of priests, as suggested by an image of Queen Amanishakheto. In this image, the queen is dressed in a leopard skin – something usually worn exclusively by priests.

HISTORY BEGINS IN THE INDUS VALLEY

Harappa and Mohenjo-Daro

When you look at a map of the world, the region in the Middle East that was home to the Sumerians, Babylonians, Egyptians and Jews is a relatively small area. East of Mesopotamia, beyond the Persian Gulf, there's a great river. This river is called the Indus, and today it forms the gateway to its namesake country: India. Along the banks of the Indus, researchers have found traces of an advanced civilisation, almost as old as Sumer.

We know very little about the scale of this civilisation, but it's thought that it may have covered an area larger than all the other early civilisations put together. It's possible too that the world's oldest written records came from here.

The climate of India is unique. Once a year, it rains constantly for three months, but it's generally dry for all the others. The monsoon rains had to be diverted into irrigation canals to water crops during the dry season and to protect the fields from flooding during the rainy season. The people of the Indus Valley built a complex system of reservoirs, canals and water pipelines that amazes architects and engineers to this day. Houses in the civilisation's two largest cities, Harappa and Mohenjo-Daro, were even fitted with baths and flushing toilets – after the civilisation's collapse, it would take almost 4,000 years for someone in Europe to come up with the same idea. The streets of Harappa and Mohenjo-Daro were as well organised as the sewers and pipes below them. Constructed in a grid pattern lined up

2600–1900 BC: Ground-breaking technological discoveries are made by the Indus Valley's Harappa culture.

with the points of the compass, from above they would have looked like chessboards made up of lines and squares.

Surviving from the Harappan period are small terracotta female figurines wearing lavish necklaces and headdresses. A small statue of bronze has even been found in Mohenjo-Daro. This statue is of a young girl, but we don't really know what she's doing. She may be a dancer.

Around 2500 BC: The Dancing Girl of Mohenjo-Daro is made – a tiny bronze statue measuring 10.5 centimetres.

After 800 years or so, the Harappa civilisation collapsed – most researchers believe this was caused by a natural disaster. A landslide may have blocked the river and the Indus may have flooded the valley. Perhaps the cities were simply subsumed by mud. Others think the settlements may have been destroyed by a nomadic people who migrated to India from the Central Asian steppes around that time.

Where these people came from is a bit of a mystery. They're known as the Aryans, and while some of them settled in India, the others would go on to conquer Mesopotamia and found the Persian Empire.

Between 2400 and 1500 BC: The Aryans arrive in the Indus Valley.

Today we can't read any of the texts left behind by the Indus Valley's early civilisations. This means we don't know very much about them. But what we do know is that after the Aryans arrived, life in India changed. The impressive buildings, sewage and water systems of the Harappa period disappeared, and with them many other aspects of its sophisticated culture, including its writing system. However, not all was lost: the customs and traditions of the indigenous Harappans merged with those of the incoming Aryans, creating a completely new society.

The caste system

What we call 'history' started the moment humans gave up their hunter-gatherer lifestyles, took up farming and invented writing. This happened in several corners of the world, at almost exactly the same time. It's tempting to think that an invention as ingenious as writing was thought up in one place and then spread from there all over the world. But that wasn't the case at all. Some ideas, such as writing or the gods, came into the world in many places independently of one another.

Even among the Sumerians and Egyptians, the differences between people were becoming greater and greater. Some were better at certain tasks than others, which made them richer and ultimately meant they usually had more influence. Society soon divided into layers. At the very bottom were the oppressed and exploited slaves. Next came the farmers, who had very little money or influence. After the farmers came the merchants, craftspeople and scholars, who had slightly more rights and opportunities. At the top there was usually a single ruler, a prince or a king, who was surrounded by a tight circle of powerful advisers and confidants. For a long time, this system went unquestioned, as people believed it was dictated by the gods.

Indian society was divided into castes. These castes weren't equal and were ordered from highest to lowest. The top caste was the Brahmins, the priests responsible for religious rites and ceremonies. They were then followed by other castes such as the rulers and warriors, the merchants and farmers and labourers.

What set the caste system apart from other class systems was its strict rules. Caste remained attached to a family through the generations. Men were expected to practise the same profession as their father and had to marry within the same caste. If the father was a warrior, the son had to become a warrior as well. The women of the family, on the other hand, were expected to be the mothers, daughters and wives of warriors. The rules even applied to food: a meal couldn't be eaten unless it had been prepared by somebody from the same caste.

Some people didn't belong to any caste. They were called the 'untouchables' or pariahs because they only did the dirtiest, most menial jobs. People believed that if they were touched by a pariah, they would become unclean themselves. They therefore made sure to keep their distance. The pariahs were excluded from all aspects of society.

Perhaps the only way of understanding the caste system is to know a bit about how the inhabitants of India viewed themselves and their place in the world. People lived according to a strict caste system on Earth, but were also part of a higher order that involved the entire universe. Everything was guided by the eternal cycle of nature, which they pictured as one ceaseless cycle of inhalation and exhalation, and all living things – plants, animals and humans – were part of it. Life didn't end with death; what ceased to exist one moment was reborn the next. All of life passed through the wheel of rebirth.

If you were poor in this life, you could gain some comfort from knowing you would come back as something else. You may die as a farmer or priest, but you could be reborn as a cat or a butterfly.

The divine breath

Around 1500 BC: The Vedas, India's oldest holy texts, are written.

In India, much like in Egypt, Babylonia and Sumer, people turned to the gods for an explanation of how the world was held together. The oldest holy texts telling of the realm of the Indian gods are called the Vedas and are written in Sanskrit, a language brought to India by the Aryans. These texts form the foundation of the Indian religion Hinduism.

The world of the Indian gods is colourful and multifaceted. The earliest Vedas tell the story of Indra, the god of war, who slayed a dragon each year. By doing this, it was said, he released all the world's water and, with it, the rains of the monsoon. They tell the story of the many-armed god Shiva and Father Heaven and Mother Earth, who are represented as a bull and a cow.

It took a long time for the Vedas to be written down. They were considered secret knowledge that could only be passed down orally in the form of songs. As far as the Indians were concerned, the creators of the Vedas were demigods. These scholars or sages were known as Brahmins, and it was their job to protect the knowledge held within the Vedas. The Brahmins were mostly men, but there were a few women too; they were known as Brahmavadinis.

These Indian scholars were especially interested in the *atman* – the breath – as the people of India believed that breath is what connected humanity to the divine. The Upanishads, another set of ancient Indian texts, describe a technique that is meant to help people become one with 'the world soul' or *Brahman*. This technique was meditation, which simply means sitting quietly and concentrating on the breath; it was also said to have powers of healing. A similar

Around 8 BC: The Upanishads are written.

practice, almost as old as meditation, is yoga. These practices required total peace and quiet, so many Brahmin withdrew from the world around them. They left everything behind, retreated to the forests and spent their days meditating.

But what did they seek to achieve by becoming at one with the divine breath of Brahma? It's difficult to say. Perhaps they were seeking wisdom and knowledge; or maybe they believed that, by devoting the whole of their being to the gods, they could escape the eternal cycle of rebirth.

THE SHANG AND THE ZHOU

A girl is not good

Around 1800 BC, while the Babylonians were watching the stars and the Harappa civilisation was entering its twilight, history was beginning again: this time in China. Here another advanced civilisation developed, but the first written evidence of its existence wouldn't be uncovered for centuries.

The story of its discovery is a strange one. Just over 100 years ago, the chancellor of the Chinese Imperial Academy in Peking was very sick. He ordered some dragon bones from the pharmacy to make some medicine. As luck would have it, the chancellor was a specialist in ancient writing, and just as he was about to grind the bones into a powder, he noticed some strange symbols on them. The bones weren't actually dragon bones, of course; they were just ordinary bones, maybe ox shoulder blades, that some farmers had gathered while ploughing their fields and then sold off as dragon bones. One thing was real, though: the writing was genuine, and it was very old indeed.

Around 1250 BC: The earliest Chinese characters are carved into animal bones.

Researchers traced the origin of the bones and started digging in the spot where the farmers had found them. They uncovered something remarkable: huge city walls and the foundations of palaces and tombs, some as large as two rooms. Those tombs contained jewellery, weapons and many other artefacts. One of China's most ancient cultures had been discovered … entirely by accident.

13th century BC: The Shang dynasty reigns in China.

This civilisation was named the Shang dynasty. The Shang carved small symbols into bronze containers, turtle shells and ox shoulder blades. These materials weren't used for writing messages to other people, but for communicating with the gods. During Shang rituals, holes were drilled in the bones and a hot poker was then used to produce cracks. The cracks were then interpreted to reveal the answers to questions they had asked the gods.

In general, the gods the Shang communed with were their dead ancestors; they believed that they were surrounded by the spirits of their dead, and that these spirits intervened in every aspect of their lives. For this reason, they cultivated close relationships with their dead relatives. They also clearly thought it was important to document the results of their ancestor rituals with inscriptions on bones. One of the inscriptions reads: 'The Lady Hao will give birth and it may not be good. After thirty-one days, she gave birth. It really was not good. It was a girl.'

The Shang asked the gods for advice on almost everything. Would it be a good harvest? Would it rain? Would it be profitable to go to war with their neighbours? How reliable the answers were, we don't know.

But one thing the inscription does tell us is that, under the Shang, giving birth to a girl was no cause for celebration.

The end of the Shang

Lady Hao, the woman unfortunate enough to give birth to a girl, was the consort of a king. Her tomb was suitably lavish and contained hundreds of carvings, jewellery and bronze art, as well as 755 pieces of jade. She even took weapons with her on her final journey – maybe so she could lead armies against the Shang's enemies.

China as we now know it didn't exist during the Shang era. Because the area that would later become the Chinese Empire is vast, with a varied landscape and climate, the region was divided into lots of small princedoms, each with its own language and customs.

Back then, a ruler's domain was only as big and powerful as their family. If they wanted to increase their power and influence, they needed a bigger family, and the best way of doing this was to get married. King Wu Ding is thought to have had sixty-four wives. There were therefore sixty-four families in his clan, and these families may also have been connected to others through marriage.

Around
1050 BC: The
Zhou overthrow
the Shang.

The downfall of the Shang is told in a legend. The last ruler of the Shang was waging a military campaign against a neighbouring state. During this campaign, he kidnapped a woman called Daji as his bride. At that time, this happened fairly regularly – when a clan like the Shang was strong enough, the leader could take whatever he wanted. This particular bride, though, was a thoroughly bad influence. They got drunk together and revelled in wild parties where prisoners were subjected to unspeakable horrors. According to the legend, the king of a neighbouring province used the pair's behaviour as an excuse to attack the Shang and bring their rule to an end. After the Shang, a new family came to power: the Zhou.

The mandate of Heaven

While the Shang used animal bones to tell the future, the Zhou put their faith in the *I Ching,* or the *Book of Changes.* The book lists sixty-four symbols, each made up of broken and unbroken lines. To find the answer to a question about the future, you would drop a bundle of small sticks and, depending on how the sticks lay, you would look up the corresponding symbol in the *I Ching.*

The Zhou stopped using writing as a means of communicating with their gods. Instead, it occurred to them that they could use it to communicate with each other. Their relationship with the gods changed, too. The spirits of the dead were replaced by Heaven, which would go on to become the highest god. The ruling Zhou family saw their rule as the 'mandate' from Heaven, a responsibility entrusted to them by a higher power. From this belief, they reasoned it was the duty of every ruler to be a paragon of virtue. If they weren't, they forfeited their right to rule.

A legend about the fall of the Zhou demonstrates this idea in action. King You, the last ruler of the Zhou dynasty, had a wife called Bao Si. Bao Si was bored: to entertain her, King You lit the beacons, raising an alarm that brought all his allies rushing to court. On their guard and armed to the teeth, his allies soon discovered the alarm was no more than an elaborate prank. Bao Si laughed, which made the king happy, so he played the prank again. Later, when the Zhou really were under attack, his allies decided they'd had enough. They refused to help, and You was defeated.

The reign of families such as the Shang and Zhou came to an end for many reasons, not just the bad influence of wives and consorts. Factors for their demise included the rise in influence and power of other aristocratic families, which diminished the power of even the strongest kings. Their leadership was also threatened by nomadic horsemen from Mongolia. The folk stories play all this down, though, and instead emphasise the role of Daji and Bao Si, the two women who are blamed for causing their husbands' downfall.

That's the point of legends: the simpler the story, the easier it is to remember and retell. However, myths and legends can also be used to spread a particular point of view, so perhaps it's no coincidence that they tend to follow a certain pattern: a wicked woman appears; she tempts a male ruler, urging him to behave immorally; disaster ensues. In this kind of legend, women become the scapegoat, concealing the real reasons for a ruler's downfall, which often include men's mistakes and misdeeds. In the words of an old Chinese song: 'A wise man builds up the walls of a city, but a wise woman knocks them down.'

ONE GOD

Fire worshippers

The religions of the early civilisations were teeming with deities. There were goddesses or gods of day and night, of fire and sea, of love and death. However, at some time or other, somewhere in the region of Mesopotamia, some people arrived from the highlands in the north (now Iran). These people were known as the Persians; they were strong warriors and their empire spanned from the Euphrates to the Tigris and eventually Egypt. The Persians had their own ideas about how the world was created. They believed in just one god, a creator who made the world in seven days. They had no images of this creator god, whom they viewed as neither human nor animal. Instead, this god was represented by the symbol of fire, and this is why the Greeks called the Persians 'fire worshippers'.

Around 1000 BC: In Persia, Zoroaster starts preaching about a single god, the creator of everything. The priests, who were known as *magi*, could only be men.

The prophet responsible for spreading these beliefs was called Zoroaster or Zarathustra. According to the religion that became known as Zoroastrianism, the world was governed by two principles, good and evil, which were embroiled in an eternal battle for domination. People were expected to contribute to the victory of good. Zoroaster's followers therefore lived according to the creed 'Good thoughts, good words, good deeds'. This concept was unusual, as it meant that people were more than just helpless victims to the whims of the gods.

Zoroaster's god was male, and his religion was a religion of men. Unlike Egypt and Mesopotamia, where there were priestesses, in Persia, only men could become priests. These priests were called *magi* and could perform magic when they communicated with their god.

Eve is weak

The Persians and the cult of Zoroaster may have influenced a small neighbouring population by giving them the idea of a sole creator god. Like the Persians, the Jewish creation story told of a god who created the world in seven days. On the seventh day, he took a lump of clay and made the first human: Adam, the pinnacle of his creation. But Adam was lonely. God placed Adam in a deep sleep and took one of his ribs to create a companion, Eve.

But the story doesn't end there. Once God had created the world, Adam, Eve and all the animals lived in a paradise where they wanted for nothing and were safe from everyone and everything. The trees were laden with ripe fruit, so they never went hungry. The only fruit off-limits were the apples of a certain tree, the tree of the knowledge of good and evil. God had forbidden Adam and Eve from eating from this tree. One day, though, the couple met a snake. The snake whispered to them that these apples were tastier than all the others, and eating them would give them a share of the knowledge that God was withholding from them. The snake's words were mesmerising, and Eve was unable to resist. She bit into the apple and then offered it to Adam. When God found out, he banished them from Paradise for daring to defy him. They had crossed a red line by disobeying God's instructions and seeking out forbidden knowledge; they had to suffer the consequences. God expelled them from Paradise to live on the Earth. Now they would have to fend for themselves and toil on the land to grow food.

This is the story of the Fall, humanity's expulsion from Paradise. It's a story with many different interpretations. One is that know-ledge brought humanity great unhappiness, as it became aware of its own imperfections. According to another interpretation, the story is mainly about the weakness and foolishness of women. After all, it was Eve who had been seduced by the snake, bringing calamity to all. This second interpretation establishes a firm link between women, the Fall and sin – this had consequences. For millennia, scholars referred back to the Fall and used it as a weapon against women. They were seen as the 'weaker' gender, both physically and mentally. Adam and Eve's expulsion from Paradise was used as justification for the oppression

Around 1200 BC: Judaism emerges in Israel.

Around 1200 BC: One of the oldest stories in Judaism – the story of Adam and Eve being expelled from Paradise – is written down. From then on, women are viewed as the weaker gender.

of women, and it was taken as proof that women were inherently inferior to men.

God is a man

The story of Adam and Eve shows how the stories people told could affect the world just as much as real events. When the Jews wrote down the stories that would later become their holy texts (and the basis of the Jewish faith), Israel was a small country and the Jews were one of many ethnic groups living there. But in their holy book, the Torah, they completely redefined humanity's relationship with God, changing the world.

The Torah tells how God entered a special covenant with the Jewish people by making Abraham their patriarch. As his Chosen People, his divine protection was offered only to them. In return, however, he demanded their absolute obedience.

Around 1200 BC: The god of the Israelites is said to have given Moses the Ten Commandments.

As time went on, the Jews' obedience to God appeared to be waning. So God spoke to the prophet Moses and gave them a new set of rules to live by: the Ten Commandments. These ten laws had a very unusual structure, as they each started with 'You shall'. This was the first time in recorded human history that God had spoken to someone directly.

Laws like the Code of Hammurabi were invented by humans and could be changed. The Ten Commandments, on the other hand, were sacrosanct because they came directly from God. 'You shall not kill'. The end. These laws were eternal and unchanging, and they applied to everyone. It didn't matter whether you were poor and powerless or rich and powerful – you had to obey. While the favour of the ancient gods could be won over by regular offerings, this new god had different ideas: he watched what you did and judged your behaviour. He wanted you to behave as you were expected to. In other words, he wanted exactly the same as the Zoroastrian god: good thoughts, good words, good deeds.

And yet, the way that the Jews pictured their god was completely new. Their god wasn't a human who had been granted immortality.

He was neither man nor woman and was everything we humans aren't. He was invisible, which is why in the Second Commandment he commanded: 'You shall not make for yourself an image in the form of anything in heaven above or on the earth beneath or in the waters below.' The god of Israel was also a jealous god who tolerated no other gods but himself. He was not one god among many, he was simply 'God'. It was forbidden to speak his name aloud, so in Jewish texts he's referred to by just four letters: YHWH.

But if God communicated with humans and humans communicated with God, how were they to address him if his name couldn't be spoken? How were they meant to pray to him? Such power was almost inconceivable, so the Jews had to make some assumptions about their god. In place of his unspeakable divine name, they started using the word *Adonai*, which means 'my Lord'. Somehow, an invisible, unnameable god became a man.

From then on, the Jews made a sharp distinction between men and women. This was inspired by the story of the Fall, and they invented laws banishing women to their houses and requiring strict obedience to their husbands. As an old Jewish prayer says: 'Blessed are You, God, our Lord, king of the universe, who has not made me a non-Jew ... a servant ... or a woman.'

Asherah, God's wife

Although centuries had passed since the time of Abraham and Moses, the people of Israel – the Canaanites – still kept some customs that were even older still. These customs endured for a while before the new god became the undisputed one god. For example, one temple was built to honour this one god, but King Manasseh decided to put a wooden pole in it, which was a symbol of the earlier religion. This wooden pole is thought to have been a representation of Asherah, a goddess popular in Canaan at the time. An inscription even survives, referring to her as YHWH's wife, 'his Asherah'. It was only later that King Josiah removed Asherah from the temple and converted the temple in Jerusalem into a place to worship the single changeless,

Around 7th
century BC:
The goddess
Asherah is
removed from
the Jewish
temple.

masculine god. With the removal of Asherah, the last goddess of Judaism is thought to have disappeared too.

The end of the goddesses

Goddesses such as the Egyptian goddess Isis enjoyed widespread fame and were honoured throughout the ancient world. For as long as there were goddesses, there were priestesses and important aspects of religion that were given over to women. With their knowledge of birth, life and death, they enjoyed the same high esteem as their heavenly counterparts.

All of this changed with the arrival of the belief in one god – monotheism, which comes from the Greek words *mono* for 'single' or 'alone' and *theos* for 'god'. The removal of the goddess Asherah from the Jewish temple marked the beginning. But the victory of the one god didn't take place overnight: for a long time the only monotheists in the world were the Jews and the Persians. Nevertheless, the goddesses of Europe, and many other parts of the world, eventually disappeared from human consciousness as well. When the goddesses vanished the priestesses did too, ushering in an era in which women were almost completely excluded from all places of worship.

THE BUDDHA DISCOVERS THE PATH TO LIBERATION

The story of Siddhartha Gautama, the Buddha

In the fifth or sixth century BC, a man appeared in northern India and founded a new religion from the country's ancient traditions. His name was Siddhartha Gautama, and he wasn't happy about the state of the world. Life, he said, meant suffering, and as humans were imprisoned by the eternal cycle of birth and rebirth, they were condemned forever to experiencing new forms of suffering. Gautama started searching for a way out.

Many years after leaving his family home, he finally attained enlightenment: he'd found a way of avoiding suffering, and he travelled far and wide to share his experience with others. He gained many followers, formed communities and founded monasteries where they lived simple lives as monks and nuns in accordance with these new teachings. They called Gautama *Buddha*, which means 'awakened' or 'enlightened' in Sanskrit. His teachings would form the foundations of Buddhism.

Around 500 BC: Siddhartha Gautama discovers a way to liberate himself from the eternal cycle of rebirth. This is the birth of Buddhism.

The holy texts describing the life of Gautama Buddha form a web of truth and myth. The same can be said of all holy texts, most of which are very old and were passed down orally for a long time before anybody wrote them down. It can therefore be difficult to differentiate between what's true and what's not.

Siddhartha Gautama is thought to have been the son of an influential warrior. His parents did their best to raise him as a good soldier, but he preferred to spend his time meditating, and when Gautama wanted to marry his future wife Yasodhara, her father demanded he prove his bravery first. Yasodhara's father organised a series of tests for Gautama, against some of the greatest warriors in the land. He won all of them.

While almost certainly a legend, one story from the holy texts in particular vividly illustrates Gautama's motivations. According to the story, the Buddha saw an old man, a sick person, a dead body and a holy man. The first three showed him that the suffering of life could be ended by age, sickness and death. The holy man, though, appeared to have found another way out.

Although Yasodhara had borne him a son, Gautama decided to set out on a religious quest, leaving his home and family behind. Back then, lots of ascetics and beggar monks wandered the land meditating because they were unhappy about the power of the Brahmins. Gautama joined them.

In accordance with the Vedas and Upanishads, he sat for a whole year, focusing his mind, eating little and denying all comforts. He believed that if he meditated long enough, he would eventually find the answer to his questions. But the answer never came.

Finally, Gautama was forced to admit that the only thing he had gained from all that meditation and self-denial was severe pain in his joints. He stopped meditating. In that very moment, he became enlightened, just as he had given up! This is hard to understand as it means you have to stop wanting things: suffering is caused by our desires.

From that point on, Gautama taught the 'Four Noble Truths':

1. Everything is suffering.
2. Suffering is caused by never-ending desire.
3. We can put an end to suffering if we stop wanting things.
4. We can learn how to do this by following the Eightfold Path.

Gautama taught his students the Eightfold Path, a series of spiritual and moral exercises. Those who followed him could achieve enlightenment as well. The goal was to attain a state after death known as nirvana. The word *nirvana* means 'blowing out' or 'extinguishing' in the sense of putting out a flame. Whoever achieved this state was liberated from the cycle of rebirth. They would never suffer again.

This new teaching was revolutionary because, unlike the caste system, it treated everyone as equals. Whether Brahmin or farmer, anybody could follow the Eightfold Path, women included. What mattered was not a person's birth or social status, but the way they led their lives and how much good karma they gathered.

The Buddha respected women. His foster mother Mahapajapati was one of his first female followers; she founded an order of nuns and became ordained. Around a third of Buddhism's first monks were women, but this didn't stop Gautama from feeling conflicted about their role. He was afraid they would tempt men to stray from the straight and narrow. He therefore decreed that women should be subordinate to all monks, right down to the youngest. His closest confidant Ananda is said to have asked the Buddha how they were to behave towards women.

'Don't look at them, Ananda,' replied the Buddha.

'And what if we have to see them?'

'Don't speak to them.'

'And what if we have to speak to them?'

'Remain on your guard, Ananda.'

Gautama was treated like a god, even though the religion he founded doesn't recognise any gods. It consists solely of exercises aimed at releasing people from suffering. A central component of its teaching is spiritual contemplation through meditation, which is why the Buddha is always pictured sitting down.

Little of what we know about the Buddha is certain because the information we have was written down many years after his death. What we do know, though, is this: in the fifth or sixth century BC, a new religion was founded in India that changed Indian society. Buddhism spread throughout south-eastern Asia with its monasteries and offered everybody the chance of a life outside the country's caste system and an escape from the goings-on of the world. For many, that also meant an escape from suffering.

THE BIRTH OF EUROPE AND ANCIENT GREECE

The abduction of Europa

While the Buddha was finding the path to enlightenment in India, the people of Greece were telling one another the following story (and they'd been telling it for a long time). Zeus, the father of the gods, fell in love with a young girl called Europa. His wife guarded him jealously, so he turned into a bull and joined a herd of cows in the meadow where the girl and her friend were playing. Europa approached the mighty bull, stroked him and then climbed up onto his back. Zeus seized his chance and kidnapped her, whisking her off to the island of Crete. Once they arrived, he revealed his true identity. The two became a couple and had three children. When the goddess Aphrodite heard the story, she prophesied that Europa would give her name to a new continent.

The Greeks also believed that the gods had created the heavens, the Earth, the oceans, the mountains and even time itself. The Greek gods lived on a mountain called Olympus, and although they were immortal beings with magic and superhuman powers, they behaved just like humans. They fell in love and fought with one another, danced, sang, laughed and had riotous parties, and they could also be vain, angry, quarrelsome and jealous.

Most of the stories the Greeks told about their past – the myths and legends – were a blend of truth and fiction. For the Greeks, there was hardly any difference between the two. After all, if a god had the power to create the Earth and give humans the gift of fire, why shouldn't he be able to turn into a bull too? It made perfect sense;

it was all a part of their world. To put things another way: if something couldn't happen in the real world, it could in the world of the gods. For example, war was traditionally the preserve of men, but in the myths, female warriors called Amazons went into battle alongside other women on horseback, armed with shields and axes. Vast armies of these women swept across the land. The residents of Mount Olympus also included Athena, the goddess of war and strategy.

The history of Europe actually started on Crete, the Greek island where Zeus held his kidnapped bride. This is a good example of how the stories the Greeks told always contained a dose of real history too. On Crete, the walls of huge 4,000-year-old palaces have been discovered, as well as the remains of the Minoans, the island's ancient inhabitants. Unfortunately, these ruins guard their secrets even more closely than the Egyptian tombs and pyramids, as no one has yet deciphered Minoan script.

2nd–3rd century BC: The Minoan culture blossoms on the Greek island of Crete. This is the birthplace of Europe.

Eventually the Minoan civilisation collapsed, war broke out and its palaces were destroyed. What followed was a time from which hardly any archaeological finds, texts or ruins have survived. This is a shame – and rather frustrating! – as we have numerous traces of earlier Greek societies. After the Minoans, however, between 1200 and 800 BC, practically everything went dark. These sorts of historical gaps have happened at other times too and have been described by some people as 'dark ages'. Some think that, after the decline of the Minoan culture, people lived as nomads and moved from place to place; some may even have migrated long distances before settling down and building permanent homes again. As a result, the later Greeks' memories of the Minoan period were hazy and survived only in their myths and legends. Travelling singers journeyed through the country, reciting them in verse and song.

Between 1200 and 800 BC: This is the time known as the Greek Dark Ages. We know very little about Greece during this era.

A good woman spins wool

At the end of the Greek Dark Ages, Greece's first written texts appeared. These texts are thought to have been written down by Homer, a travelling bard who's said to have been blind. They told

Around 800 BC:
Homer the
bard travels
around Greece,
narrating Greek
mythology in
his epic poems
The Iliad and
The Odyssey (if
he existed at all,
that is; we can't
be sure).

their stories orally, in verse with a very specific rhythm called hexameter, which made long stories easier to remember.

Homer is believed to have been the author of many of the myths and legends that were written down in 800 BC. His fame spread throughout Greece, to the Black Sea, Rome, and eventually Europe. As with the biblical story of the Fall, although the Greek myths were 'only' stories, their impact was huge. It could even be said that they were responsible for the foundation of Europe, a community of people who have told one another the same stories over and over, right up to the present day. Homer's most famous works, *The Iliad* and *The Odyssey*, describe the ten-year war against the city of Troy and the hero Odysseus's long journey home after its end.

The Trojan War was started by an argument over a woman, the beautiful Helen. Paris, the son of the Trojan king, had stolen her away from a Greek king. Of course, the gods had a hand in events too: the Greek goddess of love, Aphrodite, made sure that Helen fell in love with Paris and eloped with him of her own free will to Troy. When war broke out, with seemingly no end in sight, Helen stayed at home and spun wool, just as women were expected to. The same was true of Odysseus's wife Penelope, whose own son, Homer tells us, told her to be silent while she awaited Odysseus's return. In front of the entire court, Telemachus ordered her: 'Go home and see to your own work, the spindle and the loom ... Speech is a matter for men.'

The roles of men and women were clearly defined. The goddesses of Olympus may have had magical powers, and Zeus may have had to resort to scheming and trickery to get one over his wives and daughters, but at the end of the day, he always had the final say. The patriarch of the divine family could do as he pleased.

Women also feature in Homer's stories as brave housewives who do the right thing by staying at home. Women outside the domestic sphere posed a danger to men. When Odysseus was sailing the seas, he was ambushed by the sea monsters Scylla and Charybdis; some of his companions were turned into pigs by the sorceress Circe; and the sea nymph Calypso held Odysseus prisoner until a god ordered her to set the poor sailor free. These women were a threat to the men: they seduced them, making them submissive and weak.

Even though they didn't really exist, the stories of the bloodthirsty Amazons carry a similar message: beware of powerful women!

Sappho's lost poems

Homer's stories had a real-world impact on the everyday lives of the men and women of Greece. Gender roles in real life were divided along quite similar lines to those in his stories. That isn't to say there weren't exceptions, though. One of the most famous of these was the poet Sappho. Scarcely had anyone written about love as beautifully as she did, and for centuries her poems have inspired writers the world over. She may also have been the first to describe a universal experience of love as 'bittersweet', because although love can be sweet, it can also cause great pain. She even had a particular verse form named after her called the Sapphic stanza, which poets were still using millennia later.

6th or 7th century BC: Sappho writes poems about love on the island of Lesbos. She becomes world famous.

But almost all of Sappho's poetry has been lost to time, with only fragments and a few whole poems surviving. If only we still had all of Sappho's poetry, mused Friedrich Schlegel in the eighteenth century, then perhaps we wouldn't be so obsessed with Homer. By then, Sappho had been dead for more than 2,000 years.

Sappho lived on the Greek island of Lesbos. It was remarkable how harmonious and happy Sappho and her female companions were together, without men. In fact, the word 'lesbian' has its roots in the name of Sappho's island home; it's a reminder of the love and companionship she found within her close circle of female friends.

Cities, states and colonies

During Sappho and Homer's lifetimes, small scattered settlements started to join together to form larger entities known as city states. Many of these city states appeared on the mainland of Anatolia, the peninsula of Peloponnese and lots of the islands in between. In Greek city states, the shots were mostly called by rich men, while the poor had fewer or sometimes even no rights at all. The most powerful and influential people were the *aristoi*, the aristocrats or nobility. Sometimes a single *aristos* managed to seize power exclusively for themselves. These sole rulers were called tyrants, and everyone feared them, as many used their unchecked power for their own benefit rather than the benefit of society.

The population of Greece's cities and villages had grown, so more land was needed. The Greeks therefore started invading their neighbours and frequently took their defeated enemies as slaves. These invasions enabled the Greeks to expand into the north and the east, and westwards as far as Italy. When they arrived, they founded new settlements known as colonies. Soon, there were cities and city states all around the Mediterranean where people spoke more or less the same language: Greek. Nevertheless, these settlements retained their independence; some were ruled by tyrants, while others were ruled by a handful of nobles. The balance of power was constantly changing. Often, the cities fought against one another. More land meant more wealth, so the large city states constantly tried to gain the upper hand over their neighbours.

The Greeks defeat Xerxes and Artemisia

The further the Greek colonies spread, the closer they got to the borders of the mighty Persian Empire in the east. But the Persian kings were also hungry for new land and kept shifting their borders further westward. In fact, they had already conquered some of Greece's island and Anatolian coast colonies (now Turkey). This meant constant clashes between the Persians and the Greeks.

The Persian army was vastly superior to Greece's, so the Greek cities decided to put aside their differences temporarily and join forces against their common enemy. Together, the Greeks dealt the Persians a series of shattering defeats. This brought great shame on King Xerxes and his mighty army, so he searched the coast of Anatolia for allies to join him in his conquest of Greece. Artemisia I, the Queen of Halicarnassus, went into battle with Xerxes, bringing with her five ships, and, according to the historian Herodotus, she offered the Persian king better advice than his own commanders. Artemisia knew that attacking the Greeks at Salamis was a tactical mistake, but the king didn't listen to her. Unfortunately for Xerxes, by the time he realised he *should* listen, it was too late. The Battle of Salamis went ahead as planned and the Persian fleet was defeated. Knowing the battle was lost, Artemisia sank her own ship, preferring to drown rather than be captured by the enemy – a true Amazon. Seeing her courage, Xerxes is said to have proclaimed: 'My men have become women and my women, men.'

480 BC: The Greeks defeat the Persians at Salamis.

Who knows? If the king had followed Artemisia's advice, the Persians may have gone on to conquer the whole of Greece.

Greece's victory stopped its free cities from being subsumed into the powerful Persian Empire. This was around 500 BC. After their victory over the Persians, the Greeks had the freedom and military might to develop their own culture. This culture still forms the template for many aspects of European society to this day.

The Oracle of Delphi

Before facing the Persian army at Salamis, the Athenians travelled to Delphi. A long time ago, Apollo, the god of the sun, arts and prophecy, was said to have killed a huge serpent there called Python, and a temple was built to commemorate his victory. It was watched over by a priestess called the Pythia, whose task it was to answer complex questions. People travelled from all over Greece to receive wisdom from the 'Oracle of Delphi' ('oracle' comes from the Latin *ōrāre*, which means 'to speak/pray'). Her answers were usually cryptic and hard to understand. According to legend, a philosopher once asked the Pythia what the most important lesson was that a person could learn. Her answer? 'Know thyself.'

The Greeks took the oracle's prophecies very seriously. In fact, there may have been no higher authority in all the land, as ultimately, her mysterious predictions came from the god Apollo himself. When the Athenians went to Delphi and asked the oracle what they should do in the war against the Persians, the Pythia answered, in her usual cryptic fashion: 'Seek the safety of the wooden walls!' After a lengthy discussion, the Athenian strategists concluded that the 'wooden walls' meant the walls of their ships. They decided to attack the Persian army by sea and to fight the Battle of Salamis on water rather than on land. They won the war.

Goodness, truth, beauty and the perfect state

Around 500 BC: The Greeks invent democracy – 'government by the people'.

Against the backdrop of these violent flare-ups, something extraordinary was happening in Athens. Its citizens were coming up with a series of laws setting out how the city should be run. The difference between these laws and others was that they involved as many people as possible in the running of the state, including the poor. The purpose of the laws was to stop a single tyrant from imposing his will over the entire population. The Athenians formed a council of 500 members, which was responsible for deciding what issues to bring before the people's assembly. The people's assembly, which consisted of 6,000 members, then took a vote.

On top of the Acropolis, a rocky outcrop above the city, the Athenians had built a temple to the gods. Not far below was the *agora*, the marketplace where the citizens of Athens held their assemblies. There was a lot to discuss. Should they or shouldn't they go to war? How would they find the equipment for the army and who would pay for it? Should criminals be exiled from the city? All of these matters were decided by the people, which is where the word democracy (or 'government by the people') comes from. However, the people involved had to be able to make intelligent decisions. They had to have a good understanding of all aspects of public life, including trade, city planning and warfare, their relationships with neighbouring states and the difference between right and wrong. When a decision needed to be made, the people who argued most convincingly and persuaded their fellow citizens usually won the day.

Conveniently, the Greeks had just invented a new style of thinking that could help them do just that. They called it philosophy, the 'love of wisdom'. During the early years of democracy in Athens, teachers walked the streets of the city giving lessons to every citizen they met. One of the wisest of these teachers was Socrates, who spent his days debating in the city's squares. A malicious rumour spread that Socrates found his wife Xanthippe so unbearable that he did anything to avoid being at home. When Socrates met someone, he involved them in a deep conversation about the questions that occupied him most: what is courage (certainly pressing, given Greece's many wars)? What is justice? What is good? Through his questioning, he wanted to encourage Athenian citizens to reflect on their actions and behave more rationally.

Socrates engaged in philosophical dialogues with his student Plato, which the latter wrote down. In one of these famous dialogues, Socrates once went as far as to say that men and women were, by nature, the same. For this reason, he argued, men and women could do exactly the same things. Why, asked Plato, shouldn't women work as guards? Why shouldn't men be able to bring up children? His reasoning was based on an interesting point: if women were as dim-witted and uneducated as people believed, then why were they entrusted with raising the future citizens of Athens? The book describing Plato's thought experiment is called *The Republic*, and what he writes here must have sounded completely crazy to the Greeks. They had no reason to worry, though: the book is purely utopian, meaning it described an ideal or imagined world; Plato didn't actually think that the ideas in the book could be acted on in real life.

Life in free cities was an inspiration to the Greeks. They started to innovate in subjects other than philosophy, turning their attention to cosmology, grammar, mythology, political philosophy, religion, law, science and mathematics. They invented theatre, wrote poems and created works of art we still marvel at today. In honour of the gods of Olympus, they erected mighty buildings and held a huge sporting competition every four years – the Olympic Games. At these games, sportsmen from all over Greece competed against one another in races, javelin and other sports. All of this was in aid of one overarching goal: to promote virtuous behaviour and the creation of the perfect society.

6th century BC: The beginning of Greek philosophy.

Misogyny: the Greek word for the hatred of women

Athenian democracy was a unique invention. The citizens of Athens proudly asserted their right to participate in how society was governed. There was just one catch, though: only men were allowed to take part. A man could become a farmer or a statesman, a merchant, craftsman, poet, philosopher, speaker, sculptor, architect or doctor. One day, he could be working in the theatre and ,the next, he could go to war. Later, he could become a member of the council and discuss the political issues of the day. He could take part in sports competitions and become famous throughout the land.

Women, however, were excluded from this democracy. No matter what was planned, built, discussed or decided in the courts, they weren't allowed to be a part of it. Even in the theatre, female roles were played by men – the only role a woman could have was as a dancer. According to the Greek poet Sophocles, 'Women should be seen and not heard'.

In Greece, women's lives revolved around the home – but it's not as if there was nothing to do there. The crops men brought back from the fields were cooked by the women; they ground grain, baked bread, and made cheese and olive oil. Their most important responsibility was making fabric and textiles. The spindle had to be kept turning almost constantly to spin enough wool into yarn for fabric. The writer Xenophon once wrote that spinning was 'the work considered the most honourable and the most suitable for a woman'. Well, the reason for burdening women with this chore had to be explained one way or another, we suppose!

Men were allowed to come and go as they pleased. A woman was not allowed the same freedom, and if she did go out, she attracted unwelcome attention. A woman was always seen as the property of a man: a daughter belonged to her father and a wife belonged to her husband. It was considered very dangerous for a lone woman to meet a man in the street. When a woman did show herself in public, she was expected, at the very least, to wear a veil.

Of course, not all women were married. The elderly, who were often widows, could be seen selling their wares at market. Young, unmarried women entertained men at drinking festivals as dancers or acrobats. At these events, some women, the *hetairai*, sold their love to men.

Love and sexuality are two things that have brought much suffering to women all over the world, throughout all of history. When a woman fell in love with a man outside marriage, everyone pointed the finger and said, 'Shame on you! You've brought dishonour upon yourself!' Even when it wasn't her fault and a man had committed violence against her, a woman's life was ruined.

But these same rules didn't apply to men. If a man fell in love with a woman outside marriage, or even forced her against her will, he often had little to fear. Men *could* be prosecuted, but it was generally the woman who was assumed to be guilty, as it was assumed the woman had tempted the man to commit the crime, just as Eve had tempted Adam to taste the forbidden apple. In Greece too, the courtesans who offered men their love, the *hetairai,* made men feel uncomfortable. They were described as women who threatened to seduce them, cast a spell over them and drag them off to the underworld like the sea monsters, enchantresses and sirens encountered by Odysseus on his travels.

There were so many Greek writers who hated women that it's tempting to claim that the Greeks invented 'misogyny' (hatred of women) – and not just the word. The Greek historian Hesiod wrote, 'Zeus who thunders on high made women to be an evil to mortal men.'

Greek misogyny seems strange because, among Greek women, there were always exceptions who earned fame and recognition for themselves. One of these women was Sappho. Another was Agnodice, a doctor who disguised herself as a man so she could practise and was eventually brought before the court on no charge other than helping women to give birth.

The request made by Hipparchia, a young woman from a rich family, was also unusual. She refused money, jewellery and every manner of trinket, because there was only one thing she wanted: to become a philosopher. Naturally this meant that she was forced to have endless discussions with men who refused to believe a woman could philosophise. Aside from his fiery wife Xanthippe, Socrates knew many clever women. These included Aspasia, a woman who had taught him philosophy and whom he respected immensely.

Despite these examples to the contrary, widespread hatred of women has made a deep imprint on human consciousness. The mathematician Pythagoras summarised it like this: 'There's a good principle which created order, light and man, and an evil principle which created chaos, darkness and woman.' The contrast to the Egyptians couldn't have been starker: in Egypt, order, truth and justice were represented as a woman with an ostrich feather on her head.

The ideas remain

Even beyond Athens, Ancient Greece was a world for men, and when you consider that only three in every ten Athenians enjoyed the full rights of a citizen (the rest were either women or slaves), it was really a world made for a few privileged men. Today, this wouldn't be considered fair, but back then working people were seen as having nothing worth saying. Those who did were expected to have better things to do than waste their time on work.

The freedom from work enjoyed by Athenian citizens gave them the chance to think about how they wanted to live and how a good society should function. This was something quite extraordinary, as were the laws the Greeks introduced to prevent tyranny and the abuse of power. This complicated system lasted for almost 200 years, but then vanished into the realm of utopia for more than 2,000. For a long time, there was nowhere in the world where democracy could be made a reality.

After the Greeks' victory over the Persians, it would be almost 1,000 years until the classical world faded and gave way to a new era. But the ideas of the Greeks, their politics, philosophy, art, theatre and sport, have all endured long beyond their time. Unfortunately, so did their conviction that a woman's place was in the kitchen.

THE FIRST CONQUERORS OF THE WORLD

An underestimated neighbour

To the Greeks, the speech of people they couldn't understand sounded like a sequence of 'bar-bar-bar' noises; therefore, they called these foreign peoples 'barbarians'. However, this word soon became a term of abuse. The more successful and richer the Greeks – and particularly the Athenians – became, and the grander their buildings, theatre and art were, the more they started to look down on others. Not only could these barbarians not understand Greek, they had no culture to speak of either. They were uncultured savages.

One of the groups considered 'barbarians' by the Greeks was the Macedonians. Rather than having a democracy like the Greeks, the Macedonians were ruled by a king called Philip. Philip of Macedonia led a series of successful military campaigns, ultimately forcing the proud Greeks into an alliance with him. In the end, however, the Macedonians, who the Greeks had so badly underestimated, were victorious and the golden age of Greece's cities came to an end.

The mutilated male

Even as a child, Philip's son Alexander knew he would inherit his father's kingdom. His greatest dream was to expand the kingdom with new conquests. To prepare his son for this great task, the king asked the greatest philosopher of all time, Aristotle, to tutor his son.

342 BC: Aristotle, one of history's greatest philosophers, explains the nature of god and the world to the boy who would become Alexander the Great. His understanding of women left a lot to be desired, though ...

This may sound like an exaggeration – Aristotle himself had studied under the mighty Plato at his academy in Athens, after all – but in years to come, Aristotle would join Plato as 'a philosopher of philosophers'. For 2,000 years, all European thought started with Aristotle, and even Arab scholars were influenced by his teachings. He laid down the foundations of science and philosophy, gathered and categorised information about the natural world, its plants and its animals, and wrote about history, politics, logic (how to think correctly) and ethics (how to behave correctly). Aristotle also contemplated the nature of god, who he described as the 'unmoved mover' of Heaven and Earth.

No doubt about it: Aristotle was a great thinker. But there's one area where, for a long time, people made more mistakes than real discoveries. Despite dissecting animals and human bodies to explore their internal organs, all they found were lumps of tissue and a grey, slimy mass inside the skull. Nobody could explain how these materials and our experiences were connected. Where did our ability to see things come from, and our ability to speak, to hear words and to think thoughts? How did we come to fall in love or feel loneliness, hate, despair or pride? How was this grey blob able to conceive fantastic buildings or complex bodies of knowledge like mathematics? Even today, we still haven't found a complete solution to the puzzle of the relationship between the body and the spirit, the living body and the soul.

Today, we can explain what is going on in our bodies from birth to death; we have a thorough understanding of muscles and blood, and organs like the heart, kidneys, liver and lungs. In Aristotle's time, though, there was no such thing as microscopes or chemistry. People didn't know anything about the metabolic processes that went on in the cells or the complex relationships between the body's organs. And because they didn't know, all they could do was guess.

Aristotle observed and wrote descriptions of hundreds of plants and animals. He examined many of them inside and out, developing his own theories about how they worked. Aristotle believed that, in the natural world, all living things were placed in an order, from lowest to highest. The same order applied to men and women. In the womb, he claimed, boys were positioned on the right and girls on the

left – a crucial difference, because the right-hand side was traditionally associated with what is good and correct.

Aristotle was convinced that women had a defect that could
be traced back to a lack of heat in the womb; he believed that, as
a result of this, a girl's brain was smaller and less developed than a
boy's. A woman, he wrote, was a deformed man. They were also cold
and wet like snakes. Aristotle's observations were based on animals
not humans, but this didn't stop him from coming to the following
conclusion: 'The female is a female by virtue of a certain lack of qualities … a natural defectiveness.' For this reason, he deduced, 'A good
woman should be as submissive as a slave.' How's that for logic?

This wasn't the only way in which the great Aristotle was way off
the mark. He also believed the brain was a cold organ and that people
thought with their hearts – the worst thing was that generations of
scholars took his word for it. Many years later, an influential Roman
doctor still believed that women were less perfect than men because
their bodies were colder.

It takes some nerve to claim that women are somehow less perfect
than men (women go through the complex business of childbirth,
after all!), but that's just the way it was back then. Women were seen
as incomplete and men as the crowning achievement of creation.
With the story of the Fall, backed up by Aristotle's teachings, people
now had two reasons for believing this was the truth. It was both
nature and the will of God.

To the east and back again

None of this was of much interest to Aristotle's young pupil
Alexander. It's said that Alexander didn't learn much from his famous
teacher and that the two also disagreed about the nature of good politics. Aristotle sang the praises of democracy, where power was shared
among the many, while the king's son harboured notions of conquering the entire world single-handedly.

Alexander's story can be told quickly. After his father's death, he
took the throne and led his army to the east where he won every battle
he fought. The Persians, whose superior army had posed a real threat

to Greece a short time earlier, were simply swept aside. After that, he went to Egypt, where he made himself pharaoh. He then returned to the east, conquering one enemy after another. Along the way, he married Roxana, who, as well as already being the wife of the Persian king, was said to be the most beautiful woman in all of Asia. She accompanied him on his campaign of conquest. Alexander and his troops finally reached an uncharted region on the banks of a river Alexander called the Indus – they had arrived in India. His soldiers then went on strike. They refused to go a single step further. Sulking like a child, Alexander sat in his tent for three days before finally giving up and turning his entire army around.

335–323 BC: Alexander the Great wants to conquer the entire world, but he dies before he achieves his goal.

On the journey home, Alexander had a brainwave. He knew that a great empire was easy to conquer but difficult to govern. Macedonians, Greeks, Persians, Egyptians and Indians: they all lived a great distance from one another and were unfamiliar with one another's customs and traditions. Alexander wanted to change this. When he arrived at the Persian city of Susa, he decided to organise a mass wedding. The plan was for eighty high-ranking Greek and Macedonian governors or generals from his entourage to marry eighty Persian women. The festivities lasted five days, during which Alexander also took two more wives; he loved a good party – and a good drink.

Alexander died suddenly, never completing his journey back to his homeland Macedonia, and nobody really knows why. His great empire fell in less time than it took to conquer. Nevertheless, his spectacular campaign of conquest changed the world. Everywhere, from the Mediterranean to India, people came into contact with Greek culture. For many years to come, it would influence the lives of people in distant lands; suddenly, it was all the rage to do things Greek style. Meanwhile, Alexander, who would later become known as 'Alexander the Great', went on to become the hero of many legends and a role model for anyone who, like him, saw themselves as the leaders of a mighty global empire.

THE ROMAN EMPIRE

A sea at the centre of the world

If we could take a bird's eye view of the ancient world, at the very centre of it, we'd see a sea. That blue expanse is the Mediterranean. On its southern bank, in North Africa, was the kingdom of the Phoenicians. According to legend, the capital Carthage was founded by a princess.

Princess Dido was fleeing from her brother when she reached the North African coast. She and her entourage made land and asked the king for his permission to stay. But the king decided to play a little game with her. He told her she could have whatever land she was able to cover with a cow skin. Dido thanked him graciously, took the skin and cut it into the thinnest possible strip. She then took the strip and used it to encircle a generous plot of land, with enough space for an entire city.

814/813 BC: The city of Carthage is founded by the Phoenicians.

The Mediterranean connected Carthage to many kingdoms and city states, and a thriving trade blossomed. However, soon, one city in the centre of Italy started to outshine them all: Rome. The Romans didn't restrict themselves to trade, they also forced their neighbours to pay them tribute. Later, they started using their strong army to conquer other lands, turning them into Roman provinces. Wherever they went, they demanded taxes and soldiers; they filled the state coffers to finance their steadily growing army and continue their conquests.

753 BC: The foundation of Rome.

One region after another fell to Rome until all the lands surrounding the Mediterranean were part of the Roman Empire, the Imperium Romanum. Eventually, rather than being at the centre of several neighbouring states, the Mediterranean found itself at the heart of a single global empire. The Romans called it *Mare nostrum*, 'our sea'.

The navel of the city

The city of Rome, with its villas, houses, temples, towers and triumphal arches, sprawled across seven hills, down into a valley and a wide, open square: the Forum Romanum. This square was the true centre of the city – its beating heart.

The Forum was a bustling place. Day after day, hundreds of people flocked there to do business, discuss politics, share gossip or visit one of the temples around its edges. There were government buildings, courts, temples; all the city's most important buildings were situated around the Forum. Their magnificence was a testament to the sheer power radiating from this centre.

Here at the heart of Rome, decisions were made, the consquences of which were felt from Italy all the way to the Black Sea. Men were sent from Rome to govern the conquered provinces that made up the Roman Empire. Conversely, the city received goods shipping over the Mediterranean Sea or by land. These were stored in huge halls lining the Forum before making their way to the empire's many markets. Exotic fruit, pearls and ivory from the south; honey and furs from the east; wine and oil from the west; and wool, wood and metal from the north: the vast range of wares showed people that Rome was becoming richer and more powerful by the day. The Forum was known as 'the navel of the city of Rome', but the Romans saw it as the navel of the world.

A public affair

This navel of the world was really something special. Firstly, politics was conducted in public rather than behind the walls of a royal palace. In the Senate, senators voted on all the important issues of the day – war and peace, new laws and how taxes were to be spent. Even though the government was made up of just a few well-respected men, the Senate's business was always discussed publicly in the middle of the Forum.

It wasn't always like this, though. In the beginning, Rome too was governed by kings. All the kingdom's power and riches came from its victories at war, wars that had been fought by farmers, craftspeople, merchants and scholars, who had all put their lives on the line as soldiers. Once they realised the power this gave them, their demands to be included in governing the regions they had conquered grew louder. The king was eventually overthrown, and the Romans elected two consuls to rule in their name. Because everyone had a stake in the government, they called their state *Res publica*, 'a public affair'. The Roman Kingdom had become a republic.

Women are frivolous

The democracy of the Greeks and the republic of the Romans were both unique, as they were governed by a larger number of people than just one king. Like the Greeks, the Romans were afraid of a single individual seizing too much power for themselves; their consuls were always elected as a pair so they could keep one another in check. Their terms were also restricted to one year, and they were required to justify their actions to the Senate.

When Rome became a republic, it needed new laws. These laws were written on twelve tables and placed in the Forum Romanum so everyone could see them. The Laws of the Twelve Tables told citizens their rights and responsibilities and what punishment would be meted out for breaking them. People even travelled to Rome from distant lands to claim their rights, as Roman law applied to the entire republic.

Although all Roman citizens were subject to the same laws, it was certainly not the case that everyone enjoyed the same rights. The oldest man, the *paterfamilias*, controlled the lives of everyone in his family, particularly the women, who were placed under the guardianship of their father, brother or husband their whole lives. If anyone wondered why this was, an explanation could be found in the Laws of the Twelve Tables: 'Women, even those of full age, should be under guardianship due to their scatterbrain nature.'

Like the Jewish holy scriptures and Homer's epic poems, Rome's laws maintained that women were of lesser value than men. Children

Around 450 BC: The Laws of the Twelve Tables are issued in Rome. These laws stipulate that the *paterfamilias* (the oldest living male in a household) is the only person who gets a say in the affairs of the republic.

were also exposed to this favouritism. If a family wasn't able to feed its offspring, the girls would be killed first by exposure (they were abandoned in the open), and this decision was naturally made by the *paterfamilias* and nobody else. Even in orphanages, boys received a larger portion of food than girls.

However, putting aside their attitude to women for a moment, it must be said that the Romans got a lot of things right. Their laws were good enough that, almost 2,000 years later, many European laws are still based on them.

Hearth and home

Any self-respecting Roman citizen found Greek tutors for their children. The Romans shared many philosophical and political ideas with their neighbours, as well as their gods and mythology; they both worshipped the Palladium – a wooden statue of the Greek goddess Pallas Athena, which was one of the holiest icons in the city.

The temple housing the Palladium was dedicated to Vesta, who was goddess of hearth and home and was revered in Rome. There was a holy fire inside the temple that was kept constantly burning; the smoke from this fire rose up into the sky from an opening in the temple's domed roof and could be seen for miles around. The Romans were convinced that if this fire ever went out, disaster would befall the city.

The fire in the temple also symbolised the fire that burned in the hearth of every home. Because the hearth was a woman's domain, the sacred fire of Vesta was tended by young priestesses called Vestal Virgins, who held the fate of the entire city in their hands. The Romans' greatest fear was that one of these priestesses would forget her duties by being overcome with passion for a man. To stop this from happening, men were only allowed to enter the temple during the day.

The Vestal Virgins were Rome's only priestesses; all other activities and official offices were held by men. However, religious services and celebratory offerings were attended by lots of women. There were many goddesses dedicated to women's concerns: they helped with pregnancies and births, watched over newborn babies and made sure that husbands remained faithful. Once a year, they celebrated the festival of Bona Dea, the 'good goddess', who was associated with fertility. It was the only festival that women were permitted to take part in.

During the Festival of Bona Dea, aristocratic women gathered in houses to drink wine and dance. Every male – even the animals! – was required to leave the house during the festival and alcohol was smuggled into the abode in jugs labelled 'milk'.

Luxury in wartime

After several hundred years, the Roman Republic was hit by wave after wave of crisis. These crises changed the republic and ultimately led to its downfall.

The first of these crises was the Punic Wars. The mighty Romans experienced their first military defeats in their altercations with the *Punici* – the Roman name for the Phoenicians who lived in Carthage. Hannibal, a courageous Carthaginian general, advanced from the north over the Alps and into the heart of Rome accompanied by almost forty elephants. These gargantuan animals made a deep impression on the Romans, as did the shock of being defeated, initially, by the Carthaginians.

According to the Roman historian Livy, the impact of the Punic Wars was also felt by Rome's women. In the tense days of war, the Senate passed a law forbidding women from wearing expensive jewellery or fine clothes, and from travelling through the city in carriages. Perhaps the senators intended to use their gold and jewels to finance the war?

When reports of Rome's first victories over the Carthaginians were sent home and the Romans were able to refill their coffers with money and goods looted from their enemies, the women wanted this law repealed. But how could they get the senators to listen to them? They couldn't very well go to the Senate themselves and have the decision forced through. Their only option was to find a man to take up their complaint on their behalf.

264–146 BC: Despite initial defeats, the Romans claim victory over their strongest enemy, Carthage, in the three Punic Wars. Hannibal of Carthage rode into battle with elephants, but he didn't manage to defeat Rome.

And that's exactly what they did. To reach the Senate, all the senators had to walk through the Forum Romanum. The women stood at the entrances to the Forum and spoke to every member of Senate to win their support. Although some were convinced of the women's cause, most were outraged at the women's behaviour. The senator Marcus Porcius Cato was particularly scathing. He argued that if women were allowed to express their opinions in public once, it wouldn't be long before they wanted to weigh in on everything. The law had placed women under the guardianship of men for good reason: the whole state would be put in jeopardy if women – careless, undisciplined creatures – were included in decision-making.

The next day, the women took to the streets again, this time in even greater numbers. It wasn't just the rich city dwellers who blocked the roads to the Forum: they were now joined by farmers from the countryside around Rome, and more were arriving with each passing day. Cato's warnings were powerless in the face of this demonstration of might. In the end, the Senate gave in.

Rhetoric – the art of giving a persuasive speech – flourished in the public debates that took place in the Forum Romanum. Cicero, the greatest speaker of all, remains an inspiration to politicians to this day. Women were represented in these public discussions, and although the men preferred women to stay silent and keep out of politics, their voices continued to be heard. Hortensia, the daughter of Cicero's friend and rival Quintus Hortensius, became famous for her public speaking and for leading a protest against another tax on luxury items. Then there was Gaia Afrania, the wife of a senator, who provoked anger by continually bringing cases to court. The Roman writer Valerius Maximus wrote of her, 'It is better to record when such a monster died than when it was born.'

Cicero's sharp tongue earned him many enemies, including the many husbands of a Roman lady called Fulvia; she was the third wife of Mark Antony. Fulvia demonstrated her power by manipulating her series of influential husbands until Cicero was banished for his political scheming and eventually assassinated. His head was put on public display and it is said that Fulvia took great satisfaction in stabbing Cicero's tongue with her hair pins.

Cleopatra and Caesar

After the Punic Wars, the Roman Republic could no longer function as it had during its glorious early years. Some say this was because the land it conquered was distributed unfairly: the rich got richer while the poor got poorer.

Others say that, over time, the system of hands-off senators caused such fierce feuds among the patricians (Rome's ruling-class families) that, in the end, the senators were barely able to govern. The situation Rome had so long tried to prevent finally happened: a few individual men seized power for themselves.

The people demanded more rights for individual citizens, and this caused the Senate to become less reliable and influencial. Some attempted to remedy Rome's shortcomings with reforms, but these failed and were followed by civil war and endless power struggles. In the end, three men took advantage of the Senate's weakness. They formed a secret alliance and declared themselves a triumvirate – a government of three. Although officially the Senate continued to rule the republic, the three had in fact seized control.

They were the perfect team: Crassus was infinitely rich, Pompey had made a name for himself as the best general in the republic, and Caesar was a keen political player with a lot of clout. But the alliance fell apart when Crassus died. The remaining two squabbled with one another until Pompey was defeated and fled to Egypt.

Alexander the Great had conquered Egypt and crowned himself pharaoh, and since then the country had been governed by Macedonian generals and their descendants, all named Ptolemy. The kingdom had suffered a considerable decline in stature, and although Egypt was spared the humiliation of becoming a mere Roman province, the country was entirely dependent on Rome.

When Pompey fled to Egypt, Ptolemy XIII found himself in a predicament: should he come to Pompey's aid or side with Caesar? Ptolemy chose Caesar. As a mark of respect to Caesar and to gain his favour, he cut off Pompey's head and sent it to Rome.

By way of thanks, Ptolemy hoped to gain Caesar's support in his dispute with his sister Cleopatra. Ptolemy and Cleopatra were ruling

Egypt side by side and were each trying to oust the other from the throne. However, Ptolemy had miscalculated. Caesar fell in love with Cleopatra and, instead of getting rid of her, he supported her, helping her to become Queen of Egypt.

51 BC: Cleopatra becomes the ruler of Egypt – and Caesar's lover.

The couple went to Rome. Caesar was already married, so his arrival with an Egyptian beauty at his side sparked a lot of envy and malicious gossip. But Caesar didn't care if the people disapproved or not. If anything, he became even more reckless and had the Senate appoint him Rome's official ruler – not for a year like the consuls, but for life. This went against all the rules of the republic so, naturally, it earned him a lot of enemies.

Discontent was brewing among the senators, many of whom considered Caesar a tyrant and traitor to the republic. The Senate had given him the right to stay in office until his natural death, but some senators didn't want to wait that long and launched a conspiracy against him. On the Ides of March, the middle of the month, Caesar was assassinated at a Senate meeting.

44 BC: Caesar is assassinated.

Cleopatra and Mark Antony

The 'tyrant killers' had hoped their deed would save the republic. Instead, it ignited yet another civil war, with yet two more influential men vying for power. These men were Mark Antony and the young Octavian, Caesar's adopted son.

Mark Antony wanted to turn his attention to the matter of Egypt. This gave Cleopatra another chance to wrap one of Rome's most powerful men around her little finger. She apparently travelled to meet him on a golden ship with purple sails, dressed as the Roman goddess of love in a shimmering see-through dress covered in pearls that left little to the imagination. According to the story, she was fanned by a group of beautiful young attendants.

Like Caesar, Mark Antony fell for the Egyptian pharaoh. A commentator remarked sarcastically that Cleopatra owed this victory to Fulvia, who had already given Mark Antony a lesson in how to obey a woman. Whatever the truth, Cleopatra's new lover brought her something she had lost with Caesar's death: someone to protect her Crown. In exchange, the Romans gained a powerful ally.

Octavian and Mark Antony tried to form an alliance, but it didn't last long, as both were afraid that the other would stage a coup. As tensions rose, Octavian employed a tried-and-tested tactic: he incited the Roman people against his co-regent. Back in Rome, Mark Antony had agreed to marry Octavian's sister Octavia. Octavia was popular, so her brother made the most of her faultless reputation to smear Antony as an adulterer who had left his virtuous fiancée to cavort with a foreign barbarian in Egypt. This was a bold assertion, as Octavian himself had recently caused a scandal by leaving his heavily pregnant wife for another woman.

By now, wicked rumours about Cleopatra and Mark Antony were spreading. The Romans saw Cleopatra as the epitome of the foreign tyrant, interested in nothing but luxury and extravagance that was financed at the cost of her people. They feared that Mark Antony would force Rome to adopt the 'Egyptian way of life' and decided to follow Octavian into war. Ultimately, Mark Antony and Cleopatra were defeated, and Mark Antony was killed.

31 BC: Octavian defeats Cleopatra and Mark Antony.

Out of grief for her murdered lover, Cleopatra asked for a basket of fresh figs with poisonous snakes hidden inside. Once alone, she committed suicide by letting the snakes bite her. The story sounds very dramatic, and even then many viewed it as nothing more than a fairy tale. Whatever the truth, we can be fairly sure that, although Octavian had her under close guard, Cleopatra still somehow managed to kill herself.

The republic is dead: long live Caesar!

Octavian, who remained sole regent after his victory over Mark Antony, had learned something from Caesar's death. He avoided doing anything that could give the impression he was claiming exclusive power. Rather than openly referring to himself as ruler, or even king, he called himself *princeps* – 'first one' – and reinvolved the Senate in the governing of Rome. By doing this, he made the Romans think that he was upholding the values and traditions of the republic, even though he in fact had his hands firmly on the reins of power. He transformed his family into a paragon of Roman virtue. The women of his household in particular were expected to be the antithesis of the Egyptian queen in all aspects of life: they were expected to be modest, submissive and – above all – Roman. They shunned excess, spun the wool for their clothing themselves, and raised their children to be good citizens.

The republic began to thrive once more, and the long-awaited peace arrived at last. As a sign of gratitude, the Senate gave Octavian the honorary title *Augustus*, meaning 'venerable'. Augustus made sure the money that had been frittered away on war and disputes at the Senate was redirected into expanding the city. Now, when you strolled through the Forum Romanum, you could see that many of its old buildings had been given a facelift. With their smooth, light marble walls, they looked more illustrious and more imposing than ever.

His political successes made Augustus bolder. In public, he started presenting himself with a gravitas that, contrary to his original assertions, singled him out as the first among all venerable rulers. New monuments to the ruling family were erected, and a triumphal arch commemorating his victory over Mark Antony was built over part of the Forum. The stage, where for centuries the citizens of Rome had used their rhetorical flair to argue for the public good, was transformed into a platform for Augustus to address his people. As a reward for defeating insurgents in Spain and Gaul and securing Rome's perpetually unstable borders, the Senate also commissioned a building in his honour. The *Ara Pacis Augustae* (Altar of Augustan Peace) was the first monument in Rome to pay homage to a single ruler. Augustus, despite presenting himself as a dedicated servant of the republic in his early years of office, had transformed the Imperium Romanum into his own personal empire.

Augustus topped this all off by giving his wife Livia the title 'Augusta'. For the first time, a woman was joint head of the state, outranking everyone else. Augustus named himself Caesar after Julius Caesar, his adoptive father and the first to successfully gain sole control of Rome. 'Caesar' would enter many languages: the words for the leaders of great empires, such as *Kaiser*, *tsar* or *shah*, all come from this title.

THE MIDDLE KINGDOM

Two ancient worlds

'All roads lead to Rome', as the saying goes. It's not entirely wrong either. Roman culture may not have been as old as the cultures of Sumer, Egypt or Greece, but it was a high point in antiquity. You'd have to travel a very long way to find an empire capable of competing with the Imperium Romanum in terms of sheer size and splendour.

There was another that could, though. In China, the Middle Kingdom emerged, giving the ancient world a second great centre, this time in Asia. Caravans of merchants, traders, travellers – sometimes whole armies – crossed the vast region between these two worlds of antiquity. Their routes sometimes took them through India and sometimes through the northern Himalayas to the Central Asian Steppe and through the Persian Empire. Since one of the Orient's most sought-after goods was Chinese silk, western merchants would later name this network of roads the Silk Road. It was the Silk Road that linked the empires of Rome and China together.

The daughter of the man who damaged the pagoda tree

Rather than being a single empire, China was once made up of lots of small independent states. In one of these provinces, there lived a scholar called Master Yan. He was an adviser to the court of a duke and was held in very high esteem. In a book about his life, the following story is told.

Duke Jing of Qi had a Japanese pagoda tree. This tree was very important to him, so he placed a wooden board in front of it with a warning: 'Anyone who touches this tree shall be punished. And anyone who damages this tree shall be put to death.' One night, a drunk fell against the tree. When the duke heard, he said, 'This is the first man to disobey me.' The man was arrested and sent to receive his punishment. But the man's daughter approached the duke's adviser, the respected Master Yan, and asked to speak with him. Addressing him at length, she said she had heard that a good ruler didn't punish anyone without good reason and was concerned with governing their country well. But the duke, she argued, was exploiting his people for his own gain. The law protecting the pagoda tree went against all forms of good government: it made no sense, and the punishment was out of all proportion to the crime. She ended her speech with the threat: 'If our neighbours hear about this, they'll think our ruler values trees more than people. Is that what you want?' Master Yan went to the duke and told him everything the young woman had said. The duke realised the error of his ways and abolished the law.

Almost 400 years later, the story of the daughter of the man who damaged the pagoda tree featured in a book called *Biographies of Exemplary Women*. The book's author Liu Xiang collected 125 biographies of women who exemplified 'model' female behaviour. Sadly, Liu Xiang didn't show the same courage as the daughter did, instead warning that women shouldn't be allowed to become too independent. Their independence, he claimed, would bring nothing but pain and destruction.

Humanity and morality

Much like the girl in the story about the pagoda tree, Chinese thinkers started asking questions: what did it mean to be a 'good' ruler, and what did this ruler need to do to govern an empire effectively? The most important answers approached these questions from three different angles. One came from the philosopher Confucius, who believed that the state must be founded on morality and honesty. Then there were the ideas put forward by philosophers from the Hundred Schools of Thought, an era that flourished between 770 and 221 BC. The most well-known thinkers from this golden age of Chinese philosophy believed that law and order could only be ensured by a ruthless ruler. And then there was Laozi, who rejected all of these approaches and argued for 'non-action' – doing nothing.

Kongzi, or 'Master Kong' – known in Europe as Confucius – harked back to the ancient dynasty of the Zhou. He maintained that perfect order prevailed under the Zhou (this was only half true, but inventing stories like this can help to create a sense of togetherness): 'We're all descendants of the mighty Zhou, who were wise and model rulers.' It was this idea that ultimately may have inspired China's small states to unify.

Confucius was convinced that the Zhou's success was based on one key principle: the obedience and respect of sons for their fathers, and this led to both humanity and morality. His golden rule was: 'Don't impose on others what you yourself do not desire.'

The most important thing of all, Confucius wrote, was family. In the family, everyone had their place: a wife came below her husband in the hierarchy, but their children were obliged to obey both their parents. Confucius suggested making rules based on these relationships. If order was retained within the family, harmony and unity would reign overall.

People could learn respect for their fellow humans and become more 'noble-minded' by getting an education. Those who were clever and studied hard could achieve their goals in society, no matter how ambitious these goals were. This was a new idea as, in the past, a person's education and career were determined by their birth and family name. But naturally, the new road of education was only open to men. Confucius is reported to have said that 'a woman without talent is virtuous' – to his mind, a good wife served her husband by sacrificing her own needs.

Confucius is said to have had 3,000 students, many of whom came from humble backgrounds. They were craftsmen, farmers and merchants. The great master doesn't seem to have been that impressed by them, though, and lambasted them, saying: 'Chai is stupid, Shen is

479 BC: Confucius dies in China. Later, China declares him its greatest philosopher, and Confucianism is treated like a religion.

dull-witted, Shi is too formal, and You is coarse.' Had he forgotten his own rule about respecting your fellow human beings?

The Hundred Schools of Thought: a ruler must use violence

Confucius wasn't a particularly successful scholar or adviser – at least, that's what the little information we have about his life leads us to suspect. There were others who had more influence on China's rulers than he did. Around the same time as the Athenians were developing their idea of democracy, Chinese philosophers from the Hundred Schools of Thought were contemplating the relationship between society and state. They believed that their interests were best served by an empire united under a single ruler. But how should that ruler behave and what methods should they use to govern the country? Should they embrace education and preserve ancient customs and songs, as advocated by Confucius? Should they govern with humanity, humility and respect?

Creating a great empire and holding it together wasn't easy. The dukes and princes were constantly fighting one another, for one thing. What's more, the Chinese also lived under constant threat from horseback warriors from the vast steppes to the west. The advisers to the rich and powerful therefore believed that the only way of getting the people to fight and defend themselves was through punishment and reward.

The King of Wu once invited a very successful military commander called Sunzi ('Master Sun') to his court to ask his advice. The king wanted to know how he could guarantee his subjects' absolute obedience. Sunzi asked the king to summon 180 women from the imperial palace; he then split them into two groups and made the king's two favourite wives the leader of each. He explained the principles of military command and gave them their first order. The women started giggling. He repeated his command and, once again, the women laughed. At this, Sunzi said, 'When the orders are clear but not followed, the fault lies with the leaders of the group.' To the king's horror, Sunzi had his two favourite wives beheaded.

It's a grim story, but about 300 years later, when another ruler attempted to conquer his neighbours and form a great Chinese empire, brutal violence and oppression were precisely the methods he chose.

Laozi: it's better to do nothing

Perhaps it was this brutality that gave rise to another, decidedly unusual, philosophy alongside the teachings of Confucius and the Hundred Schools of Thought.

According to legend, there was a man called Laozi, or Master Lao, who wrote a short book about 'non-action' or *wu wei*. This teaching recommended refraining from activity of any kind and withdrawing from the world. In Laozi's view, there was only one way of escaping the suffering and injustice of the world – and that was to do nothing. The idea of isolation combined with meditation may have arrived in China from India but, regardless of how the idea spread, Laozi wanted to retreat to the mountains in the west to do just that. Upon reaching the border, he met a customs man who asked him to write down all his knowledge.

The book Laozi wrote was called the *Tao Te Ching* and told of the divine power that moved the world, the 'Tao'. The Tao defies definition: it's everything and nothing at the same time. It's 'the Way', a principle that permeates and maintains the harmonious order of the world.

The Taoists thought it was best to do nothing. They scorned power in all its forms, as well as the knowledge of books. Thinkers were ridiculed and many of the statements in texts about the Tao went directly against the teachings of Confucius, who had said that the highest goal of humanity was to educate oneself and build a good society. However, the Taoists didn't reject all ancient wisdom entirely. Some of it, such as the teaching of Yin and Yang, the complementary forces shaping our existence, tied in perfectly with the Taoist view of the world.

Around 400 BC: Master Laozi's book the *Tao Te Ching* becomes the cornerstone of Taoism, the teaching of non-action.

China's first kingdom: books are burned, and a wall is built

The first ruler of a great Chinese Empire was acutely aware of the significance of the Tao. He gave himself a new name: Qin Shihuangdi, 'the first Emperor of Qin'. The Qin dynasty successfully defeated its neighbours in northern China and the states along the mighty Yangtze River. This marked the beginning of the Middle Kingdom, at the centre of which all power was concentrated. When Qin Shihuangdi died, an inscription was engraved on his tomb: 'In every direction, the land you see belongs to the emperor.'

221 BC: Qin Shihuangdi becomes the first emperor of a unified China.

But how were the people in China's most far-flung regions to know that their land now belonged to the emperor? Qin Shihuangdi and his advisers attempted to make a new beginning. Unlike Confucius, who turned to the past for inspiration, they sought to erase all memory of history: they ordered all the books in the kingdom to be burned.

But that wasn't enough. To erase the knowledge people held in their heads, they killed 460 scholars. From that point on, anyone who contradicted the government would be severely punished.

Luckily, historical memory proved impossible to erase entirely. Books could be easily hidden, even when they were made of bamboo and wooden strips, as they were at the time, and so were slightly bulkier than later books made of paper. The Chinese Empire spread in all directions of the compass, but some regions were very difficult to reach. Therefore, many books survived; with them, the history of China survived too.

The Qin had divided the kingdom into different administrative regions and installed their officials everywhere; these officials ensured that the farmers paid their taxes and did military service. To consolidate their power, the Qin opted for brutality and violence. The vast majority of China's people were poor, and the taxes demanded of them were so high, they barely had enough to survive. Those who failed to pay were taken as slaves.

A grand construction project had been started to protect the Middle Kingdom from nomads in the north-west, and the Qin now continued this project. This would become the Great Wall of China. The world's largest man-made structure also took the longest time to complete – centuries, in fact; the final stretches were finished in the seventeenth century. As far back as the reign of the first emperor, Qin Shihuangdi, the Great Wall was built on a colossal amount of suffering; many slaves and forced labourers lost their lives in the construction of it. A woman called Meng Jiang is said to have cried so much when her husband died working on the wall that a crack appeared in it, revealing his bones.

Empress Lü Zhi

The first Qin Empire collapsed after just fourteen years, allowing a new dynasty, the Han, to seize control. The Han followed the teachings of Taoism, which meant they did as much as was necessary and nothing more; they left the governing of the empire in the hands of their officials, and the kings of each province relinquished their power. The Han emperors saw it as their duty to maintain this Taoist calm.

206 BC: The Han dynasty begins in China.

Until Empress Lü Zhi came to the throne, that is.

Before being crowned emperor, Lü Zhi's husband Liu Bang fell for a beautiful young woman, a gifted singer and dancer called Lady Qi, who bore him a son. Liu Bang loved this son much more than the son borne to him by Lü Zhi and threatened to cast Lü Zhi out so that her rival's son could become the heir to the throne. But the emperor couldn't change the line of succession without his ministers' consent, so Lü Zhi allied herself with them. She had plenty of time to work on these alliances; when Liu Bang was trying to hold the kingdom together in distant provinces, she remained at court with the ministers. Then, Lü Zhi played an ingenious move. A grand banquet was held, and at this banquet, in front of the entire royal household, the 'Four Haos' of Shang Mountain marched in with her son in their retinue. The Four Haos were a group of hermits who, like Master Lao, were very famous and well respected; according to Chinese legend, these wise men could only be summoned to court by a ruler appointed by Heaven. By having the old men enter with her son, Empress Lü Zhi was showing the entire state that her child was

195 BC: Lü
Zhi becomes
empress. She
lives up to the
stereotype
that powerful
women are
cunning
and cruel.

the legendary emperor. His father had no choice: there was no way he could present a different successor to his superstitious people.

Empress Lü Zhi also knew how to keep hold of her power. When her husband died, she banished her one-time rival to the furthest corner of the empire. There was only one way to deal with Lady Qi's son, though: he had to be put to death. However, the boy's father had taken him away to a distant province for safekeeping – Empress Lü Zhi would need a great deal of persistence and patience to bring him back to the capital. Not only that, he was also being protected by her own son, who never let him out of his sight. Just once, though, the boy's protector let down his guard and went hunting while his younger brother was asleep. This was the chance Lü Zhi had been waiting for. By the time her son returned, his half-brother was dead; he had been poisoned with wine made from the feathers of the Zhen, or 'poisonfeather' bird.

She didn't stop there. The beautiful dancer Lady Qi, the dead boy's mother, had her hands, feet and ears cut off and her eyes gouged out, and was forced to drink a concoction that left her forever unable to speak. Afterwards, she was thrown to the pigs. When Lü Zhi's son found out about this atrocious act, he's said to have shouted: 'This is not something done by a human. As your son, I'll never be able to rule the empire.' With that, he took to his bed and cried for a year. Afterwards, he withdrew from politics altogether.

These stories may have been invented to tarnish Lü Zhi's name or they may have contained a grain of truth. Either way, Empress Lü Zhi's entry into Chinese history is anything but illustrious. There's a similarly outrageous story concerning her death: she apparently died after being bitten under the arm by a blue dog. Many Chinese people believed this dog had been sent by Heaven.

The great sage

Just over half a century later, a new emperor decided to abandon the path of non-action taken by his predecessors. This emperor was called Wu, which means 'military' or 'martial'. Emperor Wu dismissed his officials and took matters into his own hands. He ruled using the same methods as Emperor Qin Shihuangdi; he was harsh and brutal. But there was another side to his personality: he had a keen interest in the arts and literature, for example, and he invited writers to his court and even set up a government department for music.

At this point, Confucius re-enters our story. By the time Wu came to power, Confucius had already been dead for almost 400 years. However, Wu and his closest advisers revisited his teachings when attempting to reorganise the country and its government, and the old master's teachings offered a lot of advice. Emperor Wu founded an imperial college where students could study China's most important texts. These texts were collected in five volumes and were thought to have been published by Confucius. From this point on, these books would form the basis of Chinese thought and Confucius was declared the founder of all knowledge, the greatest thinker in history. If you wanted to become a government official, you had to sit difficult exams and show that you knew the canonical texts inside out.

Chinese rulers followed the 'wisdom of Confucius' for almost 2,000 years. By doing this, the government made sure all their officials knew and thought the same thing for millennia.

History as told by Ban Zhao

There were lots of talented, well-educated people outside of government too, especially within the imperial court and the families in the ruler's inner circle. During the Han period, many important books were written about subjects such as medicine and a special Chinese medical technique known as acupuncture, where the patient's skin is pricked with needles. Because of Emperor Wu's love of art and literature, many writers moved to the capital city, which gave them the opportunity to start writing works of their own. These included the *Biographies of Exemplary Women* we discussed earlier, but also China's very first history book.

Around the same time, China made a breakthrough that spread across the whole world: they invented paper. Imagine how much easier it must have been to write on paper instead of unwieldy bamboo strips!

Shortly after this invention, China's first great female scholar entered the stage of history. Her name was Ban Zhao, and she was an exceptionally well-educated woman who always spoke her mind at court. Her brother, also a writer of history, was less lucky: he was executed. Back then, this could happen all too easily, especially if you had any connection to the empress. When the new ruler came to power, the previous empress was killed, together with all her supporters. And this is exactly what happened to Ban Zhao's brother, whose job it had been to record the history of the ruling family. After his death, his sister took over his work.

AD 92: The female scholar Ban Zhao writes history books and other works at the court of the Chinese emperor.

Ban Zhao titled the book *Lessons for Women*, and in it she demanded that all women should be given access to an education, just as she had. This was a brave move, as it went directly against the teachings of the great sage Confucius, who had once claimed that 'a woman without talent is virtuous'. However, so she wouldn't upset the men *too* much, Ban Zhao added that a well-educated woman would be able 'to better serve her husband'.

The end of the Han?

AD 9: The dominion of the Han dynasty comes to an end – or does it?

The rule of the Han came to an end and a new dynasty rose to power, the Xin. This gave the officials an opportunity to reclaim the influence Emperor Wu had taken away from them – soon, it would be the rulers' turn to suffer, as their policies would be dictated to them by their officials. For almost 2,000 years, the Middle Kingdom had largely retained the structure put in place by its first emperor Qin Shihuangdi and the Han emperors. This structure dictated that the Chinese emperor ruled from the centre, isolated from the outside world and surrounded by a colossal state apparatus that wielded the real power.

The new emperor was 'consort kin', related to the empress dowager rather than the emperor. He must have felt like a puppet, with his officials pulling the strings. Pressing in on him from all sides were advisers and empresses who, greedy for power and influence, con-stantly tried to outdo one another with their malicious plots. Some say that, in their constant push for power, empresses like Lü Zhi became a thorn in the officials' sides. And so, the officials soon took steps to make the rules for women even stricter.

AD 23: The Xin dynasty falls after only one emperor, and the Han re-emerge.

THE BIRTH OF CHRISTIANITY

All is well in the Roman Empire

A trade caravan setting off from China to Rome had a long journey ahead of it. The Silk Road ran across vast steppes, through boundless forest and over high mountains, and brought travellers into contact with foreign peoples. Some of these populations lived in tents and travelled from place to place on horseback. Others made a living as fishermen and farmers and lived in small, scattered settlements.

The Chinese and Romans disagreed on many things, but there was one thing they did agree on: that the people who lived in the expanse between China and Rome were barbarians. Like the Greeks, they looked down on their neighbours and saw them as uncivilised. This was also due to the dangers of travelling the Silk Road. Merchants were transporting valuable luxuries such as silk, precious stones, purple dye and spices, so as well as having to protect themselves from wild animals, they also had to defend themselves against ambushes by robbers. After months of adversity, a trader was able to breathe a sigh of relief when they finally crossed the borders of the Roman Empire. At last: paved streets! Cities with inns and taverns! Thermal baths to wash off the dirt and grime after the long journey!

This was what made the Roman Empire so unique: even in the provinces far from the capital, its citizens were able to benefit from the Roman way of life. Trade boomed, new buildings were constantly being constructed, and its luxuries and riches drew people from all over the world, who were awed by what they saw. A Roman who walked the tidy, cobbled streets of Rome could enjoy the same comfort in North Africa or along the Black Sea coast.

Queen Amanirenas contests Rome's borders

Under Emperor Augustus, the Roman Empire enjoyed a period of unparalleled peace. Nevertheless, along many of its borders, its military was engaged in warfare with neighbouring kings, sometimes even queens. One of these queens was Amanirenas, the Queen of Kush, a Nubian kingdom to Egypt's south. By this point, Ancient Egypt was completely under Rome's control; Amanirenas, however, led her soldiers into battle against the Romans to defend both herself and her kingdom. She won and returned to Kush with a bronze sculpture of the emperor's head. With great ceremony, she had it buried under the threshold to her palace so that citizens and visitors to Kush could, quite literally, trample on the Roman emperor.

The queen is said to have lost an eye in the battle, but this didn't stop her from confronting the Romans a second time. Although her army was ultimately defeated, Amanirenas successfully negotiated a ceasefire. Rome's response was unusually restrained, and the Kingdom of Kush endured for another 300 years. The wealthy Kushites were familiar with the modern amenities of the era and they built a Roman-style bath in their capital Meroë. This ancient city is a rare archaeological site, where visitors can marvel at both Egyptian pyramids and a Roman thermal bath in the same place.

The Kingdom of God is not of this world

In occupied territories at the very limits of its empire, Rome was often seen as an unpopular foreign power. In one of these territories, the distant province of Palestine, a man appeared who, much like the Buddha in India, made a new religion out of an old one. This man was a wandering Jewish preacher, and his story, the story of Christianity, is told in the Bible.

When new religions gain enough followers, they change the world. They challenge the old status quo with revolutionary ideas, and this makes them especially attractive to people who aren't very happy with the world. This was true in the case of Jesus of Nazareth, who travelled around the province spreading his teachings until finally the Romans sentenced him to death. His followers, the Apostles, convinced more and more people to follow Jesus and convert to Christianity. As with all religions, Christianity's impact on history is one of the few things we can be sure of: the new belief introduced new ideas, and these in turn changed the world. However, the religion's holy book, the Bible, tells Jesus's life story and is made up of the usual mixture of truth and myth. Only a small number of its stories are rooted in history – the rest is invention.

Jesus of Nazareth travelled through Palestine, which in those days was inhabited by the Jews. Wherever he went, he stood up for the poor and healed the sick. He shared the Buddha's belief that life on Earth brought suffering and he told people God had sent him to bring salvation – that is, to end their suffering. His idea of salvation, though, was very different.

Jesus claimed that God wouldn't deliver humanity from suffering in this world. Instead, this world would end, and another would begin. This new world would be called the Kingdom of God. It would be unlike anything humanity had ever seen; it was not of this world.

According to Jesus, suffering was largely caused by the imbalance of power between the strong (the rich and powerful) and the weak (the poor and oppressed). In the Kingdom of God, he preached, these differences between rich and poor, sick and healthy, would cease to exist. More than that, in the Kingdom of God, Jesus promised, the weak would be first.

If you wanted to enter this kingdom, you needed to prepare for it while still on Earth. Jesus was especially critical of the Jewish priests and accused them of putting power before their relationship with God. He urged everyone to look within themselves and to atone for their sins. Stop, he said, and ask yourself whether you're doing the right thing. Those who reject worldly riches, who seek no power over others and are honest and truthful would ultimately be rewarded by God.

Many people were annoyed by such talk but, to their surprise, Jesus backed up his words with actions. Poor, ordinary people flocked to him. Like him, they left all their possessions and families behind and travelled with him across the country to proclaim the dawning of a new era.

The most despised in society often became Jesus's most ardent supporters, including women. One day, the preacher arrived in a town and saw a woman being stoned after being found guilty of a crime. He placed himself between her and the crowd and said, 'If any one of you is without sin, let him be the first to throw a stone at her.' And with that, he saved her life.

Many viewed Jesus's actions as provocations, particularly when he treated women the same as men and thieves the same as law-abiding people. Nobody had ever dared to do this before. The Jewish leaders watched the wandering preacher and his disciples with growing concern. This man was calling himself the Son of God! There could only be one explanation for his behaviour: he was completely mad! But his sermons were having an effect on people. He had masses of followers and the Jewish leaders saw this as a threat to their authority. They followed the orders of Rome, and so they told the Roman governor Pontius Pilate about Jesus, burdening him with the risky task of getting rid of this troublesome preacher and his followers.

The sentence issued by Pilate was a grisly one: crucifixion. Death by crucifixion was agonising, and it usually took the victim several days to die. For this reason, it was hardly ever meted out to Roman citizens and was reserved for slaves and the basest of criminals. The message Pilate was sending was clear: Jesus, who had been brazen enough to proclaim himself the Son of God, was to be humiliated and punished like a serious criminal.

When Jesus was arrested by the Roman guards, his disciples fled. They must have been frightened they would be arrested and killed as well. The only ones who stayed with Jesus were a handful of women who followed him to Golgotha, a hill outside the city of Jerusalem, where he was crucified. To mock him, Pontius Pilate had the inscription 'Jesus of Nazareth, King of the Jews' written on the cross. A crown of thorns was placed on his head and the women, Jesus's mother Mary and Mary Magdalene, his favourite disciple, stood at his feet and wept.

AD 30/33: Jesus of Nazareth is crucified in Jerusalem. A new religion is born: Christianity. Later, the year of Jesus's birth is used to mark the beginning of the European dating system (BC/AD).

The wonder of the Resurrection

The Bible recounts the story of Jesus's crucifixion in great detail. The story may contain a kernel of historical truth, as records have been found describing the crucifixion of a Jewish insurgent, but the most important part of Christian theology is what happened afterwards.

According to the story, Jesus died before the end of the first day. Pilate gave one of Jesus's friends permission to take his body down from the cross and place it in a tomb, which was then sealed by rolling a large, heavy stone in front of the entrance. The women watched him and, on the morning of the second day, made their way to the tomb. To their astonishment, it was empty. What on Earth had happened?

The explanation later given by theologians was that the Son of God had overcome earthly life and ascended to heaven. He had risen from the dead to enter eternal life. Through the wonder of the Resurrection, God had shown humanity that Jesus was truly his son. Like Jesus, who would soon become known as Jesus Christ, everyone would be saved and enter the Kingdom of God.

These stories have to be told to help us understand the impact Christianity had on world history. Christians believe in a Son of God who criticised conditions on Earth, who preached a rejection of violence, wealth, control and power. They saw Jesus's death on the cross as proof that it was better to die than to waiver from their faith, and they also believed in the wonder of the Resurrection and God's promise in salvation after death. These ideas proved a magnetic draw for people within the Roman Empire and beyond.

The difference between fact and fiction

To the people of the ancient world, Jesus's teachings were completely alien. Unlike the old gods, who dictated the order of the world from on high and were represented in pomp and splendour by kings and queens, God chose to speak through Jesus, a simple man who had nothing. This new divine messenger travelled the country in rags and was brave enough to criticise the elite, including the priests.

While the old gods inspired fear, Jesus declared God's unconditional love for humanity. He told all the peoples of the world to give up their old gods and follow the god of the Jews.

Later, when Jesus was no longer on Earth, his story was written down by the four Evangelists: Matthew, Mark, Luke and John; their Gospels became the most important books in the Bible. However, their reports give the impression that Jesus's circle was dominated by men. They claimed that Jesus had twelve disciples – no more, no less – and not a single woman was present at the last supper before his crucifixion.

AD 33–120: Jesus's life story is written down in the four Gospels.

Events as they actually happened and events as reported by eyewitnesses are almost never the same. If Jesus wanted to rid the world of all injustice, would he really have discriminated against women? If he wanted everyone to be treated the same, if he welcomed thieves and liars with open arms and treated them with the same respect as law-abiding people, why would he have made a distinction between men and women?

The good news spreads

Jesus asked his disciples to spread the message of God's kingdom throughout the world. They called themselves Apostles, the Greek word for 'person who is sent'. With no newspapers or internet to help spread the news, Jesus's followers had to travel beyond Palestine and convince people of the Christian message themselves. Very soon, small communities who shared the new faith were popping up everywhere.

One of these Apostles was Paul. He journeyed throughout the Roman Empire and spoke in front of huge gatherings of people wherever he went. When he arrived in Athens, he stood on the Areopagus, a rocky hill that served as a public meeting place much like the Forum Romanum. There, the Greeks had erected an altar to 'the Unknown God' – the Greeks were aware that there was another god besides those of Olympus but they didn't know his name. So, to avoid incurring the wrath of this unknown god, they made sacrifices to him

From around
AD 50: Paul the
Apostle links
Christianity
to Greek
beliefs. He
travels widely,
telling people
about the new
religion.

just in case. Now Paul was telling the Athenians he could shed some light on the identity of this unknown god. This was a clever idea: far from being strange, this new faith could help the Greeks find out more about their unknown god. Paul managed to link Greek beliefs to Christianity. Not long after, Christianity took over the Roman Empire, sweeping the Greek and Roman gods aside.

A scandal with a far-reaching impact

Women also helped spread the Christian message, but it was much easier for a man to travel from city to city speaking to people. Most women were forbidden from even listening to their speeches; if they were allowed to go out in public at all, they had to do so veiled and escorted by a man. A woman who travelled alone risked being killed.

A young girl in the Greek city of Iconium was all too aware of the danger. So, by the time she was 12 or 13, she sat at home by her window and listened to Paul speak to a small gathering of people nearby. She wasn't allowed to go outside herself, but she listened eagerly to the Apostle's words from the window – and what he said left a deep impression on her.

Thecla left her parents' house to follow Paul, breaking various laws in the process and provoking outrage wherever she went. She had left her family to travel and walked along public streets on her own (despite how dangerous this was for a woman), which made people angry. But she survived it all, and for many this anger soon turned to amazement.

From around
AD 50:
Rumours about
a young woman
called Thecla
spread like
wildfire; many
women follow
her example
and convert to
Christianity.

Everything we know about Thecla's life comes from stories that were later embellished with fantastical details and transformed into legends. According to one of these stories, Thecla had been sentenced to death by burning; hardly had she mounted the pyre when she was suddenly saved from a fiery death by an earthquake and a storm. Then, in another city, she was thrown to the lions, but instead of tearing her to pieces, the lions were tamed and licked her feet. When she finally reached Paul, he too was sceptical of her, but in the end, he was forced to accept her as an Apostle.

These stories may seem unbelievable to us now, but the people of the ancient world thought the exact opposite. A miracle was proof that a story was true. After all, how else were they to know whether or not a god had had a hand in events?

When talking about the course of world history, it's not what people like Jesus, Thecla or Paul actually did that was important, but the effect they had on others. Thecla's behaviour was considered a scandal, so it shocked people and made them think. Thecla's story ultimately helped the first Christians find more followers: it was told everywhere and she soon became famous throughout the ancient world.

Thecla took a risk and showed the world that you could disobey the rules of society – which required women to marry – to obey the command of an almighty god. Many women followed her example and left their families to be baptised. As a result Christianity spread rapidly, as men often followed their wives' lead and converted. A temple was built in Seleucia (in modern-day Turkey), where Thecla was buried, and she was honoured as a saint. Centuries later, her images can still be found in churches and on souvenirs.

While the scandal surrounding Thecla was spreading through the ancient world like wildfire, Peter, one of Jesus's favourite Apostles, went to Rome, which was already home to a small Christian community. Not long after, he was joined by Paul. Christianity, a religion that had started life in Palestine, had reached the heart of the Roman Empire.

THE IMPERIUM ROMANUM BECOMES CHRISTENDOM

A heroic act

The Roman Empire was huge, and while Thecla and Paul were busy recruiting followers for Christianity, the Romans had other things to worry about: the peace brought about by Emperor Augustus was beginning to crack. In the years it had taken them to grow their empire, the Romans had got used to being more powerful, stronger and richer than all their neighbours. With every victory, more wealth flooded into Rome. They thought their empire would last forever.

Now, though, they faced an opponent they just couldn't defeat. The north-east of the empire was inhabited by Germanic tribes. The Romans painted them in the ugliest colours, describing them as massive, long-haired men with habits of being unruly and rampaging into battle half-naked. Their women and children didn't like to stay at home waiting for the warriors to return, but stood on the battlefield, cheering them on. In short, the Germans were complete and utter barbarians. But somehow, these wild men had dealt the Romans a shattering defeat. In Germania, close to the Teutoburg Forest, the German chieftain Arminius had lured the great Roman army into an ambush and slaughtered them almost to a man.

AD 9: Barbarians block Roman expansion east. The Romans are taken by surprise and defeated by the Germans.

The Romans plotted their revenge. They raised a new army to subdue the Germans and take Arminius captive. Their commander was Germanicus (whose father had been given the honorific title 'Germanicus' after beating the Germans in a previous battle). He took his wife Agrippina and their children to the Rhine, where they lived alongside the soldiers in the army headquarters. The family stayed behind in the barracks and Germanicus set off to defeat the Germans once and for all. But he didn't succeed either, and his soldiers fled. As they attempted to cross the Rhine to safety, their compatriots back at headquarters started to worry. They were afraid of the Germans, who were pursuing the fleeing men. Rather than help their comrades, they thought it wiser to protect the people inside the camp, so they decided to destroy the bridge over the river. But Agrippina, who was only there because she was accompanying her husband, had other ideas. Without hesitation, she gave the command forbidding the destruction of the bridge, saving the fleeing soldiers' lives. Instead of abandoning them, she let them in and tended the wounds of the injured.

Although Agrippina saved the lives of many men that day, her behaviour was criticised. Back in Rome's Senate, the debate about the role of women reignited. During this debate, a military commander – who actually owed his life to Agrippina – spoke out. He railed against women, calling them weak and stupid, and warning they would bring nothing but misfortune to the empire. He even went as far as suggesting that, in future, governors should travel to the military camps on the empire's borders alone, leaving their wives at home.

Matricide

Unfortunately, we don't know whether Agrippina was told about the discussion at Senate. After Germanicus died, she left the military and returned to the imperial court in Rome to raise her daughter Agrippina the Younger. Like her mother, Agrippina the Younger had no intention of adopting the role of subservient wife. Since Rome was now headed by an emperor rather than a team of senators, a new path into the centre of power opened up for women, albeit for very few of them. In theory, a woman could become empress. Agrippina already had one marriage behind her, as well as a son, when she married the incumbent Emperor Claudius. Of all the people in the empire, she now had the emperor's ear, and she used her direct access to interfere in matters of state.

The men around Agrippina weren't at all happy about this. Observers describe how the empress used them like pawns in a political game of chess. After becoming the most important woman in the state through her marriage to Claudius, she wanted her son Nero to become heir to the throne, and therefore needed to convince her husband to pass over his own son and declare Nero his successor. Claudius agreed to her request, which gave the people of Rome the impression he was a henpecked weakling. As the malicious rumours increased, the emperor died suddenly of mushroom poisoning. Was his death really an accident? We'll never know for sure, but Agrippina had achieved her goal: finally, the reins of power were firmly in the hands of her son.

To prepare Nero for his future role as emperor, Agrippina had hired him the best teacher in the land, the philosopher Seneca. Seneca taught his pupil the difference between a good ruler and a tyrant: a wise ruler, Seneca said, treated his subjects and defeated opponents with mercy. This way of thinking was popular with the Roman people. They liked Nero, and greeted the young, still-to-be-crowned emperor with cries of jubilation when he stood before the gates of the palace and presented himself to the public.

His mother now made it clear that she was no longer content with standing behind the throne: she wanted to rule beside her son. Once, when the young emperor was receiving an important delegation at court, she strode confidently into the hall and demanded to be seated alongside him so she could preside over the meeting. The attendees gasped in horror – a woman being involved in politics went against every rule in the empire. But what could they do? They could hardly reprimand the emperor's mother. The only person to keep a cool head was Seneca. He advised Nero to meet his mother and show her to a more appropriate seat in the background.

Scandal was averted at the last minute, but the tide was now turning against Agrippina. Her brazenness was starting to get on Nero's nerves and the tension between them was increasing. In the end, Emperor Nero forgot all about showing mercy, as advocated by Seneca, and gave the order for his mother's murder.

Boudicca and the British rebellion

Finally, Nero had got rid of his mother and her interfering – but the empire once again found itself in difficulties. Not only were its northeastern borders still under threat from the Germans but, inside the empire, unrest continued to flare up, which the Romans could only suppress by force. Sometimes, the tiniest spark developed into a real firestorm. One such flashpoint was in Britain, the site of one of the greatest revolts in all of Rome's history.

It all began harmlessly enough: Prasutagus, a British chieftain, died and bequeathed some of his land to the Romans. He did this to win their favour, so he could make sure that nothing happened to his family. The rest of the land he left to his daughters. But the Romans took all the land for themselves, ignoring the women's claim to it, and then subjected the women to cruel abuse.

Their mother Boudicca decided to fight back. Together with her daughters, she took a wagon and rode from one tribe to another, urging them to rise up against their Roman occupiers. It soon became about much more than Prasutagus's land – nothing less than the freedom of all the British tribes was at stake. 'Think about what you're fighting for!' Boudicca yelled to her allies. 'Is it not better to die free than to live a prisoner?'

AD 60–61: Led by Queen Boudicca, the British rebel against the foreign rule of the Roman Empire. The Romans defeat them.

Thousands upon thousands of warriors followed her into battle. However, for the Romans, this was just one of many uprisings that broke out regularly along the empire's borders. In the face of the empire's might, an uprising was a mere inconvenience the Romans could usually deal with pretty quickly. The Britons fought bravely but, in the end, they proved no match for the Romans. Britain remained under Roman control.

Rome burns

Poor Nero – women seemed to bring him nothing but trouble. He'd got rid of his mother, he'd defeated Boudicca's uprising in Britain, but there was still the matter of his clandestine affair with a young woman called Poppaea to deal with. Since Nero was already married, he was faced with the bothersome task of getting his wife Claudia Octavia out of the way. This wasn't too much of a problem, though. All he needed to do was accuse her of having an affair with a slave and then have her executed.

The people of Rome watched this intrigue unfold in horror, as Octavia had been very popular. They were not at all impressed by Nero's games. Civil unrest and uprisings ensued and, when a huge fire broke out, people claimed it had been started by Nero himself. This rumour spread almost as quickly as the flames, which blazed through the city on the back of a powerful wind. The damage was devastating: whole streets and entire sections of the city were burned to the ground. Many Romans suspected that Nero wanted to clear space for a huge palace, the Domus Aurea or 'Golden House', but that probably wasn't the case. The emperor is even said to have opened his doors to refugees and reduced the price of grain to ease the suffering of those who had lost everything. But it still wasn't enough to appease the people. Nero became known as one of the cruellest rulers in history.

To shift attention away from himself, Nero needed to find a scapegoat. The first to come to mind were the Christians: this group of outsiders had only just started to gain a following and the Romans hardly paid them any attention. Rome was a city full of foreigners and its citizens were used to their gods and their many names. However, over time, they realised there was something new and different about the Christian faith.

Most Romans were troubled by the ideas of the Christians, so Nero didn't have to do much to divert his citizens' anger away from himself and onto this small group of heretics. First, the Christians were rounded up and burned at the stake – in a gruesome scene known as 'Nero's human torches' – or crucified. The Apostles Peter and Paul are thought to have been among those executed. A Roman historian wrote that Nero held a circus game in his garden, where Christians were dressed in animal skins and thrown to wild dogs. Whether this is true or not, we'll never know. Nero might not have been as cruel as the legends of history have made him out to be, but one thing we *do* know is that the Christians were persecuted, and that it was a violent and bloody affair.

AD 64: Rome burns. Many accuse Nero of starting the fire, but he points the finger at the Christians.

Female martyrs

In the centuries that followed, this kind of persecution of Christians became more widespread. Whenever there were problems, and perhaps because they felt threatened by these new beliefs, the Romans pillaged the Christians' churches, took their possessions and killed them. But none of this achieved the desired effect. The spread of Christianity was unstoppable.

In fact, many people were so impressed by the fortitude of these Christian martyrs that they also converted to the new faith and went willingly to their deaths. In the city of Lyon, a young slave called Blandina was thrown to wild animals after having been roasted on a grill, during which she constantly repeated the sentence, 'I am a Christian.' In Carthage, meanwhile, a noblewoman called Perpetua struggled to decide whether to get baptised along with her slave Felicitas. While in prison, she kept a diary where she described her torment. She had just become a mother; should she really abandon her child for her new beliefs? In the end, she did and chose death.

Just like Perpetua, many Christians were martyred for standing by the Christian faith. Later, these martyrs were revered as saints.

Into the desert

Not everyone wanted to die as a martyr. The persecution of the Christians under the Roman Emperor Diocletian was particularly cruel, so some chose a different path: a sacrifice for their faith that required no bloodshed. Christ himself had shown them another way of rebelling against the evils of the world: by leading a simple life of radical poverty.

It goes without saying that this extreme abstinence, which was known as asceticism, needed a lot of practice. Instead of striving after gold, luxury and pleasure, they ate meagre meals, walked bare foot and wore simple clothes. Some came up with mad schemes to protect themselves against life's temptations. Like the hermits of India, they retreated to isolated forests or used iron chains to tether themselves by the leg to a tree trunk in the hope of reinforcing their resolve. Others climbed up onto high pillars and stood there for months on end, even years in some cases. The iron will of these 'pillar saints' or stylites was the envy of princes and kings, and those who were able to endure such trials were held in the same high regard as martyrs.

From the end of the 3rd century AD: Many Christians retreat to the desert to live a simple, ascetic life, and become the world's first Christian monks and nuns.

The desert was a lonely, desolate place. St Antonius, an Egyptian monk, is said to have been the first to retreat to the desert wilderness. While there, he was visited by the Devil himself, who attempted to lead him astray. Antonius and the other monks were known as Desert Fathers and became very famous, but their counterparts the Desert *Mothers* were less well known. These women disguised themselves as men in order to be allowed to join the religious communities in the desert. However, this sometimes led to misunderstandings. After passing herself off as a man and entering a monastery, one woman was accused of fathering a child and breaking her vow of chastity. Instead of fleeing, she accepted the accusations and left the monastery to raise the child. Only when she was buried did the monks discover that there was no way she could have been the child's father ...

The Desert Mothers were written about by the fourth-century Church Father John Chrysostom: 'Often the women have fought more bravely than the men, and their victories have been more glorious.'

One of these women, Macrina the Younger, came from a rich, aristocratic family in Cappadocia. Macrina had several siblings who taught her about philosophy and science, as well as many other subjects. Naturally, it was her brothers, especially Basil and Gregory, who would later find fame and glory; today they're ranked among the most important Church teachers of all time. But it was Macrina who showed them the way. When the young Basil returned from his studies in Greece, 'monstrously conceited about his skill in rhetoric and logic' (as Gregory would later write), Macrina cut him down to size and demanded that he follow a true Christian path. While he'd been gone, she had given away their family's possessions and told her slaves and servants that, from that moment on, they were sisters. She moved with them to a remote location outside town and founded a community of nuns. Her brother Basil listened to her and followed her example.

The Emperor Constantine allies himself with the Christians

Meanwhile, things weren't going so well for the Romans. The east was under attack from the Sassanids, a ruling dynasty that had led the Persians to renewed power and glory. Together with the Germans in the west, they were weakening the Romans on two fronts. This crisis was making itself felt inside the empire, which was increasingly easy prey for the Christians, and they told the embattled Romans, 'Your gods have forsaken you!' More and more people started to believe this and decided to join them. In the end, it seemed only a matter of time until the Roman Empire became Christian and an emperor converted to Christianity himself.

But what did this mean? Would an emperor really decide to give away all his belongings to lead a life of poverty? Could he dispense with power relationships, just as Macrina had done with her slaves? Should he take to standing on a pillar? It would all make for an interesting experiment. The problem was that, if the emperor gave up his power, he would no longer be emperor.

For a long time, not all Christians had followed the path of the ascetics; up until recently, they'd believed that the end of time was just around the corner. But they were still waiting, so they started to prepare themselves for life in the present world. Christian communities in the cities had ordained priests and chosen bishops, creating a hierarchy, even though it went against Jesus's teachings. Hierarchy was something that Jesus had expressly rejected, but clearly it was easier to find new followers than to keep to the radical rules as preached by Jesus.

The Christians kept gaining new followers and became a power in their own right. For Rome's rulers, they were a threat. So didn't it make sense to become their allies? Emperor Constantine, Rome's first Christian emperor, knew he couldn't go to the desert and become a hermit. Instead, he offered the Christians a share in his rule.

From old Rome to new Rome: Constantinople

Constantine was the illegitimate son of an innkeeper's daughter and a Roman emperor. Although his mother Helena came from a lower class, she had successfully negotiated her son's position as his father's heir. By way of thanks, upon becoming ruler Constantine gave his mother the honorary title of empress.

AD 313: The Edict of Milan is pronounced by Emperor Constantine, bringing an end to Christian persecution.

Constantine issued a decree saying that, from then on, the Christians would no longer be persecuted. He was in Milan at the time, so this law became known as the Edict of Milan. This was a significant step, as the torture and killing of Christians had so far been widespread – with the Edict, this practice came to an end.

Constantine made further concessions to the Christians. He invited more than 300 bishops from all over the empire to a council, where the bishops discussed the nature of 'right belief'. In Greek, the word for 'right' is *orthos* and the word for 'belief' is *dox*; from then on, every church in the empire would follow the Orthodox faith.

Everything was turned upside down. After being persecuted by Rome's emperors for centuries, the Christians now had a Roman emperor telling them what the correct faith was. Constantine had simply placed himself at the head of the council. Attempts at forming a united Church fell at the very first hurdle, as some of the bishops refused to compromise on controversial issues and clung instead to their own tradition. These people were called apostates and the Orthodox Church had no choice but to exclude them. They went on to form a Church of their own. Christianity had had its first schism.

When something stops working like it's meant to, it makes sense to change it. Constantine's predecessor Diocletian had attempted to overcome the empire's many problems by sharing power between four rulers: two emperors (Augusti) and two co-emperors (Caesars). He thought this system would make it easier to hold back the Germans in the west and the Sassanids in the east – a logical solution, but Diocletian hadn't bargained on his successors' reluctance to share power. Instead of focusing on their external enemies, Constantine and his co-emperor locked horns. In this altercation Constantine was the ultimate victor and moved to the eastern half of the empire, founding a city in his own name: Constantinople. This city was to become the Roman Empire's new capital.

As far as the Romans were concerned, there could only be one eternal capital: Rome. So Constantine simply built a new Rome. He based his new capital in Byzantium, an ancient Greek colony situated on the Bosporus, a narrow channel of water between the continents of Europe and Asia, offering access to both the Black Sea and the Mediterranean. This new Rome was to emulate the old as closely as possible. The emperor had a great palace built, as well as a forum and circus for games and chariot racing.

Back then the new 'Romans' of Constantinople had no idea that their city would become the heart of a new empire, which historians would later call the Byzantine Empire. Constantinople would become one of the most beautiful metropolises in the world.

AD 330: Constantine founds a new Rome on the shores of the Bosporus and names it Constantinople.

Splinters and bones

While Constantine and the bishops were forging their alliance, Constantine's mother Helena set about raising the profile of Christianity across the empire. To the empress, the message of Christianity was that she should be charitable and humane to all the empire's citizens: everybody, from the poorest beggar to the worst criminal, was be worthy of her compassion. Helena travelled all over. She went to the local churches and, instead of waving to the people from a balcony in splendid robes, she dressed in simple garb and mingled among them, chatting. In many places she travelled to, she founded new churches. Wherever she encountered poverty and suffering, she donated money and did what she could to alleviate it. She cared for the sick and even the criminals who had been outcast from society.

Empress Helena's actions seemed to be driven by a real love of people, so she was respected and incredibly popular, and it sounds like she must have been a strong and imposing figure. In her late seventies, she travelled to Palestine and wrote an account of her trip; this was the very first time any ruler had deliberately sought out the places

AD 326: Empress Helena goes on a pilgrimage to Palestine in search of the cross of Christ. In Bethlehem, she builds the Church of the Nativity.

from Jesus's life. While there, she also visited the point from which the first Christian Apostles set out on their journey to Rome.

Helena had a church built in Bethlehem, the place of Jesus's birth. In Jerusalem, she also excavated the site where Jesus had been crucified and buried. During the excavation, it's claimed that she discovered the 'True Cross' – the cross on which Jesus had died three centuries earlier. The truth of this claim is highly contested, though Helena is later said to have divided the cross into three parts. She took one bit to Rome, she sent one back to her son in Constantinople and she left the last in Jerusalem.

Back then, people's connection to God was as important as the bread they ate and the air they breathed. They couldn't see God or touch him with their own hands, so they kept objects that had a symbolic link to him instead. Believers collected relics: the bones of saints or objects that had once belonged to them. Around the time of Helena's journey to Jerusalem, bits of wood supposedly from the True Cross had started to circulate among Christians all over the world; splinters no longer than a finger were highly sought after and guarded like treasure. Relics were bought and stolen, and churches – sometimes whole cities – were founded around them, as people hoped the holy objects would bring them protection, safety, happiness and prosperity.

Female Apostles

Christianity's astonishingly rapid spread also owed something to how far the first Apostles travelled. Once at their destination, they gained new followers very quickly, so Christianity spread more rapidly at the edges of the Roman Empire than at its centre. As Constantine was ending the persecution of Christians in Milan, Armenia was already a Christian state, with the new religion accepted by the king and his people.

Around the time that Empress Helena was setting off for Jerusalem, a wandering preacher from Syria arrived in the small kingdom of Iberia, today part of Georgia. Her name was Nino, and she'd spent many months walking east, crossing 3,000-metre-high mountains on the way. Upon reaching Iberia, she withdrew to a hut, where she devoted her time to herbal medicine and treating the sick. She became well known for her success rate, and when the queen became seriously ill, they went to Nino for help. Under her care, the queen got better – the people's respect and awe grew for this foreigner, who had arrived in their country so destitute and alone.

Around AD 337: Nino migrates from Syria to Georgia, where she spreads Christianity.

King Mirian III wanted to offer Nino his thanks. She refused and explained that the healing had come from her god. Her humility and modesty impressed the king almost as much as her powers of healing, so he decided to convert to Christianity as well. Nino asked him to build a church and also suggested that he send a delegation to Rome to ask Constantine for priests. By this time, she'd become one of the most important people in the country. She had so much authority that, before her death, she was even given the task of choosing the next bishop.

It was Nino who had converted King Mirian and the whole of Georgia to Christianity, of that there could be no doubt. Yet, not long after her death, the Georgians found it difficult to reconcile themselves with the fact that a woman had become one of their state's most important saints. Just over 100 years ago, some theologians were still claiming that Nino was a man, while others claimed that her entire story was a fabrication. The same thing was said about many of the female preachers who travelled from town to town during the early years of Christianity. The Apostle Junia, who was highly regarded by Paul, was also described as a man by historians, who placed an 's' at the end of her name, changing it to Junias. Only in recent years has this claim been corrected by researchers: Junia was a woman (with no 's'), and the fact that she was an Apostle is proof that the early Christians treated men and women as equals.

Women on the road to Palestine

In the early years of Christianity, women enjoyed unprecedented freedom. Suddenly, other paths were open to them apart from marriage: as Christians, they could learn to read and write, study foreign languages and holy scripture. Not only that, they could also travel to far-off lands.

Many of them followed Empress Helena's example: they went on pilgrimages to Christian sites, founded monasteries, and cared for the suffering and the needy. They built institutions to care for these people, as well as lodgings that offered food and shelter to pilgrims. These hostels were what enabled women to travel: without them, they most definitely wouldn't have ventured out on the road. Not so long ago, St Thecla had put herself in great danger and was punished wherever she went just for being a lone female traveller. That was changing now.

At this time, one story in particular was causing a stir: the story of a Roman woman called Melania. The daughter of a rich senator, Melania grew up in a magnificent palace and listened with envy and admiration to the adventures of her grandmother, who had recently returned from a pilgrimage to Palestine. When Melania was 20, she decided to follow in her grandmother's footsteps and became an ascetic. Her family found her decision hard to come to terms with at first, but eventually Melania managed to win over her mother and her husband, and the two accompanied Melania on her journey east. In North Africa, she visited Augustine of Hippo, one of the era's most important Doctors of the Church. As a young boy, he had led a feral life as part of a street gang. When he was older, though, he wrote a text about his conversion, the *Confessions*, consolidating his fame as a Church philosopher. Melania continued to Jerusalem where she and her husband built two convents on the Mount of Olives. By the time she died, Melania had donated a vast sum of money to church building and the poor.

Many rich Roman women gave their possessions to Christian organisations. They were able to decide for themselves what they did with their money – something that would have been unthinkable in old Rome. These women did more than just fund the monasteries, convents, hospitals and poor houses: they usually insisted on running them too.

Some of the most important men in the Church were helped by wealthy women. One of these men was Paul the Apostle, who received both money and legal advice from them. Another was St Jerome, who translated the Bible into Latin. He was reliant on support from others and was helped in Rome by a woman called Marcella, who had turned her house into a meeting place for Christians. Here he met Paula, who later became St Paula of Rome. Jerome and Paula went to Palestine, where they founded four monasteries – with Paula's money.

Farewell to the ancient gods

Around fifty years after Constantine's death, Emperor Theodosius the Great made Christianity the official state religion of the Roman Empire. This was little more than a formality: by now, Christian communities had become large and powerful, and had started to put pressure on those who still worshipped the old gods. The former persecutors were now the ones being persecuted. In Alexandria, there lived a Greek philosopher called Hypatia, who was revered far beyond the city for her wisdom. But even the most respected individuals struggled to resist the tide. Hypatia was an advocate of paganism and the Greek priestess tradition. A Christian priest called Peter the Lector stirred up so much animosity towards her that a mob of angry Christians chased her into a church and murdered her.

AD 381: Under Emperor Theodosius, Christianity becomes the state religion of the Roman Empire.

To the Christians, the worship of the old gods was wicked sorcery. However, this didn't stop them from communicating with their new god using rituals that were sometimes identical to the old ones. Up until now, people had been used to worshipping their guardian spirits at a small altar set up in the corner of a room, where they burned candles and made small offerings. Couldn't they pray to the new Christian god here as well? And to his messengers, the martyrs and the Apostles? Of course they could! Images – this time icons (portraits of Jesus, his disciples, or saints like Thecla and Nino) – once more adorned the alcoves of houses, as well as public spaces, offering believers a window into the invisible world of God.

Although the old gods gradually disappeared, a handful of their rituals remained. Emperor Theodosius the Great put out the eternal fire in the Temple of Vesta and banned her cult. This was also the end of the Oracle of Delphi. A historian of the time reports how the Pythia predicted her own downfall in her last oracle:

Tell the king, the fair-wrought house has fallen.
No shelter has Apollo, nor sacred laurel leaves;
The fountains now are silent; the voice is stilled.

Theodosius's descendants were Christians and members of the Church. Comparisons were drawn between Theodosius's grand-daughter Pulcheria and the Virgin Mary, the Mother of Christ, and Pulcheria founded three churches in Constantinople in her honour. By this time, decisions on matters of belief were taken by the bishops at their assemblies, and Pulcheria accompanied her brother to a council of bishops in Ephesus in AD 431. At this council, the bishops passed a new doctrine that gave special significance to the Virgin Mary. With this doctrine, they decreed that Mary had given birth to the Son of God; she was given the official title Theotokos, which means the 'God-bearer' or 'Mother of God'. The bishops elevated Mary from the status of ordinary saint to something more. Even though the theologians themselves didn't make her a goddess, in the centuries that followed, Christians started to pray to and worship her like a female deity.

AD 431: At the Council of Ephesus, the Virgin Mary is proclaimed the 'Mother of God'.

Migration

The Roman Empire was changing, and not just because of the Christians. Constantine had moved the capital to the Greek part of the empire because it was becoming ever more difficult to defend the empire's western front from the Germans. Initially, all the Germans had done was prevent the Romans from expanding their territory, but now the tables had turned and they were making their own incursions into Roman territory.

AD 375: Attila, King of the Huns, and his army of horsemen advance west. The Great Migration begins.

And for good reason too. Their migration was triggered by events in the east, far beyond the Roman world, where the Huns were continuing their westward advance in search of fresh spoils. The Huns were a nomadic horse people from Central Asia and they spread fear and terror wherever they went. Their distinctive battle tactic was to overwhelm their opponents on horseback, unlike the Romans and

Germans, who marched into battle, these fearsome warriors shot bows from the backs of galloping horses.

The Huns conquered one land after another, forcing the tribes who lived there to search for new territories. The embattled tribes of Germany moved from east to west and from north to south, reaching France, Italy, Spain and even North Africa. In no time at all, the old order had been thrown into disarray. Huge populations left their ancestral lands, in a movement of people known as the Great Migration. Rather than letting themselves be conquered and enslaved by the Huns, the Germanic tribes pushed into the territories of their neighbours. Not even Rome was spared. The Visigoths and Vandals plundered the city three times, which is why we now use the word 'vandalism' to describe any kind of senseless destruction. In this case, though, the word is misleading: the Vandals stole lots of valuable objects but, in reality, they destroyed very little.

The fall of the Roman Empire

As the Huns moved west, clearing the map of the tribes before them, the pressure on Rome's borders increased. Shortly before his death, Theodosius the Great decided to divide the Roman Empire between his two sons. Like Diocletian, he believed this was the only way of resisting Rome's enemies, who were now attacking from all sides. Just as there were now two Romes because of the new capital Constantinople, now there would be two emperors: Honorius in the west and Arcadius in the east. However, the old Rome was no longer safe, so Honorius fled with his imperial court to the coastal town of Ravenna.

Shortly after, the Visigoths plundered Rome. Much to their own surprise, they managed to capture a particularly valuable bit of booty: Galla Placidia, daughter of the deceased Theodosius and sister of the two ruling emperors. The Visigoth King Alaric planned to marry her, so he also stole gold and jewels to give to her as a wedding gift. A few years later, though, he suffered the same fate as many warriors: his horde set out for Sicily, where he died in the thick of battle.

AD 410: During the Sack of Rome, the Visigoths kidnap Galla Placidia, the sister of the Roman Emperor. They also steal jewellery; the Visigoth King Ataulf later gives it to Galla as a wedding gift when he makes her his new queen.

His brother-in-law Ataulf took command and also seized Alaric's bride. Galla Placidia, the sister of both Roman emperors, was now the wife of a barbaric tribal chieftain. There could be no clearer sign: Rome's days were numbered.

Galla married both her spouses against her will and became a Germanic queen against her will too. Despite this, she seemed to get on well with her husband: Ataulf promised her that, in the event of his death, she could return to her family in Rome. As it happened, she returned to Ravenna within just a few years.

Back at Honorius's court, she was received with suspicion by some of the emperor's courtiers. After all, she had just arrived from an enemy camp, the widow of a barbarian king. When a power struggle broke out between the siblings, her brother tried to use this against her. However, Galla Placidia was cunning, and when Honorius died, she positioned her own son as his successor. Since her son was only 6 years old, she ruled on his behalf. The one-time Germanic queen had successfully seized the imperial throne of Rome.

Later, malicious rumours would blame her for the fall of the Western Roman Empire. But, of course, this was nonsense: under pressure from various Germanic tribes pushing southward, like a well-used map, the empire was already in tatters long before her reign.

There was something unusual about the Visigoths' victory, though. The Germanic tribes were in awe of Roman culture and its public squares, their multistorey houses, aqueducts, streets and complex economy. So, rather than making the territory they had won Germanic, they tried to make *themselves* Roman. After all, when in Rome … When the Germanic chieftain Odoacer usurped the last Emperor of the Western Roman Empire, he sent his insignias to Constantinople, explaining that, from then on, he and others like him would rule as kings and bear allegiance to Constantinople.

The Roman Empire of antiquity was no more.

AD 476: The collapse of the Roman Empire of antiquity.

EVERY END IS A NEW BEGINNING

After Rome fell to the Visigoths, there was just one emperor left in the Roman Empire: the Byzantine emperor. The citizens of Constantine's city didn't realise it at the time, but a new empire had been born, and that empire would be called the Byzantine Empire. The heart of this empire was to be found not in Italy but in Greece, and these new Romans spoke Greek not Latin. They no longer believed that the emperor was both ruler and god in one person either.

Christianity had changed too. Through its alliance with the emperor, it had effectively switched sides. During the first three centuries, Christianity had been a symbol of rebellion against the established elite, but now it was part of it. The Church became rich, and it became powerful. Now it was official: the ruler of the Christians was appointed by the Christian god.

The freedom that Christianity had given women soon disappeared. Some even started to doubt the existence of St Nino and the other female saints: Tertullian, a Carthaginian lawyer, had already claimed that the texts describing the joint travels of Paul and Thecla were nothing more than fabrications. According to Tertullian, Paul had been an important Apostle, but the story of Thecla was best forgotten. Warning of women in the Church, he said, 'The impudence of females assuming the right to teach must not be allowed to go so far as their claiming the right to baptise.' Many other influential Church scholars expressed similar views.

There were opposing voices as well, though. The Church Fathers Gregory of Nyssa, Gregory of Nazianzus and Ambrose of Milan all celebrated Thecla as the first female martyr and were greatly impressed by Macrina's intelligence, while the Byzantine bishop John Chrysostom praised these Christian women for their dedication and spoke constantly of their courage and wit. But these

AD 365: At the Council of Laodicea, the bishops forbid women from becoming priests.

scholars weren't able to stop the men of the Church from gradually reinstating the old order. Tertullian could rest easy in his grave: women wouldn't be given the right to baptise. As Macrina, Melania, Nino and many other women travelled the land converting new followers to Christianity, the bishops decided to forbid women from becoming priests at the Council of Laodicea. This was one of the many decisions bishops took to try to put women back in their place. Women should be kept at arm's length from power, and that included the power of the Church.

Around this time, people started quoting a Bible passage traditionally attributed to St Paul the Apostle:

> Women should remain silent in the churches. They are not allowed to speak, but must be in submission, as the law says.

Today, there is some doubt Paul really wrote these words at all. However, the quote still proved to be just as effective as the story of Adam and Eve. Whenever somebody wanted to shut a woman up, all they had to do was mention the story of the Fall, and this quote supposedly written by St Paul.

Despite all this – and perhaps for the first time in history – early Christianity opened a back door for women that has never fully closed since. A woman who lived a virtuous life in accordance with Christian teachings was capable of achieving fame and recognition. This applied to everyone. Christians who heeded the teachings of Jesus himself rather than the decisions of the Church found in them many good arguments for treating everyone as equals.

It didn't take long for women to use that back door to reach unprecedented levels of power and glory. One of these women was Theodora, the Empress of the Byzantine Empire.

THE BYZANTINE EMPIRE

From circus performer to empress: Theodora's unlikely rise

The Bosporus is a strait that runs like a fine line between the continents of Asia and Europe. It was here that Constantine decided to build his new Rome. At the strait's narrowest point, the western and eastern shore are separated by just 700 metres of water. After a short crossing by boat, you're on Asian soil.

The Roman Empire stretched far beyond Europe. Once on the Asian side of the Bosporus, travellers had to journey hundreds of miles, across Asia Minor and Syria, before they reached the edge of the empire. The eastern frontier would see 1,000 years of gruelling conflict between the Greeks, Romans and Persians.

Asia Minor and Syria were the location of Christianity's earliest beginnings. Soon this region would be host to great changes. It was still part of the Imperium Romanum and, as everywhere, all eyes were focused on its heart: Constantinople, the new Rome on the Bosporus.

Back in antiquity, all self-respecting cities had a circus – an open-air entertainments arena. In Constantinople, the Hippodrome was an enormous stone building with a U-shaped racetrack inside for horse and chariot racing. There was a box for the emperor on one side, topped by four golden horses that had been ordered from Rome by Constantine himself. The circus could seat an audience of 100,000 – more than most modern football stadiums. If you wanted 'bread and circuses', as one Roman poet once dismissed such forms of entertainment, then you had to be prepared to put up with the deafening noise, the formidable stench and being crushed from all sides by hundreds of people. Most of the audience sat on wooden benches, while the senators and the city's movers and shakers followed the action from seats made of marble. Women and children, on the other hand, had to make do with standing; after all, they should have been grateful that they were even allowed in.

Life in Byzantium revolved around the circus, not the Imperial Palace. Two factions, the Greens and the Blues, competed against one another in horse and chariot races, and people bet a lot of money on their favourites. The games also gave them plenty of time to talk about their dreams and ambitions, as well as to criticise the government. The circus was where the emperor came face to face with his people, and by keeping his ears open, he could get a feel for the mood in the city.

In the interval between the chariot and horse races, the audience was kept entertained by artists and actors, wild animals, boxing matches, dancing, singing and gymnastics. These entertainers were accompanied by music played on a pipe organ – an instrument with bronze pipes that produced sound by having air pumped into it with bellows. These organs were popular and an essential accompaniment to any sporting event.

The actors and acrobats were on the lowest rung of society. They had to work hard for their bread, and few professions were as poorly regarded; preachers constantly railed against the immorality of the circus. In their opinion, it was damaging to the Christian soul. This didn't stop them from joining in, though.

Once, one of the dancers found herself in dire straits, after the death of her husband, a bear tamer. He was the father of her three children and a member of the Green faction. With his death, the mother lost her entire livelihood. In desperation, she draped her three daughters in garlands and told them to sing songs for the spectators. She then turned to the public for help, and in the end found a new job with the Blue faction. Her family was saved.

As was usual at the time, the daughters followed in their mother's footsteps. Theodora, the middle daughter, was an extraordinary beauty, and her dance and pantomime performances were so enthralling that she became a celebrity in her own right.

But then Theodora's life saw an unlikely turn of events, like something out of a fairy tale. She travelled to North Africa with a man whom she is said to have freed from the circus by buying his freedom. This man eventually spurned her, so she returned to Constantinople on her own. On her travels, she met a number of priests, whose talk of Christianity made a deep impression on her. When she finally arrived back in Constantinople, she moved into a simple hut, swore to live a pious Christian life and made her living by spinning wool (remember, according to Ancient Greek philosophers, this was the most honourable occupation for a woman).

One day, the beautiful Theodora met Justinian I, the emperor's nephew and the successor to the throne. The love that blossomed between the two was strong, but it was also impossible. Theodora couldn't just forget about her oath of penance; she'd risk the wrath of her neighbours and be in danger of being cast out. For Justinian, too, nothing less than the throne of the empire was at stake. According to a 500-year-old law, a man of his status was forbidden from marrying someone as lowly as an actress.

But Justinian wasn't to be dissuaded. The empress wanted to thwart his marriage to Theodora at all costs, so he waited for her to die and then convinced his uncle to change the law. In the end, he and Theodora were married at a lavish ceremony in front of the entire city. The girl who had once stood in the circus begging for money moved into the magnificent Imperial Palace. In pre-Christian Rome, such a rise would have been unthinkable. But Theodora walked through the back door that Christianity had opened for women: if you repented for your sins and were well behaved, you could overcome any and all obstacles.

The city of Theodora and Justinian

The people suspected Theodora of being a sorceress. Some even believed the emperor had supernatural powers as well. Rumours spread that Justinian could take off his head and put it back on again, or make himself invisible.

Soon, the emperor became embroiled in a vicious conflict with his people. The two circus factions joined forces and turned against

AD 532: The
Nika riots
take place in
Constantinople;
Justinian and
Theodora are
lucky to escape
with their lives.

the state. With one voice, the Greens and the Blues demanded a new emperor. When their demands were rejected, they went on a rampage, setting fire to houses. The angry townspeople shouted 'Nika!' ('Victory!') and threatened to cut off Justinian's head (a terrifying prospect, it has to be said, even for someone who could reportedly take it off without anyone else's assistance …).

As the situation became more perilous, Justinian's advisers urged him to flee Constantinople by ship. Preparations were made, but just as he was about to depart, his path was blocked by Theodora. She persuaded her husband to stay and stand up to the rebels. His purple robe would make a noble shroud, she said, and death would be preferable to an impoverished life in a foreign land.

Justinian gathered his composure. With every ounce of their strength, he, his general and his soldiers defeated the angry mob. The circus became a bloodbath. By the end of the conflict, some 30,000 people had been killed, and half the city had been burned to the ground and destroyed. But the imperial couple survived, their power confirmed.

Justinian was a competent ruler, with a strong woman by his side. He started to consolidate the new Roman Empire from within, and began to write out his own laws. The Romans had long outgrown the Twelve Tables – the laws that had been written almost 1,000 years ago. When the emperor had all the latest laws written out in one place, the Code of Justinian came to almost three Bibles in length.

Theodora and Justinian rebuilt their city, transforming it into a buzzing metropolis. From Africa to Ravenna, they set up new churches, decorated with Byzantine mosaics. One of the most beautiful of these mosaics is the portrait of the couple in the Basilica of San Vitale in Ravenna, which can still be seen there today.

As empress, Theodora was responsible for laws concerning actresses and women in need. She also built an institution similar to a convent, for women seeking refuge from the hardship of their profession. Later, the citizens of Constantinople would show tourists the hut where Theodora had once lived and worked as a spinner: it had become a source of much pride.

But by far the most beautiful gift Justinian gave to the city was Hagia Sophia, a new church and a true marvel of construction. It was dedicated to 'Divine Wisdom' – *Sophia* – a concept identified with God right back to the time of the Old Testament. For almost 1,000 years, no other building in the world could match it in terms of size or splendour.

AD 532–537: Justinian orders the construction of the church Hagia Sophia.

SPLENDOUR AND DARKNESS

The golden city: the last bastion in a declining empire

Once you'd been to Constantinople, you never forgot it. It wasn't just the Hagia Sophia that left visitors breathless; everything around them seemed to dazzle with gold, and wonder after wonder was revealed before their eyes. Extravagant terraces and gardens offered a glorious backdrop for walks, accompanied by the sound of organs and the song of mechanical golden birds. Automated fountains and water features provided amusement and, every hour, one of the twenty-four doors on a clock would open to tell the time. For foreign diplomats, an audience at the palace was the highlight of their visit: the Byzantine emperor received them from a hydraulic throne that lifted him high up into the air.

But it wasn't enough to simply possess power: you had to demonstrate it too. Secretions from sea snails were used to dye the imperial family's clothing purple, a vibrant colour that made them stand out against the drab clothes of the masses; that way, everyone knew they were a member of the court. This symbol was so effective, the emperor decided to decorate an entire room in purple. This was where the emperor's sons and daughters would be born, securing their claim to the throne from birth. This strategy seemed to pay off. Soon, the people of Byzantium were convinced that worthy rulers were always born in purple.

When forging alliances with foreign rulers, the most precious negotiating tool in the emperor's arsenal was a princess born in purple. Girls were usually married to foreign rulers as ambassadors of the realm and sent away to distant lands while they were still young.

It was their job to make sure their husbands kept their bargains and didn't turn against Byzantium.

This task required women who were clever, capable and well educated. They were raised in the palace of Constantinople, which had an enormous library filled with thousands of books. But when the princesses arrived in another king's court, they found it difficult to give up all the comforts they had been used to at home. They missed the intellectual conversation, the books and the little luxuries. According to one story, a Byzantine woman visiting Venice decided to eat her meal with a fork she had brought from Constantinople (quite understandably). A doctor of the Church berated her for this sinful luxury: the fork, with its three prongs, was apparently a symbol of the Devil. As was so often the case, though, comfort got the better of superstition in the end.

Famed for its wealth, magnificent art and architecture, people from Spain all the way to the border with China dreamed of visiting Constantinople one day. The city was the jewel of the era we call the Middle Ages; from here looking out, the world appeared to be languishing in decay.

Western Europe seemed to be plummeting into a 'dark age'. The most striking thing about the first few centuries of the Dark Ages was that many things simply disappeared. The once-mighty Roman Empire had been brought to its knees by the invasion by the Germans and the Huns. Princes now ruled over small regions called principalities and no longer felt bound to a central power. Farmers and landowners were reduced to poverty, and the houses and roads of the cities crumbled. The multistorey buildings, aqueducts and thermal spas that had once left visitors awestruck now fell to ruin. The impact was most obvious of all in Rome. Of a population of almost 1 million, only 50,000 remained – equivalent to a class of twenty pupils with nineteen missing.

Things weren't looking much better in the Eastern Empire. The civilisations of Egypt and Mesopotamia had long ago lost their lustre. The Vandals had left their mark in North Africa, and the scarcity of gold and goods was felt throughout the empire as far as Syria and Palestine.

From the ruins of the Roman Empire, Byzantium shone like a lone golden beacon. Soon, people were no longer able to remember what had gone before, as they had never seen it with their own eyes. Constantinople must have seemed like a paradise, an oasis in a desert.

But Byzantium too was fighting for its survival. Little more than fifty years after the rule of Justinian and Theodora, the empire came within a hair's breadth of total collapse. The Persians had already conquered Syria, Armenia, Jerusalem and Egypt for their Sasanian Empire, even seizing the True Cross of Christ, one of Christianity's most holy relics. The Persian King Khosrow II gave it as a gift to his beloved wife Shirin, a Christian.

The citizens of the new Rome were convinced the Virgin Mary was watching over the city, interceding to fend off its enemies. Pilgrims had brought the city two priceless relics, Mary's veil and girdle, which were kept in a jewel-encrusted shrine. The Persians, when they finally laid siege to Constantinople, proved no match for the Virgin Mary's protection (the strength of the Byzantine navy may also have had something to do with it), and the city was saved at the very last second. The Romans and the Persians later agreed a truce, and the True Cross of Christ was returned to Jerusalem in a jubilant procession.

AD 614: The Sasanian Persians conquer Jerusalem and steal the True Cross of Christ, but Constantinople's defences hold.

CHINA'S MIDDLE AGES

Lands of the rising sun

In the days when some people believed the Earth was flat, they thought there were certain countries in the East where the sun rose in the same place every day. They called the land where the light came from every morning 'the Orient'. Like the Romans, they said, '*Ex oriente lux*', which means 'from the east comes light'. As far as the Romans were concerned, the Orient started beyond the Mediterranean, in modern-day Turkey, Syria, Palestine, Iraq and Iran. The people of Assyria, as this region used to be called, believed that the rising sun was controlled by the god Asher. This is where the word 'Asia' came from, which would later become the European name for the continent where the sun seemed to rise. In the Far East of Asia was China, and after China was the edge of the world.

Today we know that the Earth is a sphere and that, rather than rising in the same position over the Middle East or China each day, the sun's position over the Earth changes depending on the time of day. From China, people can also look to the east and instead of seeing the edge of the world, they see a vast ocean. At this point in history, the Chinese weren't doing much sea travel, so it took them a while to discover a large group of islands off their coast. These islands – which we now know as Japan – were home to a people with tattooed bodies and faces who called themselves a name the Chinese understood as meaning 'elves' or 'little sprites'. Then, the Chinese did what the Assyrians and the Romans had done before them: they named this land in the east 'Nippon', 'Land of the Rising Sun'. This is still the Japanese name for their own country.

The 'little sprites' of the Land of the Rising Sun were the ancestors of the Japanese. When the Chinese first came into contact with them, they were ruled by Queen Himiko. Weary of war, some tribal chiefs had united around her and elected her to the throne.

AD 239: Queen Himiko of Japan sends a delegation to China to establish contacts with the Chinese.

During Himiko's rule, she sent four delegations to China. Back then, the Japanese led very simple lives and survived through fishing. However, Himiko soon discovered that the Chinese did things very differently. Her ambassadors must have been astounded by their technology, their sprawling cities, their huge buildings, towering temples, paved streets, thick walls and the cornucopia of produce for sale in their markets. China showed respect to Queen Himiko, and as a parting gift, the emperor gave her ambassadors 100 bronze mirrors. Vibrant exchange flourished between the two countries; from China, the Japanese inherited writing, and innovations in architecture, religion and clothing, which they then absorbed into their own culture.

Himiko was a successful queen, so after her death, another woman was soon chosen to succeed her. Her name was Toyo, and she was just 13 years old.

A melting pot of religions

AD 208: The Chinese Empire falls after the Battle of the Red Cliffs, and for centuries the country is governed as individual kingdoms rather than a unified state. China opens up to Buddhism, which is brought to the country by monks and migrants.

While Queen Himiko was establishing friendly relations with her neighbours, the great Chinese Empire of the Qin Shihuangdi and the Han emperors was falling apart. The final battle in the civil war, which would later become known as the Battle of the Red Cliffs, was fought by the empire's last great generals. They weren't strong enough to repel their adversaries, and the fate of the empire was sealed. Uprisings, epidemics of disease and famine decimated the population, and whole cities and the roads linking them fell to ruin. For around 400 years, the empire was reduced to individual territories controlled by military commanders; some of these commanders even claimed the title of emperor, even though the rest of the kingdom was outside their control. And as you can imagine, there were occasions when several rulers declared themselves emperor at the same time.

During these years of turmoil, there was no state apparatus to control the furthest corners of the kingdom. People were no longer forced to follow the same strict rules and standards as before and had space to try out new things. This meant that, for 400 years, China was very open to foreign influences. One of these was a new religion from India called Buddhism, which was brought to the country by travelling monks.

Let's go back in time 700 years or so and remind ourselves what Buddhism is. The Buddha was a monk who taught his followers about the Four Noble Truths and the Eightfold Path; under his guidance, believers successfully left the suffering of the world behind, freeing themselves from the cycle of death and rebirth. When Buddhists wanted to remember the Buddha, they visualised an empty throne, or sometimes footprints or a horse without a rider. Through these images the invisible nature of the Buddha was made visible: the enlightened one wasn't a god, but a human who had 'dissolved' forever into nirvana – a state beyond the cycle of death and rebirth.

Then, about 200 years after the Buddha's death, Alexander the Great and his Greek army arrived in north-western India. Some of his Greek generals stayed there and taught the Indians how to sculpt statues from stone. Soon they began to carve statues of the Buddha, as tall as church spires, into the rocky walls of caves. Somehow, people started worshipping these gigantic cliff statues as gods. It turned out that a religion with no god or images wasn't very practical.

A new Buddhist teaching was also born, 'the Mahayana', which means 'Great Vehicle' or 'Great Road'. Followers of Mahayana Buddhism cared about more than just their own individual liberation from suffering. They were troubled by the suffering of all living things and devoted themselves to caring for the people and animals around them. By becoming enlightened themselves, they could heal others.

Since its beginnings, Buddhism had changed a lot. Although it seemed strange to the Chinese at first, its teachings on nirvana and emptiness seemed very similar to the Taoism message of non-action; in fact, Buddhism merged with Taoism when it arrived in China, and they both influenced each other. This situation must have led to lots of misunderstandings, though, as very few monks were able to translate the ancient Buddhist texts from Sanskrit into Chinese.

Empress Wu Zetian

Buddhism and Taoism changed China. In the beginning, these two teachings were little more than a collection of wise sayings, guidelines for living and exercises, but they eventually evolved into religions. Temples were built to Buddhist and Taoist gods, as well as monasteries for monks, led by abbots. The bones of saints were collected and worshipped as relics, and when believers strayed from the path of virtue, they were threatened with all the agonies of hell. This was similar to other religions – but very different at the same time. The overt blending of two religions, for instance, would have been unthinkable in other cultures. However, the Chinese didn't necessarily see anything wrong with lighting a candle at a Taoist temple in the morning and making an offering to a Buddhist god in the evening. When temples to the wise man Confucius started being built in the cities, believers could worship the old philosopher as a god, too.

The differences didn't stop there. While the Roman Empire of old had disappeared forever, the separate kingdoms of the former Chinese Empire started to come together again. The person responsible for uniting them was an emperor called Wen of Sui. Wen was succeeded by the first of several emperors from the Tang family, a very successful ruling dynasty who drastically expanded the kingdom's borders and oversaw a period of great prosperity in China. The new Chinese Empire became strong and powerful.

In the midst of this unprecedented boom, something unheard of happened: a woman dared to lay claim to the title of emperor, entering the history books as an 'Emperor of China'. This was very different from being an empress: the empress's only responsibility was to be the emperor's wife and bear him children. Her other main concern was ensuring – by any means necessary – that she wasn't usurped by one of the emperor's concubines. Only the emperor, the 'Son of Heaven', could rule over China.

AD 618: The Tang dynasty comes to power in China, and their capital Chang'an becomes the largest city in the world.

However, one woman did succeed in becoming emperor in her own right (also called an empress regnant). Her name was Wu Zetian, and she was one of the emperor's concubines.

The chroniclers of the time turned their noses up at her. One poet wrote that Wu Zetian had 'the heart of a serpent and the disposition of a wolf' and that 'both gods and men hate her, and heaven and earth cannot allow her to exist'. In reality, the only way Wu Zetian could enforce her rule after her husband's death was through uncompromising violence. She set up a secret police force who then hunted down and tortured her opponents to death. Back when she was a lowly concubine, she was also alleged to have strangled her own child and blamed it on the empress. The emperor, oblivious to her scheming, divorced his wife and declared Wu Zetian her replacement. And then, when her husband died, Wu Zetian was even accused of poisoning him so she could take the throne for herself. But, as we've seen before, we should take claims like this with a pinch of salt …

Empress Wu was beyond doubt a talented ruler, and once she had overthrown her sons, she ruled alone. She defended the empire against attacks from the Tibetans and Turks and brought peace and prosperity. She also took an unusual step in governing her people, by setting up a letterbox in the city so the denizens of the empire could send her feedback and suggestions. If they weren't able to write, a scribe was provided at the cost of the state. These suggestions were reviewed regularly by Wu Zetian's officials. Even her harshest critics had to admit that, since taking over government, she had been clear-sighted about the best measures to take, and the greatest of officials were falling over themselves to work for her.

One of these great officials had Wu Zetian's undisputed trust. His name was Di Renjie, and his career was the stuff of dreams. As a young man, he had passed the challenging Chinese civil service exams with flying colours. Like all officials, he was sent to work as an administrator and judge in provinces all over the empire. However, officials couldn't hold office for longer than four years, and once this term was up, they had to move on to a new one in another province. This was done to stop officials from giving favours to their relatives and friends.

AD 690: Empress Wu Zetian becomes the 'emperor of China'. The country becomes a religious melting pot of Buddhism, Taoism and Confucianism.

Di Renjie must have been a very competent and clever man: centuries later, people would still remember how easily he was able to resolve the most difficult disputes. By the time he took up his high-ranking post in the capital, he had behind him a long career that had taken him all over China. By appointing him, Empress Wu placed her trust in a man who hadn't been living at court for decades and didn't have any connections to its various players. Rather than focusing on the interests of his own people, she hoped he would act entirely in the interests of the state.

The empire of the Tang

Under the Tangs' rule, China experienced a golden age. Its capital Chang'an, which translated means 'Eternal Peace', became the largest city in the world. As promised by this name, the Tang dynasty ushered in a long period of peace and stability. They successfully defeated the Turks, a new people who had arrived from Central Asia, and very soon, Chinese rule extended to the west as far as the border with Persia. This was the furthest Chinese territory would ever stretch.

This blossoming empire was a colourful world. Chang'an, the new capital, was a cosmopolitan city where Turks, Indian Buddhist monks, Armenian traders, Japanese people, Jews and Christians all lived side by side. The empire's leading generals included Turks and Koreans, while the civil service included Persians, Tibetans, Indians and South East Asians among its ranks.

The new emperors built great canals between the rivers in the south and the north for transporting goods. These canals ensured that the markets were constantly supplied with pottery, silk and other precious fabrics; with carpets from Persia, spices, medicines, ivory and pearls; with ceramics, damask, bronze mirrors and slaves. You could buy everything from incense, gold and precious stones to dates, lion skins, peacock feathers and even golden peaches from Samarkand. Persian dancers and acrobats provided street entertainment, and the inns were filled with people drinking wine. Trade was flourishing, and people started to pay with paper money. The very first books were also printed and the treasury's coffers were boosted by taxes on the salt trade and the new fashion for teahouses.

The variety and colourful goings-on in China's cities made the empire rich. But what its rulers were really interested in was keeping hold of power. Rather than protecting individual citizens, the aim of the legal system they set up was to maintain the status quo. China's cities were organised along entirely different lines to the cities of Greece or Rome, as their main purpose was to control people. The streets and houses were arranged into a system of squares, and each quarter was surrounded by thick walls. Artisans and traders, Chinese, Jews and Arabs: every group had its own quarter. In the evening the gates to each were closed, and anyone found outside the walls faced severe punishment. The government of China did this to stop too many people from gathering in one place – and also perhaps to stop them from taking an active role in shaping public life.

The Buddhist queen

Empress Wu knew that, as a woman, it was impossible for her to become the 'Son of Heaven'. But miraculously, against all the odds, she managed to do just that. She didn't believe the Tang would accept her as the leader of their dynasty, so she decided to declare her own – the second Zhou dynasty. She also moved the capital to Luoyang because she didn't have enough close allies in Chang'an.

Many rulers supported Buddhism, Taoism or both, and presented themselves as enlightened beings who would bring salvation to their people. At court they surrounded themselves with monks and had countless texts translated from Sanskrit into Chinese. Across the land, *stupas* were built; these were symbolic representations of the Buddha and his teachings, and were used to house relics. During festivals, people carried statues through the streets to stand in the temples and *stupas*, where they placed offerings at the feet of the statues.

Religion had the power to set large crowds of people in motion, and when these crowds became angry, things could get dangerous for the ruler. It was vital for those in power to make themselves a part of the religion. This was the same in China as it was in Rome. So Wu Zetian promoted Buddhism, founded monasteries and had 10,000 Buddhist texts published. She also portrayed herself as the queen of the sun; in the Longmen Caves, visitors can still marvel at a 17-metre-tall statue of the Sun Buddha, which may have been carved in her image.

The end of the Tang

The empress's death at the age of 80 triggered bloody battles for the throne, and peace was only restored when her grandson Xuanzong became emperor.

In the beginning, Xuanzong's reign was a great success. He returned the capital to Chang'an and restored the Tang dynasty – brought to a premature end by his mother – to its former glory. His appreciation for the finer things in life was on full display at court: horses were popular, and courtiers spent their time playing polo. The emperor was also a patron of the arts, supporting many singers and poets.

But this success didn't last long. Xuanzong fell into the same trap that all great leaders eventually fall into. He decided to push the empire's already far-flung borders even further. Just as a balloon bursts if you fill it with too much air, the empire expanded too far and collapsed. We've seen this happen many times before: the Roman Empire and the Chinese Empire of the Han dynasty had met the same fate, while the collapse of Alexander the Great's empire was the quickest of any in history. The Tang dynasty came to an end when they lost central control over their colossal territory.

As with other empires, the downfall started with a series of military defeats at the most distant fringes. In China's far west, a new people had arrived, the Arabs. They stormed the Chinese border, thrashing the Tang troops. Emboldened, others followed their lead. Now the Turks and the Tibetans made their own stand against their occupiers and won.

Rumour has it that Xuanzong – after such an auspicious start – had simply become lazy and overreached himself. In the end, one of his own generals rebelled against him, forcing Xuanzong to flee. Chaos spread, rebels plundered the great cities and the state collapsed, bringing an end to the golden age of the Tang.

These events were an important turning point, and not just for China. The battle between the Arabs and the Tang in Central Asia, in modern-day Kyrgyzstan, decided the future of an entire region. As the Chinese Empire diminished, so too did the influence of Chinese culture in the lands between China and the Roman Empire. Central Asia came under the influence of the Arabs and their new religion: Islam.

AD 751: The Arabs defeat the Chinese at the Battle of Talas River. They push Buddhism out of Central Asia and introduce a new religion: Islam.

MUHAMMAD HEARS THE VOICE OF GOD

A letter

The feuding colossi of Rome and Persia were finally making peace with one another when their rulers received a letter. The letter's author introduced himself as 'Muhammad, servant and messenger of Allah', and he called upon them to accept a new religion – Islam. There was nothing out of the ordinary about this, so the Byzantine emperor decided to find out whether Muhammad was a real prophet, a true messenger of God. His conclusion: Muhammad was the real deal. However, the Persian King Khosrow II reacted furiously to the letter, tearing it to pieces and angrily dismissing the messenger who had delivered it. In a letter to his governor in Yemen, he wrote: 'This Arab ... has sent us an insolent letter. Send out two intelligent men and bring him to me in a cage ... If he resists ... then send an army to track him down and send me his head.' But the Persian generals couldn't find him.

The Prophet of Islam

Muhammad was born in the city of Mecca. Up until then, his homeland, the Arabian Peninsula, had been almost entirely ignored by the world's great powers. The Romans and Persians had conquered parts of it but were never truly able to control its people. The Arab tribes preferred to fight one another instead of the outsiders. Most of them travelled from place to place as nomads, and cities were only founded at the intersections of trade routes between China, Africa, India and Europe.

Even as a young man, Muhammad attracted the attention of the people around him; they valued his intelligence, his strength and his sense of justice. Everyone who knew him said he was very gentle compared to other men his age. He was poor until he married the rich widow Khadija. She was older than him and owned a fleet of trading caravans; the two got on well and they ran her business with great success.

But Muhammad was troubled by the situation in Arabia. His travels with the caravans took him to different cities, where the achievements of the Jews and Christians were on full display, and he felt that these neighbours were superior to the Arab tribes. He asked himself why, unlike the Jews and Christians, the Arabs worshipped many gods rather than one, and why their religion wasn't based on a holy scripture.

Later, Muhammad recounted how he climbed to the top of a mountain, where he suddenly heard the voice of God, or Allah. He was incredibly frightened. Shaking with fear and scared he was losing his mind, he returned home. His wife Khadija told him he had been visited by the angel Gabriel, who had whispered orders from Allah.

Khadija comforted and encouraged him and told him to trust in the word of God. Muhammad followed her advice and let himself be guided by the voice that would give him new instructions over the course of the next twenty-two years. Soon, he gained his first followers, who confirmed their belief in the new god with one simple sentence, first spoken by Khadija: 'There is no god but Allah, and Muhammad is his messenger.' To this day, that is the statement of faith for all Muslims. The prophet's students wrote down everything God revealed to Muhammad, producing the Quran, the holy scripture of Islam.

The powerful clans in Mecca weren't happy about Muhammad's arrival. In the Ka'aba, their temple – a large, black, stone, cube-shaped building – the city's inhabitants worshipped more than 300 gods. Once a year, Arabs from all over the peninsula made a pilgrimage to Mecca to do the same. Now, Muhammad was demanding that they give up their false gods to follow Allah, but the people of

AD 622: The Prophet Muhammad and his followers flee from Mecca to Medina, where the world's first Muslim community is established.

Mecca ignored him and threatened Muhammad and his followers with harsh punishment. The situation became dangerous, so the prophet decided to leave the city and his small band fled to Medina. In Medina, he established the first Muslim community or *ummah*; here, he could make his ideas a reality.

Muhammad, whose gentle nature had made such an impression on people in his early life, detested violence. His new society would be just and fair, without resorting to cruelty. People wouldn't be forced to accept Islam, and there would be no harsh punishment or oppression. Instead, Muhammad advocated mutual respect. The leader of the community should value all its members equally; he should listen to them, discuss decisions with them and act in their interests. Muhammad also extended these rights to slaves. Whenever he could, Muhammad helped them win their freedom and, as a sign of his sincerity, he even entrusted them with leading his soldiers.

In Medina, the Prophet built a mosque where he could converse with his followers every day, from morning to night. Everyone could say what they thought and ask questions about how a devout Muslim should live. Muhammad received his answers straight from God. Nine days before his death, he heard God's voice for the last time.

Muhammad hoped to set an example. Everyone in his society was expected to behave just like him. This wasn't always easy for his followers, as lots of the things he advocated were new and unfamiliar to them: for example, the Prophet refused to force a woman into marriage, regarding this custom as un-Islamic. Muhammad himself had nine wives who he loved very much. He built them each their own house close to the mosque and they travelled with him when he went to war, as he didn't want to be without their help or advice.

Although some believe it went against his pacifist beliefs, Muhammad still fought in wars. He knew that Islam would only prevail if he succeeded in conquering Mecca – and so he and his army set off to unify the feuding tribes of the Arabian Peninsula. After eight years, the long-awaited victory came. The Prophet and his followers were able to win by force of arms, leaving the powerful clans of Mecca no choice but to ally themselves with the new faith. Their temple, the Ka'aba, was dedicated to one god: Allah (the Arabic name for God).

Aisha

In keeping with Arab custom, women were an important part of the booty in times of war. The victors kidnapped them from their opponents and married them, kept them as house servants or set them to work as slaves in the fields. Sometimes, they even sold the captured women to fill their coin purses. Muhammad deeply resented this practice and wanted to put a stop to it, as it treated women as objects and he greatly respected his wives and his daughter Fatima. Many of the men in his community couldn't see any reason for changing their behaviour, but as the Prophet received his instructions from God, they couldn't contradict his authority. It wouldn't be long, though, before they would get a chance to try to ruin the reputation of Muhammad's favourite wife Aisha.

The incident took place on a military expedition. The caravan had stopped for a break and was preparing to set off again when Aisha noticed her necklace had gone. The necklace was special to her, so she started looking for it. Her porters didn't notice that her *howdah* (like a sedan chair) was empty when they lifted it up onto the camel, so the caravan left without her.

Aisha went on alone, but luckily was joined by a young Muslim man who had also missed the caravan and who offered to act as her escort. When Muhammad realised she was missing, he stopped the caravan. Soon, though, he caught sight of the two in the distance and breathed a sigh of relief: Aisha was safe. However, some of the men in the community accused Aisha of having an affair with her escort. It wouldn't have surprised them if Aisha had been unfaithful, they said; after all, Muhammad was far too old for her.

Enraged, Muhammad confronted her accusers in the mosque. He was convinced of Aisha's fidelity and defended her honour, ordering the families of the troublemakers to punish them for stirring up these rumours. This case of slander – making malicious, false, and defamatory claims about someone – was also said to have incited the wrath of God himself, who dictated seventeen verses to Muhammad about Aisha's innocence.

But the men still didn't want to give up their power over women. One of them complained bitterly to Muhammad about his wife:

'What should I do if she doesn't obey me?' Some men even started attacking women on the streets; they wanted to show Muhammad that it was too dangerous for women to travel without a male escort. They refused to accept that they were the source of this danger and that they had a responsibility to change their own behaviour. The attacks escalated and Muhammad was forced to act.

According to some, the only time God dictated Quranic verses against women was during this critical time for the new faith, as it was essential to placate these angry men. We don't know if this is true, but what we do know is this: the Quran contains verses that have been used by some Muslims for a long time – in some cases to this day – to force women to obey men, with violence if necessary. They reintroduced the old rules.

In this dispute, Muhammad discovered his authority had limits. After his death, slavery and customs such as forced marriage, which Muhammad had denounced as 'un-Islamic', were brought back into practice. His followers had abandoned the issues that had mattered most to the Prophet. Today debate still rages about whether or not these verses are misogynistic, or whether it's a question of interpretation.

What did the Prophet himself think? When the Muslims oppressed women, kept slaves and went to war were they betraying the Prophet's ideals? Or had the Prophet sanctioned this with instructions from God? Many say that Muhammad rejected forced marriage and violence towards women entirely, and lots of the things we know about the Prophet's life confirm that he valued women, not just as wives and mothers, but also as confidantes and advisers.

The Battle of the Camel

The Arabs followed Muhammad's god and recited the 'Tawhid', the Declaration of Faith. They turned to face Mecca when they prayed, they fasted during the month of Ramadan and went on pilgrimage once a year to the Ka'aba. But when Muhammad died, their direct link to God was severed. The Prophet, who used his authority to bring unity, left a void and God hadn't nominated a successor.

The community decided that, in future, the Prophet's successor would be chosen from among its own ranks and would be called 'caliph', meaning 'representative'. The first two caliphs were accepted with varying degrees of approval, but disputes broke out by the third – who was actually murdered. Now the bad blood was really flowing between the believers, and the fourth caliph, Muhammad's son-in-law Ali, had as many enemies as he had supporters.

Then Aisha, Muhammad's favourite wife, waded in. In her opinion, Ali had been too lenient on the third caliph's murderers; he was unjust and unable to fulfil the duties of his office. So Aisha gathered an army and declared war on Ali. Riding in a *howdah* on the back of a camel, she led her soldiers into battle. But Ali's army were stronger, and Aisha watched helplessly as her men suffered a devastating defeat. By the end, the battlefield was littered with thousands of corpses.

Soon after, Aisha's allies remobilised against Ali and his followers, and this time they defeated the caliph's troops. Ali's followers were forced to flee and, from then on, the Muslims were forever divided. The 'Sunnis', the followers of Aisha, and the 'Shia', the followers of Ali, became bitter enemies. Some of those who rushed to Aisha's aid belonged to the powerful Umayyad clan from Mecca. After their victory over Ali, they selected the first caliphs, who tried to defeat their opponents using all the means at their disposal. The conflict split the Muslims into two sects, and the divide between the Sunni and Shia continues to this day.

AD 661: After the assassination of the third caliph, the Muslims are unable to agree on a successor. They split into two different sects: the Shi'ites and the Sunnis.

For Muhammad, there could be nothing worse than *fitna*, a war between Muslims. Yet in less than twenty years, his dream of a peaceful society for all Muslims had turned into a nightmare. Violence and injustice had prevailed, and the wisdom, gentleness and courage of the Prophet seemed long forgotten. But Muhammad hadn't shied away from war as a tool for paving the way for the God of Islam, and this might not have helped the situation either. Some came to the conclusion that violence against non-believers was permitted – another area that Muslims disagree about even now.

The map of the world is redrawn

Under the leadership of the Umayyads, the Sunnis were so strong that the conflict with Ali and his followers didn't leave much of an impression on them. The vast majority of Arabs followed them and, together, they set out to conquer the entire world for Allah. From Iran, they spread throughout Central Asia, heading north-east to the city of Samarkand and the fringes of China and south towards northern India.

Their advance to the west was just as successful; only six years after Muhammad's death, they had conquered huge swathes of the ancient Roman Empire. Jerusalem, the city where Jesus Christ was crucified and buried, became Muslim. The caliph left the Arabian Peninsula, moving his court to the Syrian city of Damascus, perhaps because it was easier to plan his military campaigns from there. Next, the Arabs seized Egypt from Byzantium and from there advanced further into western North Africa. Their goal was to conquer the whole of the ancient world, so they set sail across the Mediterranean from North Africa to Spain. At first, it looked as if they would get even further than that, but the Arab fighters were stopped at the peaks of the Pyrenees, on the border of Spain and Francia, a predecessor to modern-day France. Charles Martel, one of the Frankish king's leading statesmen and military commanders, blocked their path, securing a decisive victory. They would have to be content with occupying Spain.

The ambitions of the Arabs in the east were also scuppered at the walls of Constantinople. The city was simply too well protected, maybe by the watchful gaze of the Virgin Mary but certainly by its fortifications and fearsome weapons. The Byzantines had machines that could project something called 'Greek fire' over the walls at

From AD 637: The Arabs conquer half of the world, from Samarkand to Spain, and the Muslim capital moves to Damascus.

enemy ships; it didn't go out when it hit the water, so it would send the attackers' wooden ships up in flames.

The Arabs' campaigns of conquest ended in northern Spain; Christianity remained at the walls of Constantinople and the rest of Europe. But the rest of the known world, from North Africa and the Middle East through to northern India and up to the borders of China, was now under Arab Muslim influence. In the following centuries, progress – that pulsing engine of world history – would mostly be found in Arab cities.

Aisha's testimony

Muhammad's dream of a just and peaceful Muslim society might not have come true, but he had achieved his goal of changing the ways the Arabs lived. These desert nomads had become strong conquerors and powerful leaders, and now, after bringing half the world to its knees, they wasted no time catching up on what they'd previously been missing. They founded cities and built magnificent buildings decorated with mosaics and ornaments, and Greek Christian culture found new centres in the Muslim capitals of Damascus and Baghdad, bringing with them the writings of Plato and Aristotle. The Arabs produced rich literature that was admired far and wide for its beauty. Contact with India brought them numbers and algebra, and from a melting pot of all the world's knowledge, a new Arab culture emerged that would soon surpass all others.

One of the culture's most famous scientists, the Persian physician and philosopher Avicenna, significantly improved humanity's knowledge of medicine with his research and treatments. In Andalusia, the Muslim philosopher Ibn Rushd (also known as Averroes) studied the writings of Aristotle and enhanced them with his own illuminating commentaries, helping the Europeans rediscover wisdom from the great thinker they had long since forgotten. Averroes also debated aloud – perhaps for the first time in history – whether it was rational to believe in a god at all, but this was too much for many Islamic scholars, who urged the caliphs to banish Averroes and burn his books.

The religious teaching of Islam was developing too. After Muhammad's death, extra texts reporting the words and deeds of the Prophet had been added to the Quran; these reports were called Hadith and they were statements from witnesses who had known the Prophet in day-to-day life. The Hadith were considered as important as the Quran itself: if a Muslim wasn't sure what to do, the best course of action was to follow the Prophet's example. When the first generation of witnesses started to die, the Hadiths' writers relied on witnesses to witnesses and then on witnesses to witnesses of the first witnesses. This is why most of the Hadiths began with long explanations of who's quoting who, e.g. 'Qutayba ibn Sa'id narrated of al-Laith of Yazid bin Abi Habib of Irak bin Malik of Urwa of Aisha that …'. The Prophet's words were only reported once the chain reached a first-hand witness who actually knew him.

With time, Islamic scholars realised that these reports weren't always reliable. It was clear that some of the witnesses were being economical with the truth; indeed, some of them recalled Muhammad's words in a way that most benefitted them. For example, one man put the following words into the Prophet's mouth: 'Never will a nation prosper that makes a woman its ruler.' The alleged witness was caught up in the gears of the war between Aisha and Caliph Ali, so he may have said this to save his own skin. Meanwhile, even the genuine Hadiths were also embellished with fabricated quotations. Some influential people even paid scholars to write them so they could strengthen their own position with a 'genuine' statement from the Prophet.

Some 200 years after Muhammad's death, a scholar set out from Bukhara, a city in Central Asia, to travel the entire Islamic world. Bukhari, as this scholar was called, asked people about the Hadiths they told one another or wrote down, collecting a total of 600,000. Out of these he developed a complicated method of determining which Hadiths were genuine and which weren't. He came to an astonishing conclusion: of the 600,000 Hadiths, approximately 590,000 were false. By this time, hostile attitudes towards women were once again on the rise, so unsurprisingly, the Hadiths Bukhari believed to be genuine included the ones vilifying women.

From AD 637: After Muhammad's death, Muslims collect witness accounts of the Prophet. In the ninth century, Bukhari discovers that 590,000 of the 600,000 witness statements are false – but he doesn't reject the ones vilifying women.

Five hundred years later, a Turkish imam was frustrated at how Bukhari and other scholars had completely ignored Aisha, so he put together his own collection, this time made up exclusively of reports from Muhammad's favourite wife. He discovered that she was a very trustworthy witness. For example, one of the Prophet's students claimed that Muhammad had said, 'Three things bring bad luck: house, woman and horse.' When Aisha heard this, she said, 'The student clearly didn't learn his lessons well enough. He came into our house when the Prophet was in the middle of a sentence and he only heard the end of it. What the Prophet said was this: "May God refute the Jews; they say three things bring bad luck: House, woman, and horse."'

It's difficult to tell whether a Hadith is genuine or not. However, the two collections met with very different fates. For many Muslims, the Hadiths collected by Bukhari carry the same authority as the Quran, but the manuscript of Aisha's commentary was filed away in a library in Damascus, where it lay virtually ignored for centuries.

Al-Khayzuran and *The One Thousand and One Nights*

In the palace of the caliph, power was shifting – and it wasn't happening peacefully. One day, Abu al-Abbas as-Saffah (later the first caliph of the Abbasid dynasty) invited the caliph and his male relatives to a banquet. The guests arrived to find a feast laid with sumptuous dishes, waiting to be served. But no sooner had the caliph's entourage sat down to dine than their hosts burst in, drawing their weapons and slaughtering them to a man. They then sat down and ate the meal themselves. With this, they assumed control of the Islamic Empire.

AD 750: The Abbasid family seizes power from the Umayyads. An Umayyad prince flees to Spain, where he founds a Muslim caliphate.

The Abbasids moved the caliph's capital from Damascus to Baghdad, and this city became the new centre of the Arab Empire. Here, Muslims and Christians, Jews and Buddhists lived side by side, each group in its own quarter. Artists, scientists, writers and lawyers moved to the city, bringing their knowledge and expertise with them.

As a result, Persian literature experienced a renaissance. One of the first to write in the modern Persian language was a poet called Rabia Balkhi; she was the daughter of a Samanid prince, who was a vassal of the Abbasids in Baghdad at the time. Centuries after her death, a tragic story was told about her, although the legend and the reality were probably very different. It is said that Rabia fell in love with a slave. When her brother found out, he arrested the slave and locked his sister in a bathroom, where he cut one of the main arteries in her neck. Before she died, Rabia is said to have used her own blood to write a final verse on the wall.

Stories like this were brought to Baghdad by travellers from Persia and India, and they were soon collected together in a famous tome called *The One Thousand and One Nights.*

A similarly fantastical (but nevertheless true) tale was told about the slave al-Khayzuran. She was sold at a bazaar, where there was a booming trade in slaves and, like many others, she ended up as one of the caliph's hareem (his wives and consorts). Around this time, a young musician called al-Mawsili had started giving tuition to young slaves; by teaching them to sing, dance and tell stories, he increased their value before selling them on again. Other traders followed al-Mawsili's lead, teaching their slaves about religion, chronicle writing and astronomy. The number of beautiful, educated 'singing slave girls' grew.

As in China and Europe, the Islamic golden age largely revolved around men. While the men were busy gathering knowledge and making art, strict rules prevented free Muslim women – those who weren't slaves – from leaving the house. Girls generally weren't taught how to read or write. The singing slave girls were an unusual exception; they made up a small minority of women who were educated for the sake of entertaining men. A singing slave girl could be sold on if her master wished or he could offer her services to other men in return for payment. Sometimes, erotic verse was written in musk on the slave's forehead, palms and feet, as a way of enhancing her appeal and value. A slave's beauty, education and skill in poetry and storytelling increased her value – but rather than earning respect, they were accused by scholars of being dishonest, disloyal and devoid of morals.

Given this context, al-Khayzuran's story is rather amazing. Al-Mahdi, the caliph's son, preferred her to all the other women at court, and al-Khayzuran convinced him to set her free and marry her as soon as he became caliph. Al-Mahdi valued her judgement and education, so they ruled together. Al-Khayzuran had achieved something truly remarkable: she was educated, free and now she was respected as well.

AD 786: Harun al-Rashid takes the throne of the Arab Empire.

When al-Khayzuran's second son Harun al-Rashid followed his father to the throne, he had no qualms about involving his mother in all matters of state. He would go on to become one of the most famous caliphs of all time. Under his reign, Baghdad shone, emerging as the cultural hub of the Middle East. Harun al-Rashid set up the House of Wisdom, where scholars translated books from all corners of the world. He also built a paper mill, helping this Chinese invention spread throughout the West.

Many of the stories in *The One Thousand and One Nights* are set at the court of Caliph Harun al-Rashid. Sometimes, he even features himself. So does his mother, as she is the stories' narrator: Scheherazade.

Rabia of Basra, Rabia of Syria and Fatima of Nishapur

A Muslim woman could be free, which meant she couldn't get an education and was rarely allowed to leave the house, or she could be a slave and the property of a man. However, there was also a third, albeit uncommon, possibility: free women who rejected the role of wife and mother. These women were the followers of Islamic mystics who later became known as Sufis. The Sufis were people who lived in strict, almost ascetic, piety every day of their lives. Just like the Desert Mothers and Fathers of Christianity, most of them refused to marry and dedicated their lives to meditating on God. This gave women a chance to gain an education, preach, debate and even travel. Many female mystics even went on pilgrimages to Mecca.

Some of them were so well known, their memory still lives on to this day. A poem surviving from this time is very likely to have been penned by Rabia of Basra, who not only made a name for herself as a mystic but as a writer of secular poems. Fatima of Nishapur was a respected scholar and the daughter of an *amir* (prince). And Rabia of Syria convinced a mystic – who up until then had been determined to stay single – to marry her so he could benefit from her money. She promised him they would spend their married life together like brother and sister. Later, however, her husband took a second wife and gave up his life of asceticism; Rabia was said to have been so shocked that she staggered all the way home, and was afraid of being mistaken for a drunk by the men on the street.

Later the mystics introduced a code of conduct and established communities, essentially transforming Sufism into a movement – and women were no longer welcome. In desperation, the mystic Maymuna bint Sakula tried to prove her devotion: 'I've worn my shirt for forty-seven years without a tear; my mother spun it for me. A dress worn by the pious never tears.'

But, despite her assertions, fewer and fewer women trod the path of the mystic, even though they continued to be respected as scholars. Just like the Buddha and the Christian bishops who denounced Thecla, the Sufis saw women as one of the three great threats capable of distracting them from God. In their animosity towards women, all religions were remarkably alike.

GREAT THINGS COME FROM AFRICA

Progress

When we think of the word 'history' – or 'world history', even – we tend to think of time moving in one direction only, as though it were a line starting somewhere in the past and ending with the present day. However, this idea is a relatively recent one. The ancient Egyptians, who had an empire lasting over 3,000 years, had no such concept. On the contrary, all Egyptian knowledge was based on the idea that most things remained the same, that *maat* or 'order' remained intact. Time flowed in a circle, forming loops of repetition. People could see that, year after year, like clockwork, the Nile broke its banks; that growth was followed by decay and birth by death. In China, people saw a harmony between heaven and earth that seemed total and eternal, and they believed it was the emperor's job to maintain this harmonious equilibrium. In the Hindu wheel of rebirth, the flow of time was also depicted as a circle.

There were many different ways of linking together the past, present and future. Each way of looking at time has its own internal logic. The internal logic of 'world history', as narrated in this book, is change. Back when the concept of history was born, these changes were called 'progress', so world history is really the story of progress. From this perspective, the new always gives the impression of improving on the old.

In the centuries after the fall of the Roman Empire, the Arabs took their knowledge and discoveries with them on their campaigns of conquest. That's how, during the reign of Caliph Harun al-Rashid, the centre of the progressive world moved to Baghdad with its modern paper mill (advanced technology by the standards of the day) and Grand Library of Baghdad, where books were written and translated.

Continuity

However, we should also look at history's continuities – the things that have stayed more or less the same. For instance, the golden age of Arab culture was based on the very same foundations as the wealth of the Roman Empire. Both took huge quantities of resources from Africa – in fact, throughout almost the whole of history and up to the present day, Africa has been treated like one gigantic larder for the world. Raw materials such as salt, gold, slaves, cedar, cola nuts, animal skins and ivory flowed constantly out of the continent to other parts of the world. During antiquity, it was mostly the Romans who took advantage of this bounty but now, after the Arab conquest, resources from Africa were transported to Damascus, Baghdad and Bukhara.

While this progress changed lives – giving birth to new cities, states and new technologies, and bringing new religions, such as Buddhism, Christianity and Islam – most Africans continued living as farmers and shepherds, either in settlements next to oases or travelling as nomads from place to place with their sheep and goats. They retained their traditional spiritual connections to their ancestors and viewed nature as infused with magic. To this day, many Africans still speak languages that are at least 5,000 years old. Most people lived in tribal communities, where work was divided equally between men and women, often headed by a chief referred to as the 'big man'.

Yet these disparate regions of the world were linked by a constant bond: an ever-expanding trade network. Even before antiquity, Berber tribes began raising horses in the Maghreb, north-western Africa, and harnessed them to war chariots. Their army became so strong, they easily defeated other clans and took slaves to sell, driving neighbouring tribes into the continent's interior. During the reign of Emperor Augustus, merchants started using camels to transport their goods through the Sahara, and the North African tribes' way of life gradually spread southwards through war and trade.

Unlike the Romans, who always bought their gold, salt and slaves from the countries around the Mediterranean, the Arab merchants' travels took them to the regions south of the Sahara. Here, vital hubs had been established for commerce and trade, such as the cities Djenné-Djenno and Gao on the banks of the River Niger, which was a busy conduit for ships and goods at the heart of the Mali Empire. Arab traders settled here and in other places, and mostly lived peacefully alongside the native population as a minority. Sometimes, they took control of an area, establishing an Arab principality, and the ancestral population eventually converted to Islam.

Of course, Africa changed too. In the eighth century, an Arab historian made the first reference to the 'gold country' Ghana, one of the first empires south-west of the Sahara to become wealthy from the gold trade. Later, the kingdom of Ghana, also known as the Soninke Empire of Wagadou, would be overtaken by its neighbour Mali, and that in turn would be surpassed by a third empire known as Songhai. Slightly farther east on Lake Chad, the Kanem Empire had emerged. The rulers of Kanem traded slaves they had purchased for horses from the north, using violence to consolidate their power over the area.

In eastern Africa, ancient trade routes crossed the Red Sea, from Ancient Egypt to the south via Kush, connecting the East African coast with the Jews in Palestine and the Arabs on the Arabian Peninsula. Christianity reached these areas very early in history, and the Christian communities of Egypt and Ethiopia are some of the oldest in the world.

Around 100 to 200 years after the death of Harun al-Rashid, the Abbasid Empire was once again in decline. Meanwhile, in Abyssinia (the country we now call Ethiopia) a female ruler ascended the throne. As we've already seen, the situation of women is one of history's great continuities – in almost every era, they were mostly excluded from public life. Nevertheless, in almost all the chronicles, at least one princess, queen or empress always manages to challenge the status quo.

In Abyssinia, it was a woman called Gudit. She is said to have ousted an incompetent king and taken over government herself. The information we have on Gudit comes from later sources, which refer to her by a variety of different names. She's likely to have been portrayed in a pretty negative light, so stories of how she laid waste to churches and monuments during her coup should be taken with a pinch of salt.

However, there's one thing we're relatively certain about: Gudit's rule lasted a good thirty years. She founded a new Christian dynasty, the Solomonic dynasty, and soon Abyssinia became Africa's largest empire. It was one of the longest-lasting empires in history, surviving almost to the present day.

THE ROMAN EMPIRE BECOMES TWO

Byzantium enters stormy waters

Vanity can be deadly. The Byzantine Emperor Leo IV the Khazar fell in love with a precious crown from the treasury at Hagia Sophia. He couldn't help himself and wore it at every available opportunity. As historians later reported, this crown would become his undoing. The gold and jewels shone magnificently, but the crown was heavy and the hard metal pressed into the emperor's forehead, causing wounds and abscesses; these wounds became infected and are suspected of causing the emperor's death. However, this unexpected outcome paved the way to a glorious future for his wife Irene. Since the couple's son was just 9 years old, in AD 780 she accepted the imperial sceptre – officially as her son's co-emperor.

When Irene ascended the throne, the Byzantine ship of state had once again found itself in stormy waters. But before she could do anything about it, she had to deal with her opponents, who contested her claim to the throne. As her son approached adulthood, he demanded the title of emperor, and many in the imperial court supported his claim.

However, Irene had already been on the throne for over a decade and wasn't going to give it up now. She clearly valued her power more than her son, because she gave the order for his eyes to be plucked out – for the Byzantine people, a blind emperor was much worse than a woman on the throne. In the end, Irene became more than just the guardian of the young emperor. Now, she was empress in her own right.

Irene had won the battle for the throne, but soon there were other matters to see to. When the Arabs arrived at the gates of

AD 797: Irene of Athens becomes Empress of the Roman Empire, Byzantium.

Constantinople, they instilled panic and terror in the guards. Muhammad's warriors had seized large swathes of the empire – Syria, Jerusalem and Egypt – and they seemed undefeatable. A volcano had recently erupted, projecting huge boulders into the air, which was taken as an omen. The Byzantines searched desperately for an explanation for their plight. Could it be that God was punishing them for abandoning the second commandment, which forbade religious imagery?

Many believed this explanation, and the emperor ordered the destruction of the icons that the Christians kept in their churches and homes. This led to a frenzy of iconoclasm as vigilantes burst into churches and houses to rip out the icons and destroy them, desperately hoping to regain God's protection. And, as chance would have it, shortly after this, the Byzantine army had a run of good fortune. This seemed to confirm the military leaders' belief that the worship of false idols had been to blame for their bad luck.

Many outside the army, however, resisted the move to destroy everyone's icons. For centuries, these artistic images of Christ and the saints had offered a window to God, acting as intermediaries in believers' dialogue with Heaven's higher powers. Some loved their icons as much as their nearest and dearest and refused to give them up. It was a bitterly fought struggle.

Irene stood to gain nothing from the rampant destruction either. She summoned the most important men in the Church to a council in an attempt to end the prohibition, but the military, emboldened by their brief spell of fortune on the battlefield, were afraid that God would punish them again. To stop the decree, they galloped to the council, stormed in and expelled the bishops. The commanders deposed Empress Irene, who was against them, and placed their ally on the throne.

Eventually, a new council was summoned, which reinstated the icons. The era of iconoclasm was over and the icons returned to their former places in churches and on household altars.

A second emperor

It was high time for these internal squabbles to be put to bed: Irene only just managed to fend off the enemies at Byzantium's gates. Through a generous bribe, she had convinced the caliph of the Islamic Empire, Harun al-Rashid (the son of al-Khayzuran), to hold back his troops from pressing further into Byzantine territory. However, trouble was threatening to flare up in the west too, and that had started even before Irene became empress.

Rome was the seat of a bishop who called himself the Pope, but he still served the emperor in Constantinople just like the other bishops of the empire. Rome had been teetering on a precipice ever since its conquest by the Germans; again and again, new people appeared at the city gates determined that it was their turn to conquer the ancient capital. Irene's predecessors had failed, on several occasions, to protect the Pope from these attacks. The Byzantine Empire was simply fighting its enemies on too many fronts; even an army with a weapon as fearsome as Greek fire was finding itself overstretched.

The Pope had to seek protection elsewhere. He was surrounded by enemies in Italy, so there was only one way out: he had to find allies further afield. In northern Italy lay the Alps, a natural border that couldn't be crossed without serious preparations. Nevertheless, in his desperation, the Pope crossed the mountains to meet Pippin III, King of the Franks (also known as Pepin the Short). His father Charles Martel was the one who had stopped the Arabs from invading France from Spain, so the Franks had proven themselves as strong allies.

The Pope and King Pippin formed an alliance; for the emperor in Constantinople, this was dangerous competition. The emperor sent a delegation of envoys to the Frankish court, and attempted to influence Pippin with the gift of a valuable organ. This seemed to work for the time being.

AD 756: The Franks and the Pope join forces against the rulers of Constantinople.

But it wasn't long before the Pope found himself in dire straits again. Rather than turning to the emperor in Byzantium, he made a second crossing of the Alps to seek the protection of the Franks. By now, Pippin's son Charles, who would later become known as Charlemagne, was on the throne. Charles had led many successful military campaigns and his kingdom now extended in all directions.

AD 800: On
25 December
the Pope
crowns
Charlemagne
emperor of the
Roman Empire,
even though
Empress Irene
is still on the
throne in
Constantinople.

For the first time since the fall of Rome, a new Western empire had been born; it didn't have a name yet, but its size, which included France and most of Germany, was formidable.

Charles hurried to Italy to defend the Pope from his enemies. Then the pair did something unheard of. On Christmas Day AD 800, during the reign of Empress Irene, the Pope crowned the Frankish Charlemagne Emperor of the Roman Empire. The throne of Constantinople might as well have been empty! With this second alliance, the Pope had shifted his allegiance and promoted Charlemagne's Frankish Empire to the status of a rival Roman Empire. All of a sudden, there were two empires claiming the same title – and two emperors.

This couldn't be, of course, so the Pope had to come up with a plausible explanation for his *coup d'état*. His explanation was that he disapproved of a woman – Empress Irene – holding the office of Roman emperor. Having a woman on the throne, he argued, was as good as having no emperor at all.

Naturally, people expected resistance from Constantinople. The whole situation was just too crazy for words. The Arab conquests had changed the Mediterranean, once the heart of the Roman Empire, into a border between Christian Europe and the Arab Muslim south. Shouldn't this have brought the Christians closer together? Didn't the Pope and his newly crowned Frankish emperor realise they were splitting the Christian empire in two?

A marriage is called off

The emperor's advisers did all they could to stop the Roman Empire from splitting. To limit the damage, Charlemagne and the Pope sent a joint delegation of envoys to Irene's court; they aimed to negotiate a marriage between Charlemagne and Irene, which, it was hoped, would mend the rift.

However, Charlemagne had also sent ambassadors to Baghdad to form an alliance with Harun al-Rashid. Irene felt cornered, but a marriage to Charlemagne could offer a way out, so she wasn't entirely opposed to the idea – some even say it was she who proposed the marriage to Charlemagne. But her advisers at the Byzantine court flew into a panic; they knew what the match would mean for Constantinople. After Irene's death, the new emperor would be crowned in Charlemagne's seat in Aachen and Constantinople would cease to be the centre of the empire. If the Franks took over, the city on the Bosporus would be pushed to the empire's edge. This had to be stopped, and there was only one way to do it: Byzantium needed a man at the helm, and quickly.

Empress Irene's finance minister rallied together a small group of soldiers and planned a palace coup to replace her on the throne. Early one morning, he and his men sneaked into the empress's apartments and took her prisoner. A few hours later, the finance minister crowned himself emperor. Irene was banished to an island and cut off from the outside world for the rest of her life.

AD 814: Charlemagne's Frankish Empire collapses again after his death.

The Frankish Empire, though, which had seen itself as the continuation of the ancient Roman Empire, collapsed again after Charlemagne's death. His sons and grandsons divided the land into a western and eastern region. These regions would later become France and Germany but, until then, Europe would be made up of lots of tiny individual kingdoms that posed no threat to Byzantium.

The end of Byzantine iconoclasm

After Irene's banishment, the fierce debate about icons reignited. Yet again, an emperor appealed to God for clemency and victory in battle by banning icons. Yet again, the citizens of Constantinople split into two camps. And yet again, the feud raged from one emperor to the next.

One of these emperors, Theophilos, waged a particularly grisly campaign of persecution against the iconophiles (those determined to keep their icons). While searching for a wife at a bride-show, a woman called Kassia caught his eye, and he attempted to chat her up with a line inspired by the story of Adam and Eve: 'Through a woman came forth the baser things.' Kassia was as clever as she was beautiful and, thinking of the Virgin Mary, she retorted: 'And through a woman came forth the better things.' The emperor, shocked that somebody had actually spoken back to him, decided to marry another, while Kassia went on to found a convent, where she wrote poetry and composed hymns. It was a tragic situation, as the pair were attracted to one another, but their happiness had been thwarted by Kassia's wit and Theophilos's pride. Theophilos is said to have tried to visit her once, but Kassia hid from him: she didn't want to be reminded of what her answer had cost her. But perhaps she could draw some comfort from the seclusion of the convent, which allowed her to dedicate herself fully to her poetry.

Instead of Kassia, Theophilos married Theodora, and when the emperor died, she took over the business of state. Theodora followed Irene's example and convened a council aimed at finally bringing an end to the destruction of icons. And yet again, the fire of iconoclasm was lit by a superstitious military and stamped out by a woman, who returned the icons to their rightful place.

AD 843: Empress Theodora brings an end to the era of Byzantine iconoclasm.

A NEW STATE IN EASTERN EUROPE

Princess Olga reforms Rus

In the Middle Ages, the map of the world was constantly changing. No sooner had the Arabs spanned the vast expanse between
Constantinople and China, than other new peoples started appearing
– often, nobody really knew where they had come from. The Turks
had suddenly regained their strength and were threatening the borders of China while, north of the Black Sea, a new state had formed
called Kievan Rus. Centuries later, this small principality would
become Russia.

Now Constantinople faced yet another enemy sending its fleet
across the Black Sea. However, the Russians' wooden ships were no
match for Byzantium's Greek fire. So Olga, the Princess of Kievan
Rus, set off on a peace mission to Constantinople, where she was
received by the empress in the women's quarters of the Imperial
Palace. Because she was visiting as a ruler and not as a wife accompanying her husband, the court somehow needed to show that she
was representing Kievan Rus as its head of state, so Olga was given an
official belt to wear. A sumptuous banquet was also held, where the
usual restrictions on men and women eating together were lifted and
Olga was seated beside the emperor.

Perhaps Byzantium had heard the rumours about Olga's past.
When the princess married her husband Igor, Kievan Rus wasn't yet
a real state. It began, as was so often the case, when a ruling clan laid
claim to a certain area and forced the resident tribes to pay tribute. If
they refused, there would be war. Igor was killed by the Drevlians, as
they wouldn't submit to his demands for furs, wax, honey and even
boats, all of which he needed to maintain his trade with Byzantium.

Just because the Russians attacked Constantinople every now and again didn't mean they intended to stop trading.

Igor's son Svyatoslav still wasn't old enough to rule, so as regent Olga of Kiev had to keep hold of the lands conquered by her husband for her son. She showed her opponents no mercy. In Russia, people later told fantastical and bloody tales about how she lured the Drevlians into an ambush and wrought her revenge. Her power assured, she carried through the first political reform in Russia's history, ending this system of paying tributes. With this she began to mould Kievan Rus into a fully fledged state.

The baptism of Kievan Rus

When the princess looked to her neighbours, she realised that great empires were held together by one unifying religion, so she asked the Byzantine emperor to help baptise her people by sending priests. But she took pains to ensure she had links with other places besides Byzantium – she had heard that the Pope and his Frankish allies were competing with Byzantium for power. So she also sent her ambassadors to speak with Otto the Great, the ruler of the crumbling Frankish Empire, asking him to nominate a bishop to help her spread Christianity throughout Rus.

AD 957: Olga of Kiev asks Constantinople and the Franks for Christian bishops.

Soon the Crown passed to her son Svyatoslav. To Olga's sorrow, he renounced Christianity and focused instead on waging new wars on all fronts. The Frankish bishop was expelled, and on the return journey some of his men were killed. When Olga's son died, her grandson Vladimir took up her plan again: the people of Kievan Rus would become Christians.

Vladimir's baptism was also important for tactical reasons. He wanted to enter an alliance with Byzantium as equals. Vladimir was a strong ruler and Byzantium faced a constant threat from its enemies, so he succeeded in doing what no other European king had ever succeeded in doing before. As the price for his army's support, he managed to get the emperor to promise him a real-life imperial princess, born in purple. In tears, the emperor's daughter Anna departed for Kiev to marry Vladimir. Her task was to act as an adviser to her husband and convert the state of Kievan Rus to Christianity.

Later, a legend was told about the baptism of Rus. Vladimir sent his ambassadors to a number of different countries to find out more about their religions. Back in Kiev, his men advised him against converting to Islam as it forbade the drinking of alcohol. The informants didn't have anything good to say about the church services they witnessed in the Frankish Empire either. Upon returning from Constantinople, however, his messengers said: 'We didn't know whether we were in heaven or on earth.' And with that, Vladimir decided to have himself and his subjects baptised. The splendour of Constantinople had won him over.

It's an appealing story because it really does give the impression of a newly formed state taking their pick of the religions, as each courted the Russians with their promises of salvation. What must have surprised the Russians, though, is how the Pope in Rome and the Church in Constantinople seemed to be in competition. Weren't they both representatives of Christianity, after all? The rift between the Christians in the west and east was clearly growing deeper, and the Church couldn't agree on who was in charge. Increasingly, the Pope was making decisions without consulting Byzantium, so the rulers of each city started to drift apart, as well as their Churches.

AD 988: Olga's grandson Vladimir is baptised and marries the Byzantine Princess Anna.

THE ROMAN EMPIRE SPLITS ... AGAIN

The birth of the Holy Roman Empire

After the collapse of the Frankish Empire, Europe once more fractured into many small independent territories. The continent was divided up like the squares of a chessboard. And like the pieces in this Arab game, the powerful manoeuvred themselves across the continent, fighting one another and seizing their opponents' land. This continued until one of the princes was able to successfully renew his alliance with the Pope, reunifying the fractured kingdom.

Otto the Great had a strong army and entered a mutually beneficial marriage with a widowed princess named Adelaide. The couple finally travelled to Rome to be crowned by the Pope, just like their predecessor Charlemagne. Here Adelaide made sure she was named co-regent at a lavish ceremony. This had never happened before; in the past, the Pope had only ever crowned the emperor. From this moment on, however, the coronation would be of the emperor and empress together.

AD 962: The Pope crowns Adelaide and Otto empress and emperor of the newly independent Western Roman Empire, later known as the Holy Roman Empire.

This was the second time that the Western Roman Empire was founded as a separate state, even though officially the emperor in Byzantium was still considered the ruler of the whole empire – it amounted to a declaration of war. This time, though, the Pope couldn't claim that the throne of Constantinople was empty, so yet again, the Western Empire had to find a way of appeasing the Byzantines. They sent a negotiator to the court of Byzantium and requested a princess to marry Otto and Adelaide's son Otto II. Their hope was that the Eastern emperor wouldn't want to attack a country that was ruled by his own daughter.

The negotiations were a success. Princess Theophanu travelled from Byzantium to the Western Empire, inspiring awe with her gold-woven silk clothes and the treasures she brought with her, which included silver crockery and crystal glasses, combs, sweet-smelling perfumes and chess sets carved from semi-precious stones.

However, the pomp and splendour of Byzantium wasn't the only thing that attracted people's attention. Princess Theophanu, it turned out, wasn't the promised bride – instead of his purple-born daughter, the emperor had sent his general's niece! In the meantime, this general had murdered the monarch and taken his place at the head of the empire. Outraged, many of Otto's courtiers demanded that the false bride be sent back to Byzantium right away. But Adelaide and Otto didn't want to jeopardise their peace treaty with Byzantium. Their kingdom and was on the line. The wedding went ahead as planned and was celebrated in suitably grand style.

By marrying his son to Theophanu, Otto I – unlike his predecessor Charlemagne – had brought long-lasting stability to his large empire. He also bound the nobles in allegiance to him. But even more crucial to consolidating his power was his alliance with the Pope and the Church. All over the kingdom, he gave the bishops and monasteries land, binding them even more closely to the state. When Otto the Great died, the Western Roman Empire – later known as the Holy Roman Empire – was recognised as a distinct empire far and wide.

THE CALIPHATE OF CAIRO

A very secret secret

The great Arab Empire, ruled by the caliph in Baghdad, was in disarray. Many had been reluctant to submit to the powerful Umayyad and Abbasid clans in the first place. And since the Arabs had conquered half the known world in the name of Islam, the provincial princes had become stronger and were starting to break away. All Baghdad could do was look on helplessly.

The caliph was much more than a ruler and the leader of all Muslims. He was also Muhammad's successor, and there could only ever be one – anyone who turned against the caliph had to justify how their actions tallied with their Islamic beliefs. But the caliph did have opponents and their explanation was linked to Ali, the caliph who was once attacked by Muhammad's wife Aisha and eventually murdered by the Umayyads.

Ali had married Muhammad's daughter Fatima, which meant Ali's sons were the Prophet's grandchildren. The enemies of the Abbasid caliph in Baghdad declared Ali to have been the true caliph, so the only ones who could lay claim to this great office were his descendants, the children and grandchildren of Ali and Fatima. In short, they accused the caliph in Baghdad of being a false caliph.

However, doctrine was decided by whoever had the strongest weapons. The followers of the Abbasid caliph became known as Sunnis, and those who believed Ali had been the rightful caliph were called Shi'ites. In the Sunni army, declaring yourself a follower of Ali and Fatima could get you killed. Because of this, the Shi'ites kept themselves to themselves and were very secretive about their doctrine. A Shi'ite imam wrote: 'Our cause is a secret within a secret, a secret that only another secret can explain; it's a secret about a secret that is veiled by a secret.' So the caliph's enemies kept their belief that the true caliph had to be a descendant of Muhammad's daughter Fatima a closely guarded secret, and would only declare it openly when they could be sure that their own weapons were a match for the army in Baghdad.

At last, in the tenth century, their moment came. The Shia founded a new state in Egypt (the Fatimid dynasty) and installed their own caliphs. Even though it was forbidden, there were now two caliphs.

AD 969: The Shi'ites in Cairo declare their own caliph. Now there are two: one Sunni and one Shi'ite.

The caliph's mysterious disappearance

The Shi'ite imams had long criticised the caliph in Baghdad for his extravagance. In their opinion, such wealth was out of keeping with the simple life advocated by the Prophet. But then they became rulers in their own right and so were conscious of their power. They draped themselves in silver- and gold-woven robes, built roads and canals, and constructed magnificent palaces so that soon their caliphate in Cairo outshone Baghdad.

Then something happened that should have been impossible. Sitt al-Mulk (whose name means 'Lady of the Empire') took over the government and, with that, the role of Fatimid caliph. This event is usually played down in the history books, of course. According to many historians, Sitt al-Mulk held office for a very short time as regent on behalf of a child – but, in fact, she was the legitimate and sole leader of the Shi'ites in her own right.

This remarkable event was preceded by even more extraordinary events. Sitt al-Mulk's father had been an extremely capable caliph but, when he died unexpectedly after an accident in a bathhouse, his son and successor, Sitt al-Mulk's brother al-Hakim, was only 11 years old. The boy didn't have a clue what was going on, and before he knew it, he was being introduced to the crowds of Cairo as the new caliph. Under his rule, however, the mood of the city soon darkened.

The new caliph was clearly out of his depth. Lonely and unhappy, he walked through the city's streets at night. To start off, he demanded that the citizens of Cairo do the same as him and turn night into day; they were to prove their devotion to him by keeping their shops and businesses open. Then he withdrew and turned his attention to his own petty grievances, at one point deciding to kill all the dogs in the city, possibly because he couldn't bear their barking. Then the focus of his strange demands settled on women. He forbade them from laughing, crying or walking in the street and made them wear the veil. He closed their bathhouses and even forbade shoemakers from making them shoes; if women dared go outside, they were killed. For seven years, women became prisoners in their homes; Cairo's streets were drained of life.

According to rumours, al-Hakim believed he was God. This suited some scholars, as the second coming of God had long been prophesied. For most people, however, the caliph had clearly lost his mind.

One day, Cairo was suddenly liberated: al-Hakim vanished from the face of the Earth and nobody knew what had happened to him. Had he been murdered? Perhaps he had been killed in an accident? And if there had been a plot against him, had his sister Sitt al-Mulk been involved? His body was never found, and so the mystery of his disappearance was never solved.

Nobody could have predicted that a caliph would just vanish like that. Islamic law offered no guidance on what should be done. So Sitt al-Mulk took over as leader, as it was preferable to having no leader at all. As the daughter of a well-respected caliph and a Christian slave, she had been raised a tolerant and open-minded young woman, so she probably wanted to reinstate the old order as a matter of urgency – and she succeeded. Cairo recovered from its ordeal with the mad caliph al-Hakim and flourished once more.

1021: After the mysterious disappearance of her brother, Sitt al-Mulk takes over as de facto caliph.

Asma and Arwa

The power of the caliphs in Cairo relied on a network of allies. Many Arab provinces were eager for independence from Baghdad and, in return for Cairo's support, they agreed to recognise the Shia caliph as their religious leader. With their approval, one of these allies conquered Yemen and even Mecca, the Muslim holy city.

The new Yemeni king's first act in office was to publicly announce that he would share power with his wife. Queen Asma attended talks without a veil and travelled everywhere with her husband. Thirty years later, when he set off on a great pilgrimage to Mecca, she went with him in a caravan comprising 1,000 members of their court.

While in the desert, the king was assassinated when an enemy snuck into their camp and stabbed him as he stood talking to his brother. Although his attackers were outnumbered, they took the caravan hostage and kidnapped Queen Asma. The assassin cut off the king's head and placed it on a stake in front of her prison window so she could see it.

It took Asma a long time to get news to her family that she was alive. Eventually, though, the information reached her son al-Mukarram, who then set off with a troop of fighters to free his mother. When he finally found her, he was so overcome with joy and sorrow that he went into shock and couldn't move; he was to remain paralysed down one side for the rest of his life.

Because of her son's paralysis, Asma was given the throne. This was unusual, especially as a male cousin from the ruling house put himself forward as the new king. But nevertheless, Asma became queen, and when she died, power passed to her daughter-in-law Arwa, who Asma's murdered husband had once described as 'the only one who can secure the survival of our dynasty, if something happens to us'. So, things were simply turned upside down in the Yemeni dynasty. Power passed down from woman to woman, and this didn't seem to offend anyone.

Queen Arwa decided to avenge her father-in-law's death. She knew that the assassin was still alive, so she claimed an eye for an eye: she had him murdered, took his wife prisoner and stuck his head on a stake in front of her prison window.

Arwa lived up to her father-in-law's expectations and proved to be an exceptional ruler. She waged wars, constructed huge build-ings and championed education and culture. From Yemen, Shi'ite scholars travelled across the sea to India, where they helped spread Islam to the north.

All over the Muslim world, it was customary for the imams to call out the name of the caliph, followed by the name of the monarch, during Friday prayers. This honour was never extended to a woman, even though there were several female sovereigns who ruled alone for a considerable length of time. Sitt al-Mulk didn't insist on being named during Friday prayers, perhaps because she knew very well how many feathers her appointment had ruffled among the men. But Asma and Arwa were exceptions. Both were hailed as 'al-Hurra', meaning they were free and needed obey no one but themselves. Their reign was reaffirmed every week during the Friday prayer.

Although the men of Yemen didn't seem to mind having female rulers, the caliph in Cairo took it as a great insult. When Arwa's husband died, the caliph turned against her and, after some parrying back and forth, it finally came to a confrontation. The caliph sent an ally to Arwa's court to remove her from the throne, confident that he would find support against a ruler who by now was old and unpopular. But both the military and the people stood united behind their queen and the caliph's army was forced to give up.

Arwa remained queen for another twenty years. By the time she died, she had reigned for almost fifty – the long reign that believers had wished for every Friday with their prayer for her: 'May Allah prolong the days of al-Hurra the perfect, the sovereign who carefully manages the affairs of the faithful.'

Upon Arwa's death, the balance of power between the Sunnis and Shi'ites shifted once more. The Fatimids – the Shi'ite caliphate in Cairo – couldn't hold their ground much longer; the Sunnis regained the upper hand and drove the Shi'ites out of North Africa. Later, they found a new home in Persia, and the Muslims of Iran remain Shi'ite to this day.

The stories of Sitt al-Mulk, Asma and Arwa prove that Muslim women could at times gain access to education and power; during those times, they could achieve almost anything. These three queens were only the most famous, but there were many more influential women in the medieval era. A British researcher counted the female Muslim scholars up to the twelfth century and discovered that there were approximately 8,500. One of them, Fatima al-Fihri, founded one of the oldest universities in the world, the University of Al Quaraouiyine, in ninth-century Morocco.

AD 859: Fatima al-Fihri founds a Quranic school in Morocco; today this institution is one of the oldest universities in the world.

THE INVENTION OF THE NOVEL

At the court of Heian-kyō

Japan, as we've already seen, learnt a lot from China. For centuries, the island state's rulers sent ambassadors to its neighbours to learn about the latest innovations in city planning, architecture, art and literature. The Japanese even adopted Buddhism after it had made the journey from India to China.

Then, under the Tang dynasty, when China was at its most powerful, Japan began to step away from the influence of its huge role model. The Japanese emperor and his court at that time were based in the city of Heian-kyō, which means 'city of peace and tranquillity'. The Heian period, named after the city, lasted for around 400 years; by the end of the era, Japan had its own script and literature. This was when *The Tale of Genji* was written – Japan's first novel and perhaps the first in the world. In its English translation, the book is almost 2,000 pages long!

The world's first novel was written by a woman. Her name was Murasaki Shikibu and we know she was a noblewoman at the imperial court in Heian-kyō. As well as writing stories, she also kept a diary; within its pages, she described how she watched her brother at his Chinese lessons. He was expected to become an official or a judge, and because Japan didn't have its own script before the Heian era, all future civil servants had to learn Chinese and its complex system of characters. This education wasn't intended for girls, but Murasaki Shikibu's brother was a much slower learner than his sister and she was able to overtake him. In her diary, she notes, 'My father sighed and said to me: "If only you were a boy – how proud and happy I would be!"'

But it was frowned upon for a woman to know Chinese; it was better for them not to be educated at all. The author of *The Tale of Genji* knew this too and advised her female readers: 'The best way is ... to pick up a little here and a little there ... Let her be content with this and not insist upon cramming her letters with Chinese characters, which aren't at all in keeping with her feminine style.'

The ladies of the imperial court occupied themselves with other things. They passed the time reciting elaborate poems, singing songs, painting and storytelling. But how could they write down these stories? Since they weren't allowed to learn Chinese, they invented a new alphabet based on syllables, which is still used in Japan to this day. In an ironic twist of fate, the decision to exclude women from education led to the development of a Japanese script invented by women.

FROM CASTLES TO TOWNS

The Great Countess of Canossa

In northern Italy, perched up high on a well-fortified rocky hill, was Canossa Castle. From here, Matilda of Tuscany – known as the 'Great Countess' because of her power and the number of estates she owned – stood on the turrets of her castle and saw all her kingdom laid out before her like a miniature world. To the south were the hills and valleys of Italy and, to the north, the Alps. Beyond them was the realm of Germany.

Adelaide and Otto had renewed the alliance between the Frankish monarchy in Germany and the Pope in Italy, forming the Holy Roman Empire. The empire consisted of two kingdoms divided by the Alps and was also ruled by two powerful lords, the king and the Pope.

The king was lord of the land but, instead of keeping it all for himself, he divided it between several princes. This was practical, as the princes then took responsibility for looking after the land – the fiefdoms – that had been granted to them. To protect their fiefdoms, the princes built castles on high rocks. Constructed with thick walls, a keep and a dungeon, with a bridge across a moat as the only entrance, these castles were practically impenetrable. The princes' fields were tended by peasant farmers who were usually serfs, not free men who could come and go as they pleased. The feudal lord might not have bought these peasants as slaves, but their lives were still at his mercy. The peasants had to feed themselves from whatever they could grow and give a tenth of their harvest to the prince – this is how he amassed his wealth.

With serfs to tend their land, the princes and feudal lords could while away their days hunting and jousting, or going off to war. Knights, dukes and barons made up the nobility: the upper ranks of the social order that people in the Middle Ages believed was ordained by God. The farmers worked the fields, the priests prayed, ensuring everyone's souls could be saved, and the nobles – courageous knights in heavy armour – protected them.

The prince or nobleman treated the land loaned to him by the king as his own property and, upon his death, his son inherited it. In return, the prince pledged the king his loyalty and support in war. For the king, though, this line of inheritance wasn't very practical. After all, if the fiefdom passed down from father to son over many generations, how could it still be considered a 'loan'? For this reason, Otto the Great preferred to give his land to bishops and monasteries. Because the clergy didn't marry, they couldn't pass down their property to their children, so the king got his land back when the bishop died.

However, this led to an unusual situation. If the king loaned his land to the Church, this meant that the bishops were serving two different masters: the king as the owner of the land and the Pope as the head of the Church.

Constantinople watched in surprise as the Pope and his bishops gradually became as wealthy and powerful as the kings and princes. Back in Constantinople, monasteries were still places of abstinence and tranquillity; seeking the refuge of the cloister meant turning your back on earthly life and devoting oneself to prayer. It must have seemed very strange to the Byzantines that some bishops in the West would so openly crave power and influence. Some of these bishops were even riding through the land and fighting like knights.

The differences between Constantinople and Rome became more and more obvious. They squabbled over the wording of religious creeds and also over whether priests could marry. Over time, these disputes became increasingly fraught. Finally, the Pope and the patriarch of Constantinople even went as far as excommunicating each other from the Church. Little did they know how far-reaching the consequences would be: this created an irreparable split, or schism, in the Church. Christendom was now divided into the Roman Catholic Church in the West and the Greek Orthodox Church in the East.

The Pope's increasing power also threatened his alliance with the king. Pope Gregory VII believed that, as lord of all Christians, it was

1054: The Roman Catholic Church and the Greek Orthodox Church go their separate ways in the East–West Schism.

his right to elect the empire's bishops. This ignited a bitter conflict: previously, Church officials had been elected by the king, as it was *his* land that they lived and worked on. The Pope was now challenging the status quo. This was the beginning of the 'Investiture Controversy', a disagreement that rumbled on for decades, and at its peak, ended up at the court of Castle Canossa, directly at the feet of Matilda of Tuscany.

Investiture means the right to appoint a bishop or Church official, and German King Henry IV (who later became Holy Roman Emperor) refused to grant the Pope this right. So, Gregory VII did something drastic: he excommunicated all the bishops nominated by Henry IV and then even the king himself, declaring that, from now on, no pious Christian should serve Henry IV and his lords, but instead should answer directly to the Pope himself. This was the first time in history a pope had made such a power grab.

1076: The Investiture Controversy erupts around one key issue: who has more power, the Pope or the king?

Henry now found himself in a dangerous predicament. Many of the princes had chosen to support the Pope and turned their backs on the king. He had to do something. Soon, the Pope was on his way to Germany to meet his new allies, so Henry hurried over the Alps towards Italy to meet him on the way.

When the Pope heard about Henry's plan, he grew anxious. He knew Henry could attack him, remove him from office and appoint a new pope. So, he sought refuge with his confidant Matilda at Castle Canossa in Tuscany, northern Italy.

But Henry didn't attack. Instead, he entered the castle's courtyard dressed as a penitent and fell to his knees to beg Gregory for forgiveness – or, at least, that's what we're told. Today, the phrase 'to go to Canossa' is still used in some countries as a metaphor for making a grovelling apology to someone, which gives you an idea of just how significant this entire episode was. It was later said that Henry was made to wait outside in the courtyard for three days – it was winter, so the king must have been absolutely freezing. Matilda's tears were the only thing that made Gregory relent.

Henry's journey to Canossa may not have happened quite like this; the story may have been embellished for political purposes. But the image conjured up by this legend delivered a clear message: the king had fallen to his knees before the Pope. The most powerful man in the land had bowed before the power of the Church. The row calmed down after this, but it wasn't over yet. The supreme leader of Christianity still hadn't been decided once and for all. Was it the Pope or the king? (The emperor in Byzantium was out of the picture by now, of course.)

Henry, Gregory and Matilda didn't live to see the end of the feud. Their successors agreed a compromise and the Pope received the right of investiture. As a result, the Pope significantly increased his power at the expense of the kings, who found theirs weakened by the conflict.

Perhaps nobody realised back then what the consequences of the power struggles of the Middle Ages would be. In England, around 100 years after Matilda's death, the nobility tried to wrest away power from the king, which resulted in King John of England (also known as John Lackland) signing Magna Carta. Magna Carta decreed that no one could be 'seized, imprisoned or stripped of his rights or possessions' or otherwise mistreated without a court judgement – this was a major change to the law of the land. It essentially meant that there were limits to the power of the king (and all other rulers) over their subjects; he couldn't just do whatever he wanted. He had to respect the protection of individuals and their property under the law.

The Investiture Controversy, Magna Carta and many similar events over the centuries gave rise to two ideas that would gain ground in Europe: that individuals – no matter how insignificant they might seem – had inalienable rights, and that power should be distributed among as many people as possible. Whether it was the Church, the nobility, merchants, courts or universities, the more independent these institutions were, the less there was a concentration of power in the hands of very few at the top.

The structure of the medieval town

If Matilda had been able to see beyond Castle Canossa and over the Alps into Germany, all she would have seen was a sea of green: vast expanses of forests, dotted here and there with a castle, a monastery or a scattering of villages. Some settlements had even survived since the time of the Romans and had grown into towns.

This was now changing. Unlike a castle, designed as it was to protect its occupants from the outside world, towns made trade easier and helped people to get very rich. Feudal lords increased a town's wealth by taxing its citizens and, realising this, they encouraged people to found new towns. To make this idea even more attractive, serfs were promised freedom and other benefits known as privileges. 'Town air makes you free,' the lords proclaimed.

Town founders divided their land into plots and built streets and houses on them. In the centre they built a church with a big marketplace that was surrounded by roads; the town itself was encircled by a wall that separated the town's citizens from outsiders, who could only enter through a heavily guarded gate as visitors or travelling merchants. Radiating from the marketplace were narrow lanes where the different professions plied their trades. These were mostly crafts, so the streets often had names such as Weaver Street, Cobbler Street and Baker Street, and most people couldn't read, so pictures were used to tell them where they could buy bread or weaving frames.

If a feudal lord – who might have been a woman, like Matilda of Tuscany – granted a charter for a market town to be founded, its inhabitants could set their own rules. They elected a mayor and a council and built a town hall in the central marketplace for holding meetings and voting on key issues. Soon, the hard work and skills of some of the town's citizens made them very rich and they were appointed to the most senior positions in the town; they later became known as 'patricians'. The patricians had very little in common with the majority of people, who got by on a modest income. The towns were populated by merchants and grocers, lords and servants, married women who looked after the home, and simple maidservants who worked for these women. And then there were the beggars, outcasts, the poor and the sick, who relied on charity and alms. Women could run their own businesses but weren't allowed to participate in public affairs. Public offices, the courts, the treasury, the town council, the mayor's office and schools all remained the sole preserve of men.

Life in the medieval town was governed by strict rules, and there were usually separate regulations for Jews. Since the Romans' destruction of their temple in Jerusalem, the Jews had scattered throughout the world and kept the religion of their ancestors going. They were assigned their own quarter, which often included a lane called Jewish Street.

In medieval towns, antagonism towards the Jews grew. This hostility was different to the centuries-old resentment harboured by many Christians against the people of Israel. This time, it was fuelled by lies, rumours and misunderstandings, and became a hostile feeling permanently lodged in people's minds. The Jews started being accused of all kinds of awful things; they were described as avaricious and miserly, cunning and deceitful, and people that Christians needed to protect themselves from. One of the worst rumours of all was that Jews kidnapped Christian children and used their blood in their religious ceremonies. This was called blood libel and, although there was no evidence of it ever taking place, this irrational fear persisted among Christians for centuries.

Local rulers knew about the population's resentment and responded to it with measures restricting Jews' rights. For example, Jews were forbidden from practising most professions, apart from those involving money, and sometimes they were even forced to wear special clothing so people could identify them more easily. Because the law forbade them from doing anything else, many Jews became experts in finance, which only reinforced their image as avaricious misers. Knights and merchants were lent money, and when they got into debt, they became envious, angry and resentful towards the people who had lent them the money in the first place. This medieval resentment evolved into anti-Semitism: the hatred of Jews fuelled by vicious rumours and lies that would bring endless suffering throughout history.

Héloïse and Abélard: forbidden love and the beginning of scholasticism

Even in the Middle Ages, there were small towns and there were large towns and cities. Some became huge, dazzling metropolises that attracted people from all over the world, including travellers, traders, artists, scholars and many with no goal other than seeking their fortune abroad. Paris, an old settlement dating back to Roman times, had become one of these magnets.

One of the main attractions of Paris was its cathedral school. Charlemagne had decreed that every bishop should set up a school alongside his church, transforming the churches into centres of learning; these cathedral schools not only educated priests and monks, but also the next generation of lawyers, treasurers, officials and doctors. In the Middle Ages, these cathedral schools became universities, and initially, it was difficult to tell them apart. Like the cathedral schools, the universities also revolved around communities of unmarried priests or bishops and their students. They were, to all intents and purposes, religious brotherhoods.

The fame of the Paris cathedral school spread far and wide thanks to the reputation of its teachers. Its students thronged the streets of a district known as the Latin Quarter, as Latin was the only language spoken and written in the universities. The benefit of this arrangement was that students from Poland, Spain or Saxony could come to the university and learn the same things, as they all had Latin in common. The students' basic tuition focused on the seven liberal arts or *Septem Artes Liberales*: Latin, logic, rhetoric, grammar, astronomy, philosophy and mathematics. Music fell under mathematics, as, after all, it involved counting notes and measuring the spaces between them.

One student at the Paris cathedral school made a name for himself by arguing so effectively that he could tie his teachers into knots and make them contradict themselves. Eventually, this student was allowed to give his own lectures. His name was Abélard, and he maintained that questions of belief should also be subjected to logic and reason. Many thought the old Church Fathers had already said everything there was to say on this matter, but Abélard thought otherwise – after all, he argued, it was our ability to think logically that enabled us to experience God's essence. Abélard promoted Aristotelian logic and argued that every thought should be able to stand up to logical scrutiny, which led to a new method of critical thinking that became known as 'scholasticism'. This approach was founded on the idea that thinking only brought about knowledge if it followed the rules of logic. In other words, that logic was the foundation of all knowledge and of science.

For women, basing medieval science on the writings of Aristotle wasn't particularly helpful. Like the Ancient Greeks, who believed women were defective versions of men, Thomas Aquinas – scholasticism's most important thinker after Abélard – maintained that 'the defective woman is God's purpose; her sole purpose is procreation'.

Around 1120:
The philosopher
Abélard sparks
controversy,
first by saying
that logical
thought should
be extended to
matters of faith,
and second by
starting an illicit
affair with his
student Héloïse.

But Abélard, who had reshaped the way people thought, now also thoroughly disrupted the decorum of medieval society with, of all things, a love affair. Soon, passionate love songs were making the rounds among the students, with lyrics that weren't at all appropriate for the high-minded environment of the university! These baudy songs sang the praises of a young woman named Héloïse – and were written by none other than her lover, Abélard. This romance between a priest who had taken the vow of chastity and a 20-year-old girl was a scandal.

Héloïse was raised by her uncle Fulbert, who worked at Notre-Dame Cathedral, the home of the school made so famous by Abélard. He wanted to give his niece the best possible education, but as Héloïse was a woman, she was forbidden from entering the lecture halls. Instead he invited the celebrated Abélard to his home to be her private tutor. 'Need I say more?' Abélard wrote. 'We were united, first under one roof, then in our hearts; with our books open before us, more words of love than of reading passed between us, and more kissing than ideas.'

Rumours soon spread among the students, and the couple's love could no longer remain a secret. Héloïse and Abélard became the most famous and most envied couple in all of Paris. Word finally reached Fulbert, and he was not amused. He hired some men to sneak into Abélard's bedroom at night and cut off his penis – the last thing he was expecting! After this painful shock, Abélard retreated into isolation as a monk.

Héloïse would spend the rest of her life in a convent. Upper-class women who didn't need to earn a living as farmers or servants had only two options: marriage or the convent. Héloïse, who suffered greatly from the loss of her lover, soon rose up the ranks to abbess, but her career brought her little comfort. She continued to send Abélard gushing love letters, even though he several times asked her to stop.

Abélard returned to his studies, but this created even more anguish. Bernard of Clairvaux, an influential abbot and Abélard's greatest rival, accused him of spreading false teachings about God and brought him before the ecclesiastical court. False teaching, or what people *took* for false teaching, was called heresy, and anyone accused of it could easily be sentenced to death. Abélard was lucky to escape with his life, but his writings were burnt and he was sentenced to perpetual silence.

Hildegard of Bingen

While Héloïse was mourning for her lost love, the fame of Hildegard of Bingen, a nun from Germany, was spreading. In the spirit of Aristotle, the official Christian doctrine said that women couldn't have theological revelations; their minds just weren't sophisticated enough. Hildegard, of course, was aware of this, so to make herself heard, she presented herself as a humble innocent. Her revelations, she said, were visions from God. Sometimes, she saw a blinding light and God then dictated word for word what she was to write down. The word of God couldn't be ignored, even by the most learned of men, so there was nothing else for it: they had to take Hildegard's writings seriously.

Hildegard had contact with many famous scholars, including Bernard of Clairvaux, Abélard's great rival. When the Pope gave Hildegard permission to share her visions publicly, her fame increased even more, and she founded her own convent. Hildegard's comprehensive knowledge of medicines also attracted awe – to this day, you can still find herbal remedies made according to her recipes, such as 'heart strengthening parsley wine' and 'colon detoxifying spicknel pear honey', which were both products of her own convent apothecary.

However, some even went as far as denouncing her as little more than a 'herb wife' or a witch doctor, and emphasised her cooking skills rather than her medical knowledge. By highlighting her famed recipe for spelt biscuits, Hildegard was gradually moulded into the

Around 1150: Hildegard of Bingen founds St Rupertsberg Convent, and becomes famous for her divine visions and knowledge of medicine.

typical female stereotype, but she was much more than a well-educated nun with a deep understanding of herbal healing. She was a philosopher, an abbess and a composer. Like Kassia, the Byzantine nun, Hildegard also wrote her own musical compositions. The first known European composers were therefore both women: Kassia of Constantinople and Hildegard of Bingen. A short time later, two monks in the Paris cathedral school invented modern musical notation.

THE FIRST CRUSADE

The testimony of Anna Comnena

Unlike Hildegard of Bingen, Anna Comnena, the daughter of the Byzantine emperor, didn't need visions to have her writings accepted by men. She founded a reading circle so she could discuss her ideas with other scholars and, just as Abélard and Thomas Aquinas had done, she drew a parallel between the writings of Aristotle and Christian theology. At the same time, she proved that the scholastics' view of women's abilities was just as mistaken as that of their Ancient Greek role models. Anna wasn't just well read in theology, she had also studied philosophy, mathematics, music and medicine. She was also very hands-on and ran a hospital with other philosophers from her circle.

Anna was a princess born in purple, and even as a child, she had dreamt of one day becoming empress. But her father, who had originally wanted to make Anna's betrothed his successor, suddenly changed his mind and placed her brother on the throne instead.

Anna refused to accept this and hatched a plot against her brother, but the plot was discovered, and Anna was banished to a convent. It is said that she became very bitter about the whole incident. Nevertheless, she used the peace and quiet of the convent to write a comprehensive fifteen-volume history of the era, proving that she also had at least some understanding of politics. The common thread running through all her stories was the life of her father Alexios, and it was from him that the work got its name: *The Alexiad*.

Between 1138 and 1148: The Byzantine princess and historian Anna Comnena writes her father's biography and describes the First Crusade.

The Crusaders ride to Constantinople

During the reign of Anna's father, Constantinople found itself once again at the centre of history. Another population was migrating from east to west and was now advancing in the direction of Europe. This time, the threat was coming from the Turks. For a long time, they had been contesting China's borders in the east, but then their area of dominance expanded westward, where they relieved the Arabs of much of their conquests. The Turks themselves were early converts to Islam, and now they were attacking the Byzantine Empire's eastern borders.

The Turks had already chalked up several decisive victories over the Byzantines, and Alexios Comnena was now struggling to hold them back. So, he appealed to the Pope in Rome for help; although the Churches of Byzantium and Rome had much they disagreed on, Alexios hoped the Christians could unite against a common Muslim enemy. The Pope answered his appeal for aid and ordered the rulers of Italy, France and Germany to go to war in support of their Christian brothers.

From a military standpoint, there was nothing unusual about Alexios's request. He had asked for soldiers as reinforcements in his battle against the Turks. However, to help recruitment, the Pope appealed to the Christians' pride and sense of moral duty. 'To the holy land!' he preached. 'Don't let Byzantium fall into Muslim hands!' Jerusalem had been abandoned to the Arabs for much too long, he argued. It was time to take back control of Christianity's holy city, the very place where Jesus was crucified. By doing this, he elevated a military matter into a religious one. With the Pope's words, an ordinary war became a holy war.

Soon, people started talking about a crusade. All over Europe, preachers urged people to join the campaign. 'It's the will of God,' the Pope proclaimed, promising to forgive the sins of anyone who followed him.

This religious propaganda had horrific consequences. When the time came for the great crusade to begin, a huge mob had gathered, but they weren't the noble knights the Pope had expected. An eclectic rabble of men, women and children had turned up to join the soldiers; instead of well-organised armies of knights, a chaotic, uncontrollable mass was on the move. Thousands of pilgrims left their homes and journeyed to Byzantium, fixated on the idea of confronting a powerful enemy. With weeks of travelling still ahead of them, in some of the villages en route the crowd turned against the Jews. Hadn't the Pope said that God had ordered the killing of all non-believers? After just a few kilometres, before they had even left Germany, their lust for war reached a crescendo and was unleashed upon the Jews.

When the Crusaders finally reached Constantinople, the city was suddenly filled with people who all needed food and lodging. Anna Comnena, who would later write a report on the events, was then only a girl of 13. She referred to all the Crusaders as Franks, although in fact they came from many regions of Europe, and these uneducated barbarians made her angry. Many took advantage of the confusion and marched through the streets in search of booty, simply taking what they wanted. The whole situation was chaos.

1096: Thousands of men, women and children desert the First Crusade to recapture Jerusalem from the Muslims.

... and onwards to Jerusalem

Alexios insisted that the Crusaders move on, and at last they left the city to head south on their campaign to win back Jerusalem and other places from the Turks. The journey was arduous and lasted many years. Of the poorest, only a small number survived, so for the most part, it was the knights who ultimately reached the Holy Land.

Upon reaching their destination, their contract with God and ideas of Christian fraternity were quickly forgotten; most weren't prepared to wait to be rewarded for their efforts in heaven. They wanted their riches now. Instead of giving the provinces back to Byzantium as agreed, the leaders of the Crusade divided the spoils amongst themselves, awarding themselves land and titles such as Count of Jaffa, Count of Edessa and Count of Tripoli.

Bohemond, the son of a Norman king, refused to surrender Antioch to Byzantium and instead crowned himself its new prince. He was appointed in his new role by an ambassador sent by the Pope himself. Anna met the Norman prince in person, and his charisma left a deep impression on her. Her report also describes his later capture during the Battle of Melitene and his clandestine escape from Antioch, when he hid from his enemies inside a coffin. To stop anyone from looking inside, a dead chicken was also placed in the coffin. The stench of death made the ruse all the more convincing.

With the Crusades, something changed. The Crusaders committed bloody massacres – and, for the first time, these massacres were committed in the name of their religion. Until then, Jews, Christians and Muslims had generally lived peacefully and respectfully alongside one another; Arab scholars had always openly discussed the Torah, Bible and Quran. The Crusades poisoned the relationship between the religions, and the consequences would be terrible.

IN THE MEDIEVAL COURTS

William the Conqueror and Matilda, the first Queen of England

Everybody knows the Vikings: the northern seafarers who sailed the seas and rivers of Europe, looting its population's worldly goods at sword point. Hardly anywhere escaped unscathed. But not all the Vikings returned north with their plunder. Some set up home overseas and travelled to Russia to found Kievan Rus. Others settled in north-western France. The Vikings of north-western France were known as 'North men' or 'Normans', and the area they settled is called Normandy to this day. For some of the Normans, though, Normandy wasn't enough. They headed south and conquered southern Italy and the island of Sicily. One of their descendants was Prince Bohemond, the Norman who joined the Crusade and then fled the city of Antioch in a pungent coffin.

William, Duke of Normandy, headed north, sailing across the English Channel and conquering England. After his victory, he was crowned the new King of England in London, entering the history books as William the Conqueror. Since the time of the Romans, no outsider had successfully defeated England. Just a few decades later, William the Conqueror's granddaughter Matilda became the first Queen of England.

1066: William, Duke of Normandy, conquers England; from then on, he's known as William the Conqueror.

Meanwhile, the Pope and the King of the Holy Roman Empire were still squabbling about the issue of investiture. The two rivals did something that would become the norm in centuries to come: one allied himself with France and the other joined forces with England. Once again, an alliance would be sealed by marriage. The German King Henry V took Matilda, the daughter of the English king, as his wife.

With great pomp and ceremony, the 8-year-old Matilda was sent to the Continent, where she was placed in the guardianship of the Bishop of Trier and taught German. Her marriage to Henry took place four years later. The pair then travelled to Rome where the Pope crowned Henry V the Emperor and the 12-year-old Matilda the Empress of the Holy Roman Empire.

At her husband's side, Matilda learnt a lot about politics and diplomacy – but upon the emperor's death, she lost her position at the imperial court. Luckily, at that very moment, her father summoned her back to England. His only male heir had died unexpectedly, and he was now without a successor.

Matilda's father named her his successor. Having a woman in the line of succession was very rare, so he summoned England's barons together several times to make them pledge an oath of allegiance to his daughter. However, when he died, Matilda stayed in France. Her cousin Stephen took advantage of her absence and nominated himself the new king. This divided the English barons; some remained true to the oath they had sworn to Matilda, but others hoped to gain an advantage by supporting King Stephen.

Matilda didn't want to give up the throne, so she rallied her allies to launch an attack on Stephen. A war broke out between the two that lasted almost twenty years. Matilda regained the upper hand and paraded into London to be proclaimed Queen of England – the first woman to rule England in her own right. However, her reign only lasted a few months. The Londoners didn't like her and, when Stephen attacked again, Matilda fled and sought refuge in Oxford Castle. But even there she wasn't safe. Along with her most trusted allies, she changed into white robes (excellent camouflage in England's thick fog) and fled on foot across the frozen Thames.

The drawn-out civil war between Matilda and Stephen became known as 'the Anarchy'; it brought the people of England much suffering. Nobody was in control and lots of the barons took advantage of the situation to seize land and build new castles for themselves. It was unclear who was in charge and whose law applied, so they started pillaging villages and monasteries for their wealth.

After many years, the war showed no signs of ending, so Matilda returned to France. She didn't give up, though, and insisted that Stephen appoint her son Henry his successor.

Chivalrous knights and virtuous ladies

The barons who destabilised England during the Anarchy struck terror into the hearts of ordinary people, while aristocratic knights used the chaos to oppress and exploit the poor.

During this time, Eleanor of Aquitaine, Matilda's future daughter-in-law, was still a child growing up in the south-west of France. During the lifetime of her grandfather, the Duke of Aquitaine, life at court had started to change. The knights, long admired for their courage and strength in battle, were now expected to learn courtly etiquette. It was important for a knight to excel in fencing and jousting, to be fearless in the face of death and ready to take on any enemy, of course, but other qualities were valued too. A true, chivalrous knight fought in defence of good and, instead of exploiting the weak, he was expected to protect them. He would only be thought noble if, alongside raw masculinity, he exhibited fine manners and showed good grace, particularly in the company of women. Later the idea of 'courtly' behaviour developed into the word 'courteous' – a person who is respectful and well-mannered.

The customs of the court were further refined by troubadours and minstrels, who spent their time composing songs and ambitious texts. The first troubadour is said to have been Eleanor of Aquitaine's grandfather, and from his court in Aquitaine, the art of the courtly love song soon spread through the other courts of Europe. The troubadours also poked fun at the Church and its rules, which so strictly controlled the relationships between men and women. But still the troubadour only sang the praises of his heart's desire from a distance: the noble lady was perfect only as long as she remained untouched and unattainable, and the couple's love remained unfulfilled. As is so often the case, this chaste ideal didn't reflect reality. Eleanor's grandfather was rumoured to have been involved in numerous love affairs, and so was his granddaughter.

11th century: In the noble manors and royal courts of medieval France, the troubadour is born.

The art of the troubadour emerged at almost the same time as the aristocratic women of the courts of Japan were starting to write novels and poems. But unlike in Japan, poetry was seen as a masculine pursuit in Europe. These male poets travelled through the land with their songs, and some of them, such as Oswald von Wolkenstein and the minstrel Walther von der Vogelweide, became very famous indeed. But there are some poems written by a woman from this time. The only thing is, nobody knows who she was any more. She wrote, 'My name is Marie and I come from France', so somebody named her Marie de France, and she may have lived at the court of an English king. After her death, however, she was forgotten, although her poems, which she dedicated to a 'noble king', became very popular among the aristocracy.

Eleanor becomes the first Queen of France …

Eleanor of Aquitaine liked the pleasures of the court; she loved having plenty of suitors competing for her favour. But when her father married her to a French king, she was forced to leave Aquitaine and follow her husband to Paris, where she was crowned Queen of France.

City life couldn't have been more different! In the court of Aquitaine, Eleanor had been surrounded by song, dance, courtly games and jousting, and had devoted herself day and night to winning men's hearts. But now, she had married a man who had grown up in a monastery and knew hardly anything of life except theology and scholastics. King Louis VII was a city dweller – worse than that, he had spent most of his time in the cloisters of the cathedral school. The colourful world of castles and knights was completely alien to him.

The citizens of France's cities had other concerns, though. With increasing wealth, they grew in confidence until they were able to challenge the power of the monasteries and the long-established aristocracy. Up until now, the medieval social order had only recognised the Church, the nobility and the farmers, but in future, these city people would gain their own influential position within that structure. This was the birth of the middle class – the bourgeoisie.

To demonstrate their power, they started building cathedrals so splendid and huge that they seemed to reach the heavens. New designs allowed sunlight into the nave through elaborate architecture and tall windows with pointed arches. To the people, who were used to their churches being little more than dark chapels, this was a revelation. In these grand new churches, God seemed closer than ever before.

These Gothic cathedrals, which were now popping up all over France, were modelled on the Basilica of Saint-Denis in northern Paris. The foundation stone for the basilica was laid by Abbot Suger, one of King Louis's most trusted confidants, and the Church was consecrated three years later in a ceremony led by Eleanor and Louis, shortly after they were married. However, not long into their reign, trouble was once more brewing in the Holy Land.

The Pope had sent Bernard of Clairvaux to Europe to summon up recruits for the Second Crusade, and Eleanor and Louis soon found themselves on the journey east to join other European rulers in the campaign against the Muslims. Eleanor and her attendants accompanied the Crusaders, much to Bernard's annoyance – he found Eleanor extremely irritating! When it became clear that the Second Crusade was going to fail, Bernard accused the women of distracting the soldiers and lowering their morale.

In reality, the Second Crusade failed because the Christians were outmatched by the strength of the Turkish army. This was aggravated by the fact that the Crusaders had constantly bickered among themselves on the long journey east. Louis and Eleanor's marriage didn't survive either. The Pope tried to stop their divorce, even ordering them at one point to sleep in the same bed, but it was all to no avail: just two months after their return from the Crusade, Eleanor had divorced Louis and found another great match. She married Henry, Duke of Normandy – the son of the English Queen Matilda.

1147: The French Queen Eleanor of Aquitaine and her husband Louis lead the Second Crusade to the Holy Land. This time, the Christians are defeated and the Muslim Turks hold onto their territory.

... and then Queen of England

1152: Eleanor swaps husbands (and countries!) and is now the Queen of England.

For the future King Henry II, this alliance with the heir to the powerful Duchy of Aquitaine came as a boon. He was already the Duke of Normandy and Anjou; by marrying Eleanor he owned more French territory than the King of France himself. In the years to come, this would cause severe clashes between France and England. For her part, Eleanor had cast aside the French Crown like a piece of old clothing when she divorced Louis. By marrying Henry, who was eleven years her junior, she made up for this loss. Just two years later, the couple was crowned at Westminster. From that point on, the French king's ex-wife wore the Crown of England.

Eleanor brought the courtly culture of the troubadours with her to England, and poets were commissioned to write down the old local legends. The adventures of King Arthur and his enchanted sword Excalibur, the wizard Merlin, the brave knight Lancelot and the beautiful Guinevere soon became famous all over Europe. Arthur's quest for the Holy Grail, a cup said to have magical powers, was as alluring – and as out of reach – as the love of the genteel ladies the minstrels praised in their songs.

The English king had a very lax interpretation of the code of chivalry. He was coarse and vulgar, and his behaviour caused Eleanor great offence. Eventually, she couldn't put up with him any longer. Angry and disappointed, she contacted her ex-husband Louis in France, and he, along with three of Eleanor and Henry's sons, supported her plot to overthrow the king. But Henry found out. Dressed in men's clothing, Eleanor attempted to flee, but was caught and imprisoned for twelve years. In the isolation of her prison, she was forced to calm down. She started to read a lot and corresponded with Hildegard of Bingen, who urged her to be less fickle.

But this wasn't the end for Eleanor. She outlived her husband and, after his death, her son Richard the Lionheart became King of England. Even before his coronation, he had already pledged his support to the French king in a new war against the Turks. However, Richard, who led the Third Crusade to Jerusalem, couldn't defeat the Turkish army either. Yet again, the Christians failed to win back the city.

Things would get even worse for Richard. Eleanor, who had taken over the reins of power at home, received news that her son had been kidnapped. On his journey home, he had been taken captive by Leopold V, Duke of Austria, who would only release him in return for a high ransom. With great effort, she just about managed to scrape together the money for Richard's freedom.

1189: The Third Crusade begins.

When Eleanor finally died, England and France were embroiled in a deep feud. The English King Henry came from the Plantagenet family and his ancestors were of French–Norman descent. Through Eleanor's marriage to the rulers of England and France, the affairs of the two countries had become even more intertwined. Very soon, things would come to a head in what would be called the Hundred Years War.

MARKET TOWNS FLOURISH AND CHRISTENDOM FLOUNDERS

Wealth by the water

The year of Eleanor of Aquitaine's death, 1204, would prove to be a turning point in the history of Europe. The events of the First Crusade had already shown that neither the Roman Catholic Church nor the Greek Orthodox Church could rely on the other side as an ally – the Crusaders had fought amongst themselves and kept losing sight of their 'true' enemy, the Islamic Turks. The real motivation for wars waged in the name of religion became increasingly clear: money and power, and the two often came hand in hand.

Little has changed to this day. Money, usually in the form of silver or gold coins, became increasingly important in this era. For a long time, wealth and power were linked to land ownership, but with the founding of new towns and cities, and with trade flourishing, this changed. Something also started changing in people's minds too. Until now, they'd been convinced that life on Earth meant nothing but suffering, and that beauty could only be found in heaven. Now, however, city dwellers were discovering the world of luxury and commercial goods. Ancient trade routes, such as the Silk Road, experienced a renaissance and were used to transport rare cloth and fabrics, spices and other exotic items to market, and from there to people's homes. The Turks controlled vast stretches of the Silk Road, so their interactions with Europeans were by no means restricted to war. They only fought one another when there was an advantage to be gained – sometimes it made more economic sense to drop their weapons and build trade links.

Blossoming trade gave merchants unexpected influence. Those who did business in far-off lands and sold exotic goods, such as pepper and cinnamon, became very highly respected, although in Germany, some people called them 'pepper sacks' out of jealousy, which meant more or less the same as 'money bags'. The rise of the merchant may have happened even faster if kings, princes and bishops hadn't tried to obstruct the transport of goods. They demanded a toll at every river crossing, or for every half-paved road, causing the price of transported goods to increase with every passing kilometre.

Yet money always finds a way. Merchants realised that the burdensome tolls and taxes could be avoided through sea travel, so they began investing in ships to transport their goods by sea instead. This was a major advantage for any city with direct access to the sea, or at the very least a large river, such as Venice, Genoa, Pisa, Hamburg, Lübeck, London, Bruges and Novgorod.

The wealth of these cities grew to fantastic proportions. Soon they were no longer bound to a king or a prince; instead, they were free and independent. The Germans formed the 'Hanseatic League' of allied port cities, while in Italy maritime republics were established. The lords of Venice gave their city the illustrious title of *La Serenissima*, the 'most serene'.

Europe splits in two: the plunder of Byzantium

Venice and Genoa reaped most of their wealth from trading with Constantinople. The merchants in each city were in competition and the Byzantine emperors played them off against one another to give themselves an advantage. The relationship between the Byzantines and the Maritime Republic of Venice was already quite strained when another pope decided to declare another crusade. By this time, the Pope knew how tedious the land route to the Holy Land was, so he sent some French nobles to the maritime republics of Italy to find out whether the army could be transported to Constantinople by ship. The Venetians agreed to provide a fleet of fifty galleys, which could transport over 30,000 soldiers; this was no small commitment, even for a city as wealthy as Venice. The lords of the city negotiated a deal with the Crusaders, where they were guaranteed 85,000 silver marks and half of the territory conquered, in return for their financial backing.

Once the ships had set sail, it became clear that the Crusaders would never be able to pay this fee; most of the soldiers they'd promised hadn't even bothered to show up. Who could honestly claim that, this time, they would prevail over the mighty Turkish army? The Venetians were afraid the whole enterprise would fail, to their financial ruin. If the Fourth Crusade fell apart, the huge sums of money invested in building and fitting out the fleet would literally sink to the bottom of the Mediterranean. Nobody knew whether *La Serenissima*, already under pressure from its competitor Genoa, would ever be able to recover from such a catastrophe.

Then, someone had a bright idea: they would raid the city of Zara and plunder the Dalmatian coast. When the Pope heard about the Siege of Zara he was horrified, and immediately sent a letter forbidding the army from attacking other Christians. The Crusaders carried on regardless, undeterred by the Pope's threats, and advanced towards Constantinople, where they turned against their hosts. For three days, they tortured, maimed and killed many of the city's occupants. They stole everything they could lay their hands on, from golden door handles to exquisite mosaics and relics, destroying countless artworks in the process.

The Venetians among them, however, knew a thing or two about valuable objects and sought the advice of art experts. Instead of destroying these artefacts, they took them back to Venice. If you want to see what remains of Constantinople, you can still find much of its art in Venice. These include the four life-size gold-plated bronze horses that originally topped the circus where Empress Theodora once worked as a dancer, which now decorate the main portal of St Mark's Basilica in Venice.

For centuries, the city on the Bosporus – long revered as a paradise by travellers on account of its beauty – had formed the beating heart of the medieval world. It was the gateway from the Latin West to the Muslim East. For centuries, its formidable Greek fire and the Virgin Mary's protection had fended off onslaughts from

1204: During the Fourth Crusade, the Crusaders plunder Constantinople, the city of their Christian brothers. The fraught Christian alliance collapses once and for all.

the Russians, the Arabs and the Turks, but now it lay destroyed by fellow Christians. With this, the notion of any unity between the two halves of the Christian world collapsed once and for all. After the Sack of Constantinople, the Byzantines' grudge against the Western Europeans was so great that the schism became impossible to mend. The two halves of Europe, the Latin West and the Greek East, were divided for good.

THE MONGOLS

The daughters of Genghis Khan

While Constantinople was being pillaged, something extraordinary was happening in the East. Up until now, we've encountered the Mongols as a group of nomadic horsemen roaming across the Central Asian steppes and posing a constant threat to their Chinese neighbours. But then, all at once, a strong leader emerged to unite the Mongol tribes into one gigantic empire. Genghis Khan seized vast swathes of Central Asia and the whole of northern China, elevating himself to the leader of all Mongols.

1206: Genghis Khan unites the Mongol tribes, becoming the first Great Khan.

Genghis Khan conquered half the known world and the Mongol hordes struck fear into the hearts of people from Europe to China. This also gave them control of the Silk Road, and Genghis used his access to the trade routes to secure the loyalty of the peoples he had conquered, giving them a share of the goods received from the Silk Road. These goods brought the Mongols – who had formerly led simple lives as nomadic herders – untold luxuries such as warm camel and goat hair blankets, expensive silk, ivory, pearls and coral, as well as iron that could be forged into weapons or tools.

In the long run, Genghis Khan couldn't control his great empire on his own, but promoting his sons to heirs or co-regents was out of the question. As far as he was concerned, they were good at drinking, average at fighting and terrible at everything else. However, he had a much higher opinion of his daughters. Their intelligence and talent outshone all of their brothers'. So the Khan married his daughters to the conquered rulers, declaring the women regents who ran parts of the empire in the name of the Mongols.

Genghis Khan believed that if you could manage a household, you could govern a country. He's said to have told his daughter Checheikhen, 'You're the daughter of your father, the Khan; you will be sent to govern the tribe of the Oirats.' He also gave his daughter Alakhai Bekhi the title 'Princess who runs the state'. To stop his daughters' husbands from interfering, he gave them roles in the military and took them with him on his campaigns, which took them far west into Europe.

Genghis Khan left the government of his core territory in the hands of his four wives. The states governed by his daughters formed a belt around the core, merging old and new territories into a vast family affair. This wasn't always easy, as the population naturally rebelled against the occupiers; not everyone was willing to just roll over and become a subject of the Mongol Empire. Wherever difficulties arose, Genghis Khan and his Mongol horde rode to his daughters' aid.

When dishing out retribution, he wasn't exactly known for being lenient; from China to Russia, Hungary and Poland, the Mongols were feared for their brutality. When the Onguds in China rose up against Alakhai Bekhi (the 'Princess who runs the state') her father sent in his warriors as per usual. Just as he had done elsewhere in the steppes, he wanted to kill not only the rebels, but also all the male members of the tribe. However, Alakhai stood beside her people and stopped the massacre, allowing only the initiators of the uprising to be punished.

After consolidating her rule, Alakhai sent her own Chinese troops to support her father in battle. In the meantime, she had also learnt the art of Chinese medicine, so she sent her physicians as well. Through the Mongols, Chinese medicine started spreading throughout the Muslim world and into the West.

In many areas, Genghis Khan's decision to give his daughters so much responsibility was met with deep disapproval. As in other parts of the world, men and women had set roles in Mongol society: the men went to war and reared cattle in peacetime, while the women were the mistresses of the tent.

This way of doing things couldn't simply be overturned and not many agreed with Genghis when he said that managing a household was like governing a country. They thought he was wrong. Perhaps this is why his confidants put so much effort into preserving, for posterity, their much-admired Khan's reputation. In chronicles dating from the time, a historian researching the Mongol queens found that the sections on women had simply been removed from the parchment. Most of the sources on Genghis Khan's daughters were simply destroyed.

The Mongol conquests sent shockwaves throughout the world. They destroyed Baghdad, bringing an end to the golden age of Arab culture that had blossomed under the Abbasids. The waters of the River Tigris allegedly ran blue as the furious Mongols flung books from the Grand Library of Baghdad into the river and the ink dissolved. The Mongols also defeated the Russians and made Batu Khan, the founder of the Golden Horde, commander-in-chief. His cruel domination of Russian territories, known as the Tatar Yoke, would leave a lasting mark on the history of Russia.

Genghis Khan's sons divide the empire

The Great Khan proved to be right: after his death, his male heirs really weren't capable of holding the empire together. They fought and killed their own sisters and used violence to subjugate the people their sisters had ruled. The brothers ultimately fell out with one another as well.

1279: After Genghis Khan's grandson Kublai Khan conquers China, he crowns himself Emperor of the Middle Kingdom – a Mongol has become the Emperor of China.

Despite all this, the Mongol Empire didn't fall apart right away (unlike the empire of Alexander the Great), and once again, this was mainly thanks to a woman. Sorghaghtani Beki, one of the Khan's daughters-in-law, made sure that her four sons followed in their grandfather's footsteps. All four of them became rulers of the Mongol Empire.

The Golden Horde, which ruled Russia for over 100 years, is said to have got its name from its founding ruler, Batu Khan, who lived in a golden yurt. The Mongol leader Kublai Khan became so strong that he was considered the most powerful ruler in the world for a long time. Eventually he even conquered the Song Dynasty in China and made himself Emperor of the Middle Kingdom.

A woman stops Marco Polo from going home

The areas controlled by Sorghaghtani's sons formed a triangle encompassing Persia, Russia and China. The family had fallen out after Genghis Khan's death, so now, new enemies from within the family were gathering at the centre of that triangle, the Mongol heartland. They allied themselves against Sorghaghtani and Kublai Khan.

One of the women who made life difficult for Kublai Khan was Princess Khutulun. She was the daughter of a prince and the great-great-granddaughter of Genghis Khan, as well as the daughter of Kublai's cousin. She was a more accomplished rider than any of her fourteen brothers, so her father chose her to lead his army. Khutulun is said to have been phenomenally strong and had never been defeated in the wrestling ring. In fact, she had promised to marry any man who could beat her in a wrestling match, but if he lost, he would have to pay for his defeat in horses – because of this bet, the princess accumulated a herd of 10,000 horses! Khutulun soon realised she couldn't stay unmarried forever, so in the end she agreed to a marriage that didn't require a defeat in the ring. Shortly before his death, her father asked her to rule the empire, but she refused. Married or not, she preferred to be the general of an army and that's how things would stay.

Kublai Khan wanted to marry one of his daughters to a Khan in Persia. But he soon found himself in a predicament: once the most powerful ruler in the world, Kublai Khan was no longer able to cross his own kingdom to take the bride to Persia. An uprising by Khutulun's people had made the land route too dangerous.

Marco Polo, a merchant from Venice, soon discovered this too. Polo was a 'travelling salesman', one of the few brave enough to travel alone to distant lands and do business with customers face to face. Kublai Khan liked the young Italian, so he made him a prefect and allowed him to travel across China. Long after his return to Italy, Polo wrote an account of his travels that gave Europeans a first glimpse into Asia – a world that, up until then, they knew almost nothing about.

Marco Polo travelled to China with his father and uncle, but when they wanted to return home, they found the land route

1271: Marco Polo, a young merchant from Venice, travels to China, where he lives at the court of Kublai Khan.

blocked. They had heard all about Khutulan's legendary strength and knew that she posed a serious threat. The Khan was also searching for a route west to send the Mongolian Princess Kököchin, who was to marry Arghun, the ruler of one of the Mongolian principalities in Persia. The Polos offered to take her by sea; from there, they would continue their journey back to Venice. This was the only way of avoiding the danger. However, the unpredictable seas also cost the men dearly: of the 600 men in the Polos' fleet, only seventeen survived. Kököchin also survived – but by the time she had arrived in Persia, Arghun had died.

Mandukhai rebuilds the Mongol Empire

For all Kublai Khan's strengths, he couldn't stop the Mongols from losing control of the Silk Road. Cut off from this source of wealth, the Mongol Empire collapsed.

It was women who ensured that Genghis Khan's dream of a unified Mongol state passed down from generation to generation. Like Khutulun, many of these women played an active role in resisting the rulers who had first caused a rift in the family by murdering and seizing the lands of Genghis Khan's daughters. Nevertheless, it would still take more than 200 years for a ruler to emerge who was skilled enough to reunite the Mongols.

Her name was Mandukhai Khatun, and after her husband's death, she became queen of a small principality in the Mongol heartland. To secure her role, she went into battle, carefully planning her campaigns with strategic flair. One after the other, her army defeated its opponents and conquered Mongolia bit by bit, regaining access to the Silk Road, reviving trade and bringing in a significant income.

In China, the foreign rule of Kublai Khan was brought to an end by a new dynasty. Unlike her predecessors, Mandukhai was wise enough to know she should avoid becoming embroiled in a war, and signed a treaty with the new emperor instead.

Mandukhai remarried and had seven sons and one daughter. During her final pregnancy, she fought in her most important battle yet. But then something disastrous happened: the pregnant queen fell from her horse.

Falling from a horse was taken as a bad omen, and afterwards, a ruler often lost the trust of their soldiers and subjects. But Mandukhai's power appears to have been built on firm foundations. When she fell, four of her soldiers immediately rushed to her aid, surrounding the fallen queen and rescuing her from a dangerous predicament. The episode showed that Mandukhai had united the Mongols into what we would now call 'one nation', as the four men were each from a different clan.

Mandukhai, her husband and her sons reorganised many aspects of the empire and spread this news through song. That way, humble shepherds, unable to read or write, could also be told how the empire was being governed. The couple brought permanent stability to the country, perhaps because the only thing that mattered to them was being a member of a common Mongol nation. Whether Christian, Muslim or Buddhist, everyone was free to practise their own religion.

The Mongol Empire of Queen Mandukhai was much smaller than the huge territory once conquered by Genghis Khan. Mandukhai's empire no longer posed a threat to Europe or China, and for that, it was much more stable too. This state, Mongolia, still exists today; up until around 100 years ago, it was still ruled by Genghis Khan's direct ancestors.

Around 1509: The Mongol Queen Mandukhai dies. She leaves behind a Mongolia so stable that it still exists today.

MARGUERITE PORETE AND JOAN OF ARC

The Church crushes dissent

When Europe built its first universities, a theologian posed the following question: could a woman become a Doctor of the Science of Theology? In his answer, he gave four reasons why not:

Firstly, a woman was unreliable: as Eve had demonstrated, a woman was vulnerable to temptation.
Secondly, a woman couldn't be effective because she was too weak.
Thirdly, a woman couldn't have authority as she was expected to submit to her husband.
And finally, a woman's word couldn't be trusted as she tended to choose seduction over a virtuous life.

As was usual in the Church, his reasoning was based on the words ascribed to St Paul the Apostle, who had allegedly decreed that women should remain silent.

Women weren't the only ones making Church leaders anxious. In medieval cities, people were searching for new ways of living together, and the Church didn't know how to respond. In Northern Europe, some of these people formed groups that lived communally, a little like a modern-day shared house or flat. They called themselves the Beguines (women) and Beghards (men); they didn't marry and instead lived simple, pious lives in shared communities called beguinages. Unlike monks and nuns, the Beguines and Beghards were independent of the Church, and lots of them had jobs. Their lives of poverty, penance and chastity made them very well respected, and the city or parish priest often gave them housing. In Belgium, many beguinages – some of which are more than 700 years old – are now World Heritage Sites.

In the Middle Ages there were many movements like the Beguines – people who followed their own beliefs and formed groups outside the Church. The Church responded to this perceived threat by setting up courts called inquisitions, where anyone who had a dissenting view could be accused and sentenced. The Church refused to accept that people were rejecting its control.

One of these groups in France were the Waldensians, who were led by a man called Peter Waldo. He and his followers were persecuted as heretics as their movement allowed women to preach – in doing so, they, like many others, showed that there was nothing inherently Christian about excluding women from certain activities. Another group was the Cathars, who took their name from the Greek word for 'pure' – *katharos* – because their overall goal was to achieve 'the purity of the soul'. Most of them were persecuted by the Inquisition as heretics and many were killed. This may have been what made the Beguines so pious: the fate of the Waldensians and Cathars showed them just how perilous their situation really was.

Marguerite Porete is burned

Marguerite Porete had links to the Beguines and grew up in the little town of Valenciennes, in the Holy Roman Empire. Back then, life in the city centred around orders of begging monks, beguinages and the courtly culture of the knight. At a poetry contest, Marguerite found that it was becoming fashionable to write in the local language rather than Latin, as had formerly been the case – so she boldly decided to write a theology book in French. This was unusual, firstly, because women weren't allowed to write books on theology and, secondly, because theologians always posed their questions in Latin. But Marguerite didn't care. Although aware of the risks, she decided to publish her book, *The Mirror of Simple Souls*, in her own name.

Furthermore, instead of referring to the authority of other scholars, she supported her argument with quotes directly from the Bible, ignoring the world of scholarly men altogether.

In one part of the book she writes, 'Here follow some considerations for the forlorn who ask the way to the land of freedom.' For Marguerite, her freedom as an individual came straight from the Bible.

Needless to say, the Church was none too happy about this woman and her desire for freedom. Although Marguerite showed her book to three scholars and received a positive opinion from each, it didn't take long for the Inquisition to move against her. First, *The Mirror of Simple Souls* was publicly burned in Valenciennes. Then Marguerite was accused of discussing her work with other people. As a result, she was arrested, sent to Paris and locked in a dungeon. Twenty-one theologians were summoned to examine individual sections of the book while Marguerite languished in prison for a year and a half. Some tried to persuade her to repent, but she refused to give up her spiritual freedom. On 1 June 1310, she was burned at the stake in Paris.

1310: On 1 June Marguerite Porete is burned at the stake as a heretic for publishing her book *The Mirror of Simple Souls*.

For the Church, the public showdown with Marguerite Porete and her links to the Beguines were rather bad publicity. A year later, the bishops decided to ban the Beguines. From that point on, both they and the Beghards were persecuted by the Inquisition.

Although the Inquisition tried to burn and destroy all copies of *The Mirror of Simple Souls*, many copies survived – perhaps because the book had been so well distributed by Marguerite's followers before it was banned. The text continued to be read for many centuries and had a great influence on later thinkers, although the author's name remained unknown to most of its readers.

France becomes a kingdom

England and France found themselves locked in a war that lasted over 100 years. The feud broke out because some parts of France were owned by the kings of England. Over time, the relationship between the rulers and their territories became so complex that, eventually, the French king laid claim to the English throne. The English in turn laid claim to the Crown of France.

This further complicated the conflict because, until now, aristocratic knights had fought each other for land, not for the sake of nations like England and France. They would take sides as suited them. The French Burgundians sided with the English and joined forces against the French king.

Then Joan of Arc stepped into the fray, rallying her countrymen with the cry: 'The English must be thrown out of France!' This young girl of barely 17 donned a suit of armour, took up the white flag and declared war on the English. She got what she wanted, too. The English were forced to leave and something new was formed: the Kingdom of France.

1339: The English and French kings lay claim to the other's throne, igniting the Hundred Years War.

Joan of Arc liberates a city and crowns the king

Joan of Arc was a farmer's daughter from a small village in Lorraine. As a young girl, she heard voices speaking to her; some of these voices she recognised as the Christian martyrs St Michael, St Catherine and St Margaret. The voices accompanied her when she set out on her unusual journey across France. By this point, the English king had already seized the French throne and Charles VII, who many French considered the true king, was surrounded by enemies on all sides. The voices Joan heard set her the task of freeing Charles and escorting him to Reims, where he would be crowned king.

Joan left her village and went to Vaucouleurs, the next biggest town. Wrapped in a shabby red robe, she stood at the town gate and waited for the local military commander to meet her. Nine weeks she waited as the captain turned her away twice. But Joan didn't let the time go to waste and used it to tell everyone who would listen about the mission given to her by a higher power: she had come to rescue the French king.

The people listened, and the news soon spread across the land. After nine weeks, Joan had a weapon that would make her invincible: the enthusiastic support of the people. A woman who had got the whole country talking couldn't be ignored by the king, even if she was just a farm girl, so the captain eventually decided to let her in. The citizens of Vaucouleurs made men's clothing for Joan to help her travel safely, and she was even given a horse.

Joan sent the king a letter announcing her arrival. In this letter, she prophesied that she would recognise the king immediately, even though she had never seen his picture. Then he would know she was telling the truth and had truly been sent by God.

Charles, the secret 'true' King of France, was in an almost hopeless situation. The city of Orléans, where his camp was based, had been besieged by his enemies, and an attempt to free him had ended in failure. The king only seemed to have one option left: to flee France. Faced with this dire situation, Charles agreed to meet Joan.

Upon her arrival, she recognised the king, who had hidden himself among his courtiers. He knew straight away that she must be telling the truth, although of course this detail may have been added later to embellish the story. Joan then sent a message to the English. 'Listen,' she wrote. 'I've been sent by God to throw you out of France.'

However, the nobles found the idea of expelling the English from France very strange. The king and his people wanted to negotiate and reach a compromise. Everyone should ultimately get what was owed to them, whether English or French. As was the custom among Europe's knights, weapons would only be used as a last resort.

Joan cared nothing for the knights' customs. She gathered the people behind her and simply stormed ahead. Many followed her command and, defying the military, they conquered the English fortresses. Orléans was liberated and Joan became famous all over France.

1429: Joan of Arc liberates the city of Orléans and she wants to expel the English from the rest of France.

But the Maid of Orléans, as she was now known, still hadn't achieved her goal. She had to get to Reim; one way or another, she needed to crown Charles the King of all France. Charles's generals were hesitant, so Joan had to pursue her plan without their backing. Once again, she gathered huge crowds behind her, putting pressure on the king and his advisers. In many cities, Joan's enthusiasm was infectious; some members of the enemy camp even changed sides voluntarily to support the king. Charles VII and his followers stood their ground to the last – the plan went against the rules of chivalry, after all – but Joan insisted that Charles should be crowned in

Reims. When the coronation celebrations began, she stood boldly by the altar, a white flag in her hand and dressed in her armour. It was almost as if she were placing the crown on the king's head herself.

Joan of Arc is summoned before the court

But then the tables turned against Joan.

To understand how this happened, we need to understand how superstitious people were back in her day. Joan's success rested on the belief that she had been sent by God; this idea brought hope to many people, and because of that, they were ready to follow her into battle. However, the English and the Burgundians saw things differently. They accused Joan of being a witch, primarily because she wanted to dismantle their power, but also because they were genuinely afraid of her. After all, she had snatched several victories from seemingly hopeless situations – the Devil had to be involved somehow!

The idea that people could gain supernatural powers from making a pact with the Devil was common then. The belief in witches spread, and the Church put those accused of witchcraft on trial in the courts; to this day, plenty of documents still exist where you can read about these proceedings. The first account of somebody being sentenced for witchcraft was written during Joan's lifetime; the accused in that case was a man. These witch trials often ended in death by burning.

For King Charles, the claim that Joan was a witch was doubly uncomfortable, as the English were now spreading the rumour that he had gained his crown with the Devil's help. The king refused to support Joan's campaign, so she travelled on to Paris from Reims without his permission to liberate more cities. This is when her luck ran out. She and her troops unsuccessfully laid siege to Paris and eventually she was captured by the Burgundians and put in prison. Now, the English and the Burgundians turned to the Church for help, as it was their job to investigate whether somebody was allied with the Devil.

Some spoke out against Joan. To them, the worst crime of all was that she had conducted her entire campaign dressed in men's clothing – for the Church, this was a crime in itself. She was also accused of killing people in battle, which was forbidden unless you were a soldier.

Joan was put on trial. Her responses to the judges' questions were so clever, quick-witted and assured that the trial was closed to the public and held over several days. The court was afraid she would cast a spell over her opponents. Between sessions, she was held in chains in a dark, cold dungeon.

The judges and Church officials did everything they could to extract a confession from her. They expected her to bow to the Church's authority and publicly admit that she had been sent by the Devil, and not by God. But Joan relied on her conscience and maintained that her orders had indeed come from God. If the Church wanted to dispute that, she said, she could do nothing to change their mind.

1431: Joan of Arc, the Maid of Orléans, is branded a heretic and burned at the stake. France becomes a kingdom.

Joan was sentenced to death at the trial because, behind the scenes, the English and the Burgundians were pulling the strings. They had the Maid of Orléans burned as a heretic so the whole of France would know that Charles wasn't the rightful king. When she died, Joan was just 19 years old.

However, Joan's successes on the battlefield had changed everything. One Burgundian city after another changed sides, perhaps because the idea of a French kingdom appealed to them. Those on the side of the king became stronger and stronger until, in the end, even the Burgundians deserted the English. In less than twenty years, the king's allies drove the English out of France. Joan's mission was fulfilled.

With France liberated and the Hundred Years War over, King Charles reopened the case against Joan. He wanted to show that mistakes had been made and that Joan had – in the words of one testimony – been put to death 'iniquitously and unreasonably, and most cruelly'. This was the only way he could refute English claims that he owed his throne to a woman who had been in league with the Devil. The sentence was officially repealed, and Joan of Arc entered the history of France as a martyr and a national hero.

THE END OF THE MIDDLE AGES, THE START OF THE MODERN ERA

Christine de Pizan

'I, Christine …' These were words written by an Italian woman in France in 1405. She didn't disguise herself in men's clothes, nor did she publish her writing under a male pseudonym, as many women after her continued to do. 'I, Christine,' she wrote, and with that a new era began. Maybe.

Perhaps the modern era began when the Abbess Kunigunde of Bohemia started translating religious texts into Czech at Prague Castle. After all, the nuns in her convent couldn't read most of the Latin text in the Bible. It wasn't long before a theologian followed Kunigunde's example. Jan Hus translated the entire Bible into Czech and held services where he preached in the local language. Suddenly, churchgoers could understand what was being said. He believed that people should trust God and the Bible more than the Church itself. Of course, the Church saw it differently. How much the Pope and bishops feared such radical opinions is clear from the fact that they had Jan Hus burned at the stake for heresy.

Or perhaps the beginning of the new era came when the poet Francesco Petrarca climbed the 'windy mountain', Mont Ventoux in France, and extolled the beauty of the landscape that spread out before him. The world, he proclaimed, was more than just a valley of despair where man must suffer and wait for deliverance. The world was glorious and it was waiting to be discovered.

For millennia, people had looked up to the sky and wondered how the world of the gods had been created. Now they turned away from

1405: Christine de Pizan is confident as she writes, 'I, Christine'. It is around this time that the Middle Ages ends, and the modern era begins.

1415: The Church reformer Jan Hus is condemned by the Church as a heretic and burned at the stake.

213

the sky and looked more closely at themselves and the world around them. Painters – who, until then, had focused on depicting the realm of angels and saints, setting scenes against a lustrous golden backdrop in the Byzantine style – now turned their attention to nature. They painted the sky blue as they saw it, and they developed a new drawing technique that allowed them to capture perspective and show their natural surroundings realistically on the canvas.

The Church couldn't stand in the way of this new era. People began to see themselves not merely as humble creations of God, but as the most superior beings that God had created – the crown of his creation.

All these changes ushered in a more human-centred outlook, sometimes called humanism, where scholars began to ask, 'What is man?' and 'What is his destiny?' By then, Christine de Pizan had already published her texts, which often asserted her perspective as a person by using the phrase 'I, Christine'. She had a thing or two to tell the world, as far as humanity was concerned.

This was the era of the Hundred Years War, which inflicted great suffering on the populations of England and France and their allies. Christine de Pizan railed against it. She reproached the nobility and complained that it was 'shameful that such a noble kingdom should make its poor people atone for something for which they are not to blame!'

Christine was familiar with courtly matters in France, having spent most of her life at the court of the French king. Her father was a scholar from Venice, well versed in medicine and astrology, and had been appointed to the court of King Charles V. It was there in the royal court that Christine grew up, married at 15 and had three children. Her husband and father both died in quick succession, leaving her alone without anyone to provide for her. In spite of her hardship, she refused to remarry and instead earned a modest income by translating books – until she realised that she herself could be a writer.

Writing gave her a medium to vent her anger. She was particularly indignant about the *Romance of the Rose*, a chivalrous love story in verse that was very popular at the time. In it, women were portrayed as cruel, spiteful creatures, who deserved to be scolded, beaten and abused by men. At one point, women were even referred to as dangerous monsters, who poisoned any man who came close. Christine was outraged. 'God would never have created anything as vile and evil,' she argued, 'as you depict women to be.'

It wasn't long before she wrote her most famous work, *The Book of the City of Ladies*. In it she imagined an alternative world where women were in charge.

Christine's criticism was by no means a condemnation of all men. She owed her education to her father, after all, and when her husband died early, she grieved deeply. But this didn't change her view of the suffering she saw imposed on many women, leading her to be critical of marriage. 'Alas, my dear friend,' she wrote to her daughter, 'you know yourself how many women there are who live a miserable life under the yoke of marriage, for whom the harsh ways of their husbands mean they suffer more than they would were they Slaves of the Saracens!'

In *The Book of the City of Ladies*, Christine explains why that is. Men who mistreat women and slander them, she argues, do so because they are jealous and envious, and because they are afraid of intelligent, capable women.

Christine realised what a powerful weapon her pen could be, and she directed it against the centuries-old entrenched convictions that her enemies exploited. She argued that women's souls were of no less value than men's. If women were allowed to learn and to take part, they could perform just as well as men, regardless of whether it was in science, art or politics – as demonstrated by the women who had occasionally come to power at various points in history. On the other hand, many men displayed exactly those deficiencies that women were accused of.

Christine de Pizan had an enthusiastic following among readers. She was admired by members of the nobility across Europe and had many patrons, including princes and English lords and even the Queen of France. But Christine, who had lost hope of seeing an end to the war between England and France, withdrew to a convent with her daughter. It was only when Joan of Arc liberated the city of Orléans that she regained hope: she now had evidence that there really was no domain where women couldn't match men, not even armed battle. Full of admiration, she wrote a poem about Joan of Arc.

But she did not live to see the fate of the Maid of Orléans; Christine de Pizan died before Joan was burned at the stake for heresy.

THE END OF THE BYZANTINE EMPIRE

The Ottomans take the golden apple

Let's take another look at the world map. The Roman Empire of antiquity had become the Christian kingdom, the Kingdom of God, as the Europeans believed in the Middle Ages. On the other side of the world was China. It seemed so far away that many Europeans thought of China and India as one and the same thing: vague places in the Far East where spices and silk came from.

But what about the vast area that lay between Europe and China? The peoples who lived here didn't belong to Europe or China or India, but neither did they form an independent entity. One exception was the Persian Empire, a long-standing rival of the Greeks, Romans and Byzantines. But neither Alexander the Great, nor the Arabs, nor the Mongols under Genghis Khan had succeeded in creating a permanent empire in the region south of the highlands of Persia, between the Bosphorus and the Hindu Kush. This only changed with Mehmet the Conqueror, a leader of the Turks. Like so many before them, the Turks moved west and subjugated large areas until they founded a kingdom in the fourteenth century that the Europeans called the Ottoman Empire. The Ottomans also had a covetous eye on the greatest jewel of the Middle Ages: Constantinople, the city on the Bosphorus that they called the 'golden apple'.

This time, Byzantium couldn't hold them back. Discord among Crusaders and the plundering of Constantinople had finally sealed the division between the Roman Catholic West and the Greek

Orthodox East. The Byzantine emperor lost one region after the other, and finally the Ottomans managed what no other foreign power had succeeded in doing: they took the golden apple. In celebration of their proud victory, they changed Constantinople's name to Istanbul and made it the new capital of their empire.

Greek scholars and priests fled to Italy, and those who deeply resented the Western betrayal were received by their Orthodox brethren in Russia. This led many to dub Moscow the 'Third Rome', now that the 'Second Rome' – Constantinople, founded on the Bosphorus by Emperor Constantine – had fallen to the Muslim Ottomans.

The Ottomans became serious players on the world scene. Over the next few centuries they made their way deep into Europe, conquering much of the territory between Constantinople and Vienna: Greece, Serbia, Croatia and Bulgaria. Their army was strong and their notorious elite troops, the Janissaries, were dreaded warriors. And since most of the Turks had become Muslims through contact with the Arabs, their sultan also laid claim to the caliphate and to the position as the leader of all Muslims – after all, the majority of Muslims now lived within his empire. The conquest-hungry Ottoman rulers soon had their sights on a new golden apple: the city of Vienna. But, unlike Constantinople, they did not manage to take it.

1453: The Ottomans conquer Constantinople and make it their capital, renaming it Istanbul. This marks the end of the Byzantine Empire.

THE RENAISSANCE

A time of rebirth and revival

Books can change the course of history. It may happen more often than we realise. After the Turks seized Constantinople, countless Greek books made their way to Italy, and from there the rest of Europe. These were books from Byzantium and Spain that were, like their people, displaced by ongoing conflict between Christians and Muslims. Many scholars fled from the fighting, taking their books with them.

This influx of books was rich food for thought for the painters, musicians, philosophers and poets of this new era. They discovered that much of what was occupying their thoughts had already been explored by the Ancient Greeks and Romans, and that they had forgotten their own history. There was great excitement as they uncovered the treasures of antiquity. They admired ancient architecture, studying its forms and patterns; they marvelled at how lifelike classical sculpture was; and they began to imitate the ancient world. Historians later called this 'the Renaissance', which means 'rebirth' in French; the art and literature of the Ancient Greeks and Romans was brought back to life, and so too were their philosophical and political ideas. This all fed the curiosity of scholars and artists, and inspired them to create something new.

The humanists, who were particularly interested in education, rediscovered the writings of Plato and held them up against those of Aristotle. From Plato they took on the idea that man passes through many stages of knowledge on the path towards what is good. The new man sought this goodness in himself and in nature, and it revealed itself in truth and beauty.

The artists of the Renaissance recognised not only the sublime dignity of nature and of man, but also their intrinsic value as individuals. They said, 'I, Leonardo', or 'I, Titian', but as they were painters rather than writers like Christine de Pizan, they expressed this in their painting by portraying themselves.

It is hard to imagine, but this idea of art did not exist in the Middle Ages. Until the Renaissance, craftsmen did not receive personal recognition for their work; works of art or craft were seen as creations of God. A new artistic approach had emerged with the troubadours and performers of the medieval courts, including poets like Marie de France, and by now the arts were really taking off. Artworks were created that were no longer intended purely for religious edification. There were poets writing plays, composers producing choral works and later even operas. They composed secular music, aimed solely at providing pleasure to its audiences; the same was happening in literature and painting. Art was beginning to break away from its religious purpose and develop a life of its own.

It would not have been possible for these artists to create their marvellous work, were it not for the people who recognised their talent and extraordinary achievements and sponsored them financially. These patrons, as they were known, were often women – ladies, princesses and other noble women – who had the wealth and influence to invite artists to their court. Some patrons themselves became famous for their support of the arts, such as Isabella d'Este, the sister of the Duke of Ferrara, who married the Prince of Mantua, a city in northern Italy. She made her husband's principality a centre of Renaissance art by inviting musicians, poets, painters and philosophers to their court. Leonardo da Vinci and Titian painted portraits of her in gratitude and, as she was not only highly educated but also very beautiful, she became a fashion guru for ladies across Europe. She was called *la prima donna del mondo* – the first lady of the world.

Leonardo da Vinci became famous for his paintings, especially *The Mona Lisa* and *The Last Supper*. But da Vinci was fascinated by much more than just painting; he wanted to know the causes of things. Because he dabbled in almost everything, he has been described as a universal genius. He built machines; designed buildings and bridges; and dissected corpses with doctors, because he

1484: In the Renaissance, people no longer look only to God, but to themselves. The 13-year-old Albrecht Dürer draws the oldest surviving self-portrait.

wanted to know how to draw a human being accurately, with all the details of muscles and hair and everything in proportion. He was probably one of the first scholars ever to look analytically at the female body and to test Aristotle's theory that boys sat in their mother's womb on the right-hand side and girls on the left. Leonardo da Vinci had so many ideas that he couldn't act upon most of them, so he left behind thousands of notes and sketches, some of which are still used today – to help us build bridges, for example. For this reason we tend to think of this period as the start of the modern era, an epoch of history which stretches to the present day. It began with people like Christine de Pizan and, later, Leonardo da Vinci, whose ideas are as relevant today as ever.

Even before this new era had begun, the Italian mathematician Fibonacci had noticed that the Arabs counted using digits from 0 to 9, and that they could do much more advanced arithmetic than the Europeans with their complicated Roman numerals. This counting system was one the Arabs had previously imported from India. The new numbers made it easier for European merchants to keep track of their money, and for painters and observers of the natural world to measure and to calculate. This in turn inspired the humanists in their drive to discover and change the world.

Philosophy, mathematics, art, thinking about God and exploring the world – all these things were still very closely entwined. It was a bishop, Nicholas of Cusa, who realised that, mathematically speaking, numbers carried on until infinity. He was one of the earliest astronomers to suspect that the Earth revolved around the Sun, not the other way round. This was a departure from the Church's official position that the Earth was the fixed unmoving central point around which orbited the planets and the Sun. The scientist who finally proved this misconception wrong was called Copernicus. It is the Sun that does not move, he wrote, and the Earth, like the other planets, revolves around it in an elliptical orbit.

Such ideas eroded the authority of the Church, which all of a sudden was facing competition from all sides. Suddenly, people asked themselves who could best explain the world. Was it the Church? Or was it the scientists who, with their new-fangled methods, were investigating the nature of the world and of mankind? With the

1543: Nicolaus Copernicus turns the Church's world view upside down by asserting that the Sun does not revolve around the Earth, but the Earth revolves around the Sun.

emergence of universal geniuses who prodded and probed everything, the Church was losing its claim of universality; it was no longer the master of all walks of life.

The beginning of a dispute that rumbles on to this day

This was a time of explosive new ideas – but it was still easier to accept that the Earth revolved around the Sun than to imagine that women could be equal to men. Christine de Pizan had started something completely new when she raised the question of women. She had initiated the *querelle des femmes*: the public debate about the role of women. 'The woman question' became one of the first debates to continue for centuries – it's still the focus of fierce debate today.

Around 1400: The *querelle des femmes* begins – the public debate about women.

Some say the real revolution came in 1440 when Johannes Gutenberg invented the printing press, which greatly simplified the reproduction of books. Until then, every page of a book had to be individually carved onto a wooden plate; to print an entire book, hundreds of these time-consuming plates had to be made by hand. Instead, Gutenberg had the idea of producing movable letter blocks that could be arranged on a frame in any order to make up a page of text. This invention not only made it much easier to print books, but also much cheaper, and the impact was spectacular. Small, mass-produced booklets or pamphlets could be produced quickly and distributed among eager readers – by the time the authorities heard about a publication's content and decided to ban it, they were usually too late. For the first time in history, people had a means of mass communication. While the majority of books in the Middle Ages had been written in Latin and were only read and discussed by scholars, all of a sudden anyone could learn and form an opinion about a topic, and because people could pass on the content of these short pamphlets by word of mouth, it meant everyone from the farmer's wife to the baker could keep abreast of the topics of the day, whether or not they could read.

Around 1440: Johannes Gutenberg invents a printing press with movable type.

The debate about women picked up momentum with the development of letterpress printing. In Italy, a philosopher by the name of Pico della Mirandola published a text exploring the meaning of human dignity called *Oration on the Dignity of Man*. The obvious next question was whether women should be granted the same dignity as men. Many humanists were serious about the pursuit of good, and they had to admit that Christine de Pizan was right in denouncing the way women were treated.

Now it was men who were publishing books in defence of women. In the late fourteenth century Giovanni Boccaccio, a close friend of Francesco Petrarca (who climbed Mont Ventoux to get a good view of the world), had published a work entitled *On Famous Women*. Boccaccio was highly respected at the time, and his book dealing exclusively with women – the first collection of women's biographies ever written – had an explosive impact. Another Italian author wrote *On the Superiority and Dignity of Women*, while in Germany the scholar Agrippa von Nettesheim wrote his *Declamation on the Nobility and Pre-Eminence of the Female Sex*, a work that caused such a stir it was immediately translated into six other languages.

These writings praising the virtues of women were not without opposition. One pamphlet was published with the provocative title *Are Women Human?* The author, who did not have the courage to reveal his name, answered the question with a firm 'no'. Some say the text was probably intended to be ironic, but the irony was quickly lost in the clamour of fierce debate that ensued. Many readers were outraged, others agreed with it, and it inspired several satirical parodies. But the fact that it was translated into many languages and reprinted in countless editions over the course of 200 years suggests that it was certainly taken seriously by enough readers to keep it in print. When it was published in Italian, the Church instantly put it on the Index of Forbidden Books (which banned Catholics from reading them), and in Germany, pastors produced special documentation to assert that women were indeed human.

It was 100 years after the death of Christine de Pizan, who had courageously spoken out against the unfair treatment of women, and nothing could be taken as truth or certainty. Were Aristotle and Thomas Aquinas right to claim that woman was a mishap of nature, a defective version of man? Had God created women only to bear children and to serve their husbands? Were women weaker than men, and was this true only of their physical strength or also of their character and intellect? All these questions were hotly debated, and Christian and Jewish scholars found suitable sacred texts to support any point of view. A Jewish author in the sixteenth century argued that women were of even greater worth than men, due to 'the fact that Adam was created from dust, while Eve was from Adam's rib'. He also claimed that women were just as rational as men, and he found that their strength was especially evident in the pain they suffered during childbirth. This debate about the role and status of women – the *querelle des femmes* – which began in the Renaissance, has still not gone away.

THE DISCOVERY OF AMERICA

The Catholic Monarchs

Suddenly there they are: women making world history. Christine de Pizan, who picked up her pen and launched the battle for the rights of women; Joan of Arc, who rallied the people around her against the will of the authorities; and now there was a powerful female ruler on the Spanish throne, Isabella I of Castile.

Muslims had conquered Spain in the eighth century, and the combination of Jewish, Christian and Arab influences led to a blossoming of culture. But with the Crusades, Christians had begun to reclaim parts of Spain. They called this the *Reconquista* – 'the reconquest'. When Isabella of Castile married Prince Ferdinand II of Aragon, their joint dominions made them rulers of almost the entire Iberian Peninsula. Together, they completed the *Reconquista* and expelled the last Muslim rulers from Spain after more than 700 years.

Isabella and Ferdinand, the new rulers of Spain, declared war against all who were not Christian, setting themselves up as the new protectors of the Church. This pleased the Pope in Rome, who had already sent the Crusaders against the Muslims, and he honoured Isabella and Ferdinand with the title of 'the Catholic Monarchs'. He wanted to show the entire world that the Pope and Spain were Europe's new, powerful alliance.

The Arabs would never recover from the defeats they had suffered since the start of the Crusades. Their territories in the east were conquered by the Ottoman Turks, and in the west they were pushed back by the Europeans. This led to the downfall of their culture – a culture that had given the world so much knowledge about mathematics, medicine and astronomy, and had preserved ancient texts.

Isabella and Ferdinand had no interest in the achievements of the Arabs or in the fact that Muslims, Jews and Christians had lived together peacefully in the Iberian Peninsula for many centuries. On the contrary: the royal couple intended to unite the Spaniards. To do that, they turned to religion; anyone who belonged to the Spanish nation had to be Christian. As soon as they had conquered the last remaining Muslim province of Granada, Isabella and Ferdinand issued a law that forced all Jews and Muslims to convert to Christianity. Those who refused had to leave the country.

Soon the demands became more radical. Now a Spaniard had to be not only Christian, but also of 'pure blood' – it was only possible to stay in Spain if you were a Christian by birth, and not a Muslim or a Jew who had converted to Christianity. The new laws forced many people to flee the country. Spanish Jews moved to the Balkans, Holland, France or Germany, while others, mostly Muslims, sought protection in North Africa under the rule of the Ottomans. The Arabs and Jews expelled from Spain took their knowledge and good trade relations and contributed to the increasing wealth of the Ottoman Empire. The Ottomans demanded high tariffs for the transport of goods along the Silk Road. Those who weren't able to establish strong trade contracts with the Ottomans fast enough, like certain Italian merchants, found importing goods from the East became prohibitively expensive.

1492: Isabella of Castile and Ferdinand of Aragon expel the Jews and Muslims from Spain.

New sea routes ...

It was time to find new routes. A Portuguese prince known as Henry the Navigator looked out onto the ocean from the south-western tip of Europe and wondered whether it might be easier to reach India by sea, sailing south and around Africa. Until then, the continent of Africa was largely *terra incognita* for the Europeans – an 'unknown land'. Although Egypt and the Mediterranean coasts of Africa and the Near East had long been part of the known world, it was only Arab traders who had travelled beyond the Sahara.

It was a long time until the Portuguese sailors managed to circum-navigate Africa. At the southern tip there were dangerous rocks in the sea, and violent storms drove many unlucky ships into the cliffs, where they shattered and perished. But in the late fifteenth century, the Portuguese circled the 'Cape of Storms', which they renamed the 'Cape of Good Hope' – they had discovered a new, cost-effective route to India, winning a huge advantage over the Spaniards.

1487: The Portuguese are the first Europeans to sail around the southernmost tip of Africa.

You might think that sailors would have been in high demand at the court of the Portuguese king, but when Christopher Columbus, a sailor from Genoa, proposed a new, even more daring adventure, the Portuguese turned him away. Columbus was convinced that, if the Earth was a globe, then you ought to reach India eventually if you set sail in the other direction. He failed to persuade the Portuguese to back his radical idea.

After years of trying to find a financial backer, Columbus was finally given a chance by Isabella of Castile. She was also sceptical and didn't want to pay for more than three ships, but Columbus was tired of begging for funds and so had to be content with her offer. He set sail, aiming for India or, more precisely, a port city in China; China and India were so far off they seemed like much of a muchness.

1492: Christopher Columbus discovers America.

When Columbus and his crew finally saw a large island on the horizon after seventy days at sea, they had no idea that beyond it lay America, a continent they had never heard of. They believed they had reached India, which is why they called the inhabitants 'Indians' and the archipelago the 'West Indies'. The inhabitants of America were astonished by the tall Spaniards with their pale skin, who appeared out of the blue on their wooden ships. They thought they must be supernatural beings, like gods.

... and a new world

For millennia, merchants had been travelling to remote areas. The Viking Leif Erikson had sailed with his fleet to the American continent nearly 500 years before Columbus. But when the Portuguese circumnavigated Africa to sail to India and shortly afterwards the

Spaniards set sail for America, they did not come as visitors, but as conquerors. In Spanish they were called *conquistadores*, which entered English as 'conquistadors'. Instead of exchanging goods with the inhabitants of Africa, India and the New World, they used armed force and tactical prowess to seize everything that could potentially bring them wealth. The Portuguese and Spaniards began to subjugate other parts of the world.

The Church raised no objection. On the contrary, the Pope gave the Spaniards permission to take possession of the land they called 'New Spain', and he called on the conquistadors to convert the people of the New World to Christianity. The Pope simply staked his claim to this distant territory, thousands of miles away. It didn't occur to the Christians to question whether the Pope actually had the right to decide the fate of this far-flung continent.

La Malinche helps Cortés conquer Mexico

On his first voyage to the Americas, Columbus landed on the island of Hispaniola. By the time Queen Isabella died twelve years later, the Spaniards had assumed control of this island and a few others, with Cuba as their administrative base. All they knew of the mainland that lay beyond were the rumours they had heard. It was said that there was a vast empire with a powerful king, and it seemed unlikely at first that the small number of conquistadors could prevail against such might.

The mysterious ruler was called Montezuma. He was the King of the Aztecs, who had subjugated numerous smaller kingdoms in the region and demanded tribute payments from them in the form of corn, beans, pumpkins, cocoa and cotton. The Aztecs had built their capital Tenochtitlán on a series of islands in a large lake. It was a thriving metropolis with three times as many inhabitants as the largest European cities, and at the centre were temples and palaces harbouring treasures of gold and precious stones. The temples were built as stepped pyramids, and one contained a skull platform engraved with thousands of skulls: artistic evidence of the human sacrifices the Aztecs made to their god Huitzilopochtli and other deities.

The cities of the Aztecs were not only much larger than Paris or London at that time, some parts were even older than the Egyptian pyramids. They had running water and clean streets lined with gardens, and in Tenochtitlán, people used small, narrow fields that ran in strips alongside canals to grow food in the middle of the city. The Aztecs had mastered the art of growing corn, and in the Amazon region they knew how to use the rainforest without destroying it.

Before the Europeans came, the Native Americans had never seen horses and their weapons were basic, but they were experienced warriors and vastly outnumbered the conquistadors. It was therefore almost a miracle that Hernán Cortés defeated the Aztecs with only a few ships and very limited troops. Who knows if he would have succeeded were it not for La Malinche.

When the Spaniards first set foot on the soil of the Mexican mainland, they encountered and fought a Mayan tribe. When the Spaniards triumphed, the indigenous people gave them twenty slave girls in tribute. Among them was La Malinche. She came from a noble family, but had been sold to the Maya by her mother after the death of her father. The conquistadors always travelled with priests, so they first had the girls baptised and then shared them out among the men.

Cortés soon discovered that La Malinche could speak the language of the Aztecs as well as that of the Maya, and it wasn't long before she spoke Spanish, too. With La Malinche interpreting for him, he found that many tribes within the Aztec Empire were unhappy and felt little connection to Montezuma – something that the Spaniards could take advantage of. La Malinche helped Cortés forge alliances with some of the tribal chiefs, which enabled him to develop a small army to fight alongside the Spaniards as they battled their way step by step to Tenochtitlán.

Once, an Aztec woman warned La Malinche of a plot to ambush the Spaniards at the city of Cholula. The woman offered to help La Malinche return to the Aztecs and to find her a safe place to hide during the attack, but Cortés's interpreter turned down the offer, and instead warned Cortés and his men. The Spaniards were able to resist the attack and slaughtered the plotters and much of the local population. This became known as the Cholula Massacre.

When Cortés and Montezuma first met face to face, La Malinche interpreted between them. But the two did not see eye to eye. One thing was clear: either Cortés would fail in his great adventure, or Montezuma was doomed. The Spaniards finally came out on top after many bloody battles and the Aztecs' fate was sealed. One of Cortés's soldiers wrote later about the conquest of Mexico: 'Without La Malinche, we would not have understood the Mexican language', and 'With God's will we accomplished much, but only with her help'.

Around 1520: Hernán Cortés and La Malinche conquer the Aztec Empire.

We don't know why La Malinche was loyal to the Spaniards, her new masters, but she could not have foreseen the far-reaching consequences of those events. Cortés's victory over the Aztecs was only the beginning. The European conquerors brought irreversible destruction to the cultures of the Aztecs, Maya and Inca – America's indigenous inhabitants.

Of Amazons and human sacrifices

Fate came to the aid of the conquistadors in their campaign against the indigenous peoples. The Europeans carried with them diseases which hadn't previously existed in America, such as smallpox and measles. This meant the locals had no immunity to protect them against the onslaught of these highly infectious diseases, which raged through the native population sowing a trail of destruction. By the time the conquistadors moved south of Central America to conquer the Caribbean and Mexico, the viruses were already well ahead of them.

The mood in the south was similar to that among the Aztecs. The Incas had founded a vast empire by defeating and subjugating their neighbours, and here too the Spaniards succeeded in winning allies among the locals who joined their campaign against the Incas. A man named Francisco de Orellana followed in the wake of the conquistadors, and he set off in a boat to explore the largest river in South America. A priest later noted in his diary that Orellana had described an amazing encounter on his return: he had faced an army with ten or twelve women on the front line – Amazons, as the Greeks would call them. It has been suggested that the River Amazon was named after them.

The Spaniards were intrigued by the Native Americans, but they also felt superior to them. Their lives seemed primitive to them and the Europeans were shocked by their custom of killing people in sacrifice to the gods. In the Inca culture, the chosen victims were beheaded, drowned or killed by other means, while the Aztecs cut young people's hearts out of their living bodies to appease the gods. The Aztecs waged a series of wars – known as flower wars – against their neighbours to win captives to sacrifice at their temples. Perhaps unsurprisingly, the oppressed subjects of the Incan Empire preferred to ally themselves with the Spaniards. The conquistadors felt validated in their belief that their religion of charity and tolerance was superior to the barbaric customs of the natives, but they showed little charity towards the people of America.

Las Casas fails

The conquistadors knew that their Spanish rulers were far away – too far away to be able to enforce the law across the Atlantic. New Spain belonged officially to the Spanish monarchy and the conquistadors were obliged to pay most of the silver and gold they found to the treasury, but nobody could really monitor how much wealth the conquerors were taking to line their own pockets.

Unfortunately, there was also no way of monitoring to what extent the conquistadors were acting on the Christian values of charity and tolerance. In flagrant disregard of directions from the Spanish monarchs and the Pope, the invading Spaniards enslaved the inhabitants and treated them like livestock. In fact, they regarded them with even less respect than livestock, wrote Bartolomé de las Casas, a Spanish monk who saw the injustice: 'They had less respect for them than the excrement on the streets.'

Las Casas described some horrific scenes:

A certain Spanish commander had set out with his troops to rob and plunder, when they came upon a mountain where a considerable number of people were seeking refuge, hiding from the heinous and cruel actions of the Christians. These Christians immediately fell upon the refugees, slayed those that they could, and carried away seventy to eighty girls and women. The next day the Indians rallied in crowds, pursuing the Christians with the intention of fighting for the return of their wives and daughters. When the Christians were cornered, they refused to return what they had looted, but instead plunged their daggers into the bellies of the girls and women and left not one of those eighty souls alive. The Indians, who could have torn out their bowels in pain at the sight, lamented in abject despair and shouted: 'O you wicked people! You callous Christians! You would kill even women?' By this they meant that to murder a woman was an atrocity perpetrated by only the most hard-hearted, wicked monsters.

The slaves were exploited for heavy labour, forced to chip away at the rock deep down in the silver mines and to sieve for gold from the rivers. The conquerors divided the land among themselves and set the local people to work in the fields or made them work as servants in their houses. Especially cruel masters did not even feed their workers, so they died of starvation and disease. They didn't care in the slightest about their slaves, whom they saw as property, as they could simply replace any who died with new ones.

There were more compassionate Christians like Las Casas and other priests and monks who tried to prevent abuse and injustice, but they were almost always too late to stop the conquistadors. Las Casas despaired when he realised that the Native American population of the Caribbean islands had been practically wiped out by the time he arrived there. So he travelled south, racing to catch up with the Spaniards who planned to conquer the Incan Empire next.

Since his lobbying had no effect in the New World, Las Casas kept sailing back to Spain to make himself heard there. He told the king what the conquerors were doing in the name of the Spanish Crown, and achieved at least some success. The most significant

1515–66: Bartolomé de Las Casas campaigns against the un-Christian atrocities committed by the conquistadors in the New World.

1542: 'New Laws of the Indies' are written to prevent mistreatment of indigenous peoples.

response came in the form of the 1452 'New Laws of the Indies' by King Charles V, the grandson of Isabella of Castile, which decreed that Spaniards were forbidden from taking indigenous people as slaves, and all previously enslaved people were freed. Charles V proclaimed: 'The inhabitants of the West Indies shall be treated in the same manner as the free subjects of the crown of Castile, for there is no difference between one and the other.'

But Las Casas's victory was short-lived. The wealth of the Spanish entrepreneurs was based on exploiting the indigenous people – and as the Spanish king also benefitted from their income, within three years they had managed to pressure him into completely overturning the laws.

The two faces of Janus

The ancient Romans had a god they called Janus, who had two faces which looked in opposite directions. One saw life while the other saw death; what was joy for one was grief for the other; what one saw as the end, the other saw as a new beginning.

So it was with the discovery of America. Even today we marvel at the achievements of intrepid explorers like Columbus, who set sail across the Atlantic with only three ships, or Hernán Cortés and La Malinche, who conquered the vast Aztec Empire in what is now Mexico with their miniscule army. At that time, something completely new began in world history: a long process in which the whole world became more or less European.

But where one face of Janus sees glorious victories, the other sees ruin. When the Europeans first set foot on American soil in 1492, there were millions of people living on the Caribbean islands, in Cuba, the Bahamas, Jamaica and Puerto Rico, and on the American mainland. Forty years after the arrival of the Spaniards, only one in ten had survived: the indigenous population had been decimated. We should remember not only Columbus, but also the monk Bartolomé de las Casas, who bore witness as the inhabitants of America were exploited, oppressed, mistreated and subjected to shocking violence. Las Casas documented it all so that future generations might understand that the discovery of the New World was not only the start of something new, but also the brutal end of something else. Soon there was very little left of the indigenous cultures of the Americas.

The impact of Las Casas's desperate struggle was that the Church began to discuss whether the Native Americans were *human* in the Christian sense, and whether they even deserved to be granted the same rights as Christians. Wasn't there ample evidence against it? Didn't the fact that the Americans were of a different skin colour mean something? And what about the fact that they led a more primitive life, as the Europeans were finding out?

What was said in Europe about people of different skin colours was similar to the arguments the humanists had come up against regarding the dignity of women. On the one hand, oppressors sought to justify their actions. Their brutal treatment of slaves was unprecedented, and in the centuries that followed, slavery would become far more inhumane and cruel than it was even in ancient times. On the other hand, the debate eventually led to the conviction that all people had equal rights as human beings; when this idea finally prevailed, slavery was banned. But in the times of Columbus and Las Casas, this idea of universal human rights was still far off in the future.

FROM AMERICA TO CHINA

THE MIDDLE KINGDOM SHUTS ITSELF OFF

Chinese conquest

The fact that the Europeans managed to sail around the tip of Africa and cross the Atlantic Ocean is astonishing, because they were technologically much less advanced than the Chinese, who were also wealthier. Certain inventions were made in China some 100 or 500 years before they were thought of in Europe, and others – such as the wheelbarrow or cast iron – existed an amazing 1,500 years before anything similar became known in Europe. The Chinese were printing books, using gunpowder, drinking tea from porcelain cups and playing golf long before the Europeans. They came up with practical inventions like chemical insecticides and the fishing reel, and they used a magnetic compass to find their way at sea.

The Chinese ships also exceeded anything the Europeans had ever seen before in terms of size and technical equipment. Just as the Portuguese Prince Henry the Navigator was leading his crew on their first daring expeditions along the African coast, the Chinese Yongle Emperor sent his naval commander, Admiral Zheng He, with a fleet of ships on a voyage west to explore the oceans of the world.

1405: Zheng He sets out on his first sea voyage to India. In the course of several trips he reaches Africa.

Zheng He sailed around all of South East Asia and the Arabian Peninsula, made a detour on the east coast of Africa and sailed up the Red Sea almost all the way up to Mecca. His 'treasure ship' was 120 metres in length – nearly five times as long as Columbus's ship, the *Santa Maria* – and, while Columbus had needed years to raise the funds for just three ships, the Yongle Emperor straight away provided his admiral with a fleet of 317 ships. With their multistoried treasure ships, escort ships, cavalry ships and warships, a crew of 28,000 men and countless gifts, the Chinese must have made quite an impression wherever they arrived, like something out of an epic legend. Indeed, that was precisely the purpose of the journey: Zheng He was commissioned to display the might of the Chinese Emperor. He was to impress the barbarians to such an extent that they could do nothing else but bow their heads to China.

Zheng He brought back medicines and exotic animals: ostriches, antelopes, rhinos, zebras and a giraffe from the west coast of Africa. The Chinese saw the giraffe as an embodiment of the mythical *qilin*, something like the unicorn, and a symbol of good governance. The Yongle Emperor personally welcomed the giraffe to his imperial menagerie.

Let's briefly return to where we left China some time ago: after the heyday of the Tang dynasty in the tenth century, the empire had been besieged by Turks, Arabs and Mongols, and its borders had been pushed eastwards. The following centuries were marked by constant confrontation with the Mongols, who forged a huge empire under their leader Genghis Khan, ruling half of the world for a while. Even China could not stand up to Genghis Khan's hordes and was forced to accept foreign rule under his grandson Kublai Khan. This lasted until an ancestor of the Yongle Emperor finally overthrew the Mongols and took the reins as emperor of a new Chinese dynasty, the Ming.

In spite of all the turmoil and upheavals, China remained astonishingly stable in many ways. For over 1,000 years, its inhabitants saw their country as the 'Middle Kingdom' and believed that their emperor had a 'mandate from heaven' to rule the entire world. His power guaranteed that people lived in accordance with the universe. The Yongle Emperor built the Forbidden City, so named because only members of the imperial court could enter, which encompassed the imperial palace complex in the heart of Beijing. Its most important building was the Hall of Supreme Harmony, which was surrounded by the Hall of Central Harmony, the Hall of Preserving Harmony and the Palace of Heavenly Purity. The Ming dynasty could hardly express more clearly how they understood their rule as being central to the order of the cosmos. It seemed so natural and self-evident to them that they did not even think of conquering foreign lands; after all, all humans were part of the 'cosmic order', and so it followed that it was in everyone's own interest to recognise the Chinese emperor as ruler.

After the Yongle Emperor's death, there was a sudden change in China's politics. It had always been a challenge to hold together the huge empire of the Middle Kingdom, but now maritime trade was bringing in outside influences which posed a threat to its stability. To protect itself, China sealed itself off from the outside world. This meant an end to trade on the high seas: ships were destroyed and nautical charts and logbooks were burned. The empire turned its focus to building the Great Wall of China, which became the symbol of a closed-off empire.

1434: Chinese Emperor Xuanzong forbids overseas navigation and all ships are destroyed. China closes itself off and leaves it to European sailors to discover the world.

LOSS OF POWER AND SCHISM IN THE CHURCH

One woman speaks out against the Inquisition

Let's head back to Europe now, where Marguerite Porete and Joan of Arc were burned at the stake because they ignored rules and convention, and were seen as a threat to the social order. Since then, increasing numbers of people were accused of witchcraft and prosecuted. A clergyman called Heinrich Kramer called for a mass witch hunt and even obtained a special permit from the Pope in Rome. He published a large book called *Malleus Maleficarum*, also known as *The Hammer of the Witches*, in which he explained how to identify a witch. Although men were also convicted, he argued that most witches were women – justified by referring to women's 'well-known character defects'.

Officially, the Spanish Inquisition condemned witch-hunting and this guide to identifying witches as cruel and inhumane. But the inquisitors themselves created a climate of mistrust and fear. Anyone could accuse their neighbour of witchcraft, and anyone could be suspected and accused at any moment. No one was immune from allegations; even priests and bishops could be accused. People were often tortured until they confessed. Afraid of being condemned by the Inquisition, pious churchgoers became extremely strict on themselves, outwardly at least, even harming themselves as proof of their faith. It was during this time that a nun became well known in Spain: Teresa of Ávila, the founder of her own monastic order and several new convents.

1486: The German monk Heinrich Kramer publishes the *Malleus Maleficarum*.

St Teresa of Ávila decided as a young girl that she wanted to be a nun. But when she joined a convent, she was shocked to find it was not the quiet and austere place it should be; it had been corrupted by wealth. Determined to devote her time to meditation, she had a mystical experience where she met God, and this vision gave her the courage to write down what she had learnt. But this meant treading a dangerous path. The Inquisition was quick to declare women who discussed theological issues to be heretics or witches and to burn them at the stake. Teresa knew the danger and spent a long time examining what she had experienced before she wrote down her thoughts.

Disapproving of life in the convent, Teresa wanted to leave and found her own. But, when she finally received permission, this move triggered outrage in Ávila. The abbess of the convent ordered her to return, and city councillors and Church officials were up in arms at what they saw as her acting on her own initiative and without the authority of the Church. It was only when influential supporters from higher circles intervened that she was allowed to go.

1562: Teresa of Ávila establishes her first convent.

While meditating, Teresa had learned that excessively strict asceticism could be just as harmful as too much luxury. She did not think much of the way Christians were encouraged to treat their bodies harshly, to fast, sleep on the hard ground and hurt themselves. Instead, she wrote, 'Be kind to your body so that your soul feels like living in it'. She was horrified by the strict punishments people carried out as penitence for their sins. 'God save me from the saints with their morose faces,' she once said. With words such as this, Teresa of Ávila turned against the spirit of the Inquisition, and that bleak era when even one wrong word was enough to get you burned at the stake. Even more than that, she railed against a much older Christian tradition of contempt for the body, repression of sensuality and rejection of the individual's physical needs. Daring to say, 'Be kind to your body', as she did, meant a lot.

As it turned out, there were a lot of believers who felt the same. They joined Teresa and eventually she got Church approval to set up her own monastic order and to found monasteries and convents across Spain.

Of course Teresa had her share of opponents. One clergyman called her a 'restless, wandering woman who is disobedient and stubborn'.

Others reported her to the Inquisition, but the court reviewed Teresa's writings and acquitted her on all counts. The Pope himself did not see any harm in her ideas and was impressed by her, issuing a decree that gave her monasteries official approval and secured the future of Teresa's monastic order.

The Church contradicts itself

It was a troubled time. In America, monks and priests were desperately campaigning against the atrocities committed by the colonisers. Back in Europe, meanwhile, more and more people noticed how the Inquisition was spreading fear and terror, while many bishops and priests had themselves strayed from the path of Christian virtues.

This was clear to see at a wedding in Rome that boasted such pomp and ceremony that many onlookers presumed the couple tying the knot were royalty. But the father of the bride, who paid for the flamboyant dresses, the extravagant jewellery and the luxurious festivities, was not a monarch – he was the Pope.

1501: In Rome, Lucrezia Borgia – the daughter of the Pope – celebrates her wedding in extravagant style.

Officially, of course, the Pope wasn't even allowed to have children; Lucrezia Borgia was his illegitimate daughter. But he was not alone in flouting this Church rule: many priests and clergymen had wives and children and, like Lucrezia's father, they bought themselves influence with expensive gifts or bribes, and plotted against each other. It was known for a clergyman in high office to lock a fellow Church leader away in a dungeon or even be involved in assassination plots. When Lucrezia's father – the most rich and powerful of all rich and powerful Church leaders – became Pope, he chose for himself the name Alexander VI. He wanted to be associated with Alexander the Great, comparing himself to a conqueror remembered above all for waging war. The Church seemed to have completely lost its way.

Lucrezia and her father went down in history as particularly ruthless, greedy and power-hungry individuals, in part because Lucrezia's first husband was murdered and her father, the Pope, was implicated. These events fuelled wild speculation among the Italians: rumours abounded of romance, scandal and betrayal in ever bolder colours.

But this image doesn't do justice to the Pope and his daughter Lucrezia. Pope Alexander was a hardworking and successful Church politician: he campaigned for the Christian mission overseas and granted protection to the displaced Jews in Rome, much to the annoyance of Isabella of Castile, who had expelled all non-Christians from Spain. Lucrezia, too, was described by her contemporaries as educated, warm-hearted and considerate. Like her father, she spoke up in defence of Jews, and she also invested her wealth in hospitals and monasteries.

In the end, however, all that people remembered were the suspicious rumours and Lucrezia's luxurious wedding. Both factors contributed to growing criticism of the Church and its leaders in Rome.

The Reformation

Long before the Inquisition was established, a man named John Wyclif had spoken out in England. He didn't think that the Pope should have any power – that power was for kings and princes, not representatives of the Church. He was very fortunate that many followers rallied around him, because their support meant Church leaders didn't dare condemn him to death for his views. When Jan Hus expressed similar views in Prague, he had been silenced by execution.

One hundred years later, these ideas were taken up again by Martin Luther, an Augustinian monk from Germany who had left the monastery to become a professor of theology. He argued that there was only one way out of the crisis that the Church found itself in. Wyclif, Hus and Luther all preached that believers should look to God for direction, and to God alone. 'A Christian is a free lord over all things, and his faith subjects him to no one,' wrote Luther. Everyone should decide for themselves how to behave and should be guided only by what is in the Bible. These were intoxicating words: Luther might as well have said that Christians should think for themselves, instead of believing what the Church dictated to them.

Unlike his predecessors, Luther wasn't so easy to silence. Thanks to Gutenberg inventing the printing press, it was now relatively cheap and easy to print books, and especially pamphlets, which were very popular and spread quickly throughout the population. Attempts to silence him wouldn't have helped, whether by execution or other means. His criticism of the Church had created a wide and impassioned following. Luther was well aware of this; in his *Ninety-five Theses*, he summarised his grievances with the Church in the form of a list of questions and comments. He made this document public in his hometown of Wittenberg and this, it is said, was the moment that kickstarted the Reformation.

After the *Ninety-five Theses* were published, the Pope tried to force Luther, in the presence of many bishops, to withdraw his theses. But Luther steadfastly refused, and so he was dealt a harsh punishment: he was outlawed by the Pope, which meant that no one was allowed to give him accommodation or shelter. However, a prince who opposed the Pope gave Luther a place to hide at Wartburg Castle in Eisenach. Luther lived there like a prisoner, under an assumed name, and since he was hiding for several years, he spent the time doing something else which was forbidden. He translated the Bible into German, as he felt the text needed to be available in the people's language, so less well-educated people could read the Scriptures and obey the word of God.

A side effect of Luther's work was that he unified the German language: at the time, they still wrote Saxon in Saxony and they wrote Bavarian in Bavaria. Before him, Jan Hus had had a similar impact on the Czech language; he had even introduced new letters to convey many Czech sounds. Meanwhile, in England, just eighty-five years after William Tyndale had been executed for translating the Bible into English, an officially sanctioned English Bible appeared. Ordered by James I, the King James Bible would dominate Protestantism across the world for almost 250 years, and had the same impact on English as Hus and Luther did on Czech and German.

Throughout Europe, nuns and monks decided to follow Luther and abandon their monastic vows, risking punishment, as once you had joined a monastery you couldn't leave without permission. One day at the Marienthron Monastery, near Grimma, twelve nuns disappeared shortly after a delivery cart had left the monastery. The nuns had smuggled themselves out among the barrels.

1517: Martin Luther publishes his *Ninety-five Theses* in Wittenberg. This is the start of the Reformation.

One of these nuns was Katharina von Bora. After her escape, Katharina met Martin Luther, and the two married – a former monk and a former nun. This was something else the Church reformers demanded: that clergymen be allowed to have a family. Wasn't it better to officially sanction what the Pope and bishops were doing anyway? For Luther, women were not the Devil incarnate and neither was marriage a distraction from Christian duties. Luther was a pastor, while Katharina took care of the household, had children and supported her husband in all respects. He was in dire need of the support she gave in the battle he was waging. He addressed Katharina respectfully as 'Mrs Doctor' and consulted with her on everything.

The role of a pastor's wife was something completely new. When the famous German painter Lucas Cranach the Elder painted their portraits, he depicted Katharina and Luther in the same proportions and facing each other – they were equally important, they were partners. Their marriage broke other social conventions, too: he was a monk and farmer's son, and she was born into the nobility. Even the fact that Martin Luther and Katharina von Bora were the subjects of such detailed portraits was remarkable, as paintings were an expensive luxury and the honour of being painted was usually granted only to royalty and aristocrats.

Marie Dentière describes the Geneva authorities as 'cockroaches'

The critics of the Church and those who joined their movement were called 'Protestants'. It was dangerous to be a Protestant: you faced the constant risk of arrest, imprisonment and even execution. Nevertheless, the Reformation found ever more followers.

The idea that there was no need for priests or bishops to mediate between the individual and God, and that all you needed was the Bible, seemed to have been especially appealing to women. Some followed the example of Katharina von Bora: they married pastors; opened up their home as a refuge for anyone who sought protection from religious persecution; and cared for the poor and the sick. They were also zealous in their support for the Reformation. There was Katharina Zell, who wrote letters and pamphlets to the citizens of Strasbourg, or Argula von Grumbach who – armed with quotations from the Bible – railed against the University of Ingolstadt over the arrest of a Lutheran student. Her impassioned letter was published in a pamphlet that became a bestseller; tens of thousands of copies were printed. Nevertheless, Argula von Grumbach had little success in her campaign; she was ridiculed, her husband lost his job, and the student was exiled to a Catholic monastery. This was partly because, although Luther respected his wife and corresponded with many Protestant women, he didn't overtly champion their cause. His priority was the Church, not the rights of women.

The situation of women remained difficult, and they often still needed to be married to have any kind of role. But not all women wanted to get married. As a wife, they were responsible only for the family and household, while they could get an education and study in the convents, even if the universities were closed to them. So why, some women thought, should they swap the privilege of the monastery for a marriage? As Protestants in some areas attempted to drive the nuns out of their convents by force, some resisted. This debate was particularly fierce in the city of Geneva, where an altercation between the Catholic nun Jeanne de Jussie and the Protestant Marie Dentière was said to have even come to blows.

Marie Dentière thought that if every believer had an obligation only to God then there was no reason for women to be subordinate to men. If a woman had a talent for speaking and writing, she should make use of it. Marie paid scant attention to the fact that women were not allowed to do this either in Church or in public, and preached everywhere she went, including on street corners and in pubs. Like many Protestants, Marie had fled from a convent, heading first to Strasbourg then to Geneva, where she chronicled how the city's leaders became Protestant, cementing the city's future as a heartland of the Reformation. Even here, though, there were heated clashes between the Protestants and Catholics, which Marie described as the 'war of shouting'.

Marie initially published her writing secretly and under a male pseudonym. But then she became bolder. She wrote a letter to

1539: Marie Dentière publishes *The Defence of Women*.

Marguerite de Navarre, the sister of the French king and, as copies circulated among avid readers, she revealed her identity. The letter contained a section entitled *The Defence of Women*, where Marie demanded that women should have the right to speak in public, and that they should not only be allowed to read the Scriptures but also to preach. Women, she wrote, were no more ignorant than men. After all, as demonstrated by examples from the Bible and history, men also made mistakes. And weren't the male heretics who were condemned by the Church not proof that the 'stronger sex' could err as much as women?

The Reformation railed against failures in the Church, its abuse of power and excessive wealth. But it also gave new impetus to the debate about women, the *querelle des femmes*, that Christine de Pizan had begun. Marie drew on this when she wrote to Marguerite de Navarre, 'with faith in God that from now on women will no longer be valued so lowly as in the past'.

Marie's speeches and writing unleashed a scandal. Of the 1,500 printed books containing her texts, most were confiscated and destroyed. Even John Calvin, the leader of the Reformation in Geneva, distanced himself from her, and so she was eventually attacked from all sides. But she was obviously endowed with an unwavering courage: she believed in God's power to free the oppressed – and women, she thought, were especially oppressed.

Marie could be vitriolic; she once described the Geneva city officials as 'cockroaches'. The men of the city felt assaulted. As they admitted, her criticism hurt all the more because it came from a woman. The city authorities decided to censor her, meaning that her writing could no longer be published without a thorough inspection. After they silenced Marie Dentière, not a single word was printed by a woman in Geneva for the rest of the sixteenth century.

After the death of Marie Dentière, it was several centuries before her memory was honoured. She had played a major role in establishing the Reformation in Geneva, but it was only in the year 2002 that her name was recorded on the Reformation Wall, an international monument to the Protestant Reformation.

Protestant networks

Marguerite de Navarre, who received Marie Dentière's letter defending women's rights, was the sister of King Francis I of France. Francis I was competing for supremacy in Europe with the Emperor of the Holy Roman Empire, whose power extended over Spain, Austria and Germany. He therefore welcomed the infighting among the German kings and sovereign princes that arose because of the Reformation. He knew that the Reformation could split France too, and, to stop that from happening, he established a most advantageous alliance with the Pope. According to this alliance, the Church in France and all its possessions were placed under the authority of the king.

But Marguerite de Navarre, the sister of the French king, was swept away by the ideas of the Reformation, and as she was able to speak and write in seven languages, she found a broad public to whom to express her opinion. Her religious poem *The Mirror of the Sinful Soul* made reference to the earlier text *The Mirror of Simple Souls* by Marguerite Porete – a text that was still in circulation some 200 years after it was written. Like all Protestant writings, *The Mirror of the Sinful Soul* was banned outright.

As Queen of the French region of Navarre, Marguerite had many opportunities to champion the Reformation. She founded France's first Protestant congregation, built Protestant churches and hospitals, set up charities, commissioned translations and helped reformers to consolidate the new doctrine. She also pleaded with her brother, the king, not to persecute the Protestants too severely. But Francis I had a commitment to the Pope, and after a few years, he cut himself off from the influence of his sister. Things had become perilous for the Protestants, known in France as the 'Huguenots'; the first were being burned at the stake in Paris.

Marguerite's life was also at risk as long as she continued to declare her allegiance to the Reformation. She began to attend Catholic Mass for the sake of show, causing many Protestants to feel betrayed by her, but it was the only way she could secretly help the Huguenots and protect the many refugees who she either sheltered in Navarre or helped to reach Protestant friends abroad.

Among them was John Calvin. Marguerite sent him to Geneva where, together with Marie Dentière, he fought for the city to join the Reformation. She sent other Protestants to the court of the Duke of Ferrara, who was the son of Lucrezia Borgia, and had married Renée de France, a secret Protestant, much to his displeasure.

Renée de France was a cousin of Marguerite and had been familiar with her writings and ideas even as a child. Her husband used all his power to force his wife to convert to Catholicism, but he failed in his attempts, and Renée could not be dissuaded from giving refuge to Protestants. In despair, the duke locked her up. Marguerite, Calvin and even the French king all sent envoys to protest against Renée's house arrest, but her husband was a loyal friend of the Pope and was not about to give in. And so finally Renée learned how to play the game: once she was freed, she publicly declared herself a Catholic but never stopped supporting the Protestants in secret.

1524–25: In many parts of the Holy Roman Empire, peasants rise up against their masters. They invoke Luther's essay *On the Freedom of a Christian* and call for an end to forced labour and serfdom.

Women who supported the Protestants, like Renée de France and Marguerite de Navarre, contributed to the increasingly intense public debates. The Reformation became a threat across all of Europe: the Church had split, and in many regions the turmoil was leading to rioting by the peasants. Wars broke out.

In the end, the Protestants couldn't even agree among themselves. Reformers like Calvin in Geneva or Ulrich Zwingli in Zurich proclaimed a new doctrine of faith just as Luther had done, but they quarrelled on many key issues. This eventually gave rise to one Catholic Church and various different Protestant ones.

Fighting, fighting everywhere: the Paris blood wedding

The Reformation had torn Europe apart. There are all sorts of stories that could be told about the events. We could look to Sweden and Denmark, where the Protestants prevailed over the Catholics. Or to Spain, where the Jesuits founded their own religious order and made sure that the supporters of the Pope kept the upper hand. Or we could look to the Netherlands, where the Protestants used the Reformation to liberate themselves from Spanish rule with the Dutch Revolt leading to the Eighty Years War. Religious differences were often only a pretext: the driving force behind the wars between Catholics and Protestants was always power and the struggle for sovereignty and territorial control.

In France, the clashes between the Catholics and the Protestant Huguenots reached a terrible, ferocious climax when thousands of Huguenots were murdered on one gruesome day, remembered in history as the St Bartholomew's Day Massacre.

Marguerite de Navarre had raised her daughter Jeanne d'Albret as a Protestant, which was significant as there was a chance she would give birth to a future king. The Catholics were horrified at this possibility, because they feared that if Jeanne had a son who came to the throne, it could mean the French king – and by extension all of France – would become Protestant. The Pope, the Spanish king and the French king all intervened personally and threatened Jeanne d'Albret with death if she didn't convert to Catholicism.

But Jeanne was not intimidated. She knew that noble Huguenots had already formed an alliance against the Catholics, so she gathered an army and took the lead in the Protestant revolt.

As luck would have it, there was also a woman in charge of Paris at the time: Catherine de' Medici. Hailing from Florence in staunchly Catholic Italy, she had married the French king, and after his death, she ruled France as regent on behalf of her son, who would inherit the throne when he reached adulthood.

Catherine de' Medici recognised that the dispute between Huguenots and Catholics among the aristocrats at court could be a test for France, so she tried to mediate between the two sides. It was probably her idea to marry Jeanne d'Albret's Protestant son Henry to her own daughter Marguerite. Their marriage, she argued, would be a time to celebrate the reconciliation between Catholics and Huguenots. Many Huguenot military leaders came to Paris for the occasion. But then something happened that nobody anticipated: there was an attempt to assassinate a Protestant admiral. It has long been supposed that Catherine de' Medici was behind it, that she deceived the Huguenots and lured their commanders to

1572: Thousands of Huguenots are murdered in Paris during the St Bartholomew's Day Massacre.

Paris under the pretext of a conciliatory wedding so she could have them assassinated in the capital, but this has never been proven.

Whoever instigated it, what we do know is that, after the attack on the admiral, there was a sudden eruption of all the tensions that had built up over the years of civil war. Across Paris and in other French cities, there was a wave of murderous attacks on Protestants. The royal wedding, intended as a token of reconciliation, turned into a bloodbath, with thousands killed. As this 'blood wedding' and the mass murders took place on St Bartholomew's Day, it has gone down in history as the St Bartholomew's Day Massacre.

The conflict between Catholics and Huguenots in France would last for more than 100 years. In the end, however, the Protestants were almost completely expelled from the country. France remained Catholic.

BRITAIN BECOMES A TRADING POWER

More division in the Church

In England, a pupil of Marguerite de Navarre helped expand the impact of the Protestants. The entire European nobility was related in one way or another, and so it turned out that Anne Boleyn, the daughter of an English count, spent part of her childhood at Marguerite's court, where she was lady-in-waiting to Renée de France. When she returned to England, she brought with her a good education, Protestant ideals and a copy of Marguerite's poem, *The Mirror of the Sinful Soul*.

There had long been followers of the Reformation in England, but they had to remain in secret: anyone caught with the writings of Luther or Calvin could easily end up on the gallows. King Henry VIII was married to Catherine of Aragon, the youngest daughter of Isabella of Castile, and the Spaniards (the 'Catholic Monarchs') were close allies of the Pope.

When the young Anne Boleyn came to the English royal court to be Catherine's maid of honour, she unwittingly contributed to the demise of the carefully crafted alliance between England, Spain and the Pope. It all started when Henry VIII fell in love with her. In itself, this was nothing special, as Henry was always falling in love. But Anne refused to become his mistress, reminding him how a Christian lady should behave: love should exist only within marriage.

Anne Boleyn had caught Henry's eye. The English king was ready to do whatever it took to marry her, and so he asked the Pope for permission to divorce his Spanish wife. The Pope refused. But

Henry, blind with love, disregarded the verdict of the head of the Church. He informed Catherine of the dissolution of their marriage and instead married Anne.

This love affair became a matter of state. The Spaniards and the Pope did not like the way the English king unilaterally flouted the Pope's ruling and their response was to exclude him from the Church. It was perhaps the most unusual of the many divisions and schisms in the Church in the Reformation era. For the sake of remarrying, Henry accepted the Pope's judgement and declared England's Church to be an independent Anglican Church – and he made himself the overall authority.

1534: King Henry VIII founds the Church of England and installs himself as Supreme Head of the Church.

Despite turning Henry's head, Anne would lose her own just a few years later. The fact that Anne's first child was a girl – Elizabeth – was met with disappointment at court. Catherine of Aragon had also only given the king a daughter. The problem was that, after Elizabeth, Anne didn't have any more children, leaving an impatient Henry with no male heir to the throne. Certain courtiers who had campaigned against Anne gained influence and encouraged Henry to accuse her of adultery and high treason. She was locked up in the Tower of London and sentenced to a drastic punishment: beheading.

Henry's third marriage – to Jane Seymour – finally brought the long-awaited male heir, but Jane died of complications following the birth. After her, Henry married another three women: he knew by now how to get rid of them if it didn't work out.

Bloody Mary

Three wives later, there was still just one male heir to the throne. When Henry VIII died, his son Edward was only 9, and he was a sickly child who would die six years later. The only remaining direct descendants of the king were his daughters from his first two marriages, Mary and Elizabeth. Mary was raised Catholic, Elizabeth as a Protestant.

After the death of their father, they worked together to secure Mary's claim to the throne. Together with an army of supporters, they rode to London and disarmed their opponents – then, as the elder sister, Mary was named Queen of England.

Mary intended to reverse Henry's break with the Church in Rome. She married Philip, the heir to the Spanish throne, and re-established the alliance with the Catholics. When the English Protestants resisted, Mary executed hundreds of them, earning her the name 'Bloody Mary'.

Meanwhile, the Scottish Queen Mary of Guise was similarly brutal in her treatment of Protestants while she ruled as regent on behalf of her daughter Mary Stuart. Shortly after the death of Henry VIII, it seemed that the British Isles were returning to the bosom of the Catholic Church.

1553: Mary Tudor becomes Queen of England and Ireland. She is known as Bloody Mary.

Queen Elizabeth I

The Protestant preacher John Knox fled England's Catholic rulers and travelled to Geneva, where he became familiar with the teachings of Calvin. In Geneva, Knox published a polemical work entitled *The First Blast of the Trumpet Against the Monstruous Regiment of Women*, and in it he warned his fellow countrymen against the abomination of having a woman at the helm. Knox claimed that with Mary on the throne the nation was without a legitimate ruler – had Marie Dentière known of this text, she might have threatened John Knox, and not just with words. The text, however, was initially published anonymously.

In the same year, Queen Mary died at a surprisingly young age, and Elizabeth I followed her to the throne. As far as John Knox was concerned, this was a change for the better, because at least Elizabeth was a Protestant. But Elizabeth resented him for his pamphlet against women. When Knox wanted to return to Scotland, for months she refused him permission to travel through England.

However, many of the English lords at Elizabeth's court felt the same as John Knox: they wanted a man on the throne. For years they tried to persuade Elizabeth to get married, suggesting suitable candidates from Britain and abroad. But the queen deftly eluded all hopefuls, repeatedly breaking promises and calling off her

1558: Elizabeth I comes to the throne. The Elizabethan era is a golden age for trade, literature and theatre.

engagement. Until her death she remained the Virgin Queen who – at least officially – never had a partner.

Elizabeth had been raised Protestant by her mother Anne Boleyn. By the age of 11, she had translated Marguerite de Navarre's poem, *The Mirror of the Sinful Soul*, from French into English. As Queen of England, she renewed her country's separation from the Catholic Church: England became Protestant again.

Now it was the English Catholics who secretly organised their resistance. They claimed that Elizabeth was the illegitimate child of an unlawful marriage between Henry VIII and a Protestant. The true Queen of England ought therefore to be Mary Stuart, the Queen of Scotland, as she was Henry's grand-niece and next in line to the throne.

Things were looking dangerous for Elizabeth. Her advisers urged her to have Mary executed, but Elizabeth resisted, as she was reluctant to shed royal blood. Her refusal to dispense with Mary kept her network of spies hard at work; her spy master Francis Walsingham was tireless and ruthless in his efforts to secure intelligence on the queen's enemies and to expose their conspiracies against the Crown. He uncovered and prevented several Catholic plots to assassinate Elizabeth and replace her with Mary Stuart, who had been forced to abdicate the Scottish throne after being accused of murdering her husband. Mary was imprisoned in England for almost twenty years before Parliament demanded her head on a block. There was no longer any avoiding it: Elizabeth had her cousin Mary, Queen of Scots, beheaded. Her intelligence chief, meanwhile, had established the infamous English secret services.

Joint-stock companies

The Reformation was followed by a long series of wars between the various European powers. However, this didn't prevent the Europeans from continuing their conquests overseas. Portugal and Spain had shown how it was done: their fearless mariners had sailed around the south of Africa to India, as well as west towards America, bringing their masters unexpected – and immeasurable – wealth. Envy sparked the ambitions of their neighbours, and the Dutch and the English now also wanted to reach the remotest regions of the world.

Foreign expeditions were expensive, however. There was the ship to pay for, the crew, all the technical equipment and arms to defend the ship from attack. Overseas trade was a risky venture, with fatal hazards at every turn. Who would shoulder this risk? Who took the hit of the tremendous financial loss if a ship was lost at sea along with its entire cargo?

Fortunately, for some time now real power in England was no longer vested entirely in the monarch. The royal court of advisers had gradually evolved into a parliament made up of influential noblemen, and all important decisions were made as a negotiation between them and the queen. Although Elizabeth was indeed the most powerful woman in the state, she still had to take her many courtiers into consideration, who represented various camps in parliament.

In many cities, citizens had also won the right to largely manage their own affairs. Merchants in London founded a trading company that went by the name of The Mystery, Company and Fellowship of Merchant Adventurers for the Discovery of Regions, Dominions, Islands and Places Unknown. Despite its cumbersome name, the idea behind the company was very simple: it was a safe way for a large number of merchants to pool their resources and finance an expedition to China via Russia, with the goal of establishing as many trading posts as possible along the way. Therefore, the financial risk of this enterprise was spread across many shoulders; should the expedition fail, it was a manageable loss for each individual donor, because each had only contributed a small amount to the initial outlay. In the event of success, on the other hand, each party enjoyed a share of the profits. The money that the various investors ('adventurers') paid into the pot was called 'stock', so these companies came to be called 'joint-stock companies'. They were able to raise much more money than any one individual would be willing to risk, and they could afford to embark on voyages which even a king or a state couldn't finance.

Already established by the time of Elizabeth's reign, the Company of Merchant Adventurers had achieved its first successes just before Mary I came to the throne, when it managed to establish trade

1551: The creation of the first trading company, where shareholders come together to raise large sums of money to finance ambitious ventures and expeditions overseas.

with Russia (known until the mid-sixteenth century as Muscovy). The company soon dropped its long name and became the Muscovy Company. Mary I granted it the privilege of being a monopoly – the only English company with permission to trade with Russia. With no other English company allowed to compete for trade, this special status brought the Muscovy Company untold riches.

England vs Spain

When Elizabeth followed Mary to the throne, the Spaniards lost their influence at the English court. But things got even worse for the Spaniards when English sailors began to challenge Spanish supremacy in the New World.

Queen Elizabeth I came to hear about Francis Drake, an English sailor who had been raiding and robbing Spanish ships. Strictly speaking, he was a pirate with little respect for the law, but as long as his attacks were against the Spaniards, the British government was not inclined to punish him. Francis Drake inflicted considerable losses on the Spaniards; encouraged by his success, he soon started besieging their ships off the coast of America. And then he embarked on his greatest adventure of all: he became the second navigator to sail around the world, passing through a strait at the bottom of South America – the Strait of Magellan – across to the western side of the American continent. From there he sailed on to China, before heading home to England via the Cape of Good Hope at the southern tip of Africa.

Officially, Elizabeth condemned piracy, but she also issued documents known as 'letters of marque', which gave sailors permission to attack and rob enemy ships. After Drake's return, she is said to have personally boarded the pirate's ship to have a look around. Tensions between Spain and England intensified. The Spanish King Philip sought allies throughout Europe; he wanted to attack England with his fleet and remove Elizabeth from her throne. The British genuinely feared such an invasion: the Spanish Armada, with its huge warships, was vastly superior to the English fleet. Elizabeth knew what was at stake. When the Spanish ships set a course for England, she went to rally the troops at their camp in Tilbury, against the will of her advisers. She's reported to have declared: 'I know I have the body of a weak and feeble woman, but I have the heart and stomach of a king, and of a King of England too.'

It's very possible that Elizabeth didn't actually say this, but that the words were ascribed to her in later reports by witnesses. Either way, it may well have seemed absurd to many at the time that a woman would attempt to inspire courage in an army of soldiers.

The Spaniards encountered a mighty storm in the English Channel and had a hard time reaching the coast of the British Isles. In the waters below the steep cliffs of the south coast, the small English ships were surprisingly quick and manoeuvrable, and they managed something that had seemed completely impossible in the face of a superior opponent: they inflicted a heavy defeat on the Spanish fleet. Elizabeth returned to London in a triumphant procession.

1588: Victory over the Spanish Armada makes England the most powerful kingdom in Europe.

With this victory over the Spanish Armada, Elizabeth had averted a great threat while also achieving something much more important: the Spaniards were no longer the strongest naval power in the Atlantic. And since Elizabeth stayed out of most of Europe's wars, focusing instead on supporting business and commerce, the English had the opportunity to develop their new supremacy at sea, unhindered. They began to colonise North America.

The Spaniards had not been particularly interested in this region, because there was only land, no gold and a relatively small population. This was where the English began to found new colonies. When they christened their first American colony shortly after Elizabeth's death, they named it 'Virginia' in honour of the Virgin Queen.

During Elizabeth's reign, England found new prosperity. This was an era shaped by adventurers, sailors and explorers, but also by scientists, writers and artists. William Shakespeare, England's greatest poet and dramatist, brought theatre to the masses (although female roles were almost always played by men; a woman onstage was deemed disgraceful in the eyes of society).

Elizabeth died in 1603, bringing the Elizabethan Age to a close after almost half a century. She had ruled independently for forty-five years.

EVERYTHING IS ON THE MOVE

Overseas trade

By the time the English began to expand their maritime trade, Portugal had already claimed areas in the north of India, and the Pope had divided all of Central and South America among them and the Spanish. The race was on between the European powers to find and claim unknown, undiscovered territories – whoever got there first could conquer the land and take possession of it. Now the Dutch and the English had joined the race. Merchants in London founded the East India Company, and Queen Elizabeth gave the company a fifteen-year royal charter granting the exclusive right to pursue free trade in all of Asia. The Dutch East India Company was launched in Amsterdam just two years later.

This was a fundamental turning point. It was no longer knights and adventurers who went out to conquer land and people for the Christian empire – and to enrich themselves along the way – but traders who ran their businesses with expertise and efficiency. Whether they sailed under the English or the Dutch flag, they shared their profits with the monarch of their country.

Finally, a chance to explore the ports of the legendary Asian cities. The trading posts of European merchants, known as 'factories', lined up along the coastline like pearls on a string. Soon, the Dutch and the British were joined by representatives of the Danish and the Swedish East India Company, and then Portuguese, Spaniards and French traders. In Asia, Europeans paid with silver from the mines of Central and South America for coveted Chinese goods like tea, silk and porcelain.

The Chinese participated in trade, but they wouldn't let the Europeans into their country. They were only allowed to set up 'factories' in one single port city – Canton, or Guangzhou in Chinese – and it was only from here that foreigners were allowed to trade and export goods from China. The Japanese applied similar restrictions. When they had had enough of being harassed by the pushy Christian missionaries, they shut themselves off from the outside world.

While the Europeans were spreading their reach across every corner of Asia that couldn't be defended by the locals, the colonists in America were running out of workers. The Native Americans, who were put to work in the silver mines and on sugarcane plantations, were dying in staggering numbers due to severe working conditions and viral diseases. The Portuguese began to buy slaves from traders on the shores of Africa. Now it was not only silk, sugar, spices and tobacco, but also millions of Africans that were being shipped from one continent to another in huge ships. People changed hands like goods. The voyage to America took three months; if they survived the crossing, which many didn't, the slaves faced even greater hardships on the plantations and in the mines.

From about 1520: The Spanish colonial masters are running out of local slaves. They begin to buy slaves from Portuguese traders in Africa and transport millions of people to South America and the Caribbean.

The free immigrants: America's white founding fathers

The transport routes and trading hubs established by European merchants formed a network that spanned the world. A huge flow of goods began to circulate the globe, and the more goods that were in circulation, the richer the trading companies became, most notably the British and Dutch East India Companies. Cash flowed, goods circulated – and now people began to move.

The Reformation had made many people refugees. In England, radical Protestants found that Queen Elizabeth's Anglican Church was still too Catholic for their tastes. It was dangerous to voice such views, since it amounted to criticism not only of the Church but also the government. Many Puritans – so called because they wanted to purify the Church further – felt this way and were afraid of being persecuted. Some fled to the Netherlands, but they didn't feel at home there either. They decided to leave Europe.

1620: The *Mayflower* reaches the coast of America, bringing the Pilgrim Fathers who settle permanently in North America. Their safe arrival is celebrated every year on Thanksgiving.

In 1620, the *Mayflower* reached the coast of North America, becoming the first English ship to bring not merchants but refugees fleeing religious persecution. Their destination was Virginia, but storms drove their ship farther north and they formed a new English colony there – a colony that would become the city of Boston, Massachusetts. They were joined by more religious refugees who also found a new home here. They saw the act of seizing land from the indigenous people as a necessary evil. Even before the *Mayflower*, French settlers had also gained a foothold in North America, followed by English and Dutch migrants. They founded towns, calling them New Orleans after the city of Joan of Arc, or New Amsterdam, as though the settlers wanted to build a second Europe. When Englishmen fought the Dutch and seized control of New Amsterdam, they renamed it New York after their commander the Duke of York. The citizens of the New World also sought to demonstrate their loyalty to the old European monarchs. They named one state 'Carolina', in honour of the English King Charles and Maryland after his wife Henrietta Marie. Then there was Louisiana, named in tribute to the French King Louis XIV.

The Pilgrim Fathers were fleeing persecution, but they entered the new continent as free people. In the land of the free, it was said, anything was possible. But it quickly became clear that, once again, freedom didn't apply to everyone. For, although they came to North America with their wives, the religious settlers entered the history books as the Pilgrim Fathers and, as was so often the case, only very few of the Pilgrim *Mothers* were able to make a name for themselves. The most famous of them, Anne Hutchinson, settled in Boston with members of her Puritan community. She invited churchgoers to her house after the service to discuss religious issues, and she gained many followers over time who were interested in her original thinking. But Anne was increasingly critical of the Puritans, and eventually she was put on trial, which resulted in her being convicted and banished from the colony.

Anne had confidants who shared her criticism; they moved to Rhode Island and they founded a new colony. Years later, following the death of her husband, Anne and her children left Rhode Island for New Amsterdam. There, she was killed in a raid by local Siwanoy Native Americans, alongside six of her eleven surviving children.

Her enemies in Boston believed that God himself had punished Anne Hutchinson. But they couldn't prevent Anne's criticism and calls for greater religious freedom from shaping debate among subsequent generations in America.

The unfree immigrants

Almost at the same time as the *Mayflower*, Dutch pirates brought to Virginia a number of African slaves, whom they had captured by chance along the way. Since the southern regions of North America were ideal for growing cotton, they soon found a use for these slaves. It wasn't long before millions of people from Africa were enslaved and sold to North America. Cotton production became a huge and lucrative business.

1619: The first African slaves arrive in North America – at almost the same time as the Pilgrim Fathers.

Unlike the Pilgrim Fathers, the slaves came as prisoners – they didn't create settlements, they weren't able to found cities or states, and they couldn't give their names to their new home. And while the Spaniards and Portuguese colonisers mingled with the various communities in Central and South America, settlers in North America observed a strict separation between Native Americans, Africans and Europeans. So, besides women, there was now another huge group of people that was not fully recognised as human.

THE OTTOMAN EMPIRE

The Sultanate of Women

Since the Turks had conquered Constantinople in 1453, the Ottoman Empire had grown to an impressive size. The Europeans had now discovered sea routes to India and America, so the Ottomans no longer benefitted so much from the high tariffs they could impose on the Silk Road, but they were still a force to be reckoned with. The Ottomans had conquered Greece, the Balkans and Hungary, and they had expanded their territories in North Africa, in the Middle East as far as Baghdad, and north of the Black Sea as far as Russia.

Constantinople had become the capital of the Ottomans. Now it wasn't the golden domes of the churches but the impenetrable walls of the sultan's harem that inspired the fantasies of European ambassadors. Visitors to the city had no access to the royal apartments, and thus let their imagination run wild as they reported what they supposed was going on in the women's quarters, the harem; they pictured the sultan's concubines being pampered in the mosaic-tiled Turkish baths with expensive oils and fragrant incense, preparing themselves to please the most powerful lover in the state.

The reality wasn't quite so colourful. While the sultan's concubines did indeed live in the harem, and of course, their living quarters did indeed have a Turkish bath (*hammam*), their role was much less about being the sensual playthings of a promiscuous sultan – as the Europeans suspected – and more about serving a single purpose as mothers. The Ottomans feared the lack of an heir apparent; since death was common, the sultan was to father as many male offspring as possible.

Of all the sultans, there was one who achieved the most brilliant military victories and brought extraordinary prosperity to the empire

– Suleiman the Magnificent. When he came to the throne, he was given a female slave, Hurrem, as a gift. Hurrem had been captured in her homeland Poland by Crimean Tatars and then sold in Istanbul. However, Suleiman fell in love with her and did something that even as sultan he was not allowed to do: he freed Hurrem from slavery and married her, laying on an extravagant wedding. A sultan marrying a slave from abroad! The Ottoman people were deeply troubled and could find no other explanation for their ruler's gross contravention of social rules: Hurrem must have put a spell on Suleiman. But what did it mean for the future of the country?

In fact, conditions in the Ottoman Empire changed when Hurrem became the sultan's favourite. Because of her, the women who were close to the sultan gained influence within his government – not in secret, behind curtains and locked doors, but openly and officially. Even more important than Hurrem, the sultan's favourite, was the Valide Sultan, the ruler's mother. Hurrem herself became the Valide Sultan when her son succeeded his father on the throne. The position of the sultan's mother became the second highest office of the state, and the population paid her great respect. Hurrem expressed the importance of her role by having magnificent mosques built, giving out grants and financing charitable institutions for the poor.

Hurrem and the women who became the Valide Sultan after her formed a family network which became the centre of power. They formed alliances with the most important men in the civil service and the military by marrying them to their daughters, and whenever there was an influential role to be filled, especially that of the grand vizier, the women made sure the chosen candidate fulfilled their wishes. With time, people came to accept that the highest woman in the state would take control of the government while her son, the heir to the throne, was still a minor. And so there were often periods of several years when the Ottoman Empire was ruled by a woman.

Since Muslims were forbidden from enslaving other Muslims, the sultan's concubines mostly came from abroad. Hurrem was from Poland, while her daughter-in-law Nurbanu, who would succeed her as Valide Sultan, was 12 years old when she was abducted in her home city of Venice and brought to the harem.

1521: The concubine Hurrem gives Suleiman the Magnificent his first son. The next century is remembered in history as the 'Sultanate of Women'.

The Venetians managed to exploit Nurbanu's origins to their own ends, as she stayed in close contact with the Venetian ambassador and the Doge of Venice. When she became Valide Sultan, she prevented the Ottoman military from invading one of Venice's colonies by strictly forbidding the admiral in question from proposing the idea to the sultan. The admiral didn't dare to oppose her, and Venice was spared this attack by the Turks. In gratitude, the Venetians showered Nurbanu with gifts.

The royal ladies of the harem made many contacts with Europe. Once, two Turkish women were kidnapped by the French and became ladies-in-waiting to the French Queen Catherine de' Medici. Nurbanu and her daughter-in-law Safiye protested vehemently: they lobbied and used diplomatic means to exert pressure for two years, until the French gave in and allowed the prisoners to return home.

Meanwhile the English ambassador to Constantinople managed to win Safiye's favour when her son became sultan and she became Valide Sultan. Through him, she sent a letter to the English Queen Elizabeth I, announcing the gifts she was sending: a robe, a sash, two large gold-embroidered bath towels, three handkerchiefs, and a tiara studded with pearls and rubies. However, Elizabeth did not receive the tiara – maybe Safiye's agent secretly took it to gain access to Elizabeth herself. The affair resulted in political tensions between England and the Ottoman Empire, which were not resolved until the tiara reappeared.

The first ladies at the Ottoman court intervened in the empire's domestic and foreign policy. When the Spanish Armada sailed for England to knock Queen Elizabeth off her throne, Nurbanu and Safiye called in the Venetian ambassador. Since they were on friendly terms with the English, he had to assure them that Venice would not supply even a single ship to the Spaniards.

There were precedents for the roles played by Hurrem, Nurbanu, Safiye and their successors in the Ottoman Empire – not in the West, but in the Islamic world. We might think of al-Khayzuran, the mother of the famous caliph Harun al-Rashid; or the daughters and grand-daughters of Genghis Khan, Princesses Khutulun and Mandukhai, whose fame extended far beyond the frontiers of the Mongol Empire. Nevertheless, this period when the sultan's favourite consort and the Valide Sultan enjoyed such strong political influence remained unique in the history of the Ottoman Empire. Indeed, the 'Sultanate of Women', as it became known, was an exceptional era in world history.

The triumph of coffee

The Ottoman Empire was large and militarily strong – quite unlike Europe, which was completely fragmented by religious wars. As in the ancient Roman Empire, travellers in the Ottoman Empire could walk for days along the caravan routes of the Silk Road without ever crossing a national border, and there was, as ever, a bustling trade in expensive fabrics, silk and spices along these routes.

Nevertheless, the rulers of this prosperous empire were confronted with the same conflicts as their European neighbours. Three questions in particular were vehemently debated by Muslim scholars: how much freedom women should have; whether to support modern science or to ban it; and whether the new Arab fashion for coffee drinking was compatible with the rules of Islam. Coffee and coffee houses were the 'in thing' and growing steadily in popularity in Mecca, Cairo and Constantinople.

It didn't take long for the Sultanate of Women to attract condemnation among Islamic scholars. For centuries Christians had been silencing women by quoting the story of Adam and Eve and St Paul's comment that 'women should remain silent in the churches'. Likewise, Muslims invariably invoked the comment attributed to the Prophet Muhammed (a Hadith), as written down by the scholar al-Bukhari: 'Never will a nation prosper that makes a woman its ruler.'

Since the Ottoman sultans saw themselves as caliphs – the rightful leaders of the Islamic world – many of them were open to influence from Muslim clerics, who were increasingly negative about women. They wanted to see women expelled from public life and forbidden from having any contact with men outside their own relatives. One scholar wrote, 'Unless they are related, a man should not even say "bless you" to a young woman when she sneezes.'

1515: The printing press is forbidden for Muslims in the Ottoman Empire.

The same happened with science: some imams believed that it risked becoming a threat to religion. Sultan Bayezid II banned Muslims from using the printing press at the beginning of the sixteenth century; anyone flouting this rule faced the death penalty. After all, the Ottomans could see from their European neighbours' experience how dangerous this technology could be. Printing had made a major contribution to the success of the Reformation, which had led to conflict and the division of the Christian Church.

For centuries, Muslims and Christians had been accumulating and sharing knowledge. It was therefore no coincidence that two huge observatories were built in the Ottoman and Holy Roman Empire at exactly the same time. Taqi ad-Din, an Ottoman Arab polymath from Damascus, and Tycho Brahe, a Danish astronomer, were keen to investigate the stars of the night sky. The Danish king provided Brahe with an island and the funds to build an observatory. Brahe spent twenty-one years there carrying out research together with his sister Sophie, one of many women at the time with a passion for astronomy. Tycho and Sophie Brahe together compiled a star catalogue charting the position of 1,000 fixed stars.

1580: Sultan Murad III orders the destruction of the observatory of the astronomer Taqi ad-Din.

Taqi ad-Din's observatory in Constantinople, built with Sultan Murad III's approval and funding, was only in operation for a few years; warned by clerics that the scientific observation of heaven was blasphemy, the sultan had the expensive observatory destroyed. The perception of stargazing may have changed after ad-Din discovered a comet and predicted a military victory for the sultan – which, to ad-Din's misfortune, did not happen.

Eventually, the coffee houses were also closed, as the government feared that men would meet in them to discuss politics. However, the ban didn't last long. As all of Europe got hooked on coffee, this black Turkish potion became one of the Ottomans' largest export success stories.

DEVASTATING WARS AND THE RISE OF SCIENCE

The 'women debate' rumbles on

Europe was changing, and a major driver for this change were the questions that were in constant debate since humanism, the Renaissance and the Reformation. The search for the right faith and the right way of life kept giving rise to new Protestant movements, and the debate about women continued unabated. Once again there was a female French writer speaking up for change.

Marie de Gournay had a lot of admiration for a writer and philosopher who liked to sit and write in the tower of his castle. This man, Michel de Montaigne, wrote what he called 'attempts' – in French, *essais* – and these texts became famous works of philosophy. Gournay got in touch with Montaigne, who was impressed by her wisdom. Since he was thirty-five years her senior, he declared her to be his 'adopted daughter'.

After Montaigne's death, Gournay took care of his essays and had them published as a book. Instead of marrying or moving to a convent, she went to Paris and managed to make a living with her work as a writer. Although – or perhaps because – she almost always did the opposite of what was usual, she gained recognition and, in fact, the French king is even said to have provided her with a small pension for a time.

For the thinker and writer Marie de Gournay there was only one topic on her mind: the *querelle des femmes*, the women question. She wrangled with her fate, the lot of an educated woman, and complained: 'Ignorance, slavery and the ability to play the

1595: Marie Le Jars de Gournay continues the *querelle des femmes* – the debate about women. She argues that women are no better or worse than men – that, in fact, they are the same.

idiot constitute a woman's only happiness … and her highest and only merits.'

To a learned priest who claimed that women were incapable of grasping the wisdom of the Bible, she retorted that some men were also not capable of doing so, but the priest hadn't noticed their incompetence, because men have the honour of growing a beard. Presumably it was their beards which made men look intelligent. She wrote, 'But if someone is stupid enough to imagine God as a man or woman, then … all he demonstrates is that he is as incapable of philosophy as he is of theology.'

The debate about women had thus far revolved around the question of whether men were superior to women or whether women were superior to men. Marie de Gournay brought a new idea to the table: she argued that they were equal, and one gender was no better and no worse than the other.

At around the same time, a Dutch writer by the name of Anna Maria van Schurman became well known. Intelligent and well educated, she was described as the 'Star of Utrecht' and the 'Dutch Sappho', as though she were a wonder of nature. But primarily, it all it came down to the fact that she had had the opportunity to pursue education to an exceptionally high level. A friend in academia allowed her to attend lectures at the university, although she had to hide behind a curtain in a wooden box which was built into the lecture theatre especially so her presence wasn't a distraction to the male students.

Perhaps, given these circumstances, it was unsurprising that her thesis was called *A Much-Asked Question: Should Girls Receive an Education or Not?*

A woman from England answered this question in her own way. As a young Catholic, Mary Ward saw how her fellow believers were persecuted by Queen Elizabeth's government and she fled to a convent on mainland Europe, where she founded several convent-like institutions, or institutes, where girls could receive a good education. She also argued something that was completely unthinkable for the Catholic Church: that women should also perform on the stage, and they should play the female roles in Shakespeare's plays. She argued this at a time when female actresses had a very bad reputation and were considered little more than prostitutes.

Mary Ward proved that a woman and a devout Catholic could also think for herself. She needed the Pope's permission to set up her schools and institutes, so she simply walked to Rome – a distance of nearly 1,000 miles – founding more girls' schools along the way. But the Pope didn't appreciate her activism, imprisoning her for nine weeks and ordering her schools to close.

A few years earlier, the Academy of Fine Arts in Florence had accepted its first female painter, Artemisia Gentileschi. But it turned out that women like Artemisia Gentileschi and Anna Maria van Schurman were only accepted because they were exceptions. It would still be a long time before people accepted the idea of educating *all* girls. And so, as a good Catholic, Mary Ward bowed to the Pope's command, and very few of her institutes remained.

Around the same time, a Protestant theologian in France published his views in support of women. François Poullain de la Barre argued against the idea that women were by nature weaker than men – this was nonsense, he wrote; nature was nature, and men's and women's bodies were as they needed to be for reproduction, but this didn't affect their spiritual and intellectual capacity. Voices in defence of women, however, remained the exception for many centuries.

Thirty years of war

The first half of the seventeenth century didn't just see a war of words. While France debated the *querelle des femmes* and other humanist ideas, clashes further east, between Protestants and Catholics, led to a war that completely devastated Central Europe.

This was still the Holy Roman Empire, where the emperor was elected by the higher-ranking princes and sovereigns known as prince-electors. The imperial crown had been transferred to the Habsburg family in Austria, who had forged alliances with the Spanish monarchy by means of marriage, thus establishing a new Catholic centre of power.

The Reformation made matters complicated for the Protestant prince-electors, as they now had to ask themselves whether, as

1618: The
Thirty Years
War begins
with the
Defenestration
of Prague,
when three
Catholic
officials are
thrown out of
a window in
Prague Castle.

Protestants, they were comfortable with electing a Catholic as their emperor. On 23 May 1618, this question was answered with surprising certainty by Protestant nobles in Prague, the capital of the Kingdom of Bohemia. The lords went to Prague Castle and threw three of the emperor's Roman Catholic officials out the window. All three survived, albeit badly injured, and the Catholics declared that God was on their side and had saved them. The Protestants, on the other hand, claimed they had only been saved by a heap of dung under the window that had given the three imperial officials a soft landing. Perhaps neither side was right. However, a few months later, a large comet appeared in the sky and a 'little ice age' brought about sudden climate change, causing widespread famine. People interpreted these events as a prophecy of God's judgement: it seemed certain that the conflict that started in Bohemia would spiral into a great pan-European war.

This suspicion would turn out to be right. This event, known as the Defenestration of Prague, led to armed clashes between Protestants and Catholics, and soon half of Europe would be mixed up in it. This spat developed into what would become known as the Thirty Years War.

The two warring parties, a Protestant alliance and the Catholics led by the Habsburg monarchy, formed a close-knit web of allies stretching the length and breadth of Europe. The fighting spread from Sweden to Spain, and from Poland and Bohemia to the Netherlands, with many German principalities in the middle. Vast swathes of Europe were turned into a battlefield.

It took thirty years for all the parties to realise that there was nothing to be gained from killing each other. In 1645, for the first time in history, the great powers of Europe – France, Spain, Sweden, the Netherlands, the Austrian emperor and the princes of the Holy Roman Empire – sat down at one table to negotiate: . They met in the cities of Münster and Osnabrück, negotiating for three years, and the agreement they came to was called the Peace of Westphalia. The agreement established a new balance of power among Europe's larger and smaller kingdoms and principalities.

1648: The
Peace of
Westphalia
ends the Thirty
Years War.

Peace was a long time in coming and the Thirty Years War had left a trail of devastation. Cities were ransacked, thousands had died or were left destitute, and on top of this came a plague which finished off nearly half of the population in some regions.

The triumph of science

A few years before the imperial civil servants were thrown out of the window, the Emperor of the Holy Roman Empire still had his official residence in Prague, where he employed famous astronomers at his court, including the Dane Tycho Brahe and the German Johannes Kepler. Kepler's calculations of how the planets moved around the Sun culminated in what are now known as Kepler's laws of planetary motion. However, these laws were extremely complicated and baffling to most of the people who tried to interpret them – until, in the midst of the turmoil of the Thirty Years War, a mathematician and astronomer called Maria Cunitz managed to simplify them. This was a significant scientific achievement, but it didn't stop her petty critics from accusing her of neglecting her household chores by sleeping during the day so she could stargaze at night.

Maria Cunitz and Kepler were not the only ones looking up at the sky for answers. The idea that the world might be better understood by reading not the Bible, but the 'book of nature', had sparked widespread enthusiasm for the natural sciences. New optical instruments with ever sharper lenses also contributed to this.

> By the means of Telescopes, there is nothing so far distant but may be represented to our view; and by the help of Microscopes, there is nothing so small, as to escape our inquiry; hence there is a new visible World discovered to the understanding. By this means the Heavens are open'd, and a vast number of new Stars, and new Motions, and new Productions appear in them, to which all the ancient Astronomers were utterly Strangers. By this the Earth it self, which lyes so neer us, under our feet, shews quite a new thing to us, and in every little particle of its matter; we now behold almost as great a variety of Creatures, as we were able before to reckon up in the whole Universe it self.

This was how one English scholar, Robert Hooke, described the hopes that now rested on physics and mathematics. 'We may perhaps be inabled to discern all the secret workings of Nature,' he added. Scientists came together in London to found the Royal Society of London for Improving Natural Knowledge. What they had started was something completely new, because the participants saw themselves as part of a scientific community working across all national borders towards the common goal of increasing human knowledge. Now it was not only merchants and sailors who were setting out to conquer the world – scientists were too.

1660: The Royal Society is founded in London, as scientists from across Europe research and survey the world.

The Church was quickly losing its influence but it wasn't going to surrender without putting up a fight. In desperation, the Church resisted the claim that the Sun was at the centre of our planetary system. There was quite a stir when the Pope – the same one who had banned Mary Ward's girls' schools – put the physicist and mathematician Galileo Galilei on trial for asserting this blasphemous idea. Galileo was a deeply religious Catholic; he wanted nothing less than to harm the Church. The Church, however, was forcing him to revoke his scientific findings, which brought him into a serious conflict of conscience.

But while the Church was still arguing with Galileo, their next adversary had already come to the fore. The French philosopher René Descartes declared that we needed neither God nor Aristotle to make sense of the world; it was enough to rely on one's own understanding and experience. He wrote in Latin, '*Cogito ergo sum*' – 'I think, therefore I am.' That, argued Descartes, was enough. No sooner had he died than the Pope added his works to the Index of Forbidden Books.

1641: The philosopher René Descartes writes *Cogito ergo sum* – 'I think therefore I am'. He argues that people should rely less on what the Church says and more on what can be deduced by reasoning.

For philosophy, what Descartes wrote unleashed a revolution. The route to knowledge no longer stemmed from God, but from man. He questioned whether we can confidently say we *know* something to be true: is it through rational thought and logic that we make sense of the world, or is it through our senses, our eyes and ears? Many felt too much store had been set by religion and not enough by what our senses could tell us. With ever greater zeal, scientists investigated nature not only with optical instruments such as the telescope and the microscope, but also with pen and paper, writing and drawing what they observed with the naked eye. They started measuring and charting the world in all its dimensions. People, animals, plants – everything in the natural world – was studied and described in detail, given a name and categorised within a taxonomical system of classes and subclasses.

As we might well guess, women were not generally included in this community of knowledge seekers. There were few women who had the courage to say with the confidence of a man, 'I think therefore I am.' However, one who did was Maria Sibylla Merian.

Merian clearly possessed a rare talent: not only did she very closely observe the natural world, but she had an exceptional ability to capture her observations in drawings, which brought her much admiration. She began painting flowers as a child, then as an adult, she published her first book on insects, *Caterpillars: Their Wondrous Transformation and Peculiar Nourishment from Flowers*, followed shortly after by a second volume.

Merian was aware that there were many species in the New World that were completely unknown in Europe. In her fifties, she sailed across the Atlantic with her daughter, also a naturalist, on a voyage to the Dutch colony of Suriname in South America, in the hope of finding and sketching some uncharted species. After two years of collecting, studying and illustrating the jungle's plants, insects and other animals, Merian published her most important work, the *Metamorphosis insectorum Surinamensium*, in which she described the metamorphosis of insect larvae into their adult form, including the transformation of caterpillars into butterflies and moths. Merian was the first to distinguish between moths and butterflies – a distinction that is valid to this day.

1699: Maria Sibylla Merian travels to Suriname to investigate tropical butterflies.

THE GLORIOUS REVOLUTION

New ideas about the role of the state

For a long time, England watched mainland Europe sink into the turmoil of the Thirty Years War from a safe distance, isolated by virtue of being on an island. Little did they know that the ongoing tensions between Catholics and Protestants already posed a threat to their own social order. Like one cardboard box hidden inside another, there lurked at the heart of this sprawling conflict another, smaller one: a quarrel between king and his parliament. Before either side realised what was happening, they had plunged the entire island into civil war.

The king and his followers thought that the Members of Parliament had too much influence; after all, he had the 'Divine Right of Kings' – the God-given right to rule. The Parliamentarians saw things differently. As far as they were concerned, the king had to consult the House of Commons; he couldn't simply make decisions without their consent.

King Charles I tried to enforce his claim to the throne by force. Backed by 400 soldiers, he stormed the House of Commons, aiming to arrest a handful of particularly outspoken Parliamentarians. But the Members of Parliament managed to escape, and Charles I was forced to flee London, following outrage among the citizens at his attack on Parliament. Both sides hurried to establish armies that engaged in fierce battles, spreading the conflict as far as Ireland and Scotland. After seven years of civil war, the Parliamentarians won under the leadership of Oliver Cromwell, and something happened which would once have seemed impossible: Charles I, the King of England, was beheaded.

1649: Oliver Cromwell takes over the government after the English Civil War and England becomes a republic.

Oliver Cromwell declared England a commonwealth, but it didn't last long once he turned out to be a tyrant. In the end, people felt it would be better to have a king who argued with parliament than a leader of a republic who behaved like a despot. So, two years after Oliver Cromwell's death, Parliament crowned the son of the beheaded monarch as the new King of England.

Catherine of Braganza starts a tea craze

This son, Charles II, married the Portuguese Princess Catherine of Braganza. When she arrived in England, he is said to have cried out in horror that he had been sent a bat and not a woman. He was appalled by his bride's hairstyle; it seemed the husband-to-be knew little of Portuguese fashion. It was not only her hairstyle that was unfamiliar in England. Catherine of Braganza, the new queen, drank tea that the Portuguese imported from their colonies in South Asia. It wasn't long before her courtiers imitated her and soon everyone in the nobility was drinking tea – the Portuguese queen unleashed a fashion that would later become a quintessentially English custom.

Catherine was strictly Catholic, and shortly before his death Charles also converted to Catholicism. When his Catholic brother James II came to the throne, conflict and civil war were back on the horizon. Again, the king tried to assert his right to rule over Parliament, and again, there was resistance from the mainly Protestant Parliamentarians.

Out of desperation, they turned to the Protestant son-in-law of the English king, the Dutch Prince William of Orange. This time, they hoped to have a 'Glorious Revolution' – one with no blood – an idea that soon gathered support. William brought his army to the island and James II fled to France, which Parliamentarians interpreted as him giving up his claim to the Crown.

As William was brought in from abroad, which risked being seen as a Dutch invasion, he was not crowned alone as king. Instead, William and his wife Mary (James II's daughter) were crowned as equal monarchs of England. In return for the Crown, William and Mary signed

1689: The English king and queen sign the Bill of Rights, creating a new form of government – parliamentary democracy.

the Bill of Rights, a declaration of rights that the monarchy granted Parliament. These two revolutions brought England a brand new form of government: the monarch required a parliamentary majority to pass any law and would in certain circumstances need to bow to the will of the House of Commons.

Mary's sister Anne, who had supported the Glorious Revolution, followed William and Mary to the throne. She was a skilful ruler and negotiator, and it was under her rule that the two kingdoms of England and Scotland (Wales had been part of the Kingdom of England since 1284) united to become Great Britain.

Does the state have to be a monster?

The Civil War and the Glorious Revolution both gave philosophers much to reflect on. They were shocked to see how the country's social order could so quickly disintegrate into a devastating civil war, and this led one philosopher, Thomas Hobbes, to theorise that only a strong state could prevent such a calamity. He argued that the state needed to be giant like the leviathan – a mythical sea monster that combined elements of a dragon, a crocodile, a snake and a whale.

Another philosopher, John Locke, felt that power in a state needed to be divided between various bodies, so that each side could keep the others in check. When, after the Glorious Revolution, every new monarch signed the Bill of Rights, the new system of government was more or less in line with what Hobbes and Locke proposed: it was an arrangement based on a social contract between the monarch and the people, with the people represented by Members of Parliament. The monarch was no longer free to do as they wanted; in this new constitutional monarchy, the king or queen's power was legitimised by Parliament, not the 'Divine Right of Kings' – God was out of the picture.

The ideas expressed by these English philosophers and the new democratic parliamentary structure that was enshrined in the Bill of Rights would later become the political model adopted throughout Europe.

FROM ENGLAND TO FRANCE

ABSOLUTISM AND ENLIGHTENMENT

In France, all power lies with the king

While the Bill of Rights once and for all limited the authority of the English king, across the Channel Louis XIV enjoyed absolute power. In France, there was no parliament that held the monarch to account. On the contrary, Louis had created a situation where the people – above all the otherwise-so-resistant nobility – revolved around him like planets around the Sun. He soon became known as 'the Sun King'.

Louis summoned the members of France's royal and noble classes to his court in Paris, where they served only the king; it was seen as a great honour to hold one of his stockings as he dressed in the morning or to help lace up his vest. Kept busy with such ceremonial activities, the princes, dukes and other noblemen had no time to think about their own interests.

Louis used his tremendous power to reform France. He hired capable ministers to introduce a new system of taxation, and he was the first ruler in history to succeed in making the upper classes pay their share. This new tax system worked so well that the king could afford costly wars against Spain, and still had money left over to expand his château at Versailles and make it even more extravagant. Famous architects and landscape gardeners developed Versailles into the largest and grandest palace complex in Europe. Nowhere else received such an influx of money. Nowhere were more expensive fabrics fashioned into ladies' dresses, nowhere else saw so many festive celebrations and lavish feasts. Nobles and royals across Europe were inspired to imitate Versailles, copying its symmetrical gardens, with trees, hedges and bushes cut into all sorts of geometric shapes and

1643: Louis XIV ascends the French throne. He rules for seventy-two years and shares his power with no one.

planted as ornamental mazes. Like Louis, they perfected the art of demonstrating their power and wealth.

The light of reason

The French philosopher Voltaire was always getting into trouble. As a student he disobeyed his father, who sent him abroad as punishment until he started behaving. It didn't help. As a young adult, Voltaire incurred the wrath of authorities with his mocking, satirical poetry. The authorities, however, weren't as tolerant as his father had been; Voltaire was arrested and sentenced to eleven months in the Bastille, the notorious Paris prison.

But Voltaire was not deterred. No sooner was he released from jail than he started writing new works of caustic satire, criticising the state and the Church alike. He quickly rose to fame. Again the king – by now it was Louis XV – tried to get rid of him, offering him a choice of the Bastille again or exile.

He chose exile to England, and there Voltaire became acquainted with the writings of Locke and the parliamentary system that the British had negotiated in the wake of the Glorious Revolution. He was enthused by what he saw in Britain, and it strengthened his conviction that all was not well in France. Voltaire returned to his homeland brimming with new ideas.

While Louis XV, like his predecessor, lived in luxury in the seclusion of his palace in Versailles, Voltaire and other young thinkers met in Parisian coffee houses to discuss conditions in France and to sharpen their wits and critical thinking.

The Church claimed that God had created the best of all worlds for man, Voltaire pointed out. He published a novel in which a hero named Candide embarks on a journey searching for the happiness promised by the Church, but wherever he and his companion go, all they find are the horrors of war, misery, poverty and disease. Candide scoffs at how the Church insists our world is the 'best of all possible worlds'. Voltaire argued that if we put two and two together, then reason tells us something other than what the Church claims.

The world could be beautiful and good, he reasoned, if it were fairer, and if men were free and equal. He concluded that people should listen a little less to the Church and place a little more trust in what can be deduced by reasoning.

Voltaire's caustic satire and constant resistance stirred up a wave of enthusiasm that soon spread across Europe. Reason cast light on many things that until then had lurked in the shadows. Suddenly, there seemed to be an infinite number of ways to build and shape the world. The French called this new era *L'Âge des Lumières* – 'The Age of Light' – for it was the light of reason that would show people the way. Elsewhere, people spoke of 'the Enlightenment'.

Other authors contributed to the Enlightenment with influential texts. Since people were no longer willing to accept that a king's right to rule was justified by God, they had to find new ways of organising the state. Jean-Jacques Rousseau argued that rulers should sign a treaty or social contract, through which the entire population gave the government the right to rule. Then there was Charles de Montesquieu, who felt there needed to be a separation of powers, where each of the three branches of authority kept each other in check. It was best, he argued, when there was a distinction between those who interpret and enact the law (the judiciary), those who write the law (an elected parliament) and those who enforce the law (the government).

Denis Diderot began to collect all the world's knowledge in the first encyclopaedia, an ambitious work stretching to thirty-five volumes. The articles were supplied by Diderot, Voltaire, Rousseau, Montesquieu and many other contributors, but only a single woman, Émilie du Châtelet. The encyclopaedia included over 70,000 entries. The authors wanted to collect and capture in writing all conceivable knowledge about the world, and they believed there was nothing – absolutely nothing – that couldn't eventually be explained. The Enlightenment thinkers were convinced that with reason and knowledge they had the necessary instruments to make the world into 'the best of all worlds'.

The light of reason even shone into the dark dungeons of the prisons, and harsh punishments were gradually replaced with milder ones. In Russia, Tsarina Elizabeth I was the first ruler to abolish the

1759: The philosopher Voltaire publishes the novel *Candide*. He writes that only a world ruled by reason can be good and just; these ideas kick off the Enlightenment.

death penalty. This step was repeated in Italy, then in other countries. Meanwhile, the English found a practical solution for their convicts: instead of executing them, they started shipping their prisoners to the new colonies in America.

Coffee houses and salons

People were also thinking about women, of course. Did the ideas of the Enlightenment also open up new opportunities for them?

Some women had long since found ways to participate in the world that was closed off to them. As they weren't welcome to participate in public discourse, they welcomed the public into their homes. As far back as 1610, Catherine de Vivonne, Marquise de Rambouillet, had founded a salon to which she invited the most fascinating men and women of her time. During the Enlightenment 100 years later, these salons really came into their own. Upper-class women – whose social status and financial resources meant they could afford to entertain guests – hosted afternoon tea and dinner parties. These salons became fashionable meeting places for those who were educated, enquiring and, above all, well read: you would only be invited if you were distinguished by your achievements in the field of literature, music, science, philosophy or politics. Your achievements were the only things that mattered, not rank, status or origin. What was unthinkable in public places, such as in the Church or the universities, became possible in private: discussions were now taking place between men and women, the rich and the destitute, nobles and commoners. They all argued together as if the social barriers that normally kept them apart didn't exist.

In London, the salon of Elizabeth Montagu became particularly famous. Here, too, women and men met to discuss politics and literature. The group was called the Blue Stocking Society, but historians can't agree as to why. The most popular story is that one of the gentlemen attending once made the mistake of wearing blue instead of the more fashionable black stockings. Nevertheless, from then on, educated women were called 'bluestockings'.

1610: Madame de Rambouillet hosts a salon in Paris and starts a new trend. At these salons, men and women discuss politics, science, literature and philosophy.

In Leipzig, Christiana Mariana von Ziegler founded a salon special-ising in literature and music, which became the meeting place of the brightest minds in the city. She became distinguished by her poetry and her essays, prompting one of the most prestigious literary asso-ciations, the Leipzig German Society, to appoint her as their first and only female member. Johann Sebastian Bach set her lyrics to music, and the University of Wittenberg awarded her an honorary degree.

Other universities were willing to pay tribute to the extraordinary achievements of individual women. In Halle, Dorothea Erxleben had studied alongside her father and eventually took over his practice as a doctor – the first female medical doctor in Germany. But as she was not allowed to qualify officially, she was accused of medical malpractice. Erxleben therefore wrote to the Prussian king, who then issued the university with a royal decree to allow her to study in Prussia. She became the first woman to obtain a doctorate from a German university.

The world's first doctoral degree had been awarded to a woman in Italy, some seventy years earlier. Elena Cornaro was from Venice and enrolled at the University of Padua, where her philosophy tutor proposed her for a doctorate in theology. But the Catholic Church wouldn't allow it – no doubt the clerics recalled the words of St Paul, who declared that women ought to be silent in church. The doors of the Roman Catholic Church were closed to women, regardless of what was happening in the world of academia. For Cornaro, however, a solution was found at the University of Padua: she submitted a thesis on the logic of Aristotle and received her doctorate in philosophy, instead of theology.

The Enlightenment era's exchange of ideas wasn't limited to the salons. Just two years after the end of the Thirty Years War, the world's first daily newspaper appeared in Leipzig, and soon there were daily, weekly and monthly papers popping up everywhere. These news-papers and journals vastly accelerated the spread of information set in motion by Gutenberg's developments in printing: this was the dawn of the print media. People used to speak of 'the three estates' in society (the clergy, the nobility and commoners) – now winning over public opinion had become so important that the press came to be seen as the fourth.

The first English newspaper was published by a woman. In London, in 1702 – when Voltaire was just 6 years old – Elizabeth Mallet began publishing *The Daily Courant*. In the first issue, she declared that the author would not 'give any Comments or Conjectures of his own, but will relate only Matter of Fact; supposing other People to have Sense enough to make Reflections for themselves'.

Soon, women were getting a reputation for their interest in reading and getting an education. Numerous books were published which were intended for a female audience, with titles such as *Fundamentals of Comprehensive Knowledge for Ladies* or *Logic for Women*. Schools and academies were being founded for women's and girls' education, following the example of Mary Ward. This was something that Daniel Defoe, the author of the famous novel *Robinson Crusoe*, had proposed in England as far back as 1697. A poet named Gottlieb Corvinus published the *Useful, Gallant, and Curious Women's Lexicon*, a weighty tome that contained all conceivable knowledge about women; it described every possible item related to the home, particularly the kitchen. While the great men of the age worked on the encyclopaedia of all knowledge, women got an encyclopaedia of knitting and cooking pots.

Reason and logic have no gender. This was what Montaigne's adopted daughter Marie de Gournay and her colleague Poullain de la Barre had argued half a century before. Many women demonstrated this to be true. Even so, the barrage of the Enlightenment had done little to shake the solid foundations of gender prejudice.

Many were troubled by the self-esteem displayed by the women who hosted the salons. They regarded learned women – the bluestockings in England and *femmes savantes* in France – as a threat. When asked whether women should be allowed the same rights and opportunities as men, many men responded with a vehement 'No' – if they were, who would take care of the household and the children? That was not the only argument, of course. Many simply didn't believe women had the same strength, courage or logical faculties as men, such as Rousseau, who stated that 'the Republic needs men'.

The private salons could defy many social rules. Allowing a woman to visit a public coffee house, however, would have meant more profoundly questioning the accepted social order, so women were simply denied access. Émilie du Châtelet – Voltaire's lover – experienced this when she planned to visit the Parisian Café Gradot. The mathematician Moreau de Maupertuis was a regular, and since Émilie du Châtelet had just translated Isaac Newton's *Principia Mathematica* into French – a book that caused a stir throughout Europe for half a century – she could hardly have been a better discussion partner for Maupertuis. But Émilie du Châtelet was turned away at the entrance to the café. She went away, then returned in men's clothes. It wasn't long, however, before the waiter noticed she had deceived the porter at the entrance. Later, it was said, he warned Émilie that he would have to charge her twice: once for the gentleman and once for the lady. Émilie du Châtelet is said to have replied that in that case she demanded two cups of coffee: one for the gentleman and one for the lady.

1745: Émilie du Châtelet begins translating the *Principia Mathematica* by Isaac Newton into French.

Émilie du Châtelet's translation of the *Principia Mathematica*, which she annotated with her own commentary, is to this day considered the standard French edition. Nevertheless, there was still heated debate about whether women could be considered beings capable of rational thought. One poet in Leipzig, for example, thought that the answer to this question had to be 'yes' – after all, women were 'not lifeless machines'. This is, of course, not a particularly convincing argument, as animals are also not 'lifeless machines', but we would not describe a frog as capable of rational thought. But this debate was still in its early days. We have to remember that many scholars at that time pictured the human body as a machine. They suspected that our innards were much like the inner workings of a clock, except that instead of cogs and pendulums, the mechanics of the human body were kept ticking along by organs, blood and muscles.

The Enlightenment thinkers called upon the people to place their trust not in God, but in reason and rational thought. Therefore, they could no longer rely on the Church to prove what God had supposedly intended: that women should focus on raising offspring. Instead, the Enlightenment found a new argument that allowed them to hold women back and ignore women's demands. The place for women was the home, they declared, and their role should be limited to mothers and servants – as was determined by nature.

Back to nature!

The argument on a woman's natural place weighed heavily. During the Enlightenment, nature and what was considered 'natural' became the ideal – everything that was seen as being 'too artificial' was rejected.

1750: Rousseau argues that nature is better than man-made culture.

It all started when Rousseau responded to a question posed in a magazine, asking if the sciences and arts had contributed to the purification of morals. Rousseau sent in an essay where, contrary to the prevailing mood, he argued that they had not. It was only in his natural state, at the very beginning of history, that man had lived freely and independently. Since then, farming and settlements, the emergence of larger communities, the construction of houses, streets and cities, and finally the founding of states had all led mankind into social slavery. Rousseau questioned everything men had been doing for millennia. The 'noble savage', he wrote, the hunter-gatherer of the past, was by no means inferior to the contemporary civilised man, and the history of humanity was not heading forwards, but was declining steadily.

His essay was a provocation: no one had ever doubted that people were improving themselves the more knowledge and education they accumulated. How could anyone claim that untouched nature was superior to man-made culture?

Rousseau's other work brought him widespread recognition, including the novel *Emile*, which explores how children should be educated. In this Rousseau also suggests that women should play the piano, sing, sew and cook, but that their curiosity should be curtailed. His attitude was a bitter disappointment for women hoping for greater freedom and rights – after all, Rousseau was one of the best-known philosophers of his time.

Nevertheless, the Enlightenment was a period of great change. For centuries, the Church had condemned anyone who violated God's order; it was thought that the Devil had got inside them and they were burned as witches. Such superstition was completely alien to the Enlightenment thinkers. But when a woman acted against her 'nature', it was enough to declare her an exception. This effectively meant that any 'normal' woman did not write books on philosophy or mathematics – even Voltaire is said to have described his beloved Émilie du Châtelet by saying: 'She was a great man whose only fault was being a woman.'

THE GREATS: FREDERICK AND CATHERINE

Philosophy moves to Prussia

While the Enlightenment wasn't getting much attention at the court of Versailles, other rulers in Europe were proving to be more open-minded. They were taking on the ideas of Voltaire, Montesquieu and Rousseau, and from them they were developing new ways to rule. The Prussian King Frederick the Great was the best expression of this attitude; he was the king who told the University of Halle to allow Dorothea Erxleben to study medicine. As a sign that he was serious about Enlightenment ideals (and much to the dismay of his father), he wore scruffy clothes, surrounded himself with philosophers and artists, and claimed that a crown was basically nothing more than a hat, and one that doesn't keep the rain out, at that. In other words, instead of revelling in his wealth and living a life of luxury, the king should serve the people and care for the well-being of the people in his country. When Voltaire was forced to leave France again, Frederick granted him refuge. He was delighted to personally receive the greatest philosopher of the Enlightenment at his court. Voltaire was followed by other French thinkers – and so French philosophy came to Prussia. The new centre of the Enlightenment was Sanssouci Castle, which Frederick had had built as a small private residence in Potsdam. His successors didn't maintain his sense of modesty and extended Sanssouci into a grand palace and park, which earned it the name 'the second Versailles'.

From 1740: Frederick the Great presents himself as an enlightened ruler and invites French philosophers to live in his castle.

Frederick the Great insisted that everyone should be able to practise their religion without danger to life and limb. He invited religious refugees and immigrants from other countries to settle in Prussia and saved the lives of many Huguenots by giving them a home in Berlin. He was a patron of artists, scientists and architects, and allowed people to express their opinions – not only in salons and discussion circles, but in the press as well.

People argued about religion, the state or literature, and they were open-minded and tolerant. One could almost say that Frederick's Prussia was like a Parisian coffee house, the difference being that the king was in the midst of it all.

Frederick the Great led the way: his actions were imitated in the farthest corners of the Prussian state. On the border with Russia, Caroline von Keyserling ran a grand salon that would become the cultural hub of East Prussia. She was herself an artist and her talent was so respected that she was accepted into the Royal Prussian Academy of the Arts and Mechanical Sciences. One of her portraits is of her most famous guest, the shining star at the centre of her salons: the philosopher Immanuel Kant. When asked, 'What is enlightenment?' he replied, 'Enlightenment is man's emergence from his self-imposed immaturity.' Anyone who did not want to think, reasoned Kant, was immature and only had themselves to blame. When people started to use their brains to think critically, humanity would grow up.

1784: Immanuel Kant writes that enlightenment is 'man's emergence from his self-imposed immaturity'.

The Enlightenment moves to Russia

The ideas of the Enlightenment didn't stay just in Prussia; they continued to spread eastwards to Russia. That was not an obvious development: for a long time in Russia, there had been none of the things that had changed Europe since the Middle Ages; there were no cathedral schools or universities, the places that, in Europe, had been a breeding ground for scientific enquiry, criticism of the Church and the Reformation. For many centuries the land belonged to aristocratic landowners, the peasants were serfs – workers who were legally tied to the landowner's estate – and the monks lived in seclusion in monasteries and hermitages.

Tsar Peter the Great wanted to change that. He believed Russia needed to be redesigned, following the example of Europe. He changed almost everything. From education to the military to trade, there was hardly a sphere of life where Peter didn't completely reorganise things. As France was the golden standard at that time, he instructed his people to dress in French fashions and adopt French haircuts. If you wanted to keep your traditional Russian beard, you had to pay a special tax.

As a bold expression of his country's radical fresh start, Peter the Great had a city built in the swampy landscape where the River Neva flows into the Baltic Sea. The construction of St Petersburg was an unimaginably difficult feat decreed by the tsar. Thousands of builders, stonemasons and unskilled serfs were forced to drain the swamps, build houses and roads on more than forty islands and connect them with canals and bridges, modelling it on Venice.

1703: Russia looks to Europe as a role model. Peter the Great builds St Petersburg.

Many forced labourers tried to flee the harsh and often deadly conditions of work in the swamps. When the city was finished and Peter declared it the new Russian capital, the nobility reluctantly obeyed the command and moved from Moscow to St Petersburg. But in the end, the city served its purpose. Not only was it closer to Europe, but it was also able to compete in beauty with the continent's most famous cities – and Peter the Great had managed to get his vast country to turn its attention to the West.

After his death, Russia experienced a seventy-five-year 'Sultanate of Women', with mainly female rulers at the helm. Unlike the Ottoman Empire, these empresses came to the throne by accident, but nobody was particularly upset about it. Peter had no male heirs, so his daughter Elizabeth was crowned his successor. Empress Elizabeth was the first ruler to abolish the death penalty.

Her successor, Catherine the Great, was born Sophie Auguste Friederike von Anhalt-Zerbst. She grew up in Prussia and was sent by her parents to Russia to marry Elizabeth's nephew and heir to the throne, Peter III.

When she arrived in Russia, Sophie Auguste assumed the name Catherine, or Ekaterina. She applied herself assiduously to learning Russian and she devoured the political and philosophical tracts of the Enlightenment with equal enthusiasm. Her intellect and talent didn't go unnoticed: when her husband Peter III turned out to be a useless ruler, there was a *coup d'état* to put her on the throne instead. A group of Catherine's allies in the upper ranks of the nobility and military ousted him from power after just six months, and crowned her Catherine II, Empress of Russia.

Armed with the ideas of Voltaire, Montesquieu and Diderot, she began to reform Russia as radically as Peter the Great had done. She divided the country into administrative districts, built schools and hospitals, and helped the poor and homeless. Voltaire and Diderot were thrilled. At last, they thought, here in the chilly north was a country being ruled by a philosopher. Catherine corresponded with them both; she sent Voltaire money, invited Diderot to St Petersburg, and bought Voltaire's collected works and Diderot's entire library. The French Enlightenment had arrived in Russia.

She was the only female ruler to receive the honour of being called 'the Great'. When a committee decided to grant her this title, it wasn't only modern-thinking philosophers who agreed. Catherine the Great also proved herself a strong military leader, successfully waging war on all sides, particularly against the Ottoman Turks. The territory won in these wars considerably increased Russia's sphere of influence – of course, you could debate to what extent this was *good*, and for whom.

However, like almost all great rulers of history, Catherine the Great also disappointed her admirers. There was one philosopher who she had supported, even paying for him to study in Leipzig as a young man. When, in the spirit of the Enlightenment, he wrote a very critical book about conditions in Russia, the empress could not accept this, and she sentenced him to death. Although she eventually softened the punishment to exile for ten years, this was the end of her generosity when it came to freedom of thought. Empress Catherine tightened up censorship, and by subjecting all written work to scrutiny from now on, she betrayed the ideals of the philosophers she had once befriended.

From 1762: Seeing herself as an enlightened ruler, Catherine the Great buys the libraries of French philosophers.

Conflict between Prussia and Austria

Catherine wasn't the only great military strategist of the age. Frederick the Great also knew a thing or two about war and the spoils that could be won: he saw Poland, for example, as an artichoke that was waiting to be consumed, leaf by leaf. Frederick's father had claimed his son could neither ride nor shoot, that he was slovenly and let his hair grow long 'like a fool'. But his father was wrong, which wasn't often the case when it came to military matters.

Frederick the Great's father, Frederick William I, had reformed the Prussian army to become the model for the whole of Europe. This made Prussia strong, but also meant the next 100 years were spent in combat with the Habsburgs in Austria for supremacy over the German-speaking lands. Both wanted to gain the upper hand over this region to the east of France, which was divided into hundreds of small provinces. Poland was the first victim in this protracted conflict: Prussia, Austria and Russia shared out the leaves of the Polish artichoke between themselves, splitting the country in three.

From 1740: Prussia and Austria vie for supremacy in the German-speaking lands. Meanwhile, Austria, Prussia and Russia divide Poland between themselves several times.

Empress Maria Theresa, ruler of Austria and therefore of the Holy Roman Empire, was only interested in power, with no time for philosophy. The ideas of the Enlightenment probably wouldn't have been much help anyway when Frederick the Great invaded the Austrian province of Silesia with his troops. He justified this attack by commenting that the region could hardly be ruled by a woman on the throne – a surprisingly old-fashioned explanation for an enlightened ruler like Frederick, but one that was shared by most of Europe. The fact that Maria Theresa dared to be both a woman and a ruler would lead to eight years of war.

THE FOUNDING OF THE UNITED STATES OF AMERICA

Liber-tea

One December night in 1773, a group of men dressed as Native Americans sneaked into the harbour in the English colony of Boston, on the East Coast of North America. There they boarded three ships belonging to the East India Company, all loaded with vast quantities of tea, and proceeded to throw the tea overboard.

There was historical context to this act of vandalism. There had long been disputes between the inhabitants of the British colonies of North America and the motherland. The colonies had no one to represent their interests in the British Parliament, so they simply had to accept decisions negotiated far away on the British Isles; the British took advantage of this and increased taxes in the colonies to finance their expensive wars. Now they wanted to impose a monopoly on tea sales so that their American subjects had to buy British tea, thereby paying the high tariffs which might save the East India Company from bankruptcy. The Americans had had enough; they didn't want any more taxes they hadn't agreed to. In protest, the men in disguise threw all the crates of tea on board the East India Company's ships into the waters of Boston Harbor. The event went down in history as the 'Boston Tea Party'.

The Boston Tea Party became a wedge that once and for all divided the warring parties, and sparked a chain of events that would eventually lead to war being declared. The British

1773: On 16 December American colonists protest British taxation by throwing shipments of tea into Boston Harbor. The 'Boston Tea Party' sets off a chain of events that would eventually start the American Revolution.

1776: On
4 July thirteen
American
colonies
sign the
Declaration of
Independence,
forming the
United States of
America.

and Americans had already been fighting for some time when revolutionary leader Thomas Paine circulated a pamphlet calling for the Thirteen Colonies of America to become independent of Britain. This idea spread like wildfire, and within a few months, the colonies had formed a joint committee, which composed a Declaration of Independence. This was signed on 4 July 1776, which became the most important day in American history: the day when the Thirteen Colonies broke away from British rule and founded the United States of America. However, in response, King George III sent an army, ready to use military force to prevent the American colonies from parting ways with Britain. The United States had to fight for another seven years before achieving independence.

In the face of this struggle, women began to organise themselves politically for the first time. Even before the Boston Tea Party, they had founded 'Anti-Tea Leagues', where members pledged to stop drinking foreign tea. Instead, they brewed their own 'freedom tea', which they produced from native plants.

Some women were not content to support the struggle for independence by abstaining from English tea alone; ladies of the upper classes also waged war with words. At the forefront of this movement was Abigail Adams, who later became the wife of the second President of the United States. During the war for independence, she feared that the men who were penning a new constitution for the United States might neglect to consider the rights of women. She urged her husband to bear in mind that, 'If particular care and attention is not paid to the ladies, we are determined to foment a rebellion, and will not hold ourselves bound by any laws in which we have no voice or representation.' Abigail Adams's fears would prove true. Thomas Jefferson, who was in charge, wrote in the Declaration of Independence: 'All men are created equal.' Everyone had the right to life, freedom and the pursuit of happiness, it went on to say. But 'all men' in this context meant 'all white men'. These rights did not apply to women, nor to slaves or Native Americans – and the more time went by, the clearer it became that it was going to take more than a rebellion to change things.

In the end, the colonies won, partly because the French inter-vened by sending an army across the Atlantic to support them. After all, France benefitted from anything which weakened England. A peace treaty was signed seven years after Independence Day and England had no choice but to recognise the United States as an independent country. Finally, the Americans were able to pass their constitution into law, and a few years after, George Washington became their first president.

THE LAST CONTINENT IS DISCOVERED

No man's land

For the English, the loss of their American colonies was a huge blow; they had suddenly lost control of a vast territory. Luckily, this happened just as they were developing the Royal Navy into a sailing fleet superior to any worldwide. Soon they were able to make up for their defeat in America by seizing possession of an as-yet-unclaimed continent: Australia.

Although one or two Dutch sailors had indeed already set foot on Australian soil, it was the Briton James Cook who first explored the country more thoroughly. Britain declared it to be *terra nullius* – no man's land – claiming it belonged to no one. This was of course a blatant injustice to the native inhabitants of Australia. But the British didn't stop to worry about that; after all, they had done the same to the Native Americans. Britain used their new land primarily as a colony that was populated by entire shiploads of prisoners. And since the Home Secretary at the time was Lord Sydney, the first penal colony they founded was named Sydney.

1788: The British take possession of Australia, ignoring the fact that people already live there – as usual.

OLYMPE DE GOUGES DECLARES THE RIGHTS OF THE WOMAN AND CITIZEN

Liberty, equality, fraternity

Inspired by the ideas of the Enlightenment, the Americans had formed a new, independent state. They elected a man as their leader and called him not king, but president. Although women weren't allowed to vote (meaning there were also no women at the helm), many felt that this was progress. Here, in the New World, the first modern democracy had been created.

How different things looked in France, with its ancient monarchy, extravagant court life and social structure that granted so many rights to the nobility and so few to the peasants. How far they were from a new beginning! Courtiers at Versailles seemed oblivious to the fact that a revolution was taking place in America. It didn't occur to Louis – by now it was Louis XVI – that the world was changing, and that this could also have consequences for him, the King of France.

Recent wars had cost France a great deal of money and the treasury was empty. Louis XVI was forced to convene a general assembly, called the 'Estates General', which brought together representatives of the three estates of the realm: the clergy; the nobility; and the bourgeoisie and the peasants. He needed their approval to raise taxes. The representatives didn't mind – for them, it was finally an opportunity to make their own demands of the king. They wanted more say; it was time for the king to share his absolute power with them.

Louis XVI refused but, given the state of his finances, he couldn't afford to. The representatives stood by their demands. They met in a ballroom in Paris and formed a rival National Assembly, vowing they would not be dismissed until France had a constitution. In an instant, they abolished all the privileges enjoyed by the nobility and the clergy. In the National Assembly, the parliamentarians were equal.

The king had long faced criticism from his people. The empty coffers meant a hike in bread prices at a time when poverty was on the rise, and many were starving. The story goes that Marie Antoinette, the wife of King Louis XVI, exclaimed, 'If the people have no bread, then let them eat cake!' when she heard people's complaints about the lack of bread. She probably never said that, but history shows that many believed that the king and his wife were not much moved by the plight of the people of France.

1789: On 14 July the French Revolution begins with the storming of the Bastille.

The people revolted because no one was doing anything about the rising price of bread; people's hunger and desperation led to rioting at bakeries. One thing led to another, and suddenly the citizens had armed themselves and were storming the Bastille, the notorious prison in Paris. Many state officials were attacked by the mob, and the prison governor was brutally murdered.

When people are starving, they break down the barricades. But would they also do that for the ideals of the Enlightenment? Nobody knows if the assault on the Bastille would have happened if bread prices had not risen so high. Members of the National Assembly supported the popular uprising, shouting, '*Liberté, Égalité, Fraternité!*' – 'Liberty, Equality, Fraternity!' – which became the motto of the revolution. By now the French people were not just angry about poverty and the lavish exuberance of Versailles: it had become a struggle for human and civil rights.

The revolution picks up pace

The storming of the Bastille kicked off the French Revolution and sent everything descending into chaos. Meanwhile, Louis and his court were some 15 miles away at Versailles, the king still refusing to make any concessions to the National Assembly.

There was the National Assembly in Paris, zealously working on a constitution, with the king still confident it would all soon blow over. On the streets, citizens were getting more and more passionate and vocal about the principles of liberty, equality and brotherhood. They held meetings, distributed pamphlets, published journals and published bitter polemics against the authorities and the Church.

There were women who started their own newspapers and clubs. It was high time – after all, they had even fewer rights than men of the lowest social rank. Women were finally organising themselves, participating in the meetings and speaking up in the debates. Some took up arms themselves and pushed themselves into the forefront of the action.

The revolutionaries wanted total change – they wanted to do everything differently. They deconsecrated churches and the great Parisian cathedral Notre-Dame became a Temple of Reason, a church for their short-lived 'replacement religion' that celebrated the ideals of the French Revolution. This was such a radical break with tradition and the old way of running the country – the *Ancien Régime* – that even the months were given new names.

The storming of the Bastille was followed by a long pause in the power struggle between Louis XVI and the National Assembly. But then the people couldn't wait any longer. A huge crowd marched to Versailles, led by the market women, known as the 'fish wives', who had faced some of the worst difficulties during the food shortages. Arriving before the palace, the protesters noisily settled down for the night. The next day, they forced the king to come to Paris and finally to respond to the demands of his people.

Although the women were celebrated as heroines and many of them were prepared to join the battle and die for the revolution, their concerns as women were given scant attention. And yet again, the fact that the slogan 'Liberty, Equality, Fraternity' addressed only half of the population – the brothers – and excluded France's sisters seemed to bother no one.

Women and slaves

1791: Olympe de Gouges writes the *Declaration of the Rights of Woman and the Female Citizen*. She is the first in history to express the human rights of all people.

Well, almost no one. A writer named Olympe de Gouges, previously known for writing plays, published the *Declaration of the Rights of Woman and the Female Citizen*, expressing for the first time in history the concept of human rights for *everyone*. In this manifesto, she argued for equality by referring to the death penalty: 'Women have the right to mount the scaffold, they must also have the right to mount the speaker's rostrum.' The constitution that had just been passed by the new National Assembly meant nothing unless the nation's mothers, daughters and sisters were also represented. As long as men simply excluded women, argued Gouges, the new government was just as likely as the last to descend into tyranny.

1792: Mary Wollstonecraft publishes *A Vindication of the Rights of Woman*, one of the first modern feminist texts.

Over in England, the writer Mary Wollstonecraft also noticed that, when people spoke of civil and human rights, these were exclusively male rights. She responded with a book entitled *A Vindication of the Rights of Woman*.

Olympe de Gouges confronted men with harsh accusations. Her frustration was hardly surprising considering her lack of freedom in her aristocratic family: her father didn't allow her or her mother out of the house. And by law he was entitled to control them in this way – after all, he was a man.

Wollstonecraft, on the other hand, criticised women and accused them of tacitly accepting their own lack of voice rather than rebelling against it. 'Strengthen the female mind by enlarging it, and there will be an end to blind obedience,' she wrote. The book brought her instant fame; it was translated into several languages and printed abroad. Despite this, she was ridiculed in England, and a well-known writer even called her a 'hyena in a petticoat'.

But, as has often been the case in history, there were also men who spoke up for women. The Marquis de Condorcet wrote:

> It ought to be hard to prove that women are incapable of exercising their rights as citizens. Why should one group of people, because they are able to become pregnant and feel unwell from time to time, not enjoy rights that would never be denied to those who suffer from gout every winter and are prone to catching a cold?

The marquis supported women's right to vote (women's suffrage), and called for the abolition of slavery, as did Olympe de Gouges, who wrote a play about the injustice of slavery. Condorcet and Gouges were the first to consider what it meant to make a *universal* declaration of human rights: it had to apply to everyone, women as well as slaves. At the time of the French Revolution, however, there were still extremely few people who thought like this. Gouges' play caused such a scandal that it was discontinued after just a few performances.

Off with their heads

There was no time for a detailed discussion of women's rights during the troubled and chaotic days of the French Revolution. One convulsion followed another, always on the verge of tipping into all-out war. There was too much at stake. If the king no longer had power and neither did the National Assembly, who was in charge of making sure everything was in order?

So far, the two parties in the National Assembly – the moderate Girondins who wanted to keep the king and the radical Jacobins who wanted to abolish the monarchy – had been arguing with words alone. But Louis XVI didn't trust that the moderates would prevail, and he didn't think much of the idea of sharing power with a parliament anyway. Instead, he secretly asked the rulers of Prussia and Austria for help; after all, Austria's Empress Maria Theresa was the mother of his wife Marie Antoinette.

And so, while the National Assembly debated, France was attacked by an alliance of Prussian and Austrian troops. Although they were not exactly friends with the French king, Europe's monarchs were very afraid that the revolution in France could spark unrest in their own countries. Hoping to intimidate them, the commander of the Prussian troops issued a drastic warning – known as the Brunswick Manifesto – to the citizens of Paris: if anything were to happen to King Louis, or if any of the royal family were exposed to even the slightest harm, Paris would be razed to the ground.

This threat by the foreign powers triggered a turnaround in the revolution. The revolutionaries feared a war where they risked losing everything they had achieved so far. They panicked and, since Louis had clearly betrayed them, the radical forces prevailed. Once again, angry crowds stormed the prisons. Angry protestors attacked and killed many prisoners thought to be royalists, who would fight against the revolution if they were released, but many were convicts who had no political role at all. Thousands were massacred.

After the incident that went down in history as the September Massacre, the revolutionaries deposed the king and declared France a republic. Since Louis had allied himself with France's enemies, he was charged with high treason. But while he was still king, even while he was in prison, representatives of the National Assembly tried to persuade him to approve the constitution. But Monsieur and Madame Véto, as the people started calling Louis and Marie Antoinette, refused (although 'Madame Véto' didn't have the right to sign a constitution, as she was 'only' the king's wife). The French king made the world realise the consequence of such a stubborn refusal to compromise. Louis and his wife were beheaded by guillotine.

1793: King Louis XVI and Queen Marie Antoinette of France are beheaded with the guillotine.

Charlotte Corday

1794: The Jacobins under Robespierre and Danton establish a reign of terror. In the end, they themselves fall victim to the violence.

After the execution of the royal couple, all the good intentions of the Enlightenment and the revolution seemed to be reversed. The Jacobin leaders, Maximilien de Robespierre and Georges Danton, unleashed a period of horrific violence known as the Reign of Terror. They executed anyone who voiced even the slightest doubt about the revolution and its leaders.

Many looked on in horror. Charlotte Corday, who had moved to Paris as a young woman full of enthusiasm for the revolution, saw how the Jacobins lost all sense of restraint: Robespierre and Danton were executing thousands in the belief that this was the only way the revolution could be accomplished. For Corday, however, these weren't the only culprits; she blamed the journalist Jean Paul Marat for inciting violence with his incendiary writing. She was convinced that she could save France and free the country from the Reign of Terror if she murdered this one villain. So she made contact with him and asked to visit him, claiming she had important information. Once she had entered his apartment, Corday joined Marat in the bathroom and talked to him for a while as he lay in the bath (he conducted most of his business there as he had to take regular medicinal baths to treat a skin problem). Suddenly she pulled out a knife and stabbed the unsuspecting revolutionary. She was arrested and put on trial. Just four days after the murder, she too was executed by guillotine.

1793: Charlotte Corday murders the revolutionary Jean Paul Marat in his bathtub, claiming that she wants to save the ideas of the revolution.

Corday's hope of saving the ideals of the revolution was not fulfilled. On the contrary, her act actually damaged the prospects for women. Their clubs and associations were banned, and while their efforts and battles had previously been welcomed, there were now calls for women to stay out of it and to remain at home.

Olympe de Gouges also blamed Marat, Robespierre and Danton for the September Massacre. Like many at the time, she thought it had been wrong to behead the king – she had even offered to represent him in court. She put up posters and published pamphlets against the Jacobin government and wasn't afraid to attack Robespierre in person. She must have known that she was preparing her own path to the guillotine. Shortly before she was beheaded, she wrote to the Revolutionary Tribunal:

Does Article 7 of the constitution not bless the freedom of expression, and of the press, as the most precious heritage of man? These rights, this heritage, this actual constitution, are they only vague phrases with illusory meanings? Alas! That is my sad experience; republicans, pay attention to my words, right to the end.

But the revolutionaries had had enough of women dabbling in politics. 'Remember this shameless man-woman,' they threatened. 'Olympe de Gouges, who founded societies for women, neglected her household, wanted to be political and committed heinous crimes. Such immoral beings were annihilated under the axe that avenges the laws. Would you imitate her?' Five days after Olympe de Gouges, another woman stepped onto the executioner's scaffold: Madame Roland, a famous salon host who was known across all of Paris. For years Jacobins and Girondins had met in her house, but now she too had fallen out of favour. As she stepped up to the guillotine, she is said to have exclaimed, 'Oh Liberty, how many crimes are committed in your name!'

REVOLUTION AND RESTORATION

France gets an emperor

When Robespierre, the leader of the Jacobins, had his own comrade Danton executed, he had gone too far. He himself was on the executioner's scaffold a few months later. His death was followed by chaos and confusion that Napoleon Bonaparte was quick to exploit, promoting himself to the head of a new government. This short man from Corsica was shrewd, lucky and had serious ambitions.

His quick thinking and talent helped him to climb through the ranks in the military, from being an ordinary soldier to eventually taking over the reins of government. France was still a republic, and Napoleon, following the example of the ancient Romans, declared himself consul for ten years. 'Citizens!' he announced. 'The revolution has returned to the principles from which it started; it has reached its end.' He reorganised the state and gave it a law, the *Code Civil* or Napoleonic Code, that guaranteed citizens' rights.

1804: Napoleon introduces the *Code Civil*, a legal code that guarantees civil rights to all men in France.

His first ventures were testament to his strategic skill and cunning. Glancing enviously at the wealth England, Holland and Portugal were accumulating from their overseas trade, Napoleon proclaimed that France needed colonies, declaring: 'Great glory can only be won in the Orient; for this, Europe is too small.' He prepared an expeditionary force of ships that sailed to North Africa and occupied Egypt. He presented himself as a son of the French Revolution, who wanted to carry the light of the Enlightenment to the East.

Unfortunately, Napoleon and his troops failed to appreciate how alien the European forms of government and administration were to the Egyptians. They struggled to persuade the Egyptians to accept the wonderful ideas of the Enlightenment (such ideas are less persuasive when they're introduced by coercion). This foray into North Africa ended with the French brutally suppressing an Egyptian rebellion and destroying many mosques. France defended its first colony with the tried and tested methods of brute force.

Back in France, Napoleon was helped by a little luck. The Jacobins had turned the revolution into a bloodbath and the French people were still deeply traumatised by all the violence. Many longed for a king again, but one who would accept a constitution and guarantee civil rights. Sensing this longing for a strong hand to guide the country, Napoleon had himself crowned not as king, but as 'Emperor of the French', without encountering much opposition. This was a first: France had never had its own emperor before.

France gets a king again

Napoleon had big plans and it gradually became clear just how big. Taking inspiration from Europe's mightiest generals, Napoleon wanted a legacy that put him on a par with Alexander the Great and Caesar. Following their example, he set out to conquer Europe. He led his fearsome army east and won battle after battle. The German principalities, Prussia, Austria – none could stop him. The Emperor of the French and his mighty army seemed invincible.

Napoleon rebuilt Europe from the foundations up. He dissolved the 1,000-year-old Holy Roman Empire, as well as many Church institutions and monasteries. He reorganised entire kingdoms and principalities, and he imposed the Napoleonic Code as the basic law everywhere he went. Europe became French, and because this conqueror came as the bearer of civil rights, he was met by many with great enthusiasm. He was seen as completing the work of the Enlightenment and liberating them from ancient power relations.

Like the Poles, for example. Having had their territory split three ways between Prussia, Austria and Russia, the Poles placed their faith in Napoleon to liberate them and give them their country back. 'Poland is not yet lost,' they sang, and Polish soldiers fought alongside the French. They also trusted the emperor's good intentions, because all of Europe knew that he had a Polish mistress, the Countess Maria Walewska. And since love was always a political matter in the lives of the powerful, Countess Walewska was lobbied by the Polish nobility to stand up for the cause of her nation.

Napoleon set his sights on all of Europe, and he got what he wanted – but he went too far when he crossed the border into Russia. Here he encountered an opponent even mightier than the Emperor of the French: the cold Russian winter. On their march through the vast expanses of Russia, Napoleon's troops faced a wretched fate as thousands froze and starved to death. Napoleon had to retreat, and as half of Europe had by now formed alliances against him, he finally experienced his first crushing defeat at the Battle of Leipzig.

1804: After crowning himself Emperor of the French, Napoleon conquers half of Europe; only the Russian winter stops his army.

Madame Germaine de Staël, a great French intellectual, probably breathed a sigh of relief when she heard of her emperor's defeat. She had taken part in the storming of the Bastille, she had received all the movers and shakers at her influential salon, she was the intelligent author of many texts, and she had intimidated even Schiller and Goethe in Germany with her highly erudite monologues. But she was disappointed with Napoleon. De Staël saw him as a power-hungry tyrant of the old style, whose promotion of civil rights was merely a façade. She wrote books that said as much, and became a focal point for like-minded people, which embarrassed Napoleon so much that he exiled her from Paris – she couldn't come within 40 miles of it. Whilst in exile, she wrote De l'Allemagne (Of Germany), her most important work. In Of Germany she described her country's neighbour as the 'land of poets and thinkers' – de Staël felt you could breathe more freely in Germany than in imperial France. Napoleon resented this 'anti-French' criticism and had the book censored; all the French copies were seized and destroyed, and de Staël persecuted by the police. She managed to evade them, however, and slipped away with her children, travelling to London via Vienna, Kiev, Moscow, St Petersburg and Stockholm. Of Germany was published in England in 1813, the same year that Napoleon's fortunes changed and he was defeated at Leipzig by the allied European armies.

Napoleon was exiled to the Mediterranean island of Elba as a prisoner, but he escaped after a year and resumed his throne in Paris to

303

rule for another 100 days. The allied forces rallied against him again and finally beat him at Waterloo; this time he was banished to the island of St Helena, in the South Atlantic Ocean. The French were given a king again, another Louis, and the French kingdom was welcomed back into the bosom of the European royal family.

The Vienna Congress

While Napoleon was recovering from his first defeat, the Austrian Foreign Minister, Prince of Metternich-Winneburg invited the old European powers to a congress in Vienna. The mood was strained as the parties sought to redefine Europe's states and their borders. Austria wanted to be stronger than Prussia; Russia wanted most of Poland; Prussia wanted Saxony; France didn't want Germany to become too big; and England didn't want Russia to become too strong. Britain and Russia were both eyeing up the ailing Ottoman Empire.

To lighten the mood, delegates of the Vienna Congress were treated to constant entertainments such as dances, theatrical performances, hunts, sleigh rides, fireworks displays and races. The scale of the entertainments budget was staggering. There were balls held for some 10,000 guests, where 7,000 candles were burned, and concerts with orchestras made up of 1,000 musicians – one even had 100 pianos. Several observers reported home that there was a lot of dancing going on at the Vienna Congress, but not much work. That may have been a misunderstanding. After all, the most complex negotiations were often mediated on the sidelines by the negotiators' wives: the balls were the venue for endless private conversations, cautious approaches and attempts to forge alliances. No women were present at the official discussions, but they had a key role to play at the balls and the theatre, as well as in the salons and boudoirs.

1814–15: The First Restoration begins with the Vienna Congress.

The rulers of Europe agreed on one thing: they would return Europe to the conditions before the French Revolution and restore the old monarchies where the king or prince governed by the grace of God. The Congress of Vienna marked the start of the era of restoration:, restoring the pre-revolutionary status quo.

Restoration undoes Revolution

The Enlightenment had left an emotional impact on the people of Europe. They had wanted freedom, equality and brotherhood (the voices calling for sisterhood were still in the minority), but now they experienced the same disappointment as Germaine de Staël. The restoration, spearheaded by the Austrian Prince Metternich, limited their rights, censored their texts and criminalised anyone who voiced an opinion in public. You faced a jail sentence if you were found with a radical poem in your pocket.

The Germans, Italians, Czechs, Poles and Hungarians united around a new common goal. Across Europe, where once Napoleon's French soldiers had been quartered in every village, many now became aware that they themselves were not French; they were Italians, Germans, Czechs, Poles or Hungarians. Becoming more conscious of their national identity, they developed a fascination for their own language and an interest in collecting and writing down fairy tales and folk songs, and drawing maps that defined the landscape of their homeland.

The new idea on everyone's lips was that of the 'nation' and 'nationality'. Suddenly everyone wanted to live in their own nation state. The inhabitants of the principalities of Naples, Sicily, Rome, Turin and Venice recognised their common Italian identity and wanted to form a united Italy. Likewise, in Württemberg, Saxony, Bavaria and Hesse, German-speakers dreamed of having their own German national assembly. The Irish wanted independence from the United Kingdom, while the Poles sang their anthem 'Poland is not yet lost' and continued their struggle against their Russian, Prussian and Austrian overlords. The Hungarians, Czechs, Slovaks, Germans, Italians, Slovenians and Croats no longer wanted to be part of Austria. But this was precisely their fate after the Congress of Vienna: Austria was defined as a multi-ethnic state, ruled by the Habsburg family.

Yet, even to this day there is debate about what exactly is meant by a 'nation'. Generally speaking, a nation unites people who share the same language and religion, and whose ancestors have long been associated with the land they inhabit. The nation therefore includes everyone who has 'always been there'. And this is precisely why the concept is so complicated and flawed, because throughout history people have always been on the move. For one reason or another, they move and settle somewhere else, initially as foreigners, until at some point it's impossible to say who is a foreigner and who is native. Are the descendants of Spaniards who emigrated to Central and South America 500 years ago still Spaniards or are they Chileans, Argentines and Cubans? What about the French Huguenots who emigrated to Switzerland, the Netherlands, England and Germany in the seventeenth century?

Despite this problematic aspect, the idea of the nation has become one of the most successful concepts in history. Today the whole world is divided into nation states. In countless disputes and devastating wars, long-established empires such as the Austrian Habsburg monarchy and the Ottoman Empire disintegrated, with new nation states forming in the breakaway regions. It all started in Europe in the nineteenth century.

Two concepts came to define nineteenth-century Europe: the values of the Enlightenment – the call for freedom and human rights – and the idea of the nation. As the idea that people could only live happily in a nation state became rooted, this definition seemed to contradict the concept of universal human rights. As soon as people said 'France for the French' or 'Italy for the Italians', they began to imply that, for one reason or another, there would be outsiders who were not considered French or Italian, and therefore had fewer civil rights. In the nation state, all of a sudden, nobody was equal any more.

1848: Revolution sparks in many European cities. People fight for freedom, equality and brotherhood, and to be part of a nation state.

When an idea starts to spread, it is sometimes hard to stop. The new wave of revolutionaries no longer campaigned for human rights alone, but for their dream of uniting within a nation state. About thirty years after the Congress of Vienna, crowds protested in cities across Europe, from Paris to Warsaw; they built barricades and fought street battles with the military and police forces. A few weeks later, German revolutionaries held their first National Assembly in Frankfurt. Since there was no parliament building, they met in the Church of St Paul.

The people's revolution saw some success, at first. In Austria, Prince Metternich was forced to resign, while Friedrich Wilhelm IV of Prussia was helpless as he observed the events unfolding in Frankfurt. A year later, the members of the St Paul's Church parliament offered the crown to the Prussian king, proposing that Germany become a constitutional monarchy like England – a state with a king and a constitution. But Friedrich Wilhelm refused. How could he accept a crown offered to him by his subjects? His power came from God!

Friedrich Wilhelm and the other European monarchs rallied their troops to crush this revolution by force. A year later, the revolutionary army was defeated. Europe's second revolution had failed. There would be no German state, as defined by the National Assembly at St Paul's Church. For now, anyway. Instead, thirty years later, the Prussian government would establish the Deutsches Kaiserreich, the German Empire. The many nationalities and ethnic groups who lived in the Austrian Empire had to wait even longer before they could establish their own nation states.

1871: The German Empire is re-established, with the Prussian King Wilhelm I crowned as emperor.

THE TRIUMPH OF THE MACHINE

The Spinning Jenny

Texere is a Latin verb that means 'to weave'. A text is a fabric spun from narrative threads. As with sewing, crocheting or knitting, when we compose a text or tell a story we choose the events that will be our threads and we choose how we create patterns and images from them. And so every history, including world history, is a text woven from an infinite number of threads.

Textiles and texts are among the oldest products in the world. For millennia, fibres have been spun into threads and woven into cloth, and our habit of telling stories is just as old. One such story is the great historical narrative which marginalises women and presents them as inferior and incapable; this is a fabric that has been woven and rewoven since time immemorial in the minds of men. For centuries, many women bought into this idea, like a cloth merchant buying a bolt of fabric. They believed the men who insisted that a woman's place was at home and her role in life was to sit at the spinning wheel, making yarn.

That was now starting to change. While people in America and Europe fought for freedom and civil rights, the biggest revolution was just about to begin: the Industrial Revolution. It started with the invention of machines and it wasn't long before it changed the world.

1764: The Industrial Revolution begins.

One of the first inventions of the Industrial Revolution was the Spinning Jenny, a machine that could spin four to eight threads of yarn on four to eight spools at once – the work of eight women. At around the same time, engineers invented the steam engine, which replaced human muscle power with mechanically generated energy. And since these machines were 100 times stronger than humans, there were soon new steam-powered spinning machines which could drive 100 spools, rather than the hand-powered ones that managed eight. A single spinning machine could now replace 100 women spinning with the traditional spindles.

The Industrial Revolution began in England, in the parlours where women span and in the coal mines. Until then, the coal for heating had been dragged out of the low tunnels by men and children; it was hard work, and many fell ill or died young. Now the coal was used to produce steam power, and that steam power could in turn be used to bring more coal from the mines.

The steam engine suddenly made it possible to produce unimaginable physical strength and power. New agricultural machinery lightened the load for farmers in the fields. Steamships crossed the ocean at unprecedented speed, and soon the first railways connected small English provincial towns with London.

The machines needed space and people to run them, so factories began to emerge, and with them the housing quarters for the workers. Engineers also found new uses for the earth beneath the streets. In large cities, such as Paris or London, sewers were introduced to dispose of human excrement and waste. Whole streets of houses were demolished in London, Paris and Vienna to give architects and city planners the space to almost completely redesign the old city centres. They wanted to make room for factories and sewers, for underground trains and trams, and for large town houses for the growing middle class, built with indoor bathrooms and toilets. Nutrition, hygiene and medical care all improved, leading to rapid growth in the population. For the first time, people were thinking about controlling the birth rate – a question that affected women above all. Was it right or necessary for women to get pregnant over and over? And who had the power to decide?

1798: For the first time, people consider population growth. One hundred years later, the first birth control clinic opens – birth control will fundamentally change women's lives.

DARWIN AND MARX EXPLAIN THE WORLD

The new man

Let's go back to the beginning of history. When the hunters and gatherers of the Stone Age developed agriculture and began to settle, they saw the natural world around them as inhabited by gods. Then, after about 2,000–3,000 years, the idea spread in many parts of the world that there was just one god who created the world and man. This was the age when today's major world religions emerged.

Some 2,000–3,000 years after *that*, Europe saw the beginning of the modern era. It became increasingly rare for people to look up at the sky for answers to difficult questions, and gradually the idea took shape that God might perhaps not even exist. God began to be replaced by science: scientific questioning and empirical evidence could answer our questions. It wasn't long before a naturalist gave the final death blow to the very concept of God as a creator.

The evidence encountered by scientists was becoming less and less consistent with the idea, as described in the Bible, that God had created the world in seven days and entrusted it to mankind. What were people to make of the fossils Mary Anning had dug out of the limestone at Lyme Regis in Dorset, England?

Mary Anning was still a young girl when she first discovered fossils on her walks. Since she came from a poor background and had no access to higher education, she taught herself geology, anatomy, palaeontology (the study of life on Earth via fossils) and scientific drawing. Researchers in London became aware of her work and paid Mary Anning a visit – it turned out that she had stumbled across the remains of prehistoric animals, which came to be known later as dinosaurs. However, Mary Anning's sensational fossil discoveries and her contribution to the study of dinosaurs were not recognised by the Royal Society until 2010, almost 200 years after her death.

Fossils found by Mary Anning and other researchers all contributed to the accumulation of knowledge about the origin of the world and of different species. Charles Darwin is likely to have heard about their discoveries.

Charles Darwin sailed for five years around the world, stopping to study the animals and plants of various continents. Working from the evidence, he formulated his theory of evolution, which he outlined in a book called *On the Origin of Species*. Darwin had noticed that plants could spread better and animals had more young if they were particularly well adapted to their environment. These adaptation characteristics were then passed on to their offspring, while others lacking those strengths were less able to reproduce. A process of natural selection was taking place, where 'weaker' life forms became extinct and 'stronger ones' were better placed to reproduce.

1859: Charles Darwin publishes *On the Origin of Species*, where he develops the theory of evolution.

Darwin's theory was explosive: he claimed that humans, animals and plants were not created by God. Instead, they were the result of evolution, a constant process of gradual change that took millions of years. Every creature on Earth had slowly evolved to its current form. And, as if this idea were not revolutionary enough, Darwin expressed another idea which at that point was completely unheard of: humans, too, had gone through this process of evolution from simpler to more advanced creatures, ever more sophisticated and capable. Mankind had descended from apes.

This message was not easy to digest. Many interpreted this assertion – that man was not God's most treasured creation, but was in fact a distant relation of the ape – as an assault on their dignity. Darwin had managed to insult God and mankind at the same time. But his contemporaries quickly recovered from the shock. After all, didn't evolutionary theory suggest that man was the highest level of development? Couldn't mankind still keep the crown as the pinnacle of creation?

At first, the Industrial Revolution, which was by now truly under way, seemed to support this idea. Developments in technology gave the natural sciences a boost, because the more precise equipment meant scientists could carry out better experiments. This was the dawn of chemistry as we know it. Scientists could now break everything down into smaller units; they could weigh, measure and analyse even the tiniest particles. There seemed to be nothing that couldn't be investigated, whether it was a grain of sand or human breath. The first pioneering experiments were carried out by Marie and Antoine Lavoisier, a married couple who were both chemists. They wrote everything down in minute detail and laid the foundations for modern chemistry – and as Marie was a talented illustrator, she kept accurate sketches to document their work.

Chemistry gave people insight into the world of substances that were invisible to the naked eye: the smallest particles, atoms and elements. At last, scientists began to understand biological processes in the body better, not just in the human body, but also those of animals and plants. From here it was only a few steps before medicine could hunt down bacteria, viruses and pathogens.

As fascination grew for the realm of the minute, the microscope became more important than the telescope. The sky – once seen as the realm of God – came to be seen as an entire universe, a realm whose mysteries scientists could decode with the tools of physics and chemistry.

Innovation was everywhere, changing every sphere of life, often for the better. And so, the Industrial Revolution gave people utopian dreams: many believed that, with the help of technology, they could solve all humanity's problems, eradicating hunger, disease and social injustice. After all, as Voltaire had joked at the beginning of the Enlightenment, God had obviously not succeeded.

New slaves

Although technological advances convinced many that this was the dawn of a golden age, it also became apparent that the Industrial Revolution was creating new problems. When spinning machines were introduced that could each replace 100 women working in their parlours, suddenly thousands lost their jobs. In England, where there had been centuries of cottage industries producing the finest cloths, suddenly vast swathes of the country were plunged into poverty. Farms needed fewer workers out in the fields, while in the towns and cities craftsmen were losing their work to machines. How could they earn a living to feed their family? If you didn't find a job in a factory, you starved to death. This was a disaster that soon struck the rest of Europe. Widespread poverty resulted in mass emigration, with tens of thousands of people leaving their homes to start a new life in the United States.

But even if you found work in a factory, life was harsh. Once a shoemaker would make an entire pair of shoes from start to finish, but now he was forced to stand on an assembly line, sticking soles together for hours on end, carrying out the same hand movement over and over. He often didn't even get to see the finished product at the end of the chain. Workers were alienated from their work, reduced to little more than robots.

Working conditions were appalling. Workers often inhaled toxic fumes from adhesives or other substances with no protection; they were malnourished, with very little or no access to medical attention; and they were paid a pittance. Factories were an entirely new phenomenon, so no one was thinking about how to protect workers from danger. Workers had no rights and the factory owners took full advantage of this. If you didn't want to be exploited, you could go: factory owners knew there would be plenty of other workers queuing up to accept even the worst conditions, desperate to feed their families. The impact of the Industrial Revolution gradually became clear. It wasn't just the physical world that had changed, with new houses, streets, cities, railways, canals and ships – the interactions and relationships between human beings were also changing.

The philosopher Karl Marx wrote about these changes in society. He pointed out that workers didn't enjoy much in the way of freedom, equality or fraternity when they toiled away for a pittance in the factories. They were little more than slaves, he argued. Marx devised the term 'capitalists' for the wealthy factory owners who all but enslaved their workers.

Marx observed that society had changed from the old feudal way of life where communities were based around rural estates. The old social hierarchy of nobles, merchants, artisans and peasants had evolved into a new order of masters and servants. The masters were the capitalist factory owners who ruled over the workers; they owned houses, factories and a lot of money, while their employees had nothing except their ability to work. Society was divided into different classes, with the vast majority of the population falling into the working class, which Marx called 'the proletariat'.

Marx prophesied that the future would be determined by conflict between these layers in society: a class struggle. He called on the workers to fight for a classless society, where all citizens were equal; there were no more masters and servants; and property and possessions would be distributed equally and fairly across all members of society. He popularised a new ideal for society: 'communism'.

Marx published his observations and ideas in a book called *Das Kapital*. Together he and his friend Friedrich Engels wrote *The Communist Manifesto*, published the year a new wave of revolutions broke out across many European cities. The manifesto begins with the words: 'A spectre is haunting Europe – the spectre of communism.' These words were intended to frighten the capitalists.

Marx's thinking had an incredible impact; his ideas turned society upside down. Marx had described how the Industrial Revolution had created a new social class, the proletariat, and he predicted that class struggle would be the dominant theme of the future. All political thought, argued Marx, would from now on be determined not by questions of religion or science, but by economics – that is, by money.

People tried to resist the changes brought about by industrialisation. Protestors attacked the machines and destroyed them; in some cities, weavers even staged an armed uprising after losing their jobs to the new mechanical looms. Soon, however, people started to realise there was nothing they could do to stop the onslaught of technology. Instead, they formed workers' associations, or trade unions, to put pressure on governments and lobby for workers' rights. Many saw communism as the solution. They believed that injustice and oppression would not be eradicated until all land and property was fairly distributed among the people.

1848: Karl Marx and Friedrich Engels publish The Communist Manifesto and call on the workers to engage in a class conflict against the capitalists.

Missed chances

It's quite remarkable that, after every single revolution, women still found themselves trapped at home with none of the rights of men. It was the case when the Church deprived women of a voice. It was the case in the Muslim world, even though the Prophet Muhammad had rejected customs such as forced marriage. It was the case with the Protestants, who silenced Marie Dentière. And it was the case with the Enlightenment, where leading figures such as Rousseau argued that freedoms and rights didn't apply to women. Even the French Revolution had ended with the execution of Olympe de Gouges, which warned women: look what happens when a woman abandons her responsibilities at home and interferes in politics!

Now the great thinker Karl Marx had also joined the long struggle for freedom and justice. But while he spoke up for the millions of workers who were enslaved in the factories, he overlooked the endless unpaid work that women were forced to do in the home. It didn't offend his sense of injustice that women weren't paid for the drudgery of cooking, cleaning, laundry and raising children, or that women were often treated as little more than slaves by men.

Men, as ever, continued to take all decisions on behalf of their wives, aided by the Napoleonic Code, which defined persons without legal rights as minors, married women, criminals and those who are mentally disabled. Women, according to the law, were the property of their husbands. Men also had the legal right to beat their wives; it was deemed acceptable at the time for criminals and mentally ill people to be physically abused, so why not women? They all fell into the legal category of those excluded from the protection of the law, after all.

The Reformation, the Enlightenment and the French Revolution all brought people more freedom, resulting in parliaments and civil rights that were codified in the law. But when we speak of the rights gained by 'people', it was always restricted to the male half of the population. Where were the women? Why didn't they join the struggle along with Marie Dentière, Olympe de Gouges and Mary Wollstonecraft? What would have happened if Marx had also condemned slavery in the home? Would we have to pay for housework today, just as we pay for any other kind of work?

There were men who noticed that women were generally worse off than workers in the factories. Among them was the English philosopher John Stuart Mill. He was the first to speak up for women in the British Parliament and call for women to be given the right to vote. However, his suggestion was laughed at by the entire House of Commons.

When Karl Marx was expelled from his homeland because of his incendiary writing, he recommended a newspaper to his readers. It was edited by German revolutionary Mathilde Franziska Anneke; even if he failed to recognise the work of women in the home, he did at least appreciate the work of an intelligent female activist. But shortly thereafter, a law was passed in Saxony and Prussia prohibiting women from printing newspapers. Anneke was forced to shut down her newspaper, and instead she and her husband took up arms and fought with the revolutionaries against the authorities. When the German revolution was finally crushed in the summer of 1849, they fled with many like-minded people to America.

PROGRESS AND REGRESSION

Lady Montagu and Montesquieu report from Constantinople

We live in the modern age. It's hard to say precisely what that means and when this era began because, like so many others, the term 'modernity' is the subject of much debate. Nevertheless, words like this help us to identify and understand certain changes. In this case, technology and science, the Enlightenment and the Industrial Revolution all changed the world to such an extent that they ushered in a new era.

In the Middle Ages, China and the Arabs were leagues ahead of the Europeans. In modern times, however, this relationship was reversed. Ever since the Europeans started to create new art, new technology, new ideas and new ways of trading, the large, powerful empires of China and the Ottomans started to lag behind.

Some say that the Ottoman Empire lost its lead because of religious advisers warning against innovations in science. The French scholar Charles de Montesquieu was an early observer of this decline and described it in rather unfriendly words:

These barbarians have neglected the arts to such an extent that they have even abandoned the art of war. While the European nations continue to evolve on a daily basis, they remain steadfast in their old ignorance and only come around to the idea of adopting one of the Europeans' new inventions after they have had it used a thousand times against them.

But perhaps the picture Montesquieu drew was rather one-sided. Lady Mary Montagu, the wife of an English diplomat, was in Constantinople at almost the same time as Montesquieu. Unlike him, she had access to the harem at Topkapi Palace and, in her witty and insightful correspondence, she presented the Europeans with a very different picture of the Ottomans. 'Upon the whole,' she wrote, 'I look upon the Turkish women as the only free people in the empire.' A surprising remark, perhaps – but Lady Montagu got to know the ladies in the harem as self-confident and free individuals. The grand harem she visited was for a long time the only place in the Ottoman Empire where women could receive an education, read newspapers and play the piano.

1718: Lady Montagu returns to England from the Ottoman Empire and campaigns for the introduction of smallpox vaccination.

Lady Montagu noticed something else. She had once had smallpox, which had left her face scarred, and she was astonished to see that the Turks protected themselves from the disease by variolation – injecting a mild case of smallpox into healthy people. No sooner had she returned to England than she began trying to persuade doctors, politicians and Church leaders of the benefit of this procedure. People were sceptical, so Lady Montagu had to battle to have her case heard. However, one of the people she convinced was the Princess of Wales, who helped encourage people's trust by inoculating two of her daughters.

When Montesquieu formulated his criticism of the Turks, the ideas of the Enlightenment were just getting established, and the Spinning Jenny which kickstarted the revolution in the textile industry had not yet been invented. Nevertheless, Montesquieu would prove to be right: because the Ottoman Empire hampered progress in science and technology, it missed the dawn of modernity. Only a few decades before, Ottoman doctors and scholars had been looking down on the ignorant and backward Europeans. Suddenly, they realised that they were the ones being left behind.

THE MING AND THE QING

Behind closed doors in the Middle Kingdom

The emperors of the Ming dynasty in China didn't stand in the way of progress and science, but they did seal their empire off from the outside world. For almost 400 years, the Middle Kingdom had remained closed, so perhaps it is not surprising that most of what we know of China from the time is from valuable Ming and Qing vases. They became coveted objects among European art collectors.

From around 1434: Seafaring is banned in China and the country is shut off from the outside world for 400 years.

Perhaps the most important event of the era was the change from the Ming to the Qing dynasty. In the first half of the seventeenth century, when the Ming rulers were already weak, rebels led by a man named Li Zicheng rose up to overthrow the last of their emperors. As a result, the imperial military leaders forged an alliance with Manchuria in the north-east of China – but soon these trusted allies would themselves become a threat to the Ming.

In the tumult of armed conflicts between rebels, imperial troops and Manchus, one military commander stood out. After the death of her husband, Qin Liangyu took over his rank and title and assumed command of his army. Her soldiers fought with white spears made of ash wood, which earned them the name the 'White Stick Troop'. They were a notorious fighting force; it was said that they had never lost a single battle.

However, Qin Liangyu and her White Stick Troop could not prevent the demise of the Ming dynasty. The crisis in the old government was unstoppable. The Manchus, who had been called upon to help save the empire, instead seized control and began ruling under the name Qing. As they were unsure of the loyalty of their new subjects, as a gesture of complete submission to their rule, they made everyone

1644: The Manchus take the reins in China and begin the Qing dynasty.

cut off their hair except for one braid at the nape of their neck. The Chinese were faced with a stark choice: off with your hair or off with your head. Many refused to submit and preferred to die rather than show allegiance to their occupiers.

Under the Qing, the empire grew again until its territory was almost twice the size it had been under the Ming dynasty. The frontiers of the empire were peaceful, and the emergence of trade with Europeans brought prosperity and better living conditions. Since the Chinese only accepted silver coins when they sold their goods to foreigners, the Qing's treasury was well stocked.

China managed to adapt without fundamentally changing. The teachings of Confucius still applied to the entire cosmic order, and women had their fixed place within it. The philosophy and style of government had remained unchanged for millennia, leaving no space to consider or question the role of women. It was a long-standing custom that wealthy men kept a harem of concubines or mistresses, as they had in the ancient Han Empire, and the sovereigns of the Qing dynasty also surrounded themselves with thousands of women. The concubines were the property of their master, and they could be bought, sold or given as presents. It was taken for granted that a man should be surrounded by female servants attending to his needs, and impossible that it should be otherwise. The words of one scholar captures the way in which this was deemed to be an unchanging truth: 'We know that a teapot is served with four cups. But have you ever seen a cup and four teapots?'

Ideas of what was considered beautiful were also enduring and the custom of foot-binding, which started in the tenth century in the court of the last emperor of the Tang dynasty, was still very much in vogue under the Qing. The idea that small feet were a sign of perfection was said to have been inspired by Yao Niang, a dancer in the emperor's court who had particularly small and dainty feet. From that point on, young girls' and women's feet were bandaged up tightly – to the point of breaking bones – so their feet would not grow. This brought lifelong agony for girls and women and made it difficult to walk unaided, but was in keeping with the tradition that a respectable woman didn't leave the house, and this is why the custom continued for almost 1,000 years. Since it was only wealthy men who could afford to support a wife who couldn't walk and served a merely decorative purpose, the custom of foot-binding didn't spread among the ordinary working population but was a status symbol among the wealthy elite. The working class received very low wages, not enough for a man to support his family, meaning women had to go out to work as well as men.

But things improved for women in the Qing dynasty. Foot-binding was not customary for the Manchus, the ancestors of the Qing ruling family, and they attempted to ban it. And as levels of prosperity rose, new opportunities opened up for women, who were increasingly able to leave the house and play an active part in society.

Occasionally, women would break the mould of how they were expected to behave. Not only did they dare to engage in 'male activities' like studying, they also debated the role of the female gender. One such exception was the eighteenth-century astronomer Wang Zhenyi. She taught herself astronomy and mathematics and, although she wasn't allowed to go to school or college, her scholarship had an influence on the study of these subjects. She was the author of numerous books, corrected incorrect calculations and made her own accurate observations of the motion of the stars. Her exacting, scientific approach was rare in China at that time for anyone, let alone for a woman. Wang Zhenyi wrote, 'When we speak of learning and science, it is rare to think of women. We women are expected to cook and sew, not to write articles and poetry or to engage in history or calligraphy.' And elsewhere: 'I believe that women are like men. Who says that daughters cannot also be heroic?'

Chinese–European contacts

As China had cut itself off from the outside world, Europeans knew very little about Asia's largest empire. The English philosopher Francis Bacon noted in 1620 that three inventions – the printing press, gunpowder and the compass – had changed the face of the world. What he didn't realise was that all three were first invented in China, as was the paper needed for printing.

Around 1630: Jesuit missionaries settle at the court of the Chinese emperor.

This lack of knowledge about China gradually started to change from the seventeenth century onwards, when Jesuit missionaries managed to break through the walls that sealed the country off and began to settle in China. The emperor was interested in what the Jesuit monks had to show in terms of science and the arts, and they in turn hoped to win the Chinese over to Christianity. The Jesuits returned from China to Europe with reports that gave Europeans the first glimpse of life in the Middle Kingdom. And since the grass always looks greener on the other side, to the thinkers of the Enlightenment, the Middle Kingdom seemed like a perfect utopian state.

Many Enlightenment thinkers admired the Chinese Qing Empire for its philosophy of harmony: the idea of a peaceful life that was in harmony with nature and the universe. But over time, they realised that this wealthy, prosperous state was only partially suitable as a model for other countries, because of the ancient traditions the Chinese maintained. It could hardly have been more different to Europe. In China, people practised the art of preserving the status quo, keeping things how they were and how they had always been. Europe had moved into the modern era, which meant progress and constant change.

THE FIGHT FOR CIVIL RIGHTS

The French Revolution ignites in America

Armed with the latest knowledge and technology, scientists set about measuring the human brain. They found the results were clear: women's brains were smaller and lighter than men's. From this it was concluded that women were less able to reason and to think. The German women's rights activist Lily Braun then reversed the argument by pointing out that women's brains were heavier in relation to their overall body weight than men's, but this perfectly logical argument didn't convince those who looked down on women. It would be a long time before more advanced biologists with more nuanced methods realised that the brain's output did not depend on mass, but on the number of junctions between the nerve cells (synapses) – and in this respect there was no difference between female and male brains.

You could do as much harm in the name of science as you could in the name of God. This was proven by advocates of racial theory. It was argued by racial theorists that the indigenous people of Africa, Asia, America and Australia were at a lower stage of evolution than the 'noble, white master race'. White men didn't just look down on women, but considered themselves superior to all people of other ethnic backgrounds and skin colour. The Europeans were in the process of colonising most of the planet after sailing around the southern tip of Africa and stumbling upon America, so this theory came in handy as a way of 'scientifically' justifying their rule over the locals. From the presumption of their evolutionary superiority, Europeans deduced that they had the right to seize possession of the whole world.

In 1792, as France was ablaze with the Revolution, an article in the *Encyclopaedia Britannica* described people of African descent as being afflicted by the most atrocious vices: laziness, perfidy, vindictiveness, cruelty, impudence, stealing, lying, godlessness and debauchery. The *Encyclopaedia Britannica* was a highly respected publication, but it still occurred to some observers that descriptions like this were inhumane and that slavery was incompatible with human rights. Olympe de Gouges made a point of signing her letters as from a 'mortal enemy of slavery'; during the French Revolution, she and the Marquis de Condorcet called for the abolition of slavery. And indeed, the revolutionaries had barely got their parliament up and running before they banned French involvement in the slave trade and slavery in overseas colonies.

The revolutionary call for liberty, equality and fraternity also rang out on the island of Hispaniola in the Caribbean. The French and Spaniards had divided the island between themselves – the Spanish colony Santo Domingo and the French Haiti – and they were profiting nicely from the production of coffee and sugar. But in 1804 the slave workers had started an uprising, and for the first time since the conquest of America they freed themselves from their colonial rulers, founding the independent state of Haiti. This spark of mutiny flew across to neighbouring regions. Simón Bolívar, a talented and courageous independence fighter, gathered supporters everywhere he went, and soon Venezuela, Colombia, Panama, Ecuador, Peru and Bolivia – named in honour of Bolívar – had all succeeded in liberating themselves from the Spaniards.

1804: Haiti becomes an independent state after the slaves liberate themselves from their colonial rulers, which sparks independence movements across South America.

1823: The US President James Monroe announces the Monroe Doctrine: Europeans should stay out of America forever.

Further north, after its foundation as an independent state, the United States of America began expanding its territory westwards by purchasing or simply seizing land. The President of the USA, James Monroe, delivered a speech later referred to as the 'Monroe Doctrine' in which he declared that American independence was irreversible. The Americas would from now on be a sphere where Europeans had no say – except, of course, the Europeans who now called themselves Americans. No European country should try to regain control of a now independent former colony – neither in North nor South America. Monroe was demanding the end of European colonial rule on the entire American continent.

The Underground Railroad

The people of Europe were becoming more intolerant of cruelty and injustice. Their dream of a free society had not yet come true, and since the sovereign rulers of France, Austria and Prussia had crushed the revolutions of 1848, they were again forced to wait. Full of envy and admiration, Europeans looked to the United States, the 'Land of the Free', whose declaration of independence begins with the words, 'We hold these Truths to be self-evident, that all Men are created equal, that they are endowed by their Creator with certain unalienable Rights, that among these are Life, Liberty, and the Pursuit of Happiness.'

In certain southern states of the USA, however, business was booming and slavery was at the heart of it. Africans were needed as cheap labour for cotton production, and there were laws in many states that defined slaves as objects. Since human rights did not apply to objects, their owner could do whatever he wanted with them.

It was hard not to notice how inconsistent this was with the freedoms and rights the American Constitution promised its citizens. In France and England in particular, there were increasingly loud and impassioned calls for the abolition of slavery, and a movement called Abolitionism gained momentum.

It all started with the Quakers, a religious Christian community which started in England in the seventeenth century. The Quakers believed that the light of God shone in every human being, so every injustice carried out against another person was an offence against God. English preachers such as Margaret Fell in England and Hannah Feake Bowne in the USA proved how seriously the Quakers took the principle of equality – including of women – and so it was only logical for them to also reject slavery.

The conflict between the proponents and opponents of slavery threatened to divide the USA. There was intense debate in Congress about which was the more fundamental right: the right of individual states to determine their own laws, or the freedom and human rights enshrined in the Constitution? The southern states insisted on their right to self-determination and threatened to leave the USA – they knew that the northern states would pay almost any price to avoid that happening.

Citizens in the northern states were obliged to report slaves who were on the run from the South, but many Americans chose not to. If an escaped slave knocked on their door, they gave him or her food and a safe place to hide, and a network of supporters formed over time, who helped the slaves to flee to Canada. It was only once they had escaped the country that they were safe – and truly free. Canada still belonged to Great Britain, as a colony, and the British Parliament had abolished slavery.

More and more slaves escaped. One Kentucky slaveholder is said to have complained that one of his slaves had barely crossed the river into the slave-free state of Ohio when he suddenly vanished, as if swallowed up by the ground. Or as if he had been whisked away by an underground train. In fact, the network of refugee helpers really was made up of fixed stations, which is why it was named the 'Underground Railroad'.

The slave Harriet Tubman was 5 years old when her owners separated her from her family and sent her to work at a farm far away. Later she wrote about her childhood:

> I used to sleep on the floor in front of the fireplace and there I'd lie and cry and cry. I used to think all the time, 'If I could only get home and get in my mother's bed!' And the funny part of that was, she never had a bed in her life.

1849: Harriet Tubman manages to escape slavery and becomes the most famous helper of the Underground Railroad.

Once, Tubman's supervisor ordered her to help him catch a slave who was trying to escape. She refused, and as she didn't move to help, the supervisor threw a heavy weight at the fugitive – but he missed and instead hit Harriet Tubman on the head. Miraculously, she survived the severe injury to her skull.

Tubman eventually managed to escape to Canada. She joined the Underground Railroad network and went back to the South several times – following dangerous routes across wilderness, over rivers and hiding at secret refuge places along the way – first to free her own family, and then many more slaves.

The book that leads to civil war

The South was suffering financially from the loss of slave workers, so they called on Congress to do something to stop the Underground Railroad. The Congress members who opposed slavery came under pressure, and in the end, the majority agreed to the Fugitive Slave Act, a law which made it a criminal act to help escaped slaves. This made the long journey on the Underground Railroad even more dangerous.

Many Americans were outraged. Instead of obeying the law, they did the opposite and did even more to help slaves escape. Writer Harriet Beecher Stowe was so angry about the new law that she sat down at her desk and wrote a novel about slavery – she finished *Uncle Tom's Cabin* in just a few months and it was serialised in a magazine. Beecher Stowe described the suffering of the African American slaves and showed her readers the full extent of the injustice. She was well aware of the conditions in the South, because she had travelled there extensively with her husband. *Uncle Tom's Cabin* shocked her readers with its descriptions of the cotton plantations, the 'Negro markets', auctions and slave warehouses, of handlers haggling over slaves as though they were inanimate goods, of abusive treatment and flogging.

1852: Harriet Beecher Stowe publishes the novel Uncle Tom's Cabin, which fuels outrage about slavery across America.

Uncle Tom's Cabin became one of the best-selling books of the nineteenth century, and the Abolition movement swelled in support. Eventually, Abraham Lincoln, an avowed opponent of slavery, was elected president. The South saw this as a provocation and refused to accept him as president; they declared they would leave the Union and form their own confederation, the Confederate States of America. It looked like the United States of America might split into two.

A civil war broke out, which the North won after many long battles. The breakaway Southerners returned and became part of the USA again, and this time there was nothing they could do to prevent Congress from abolishing slavery, granting former slaves citizenship and the male ones the right to vote. The story goes that when Abraham Lincoln met Harriet Beecher Stowe in person, he said to her: 'So you are the little woman who wrote the book that started this great war.'

1861–65: The American Civil War is fought between the northern and southern states of America. After the war, President Abraham Lincoln ends slavery in the United States.

327

The legacy of slavery

During and after the American Civil War, the United States was still far from reaching its eventual size. Between the Eastern states and California on the West Coast were vast swathes of undeveloped land. The cities of Europe were becoming cramped and overpopulated, and many wanted to escape hunger and poverty. Families spent everything they had on the passage by ship to North America, hoping to start a new life there. This constant stream of immigrants caused American cities to swell in size, and to grow in height; soon, Americans were building the first high-rise houses.

Some didn't stay in the coastal cities but headed west into the country's interior. New railways stretched further and further through forests and prairies, eating deeper and deeper into the territory of the indigenous people. The 'new frontier' kept pushing westward, while stories were told about lonesome cowboys and cowgirls, brave settlers, gold diggers and prospectors seeking their fortune. This was the time of the legendary Buffalo Bill and Calamity Jane, who knew no fear and could shoot faster than their shadows. There were stage shows celebrating these legendary figures, some of whom even performed on stage themselves. Women were rare in this pantheon of heroes of the Wild West, but there was the sharpshooter Annie Oakley, who could hit a playing card as it span through the air.

Many former colonies joined the United States as new states. In areas where there hadn't been colonies, the US government bought land or simply claimed it. The indigenous people could do little to oppose the immigrant settlers. Now that there was no danger of the Union collapsing, the United States grew step by step until it reached its current size of fifty states.

1876: In the Battle of Little Bighorn, the indigenous inhabitants win a victory against the US Army. Nevertheless, they are displaced by white settlers and deported into reservations.

The country was a melting pot of immigrants from around the world, but certain groups of people were still kept separate. The injustice of slavery was transformed after the Civil War into the injustice of racial segregation, and laws were implemented to keep black and white people apart. They were not allowed to marry or go to the same school. America's white founding fathers still determined the fate of the country, blocking black people's access to many areas of public and political life.

Harriet Tubman had fought on the Northern side during the Civil War, where her thorough knowledge of the South proved to be of great help to the military. After the war and the abolition of slavery, Tubman continued her political campaigning, this time fighting to end racial segregation. She was honoured for her achievements by one of the world's most powerful women: Queen Victoria, who invited her to her Diamond Jubilee, where she gave her a silk scarf. The honour and respect she was also afforded by high-ranking politicians (one even called her 'General Tubman') didn't change the fact that many whites refused to give up their privileges and wouldn't even sit next to a black person on the bus. And for all her work and strength of character, it took Americans a very long time to honour Harriet Tubman after her death for her achievements.

Society changed slowly, but eventually it did. A hundred years after the abolition of slavery, the civil rights movement continued Harriet Tubman's work and had a groundswell of support. Their most important leader, the Reverend Martin Luther King, made a speech that began with the words, 'I have a dream.' He dreamed of overcoming racial segregation. A few months later, the President of the USA signed a law that abolished it. That was in 1964 – it would be another almost fifty years before US citizens elected an African American president for the first time.

1964: President Kennedy ends racial segregation in the USA.

2008: Barack Obama is elected: the first African American president.

The fight for suffrage – the right to vote

There are people, and then there are women. After the end of the American Civil War, history once again proved they were not one and the same thing. The abolition of slavery granted the former slaves the rights of citizens – but only the men. In fact, for women things became even worse, because many who had advocated for civil rights for *all*, before and during the Civil War, now felt that the battle had been won and lost interest in the women's cause. For those who still felt the urgent need for change, it was time to take the argument beyond mere pencil and paper.

1848: Elizabeth Cady Stanton and Lucretia Mott host the Seneca Falls Convention: the first American women's rights meeting.

Even before the Civil War, women had begun to organise themselves politically in the United States. Elizabeth Cady Stanton and Lucretia Mott had hosted the first public women's rights meeting in the United States. However, the declaration signed at the end – by a total of sixty-eight women and thirty-two men – didn't get much attention. That changed when Stanton, along with Susan B. Anthony, founded the American Association for Women's Suffrage and began to travel around the country, holding meetings everywhere they went. Former slaves participated in these congresses, such as Sojourner Truth, who became famous for asking, 'Ain't I a woman?' (although she may not have used this exact phrase). As a woman, even after the abolition of slavery, she was still without rights.

Once, a man stood up at one such congress and remarked that it was not for nothing that women were by nature smaller and weaker than men. At that point the revolutionary activist Mathilde Franziska Anneke, who had fled from Germany, stood up beside him. She was a whole head taller than this man, who was short and plump, and she towered over him. Laughter broke out in the hall.

But it wasn't enough simply to hold meetings. Susan B. Anthony forced her way into a polling station and threatened to sue them if she wasn't allowed to vote in the presidential election. Instead of being permitted to vote, she was herself taken to court for threatening officials.

Anthony didn't let that stop her. On 4 July 1876, the United States celebrated the 100th anniversary of the Declaration of Independence. At that point, only a small group of women activists were troubled by the fact that this constitution ignored the rights of the female half of the country's citizenship. So Anthony caused a scandal by making her way onto the stage during the celebrations in Philadelphia and proceeding to read out a Declaration of Women's Rights. Stunts like this brought attention and gradually the suffragettes managed to win public support for their cause.

What women were demanding was entirely logical. It was obvious that women could be just as good or bad as men, just as honest or deceptive, as clever or as stupid, as helpful or as selfish. Unfortunately, whenever one woman found the courage to stand up and demand their rights, other women tried to drag her back down. This was the experience of Mary Wollstonecraft, who had been laughed at by the fine ladies of English high society, dismissed as – although this was from a man – a 'hyena in petticoats'. This was also the experience of Victoria Woodhull.

Victoria Woodhull didn't just want the right to *vote* for the President of the United States, she also wanted to *be* it. Woodhull was already a well-known American public figure, something of a celebrity. She had managed to become rich by speculating on the stock exchange, so she had already broken into what had until then been a closed men's world. But, for many people, putting herself forward as a presidential candidate was a step too far. It was seen as a joke: how could someone apply for such a position when they didn't even have the right to vote? Woodhull faced vehement opposition by Harriet Beecher Stowe, the author of *Uncle Tom's Cabin*, and her brother, the preacher Henry Ward Beecher; Harriet parodied Woodhull in one of her books, whilst Henry railed against Woodhull's support of 'free love' at his pulpit. The dispute got vicious when Woodhull revealed in her newspaper that Henry – despite arguing against 'free love' – had had an extramarital affair. Woodhull never had the chance to attempt to vote for herself; a few days before the election, she was arrested for 'sending obscenity through the post': her newspaper, which could be ordered by mail. The charges were dropped seven months later – after the election had finished.

The time had not yet come for women's suffrage, let alone for a female President of the United States.

IMPERIALISM: EUROPEANS ON THE RAMPAGE

Artichokes, cherries and melons

When the rulers of powerful countries set out to annex foreign territory, the thought of their prey seems to induce pangs of hunger. Just like Frederick the Great, who called Poland an 'artichoke' to be savoured 'leaf by leaf', British generals talked of a 'ripe cherry' that was 'ready for picking'. They were talking about a rich province in northern India – one they had long had their eyes on. As the European powers traded valuable Chinese artefacts to one another, they spoke of 'sharing out the melon'. No one stopped to question whether the prey could defend themselves against being consumed by the predator – that's how weak the Europeans thought the Indians were.

The stakes were high. Raw materials were needed – for the construction of steam engines and locomotives, houses and roads, sewers under the cities and cables under the sea, for everything from telegraph poles to shoe soles. The economy developed an insatiable hunger for raw materials, and it was with this rapacious appetite that a handful of European countries pounced on the rest of the world. After America had freed itself from their grip, they needed to find these resources elsewhere. Asia and Africa were rich in commodities: wood, stone, metals, coal, oil and gas. So the French took Vietnam; the Dutch Java; the British Burma; and the Russian Empire conquered one colony after another in Central Asia until they had reached the borders of Mongolia and China.

This was the beginning of the age of imperialism: bit by bit, the Europeans conquered the rest of the world, carving it up between themselves. They raced to grab territory, trading routes and commodities. The British were in the lead, leagues ahead of the Russians, French and Dutch. After all, they had been among the first to send trading companies to the Far East; now they were building the kingdom of Great Britain into a global empire – the British Empire. They conquered Burma and the entire Indian subcontinent, and eventually they managed to break through the walls of impenetrable China.

As boundless as Britain's success was, so was her self-confidence. The British used the term 'the Great Game' to refer to the long drawn-out war they waged against Russia in Central Asia and Africa over 150 years, as if it were mere child's play to turn entire swathes of Egypt or Afghanistan into a battlefield.

At about the same time, over the course of the nineteenth century the Ottoman Empire began to disintegrate from within. The once huge 'Sublime State', which stretched from the Balkans to Baghdad and from the Black Sea to Africa, began to fall apart. The empire became known as the 'sick man on the Bosporus', and the European colonial powers exploited its weakness to gain influence and power. The same happened in neighbouring Persia, another enormous Muslim empire: the British, Russians and French saw everywhere as a playing field for their Great Game as they battled for supremacy.

Queen Victoria was on the throne as British monarch for sixty-four years, and during her long reign, the British rose to become masters of the world. After forty years, she was the first British monarch to be given the title 'Empress of India'. Another fifty years later, an entire quarter of the planet belonged to the British Empire.

1877: Queen Victoria becomes Empress of India. In the era of imperialism, the British Empire emerges as the Europeans subjugate Asia and Africa.

Exploitation

What seemed like nothing but a game to the Europeans was a serious shock to billions of people in Asia and Africa. Huge, proud empires with ancient traditions and tremendous cultural wealth were forced to realise within a few decades that a contest had begun – one in which they were not only the losers, but also the coveted prize.

The Chinese experienced a particularly dramatic fall. Back in the late eighteenth century, Emperor Qianlong had looked down on the Europeans. A British delegation had by duplicitous means gained access to the Forbidden City. On behalf of their king, the British ambassadors had invited the Chinese to finally open up their empire and establish proper trade relations. They had valuable gifts for the emperor: telescopes, a huge glass lens, expensive instruments 'to explain and illustrate the principles of science', a planetarium and many other beautifully crafted devices. But Qianlong refused. He sent a letter to the English king, George III, declaring that China had all it needed within its borders, and had no need of England's products. China remained closed to European merchants.

1793: A British delegation travels to China bearing valuable gifts, but Emperor Qianlong rejects them.

Half a century later, these 'sophisticated objects' – particularly their military technology – had made the British so strong and powerful that they could force the Chinese to enter the global market.

The rise of the British began in India. The East India Company had brought certain provinces under their control early on in the race to claim colonies. Now Britain had claimed the entire Indian subcontinent, piece by piece – or 'cherry by cherry', to put it in the language of the imperialists.

They encountered little resistance. There was only one major revolt that spread across much of the subcontinent: the Sepoy Mutiny (the Sepoy were the Indian soldiers who served the British colonial rulers). A symbol of this mutiny and one of its leaders was the ruler Lakshmibai; by marrying the maharaja of the Jhansi province, she had become rani, or queen. However, when her husband died young, the British simply seized control of her provinces. They ignored Lakshmibai and her adopted son, the heir to the throne, and instead declared a representative of the East India Company as the chief administrator.

1857–58: Lakshmibai, the Rani of Jhansi, fights alongside her soldiers during the Sepoy Mutiny – an uprising of the Indians against the British. It is suppressed by the British.

A short time later, the Indians rose against the British occupiers in various regions. Lakshmibai claimed the throne back and summoned up troops to support the insurgents. When her army was defeated, she managed to escape with a few men and to inflict heavy losses against the British elsewhere – but her pursuers were on her trail, leading to another battle. Fighting as a soldier in men's attire, she was wounded and killed in battle.

After suppressing this rebellion, the British now controlled huge regions of India where they could grow opium, and they had the military strength to force open China's locked gates. The British had long been frustrated that the Chinese only traded their goods for silver, because the silver disappeared out of circulation and into China's coffers, and the British were constantly running out of money. But now they forced the Chinese to exchange their goods for the dangerous and highly addictive drug opium, turning the tables. As the Chinese quickly became net importers rather than exporters, China's coffers were drained of cash – in no time at all, the empire was approaching bankruptcy. This was a catastrophe for the country's rulers: they were in financial ruin, all for the sake of imported goods that had done nothing to help their people. Instead, the country's rulers looked on as part of the population became addicted to a lethal drug.

In desperation, the Chinese government tried to ban opium and to destroy supplies, but the British forced them to import the drug. An official of the emperor wrote to Queen Victoria, begging her to stop her countrymen from supplying opium. 'Do they have no conscience?' he wrote.

The British merchants seemed to have none. They waged two wars, the so-called 'Opium Wars', and France and the USA lent their support, securing themselves their share of the Chinese 'melon'. Eventually, the once proud Middle Kingdom had to admit defeat. China was forced to pay large sums of money in compensation, to open most of its ports up to trade, and to hand the city of Hong Kong over to the British Crown. The documents that sealed China's fate were later called 'unequal treaties', because the two parties to the contract were so obviously unequal in power and the ability to negotiate.

1842 and 1860: China loses two Opium Wars with the British. After the first one, she is forced to cede Hong Kong to Britain and sign several 'unequal treaties'.

In North Africa, the Ottoman Empire, Persia and Afghanistan, the residents didn't fare much better. The French and British fought for supremacy in Egypt. The Ottoman rulers suffered devastating defeats at the Black Sea and Crimea. The French invaded Tunisia. The Persians lost Georgia, Armenia and Azerbaijan to Russia. And so, ever since Egypt fell to Napoleon, at the beginning of the nineteenth century, again and again people found they were completely defenceless against the onslaught of the Europeans. They became colonies, in the possession of the wealthy Europeans with their military might.

Breaking through into a Muslim modernity

The colonised people were shocked at how brutally the Europeans turned their lives upside down. In Persia and India, simple farmers and artisans were impoverished because their fields and small businesses had to give way to large-scale plantations, modern sewers, roads and railways. But instead of developing industry in Asia in a way that benefitted the local population, the colonial powers plundered their raw materials to feed industry in Europe.

The colonised people, however, were also surprised to realise how they lagged behind in many ways. The Europeans brought not only war and exploitation, but also knowledge and ideas that had previously been completely unknown to them. Life in Europe had changed so radically that intellectuals in India, China and many other Asian countries couldn't help wondering how it had taken them so long to notice. Now, all the new ideas and innovations from Europe began to seep into the Muslim world, where they also had a tangible impact. Educated Muslims in North Africa, Syria and Lebanon, Turkey, Iran and Afghanistan took on knowledge and experience from Europe and worked towards nudging their societies to catch up with the modern age. All the topics that had been debated since the Renaissance and the Enlightenment in Europe – freedom, equality and democracy, science and empirical reasoning, education, printing and later the free press – now prompted heated discussion in Cairo, Beirut, Aleppo, Istanbul and Tehran.

It was as though the Europeans had a box full of tools to help them build a new society: the laws that protected individuals from arbitrary abuse by the powerful, and the sciences which promoted a very different understanding of the Earth and of plants, animals and humans to what was taught in the Bible and the Quran. There was medicine, human rights, parliamentary democracy, women's rights, but also countless technical inventions – with the help of all these instruments, Europeans had created new societies.

While some were enthusiastic about exploring and trying out this new European toolkit, others saw in it the work of the Devil. Clerics in Islamic educational institutions, such as Al-Azhar School in Cairo, argued that European ideas and their modern way of life contradicted the teachings of the Quran; many feared that Islam and its institutions could lose power and influence, as had happened to the Christian Church.

Others, however, saw no contradiction in reconciling the Islamic religion with scientific progress. Some scholars didn't simply adopt the new ideas from Europe, but took them on while maintaining their own tradition. They recalled the golden age of Arab culture in the Middle Ages, which proved that Muslim philosophers, physicians, mathematicians and poets had been capable of the greatest scientific achievements. There had been a time when Arab cities such as Damascus and Baghdad were at the forefront of human progress.

Among these was the Egyptian intellectual Rifa'a al-Tahtawi, who spearheaded a movement called the *Nahda*, which is Arabic for 'reawakening'. Some compare the *Nahda* with the Renaissance and the Enlightenment in Europe. Like many of his contemporaries, al-Tahtawi picked up on the question of the rights of women and, among other things, he campaigned for the education of girls. This he justified by referring to a Hadith that said the Prophet Muhammad's wives could read – surely, he reasoned, it couldn't be un-Islamic for women to be educated.

Al-Tahtawi was by no means alone in his thinking. The Egyptian lawyer and author Qasim Amin was appalled by the completely uneducated and idle women in his homeland. Amin wrote texts entitled *The Liberation of Woman* and *The New Woman*, in which he argued that Egypt couldn't possibly catch up with progress in Western countries unless women were finally allowed to gain an education and to contribute to the good of the entire society.

Meanwhile, the first women's magazine was published in Istanbul, after the Ottoman government had lifted the centuries-long ban on printing and a public printing press had been set up. The magazine was called *Progress of Muslim Women*. One contributor wrote:

Men are as little made to rule over women as women are to be ruled by men ... Are we unable to acquire knowledge and skills? What is the difference between our legs, eyes and brains – and theirs? Are not we humans? Does our gender alone condemn us to this situation? Nobody with common sense accepts that.

Another author wrote that the magazine's goal was to completely reverse the image of women: 'We are the tribe that men make fun of for having long hair but being short on reason. We will try to prove the opposite.' Articles were often printed without naming the author, because it seemed too risky to voice such views.

Nevertheless, at that time, women were becoming known throughout the Muslim world as poets, writers and commentators on day-to-day political events. Fatma Aliye, a Turkish writer, learned French as a teenager in secret, because her mother feared education might harm her daughter. Aliye published her first articles anonymously and signed them as 'A Woman', but later she found the courage to give her name – perhaps the first step towards an independent life. From that point on, Aliye wrote a lot. She travelled the world alone and set up a charity, and with her articles and novels she became an important voice in the Muslim reawakening.

Women's magazines were also set up in Egypt and Iran, following the Istanbul example. These created a space for authors and readers to discuss all sorts of questions. Just as with Europe's *querelle des femmes*, Muslims now also asked themselves: are women inferior? Should they work and do the same jobs as men? Other issues concerned Islam specifically. There were differences of opinion, particularly with regard to wearing the veil. Some women didn't see the veil as a means of oppression, but as a garment that gave them greater freedom, as it protected them from men staring at them.

Hana Kawrani, a Lebanese writer, published an article criticising the modern image of women. 'Women,' she wrote, 'cannot work outside the home and at the same time serve their husband and children.' In response, the writer Zaynab Fawwaz, also from Lebanon, pointed out that Islamic law by no means forbids women from working or doing the same things as men. In writing this Fawwaz was also defending her own freedom, as she was the first female author to write a play in Arabic. She lived in Alexandria for a while, then moved to Damascus where she started a literary salon, while the poet Maryana Marrash ran one in Aleppo. They had both heard about women in Europe hosting these private social gatherings where they took part in the lively discussions between writers, intellectuals and politicians.

The emancipation of women in the Islamic world had much greater obstacles to overcome than in Europe. It had taken centuries for Europeans to get used to things like democracy and a secular justice system; now these were introduced in the Muslim world, the locals had to adopt changes within just a few decades. For many, this was too much. When hosting her salon, Zaynab Fawwaz not only wore a veil, but the women also stayed in a different room to the men, while her husband went between the two rooms. One of the first women's rights activists in Iran, the poet Fatimah Baraghani, was concealed by a curtain when she discussed questions of religion with men.

Despite these obstacles, educated men and women found that many of the ideas reaching them from Europe were by no means exclusively European, because there were many points of reference in Islam and its history. Islam itself was not against equal rights for women, they argued: any opposition came from centuries of sexist misinterpretations of the Quran.

This was also true of the ancient Persian Empire (which later became Iran), an empire that differed in many ways from the Turkish and Arab territories of the Ottoman Empire. With a history of over 2,000 years, Persia had long existed in the form of a nation, a vast state whose population was largely unified by the Persian language, Shi'ite Islam and an ancient culture.

Here, in Persia, a small religious reform movement emerged that included the women's rights activist Fatimah Baraghani. Their members saw themselves as particularly devout followers of Islam, and it was because they took their religion so seriously that they could plainly and definitively declare that Islamic law was outdated and no longer valid. They wanted social improvements for the people, and they supported a peaceful coexistence of religions, democratic conditions and equal rights for women. They were unusual at the time in opposing the idea of the nation. They were also against weapons and wars, which were expensive and destructive – instead, they called on people to understand themselves as a world community. Their unusual ideas prompted so much suspicion that their followers were persecuted and many were executed, not least because the reformers wanted to overthrow the Persian shah, believing that only then could they restructure society according to their ideas.

Fatimah Baraghani, who as a young woman had hidden behind a curtain to talk to men, gradually found the courage to break away from the old shackles. At a conference where the movement discussed breaking away from the old religion, she finally emerged from the curtain and took off her veil. The men in attendance panicked – after all, for centuries they had been taught that an unveiled woman represented the Devil. Such a well-respected woman unveiling was an explicit challenge to their customs. From that day on, Fatimah Baraghani was persecuted until she was arrested and executed.

Human rights are universal

Among the representatives of the Islamic awakening was a thinker who travelled in all directions across the vast space we describe here. Jamal al-Din al-Afghani travelled across Persia, India, Afghanistan, Turkey, Egypt and Europe, looking for like-minded supporters. As he was a man of great charisma, many people rallied around him – from theologians and women's rights activists to wealthy patrons and influential politicians, all helped to spread his ideas from India to Constantinople. Like many other Muslim thinkers, al-Afghani was convinced that values such as human rights and the freedom of the individual were not specifically European. They were universal, he believed, and therefore there was no contradiction between them and Islam.

Jamal al-Din al-Afghani (1838–97), Rabindranath Tagore (1861–1941) and Mahatma Gandhi (1869–1948) reflect on the future of Asia, which is dominated by the imperialists.

This idea connected progressive Muslims with Indian thinkers such as the poet Rabindranath Tagore and the resistance fighter Mahatma Gandhi. They, too, lobbied for human rights, arguing that religion was no justification for inhumane customs, violence or cruelty.

One such religious custom that Tagore and Gandhi campaigned against in India was the practice of widow burning. After the death of her husband, a woman could be burned along with his body, and women who followed their husband to death in this way were worshipped as saints. This was a decision widows made voluntarily, and it was a very rare event, but nevertheless, they called for such cruel customs carried out in the name of religion to be prohibited.

The white man's burden

Al-Afghani, Tagore and Gandhi admired the Europeans for having created civil rights, parliamentary democracy and the rule of law. At the same time, they questioned whether their people had to adapt to European civilisation in all respects in order to live by these values. Did they have to think like the Europeans, live like them and dress like them too? Had European modernity produced a civilisation that was better in *all* respects than the way of life practised in other parts of the world?

To most Europeans the answer was clear: it was their society that had given rise to the ideas of the Enlightenment. Where these ideas were unknown, it must mean people were uncivilised. The Europeans condemned and looked down on almost everything they encountered in Asia, Africa and Australia, seeing it as their duty to bring law and order to the 'less civilised peoples'. Rudyard Kipling, the author of *The Jungle Book*, wrote of the 'white man's burden' – a convenient guise to dress up imperialist crimes as a moral duty.

But this narrative was thinly woven loth and it was all too easy to see through. The injustice was glaringly obvious. Instead of bringing law and order, 'white men' brought destruction; instead of giving the colonies the means to develop as self-sufficient, free societies, they turned the inhabitants into slaves. Millions of Indians and Chinese workers slaved away on plantations, factories and mines whose products and profits flowed to Europe. It was not only in Asia that people were appalled – and disappointed – to realise how uncivilised the Europeans proved themselves to be.

Many Britons who travelled abroad could see clearly what was happening in the colonies and they described it in letters they sent home. One such correspondent was Lady Lucie Duff-Gordon, who spent several years in Egypt, learned Arabic and earned the trust and admiration of locals. She was horrified by her compatriots' behaviour. 'What chokes me,' she wrote, 'is to hear English people talk of the stick being "the only way to manage Arabs" as if anyone could doubt that it is the easiest way to manage any people where it can be used with impunity.'

When students or scholars from one of the colonies travelled to London or Paris, they might have recognised the advantages of

1899: Rudyard Kipling's poem 'The White Man's Burden' is published; many people read it as an attempt to justify European imperialism.

European life: cobbled streets where women and men mingled infor-mally, railways that let people travel quickly from place to place, schools and universities, medical care, the rights enjoyed by citizens, and democratic political debate in parliament. In their home coun-tries, however, they would have seen a completely different side to the Europeans. Their morals, and in particular the claim that every human being deserved dignity and respect, proved to suffer from double standards. Whatever was true in Paris and London was soon forgotten when they interacted with people outside Europe. The threadbare excuse was that the inhabitants of the colonies were not born as the equals of Europeans, but were of an inferior status due to their race.

It took less than 100 years of colonisation for Rabindranath Tagore, once an admirer of European civilisation, to realise that Europe had completely lost its moral authority in Asia. Tagore wrote that Europe could no longer be considered a champion of fair behaviour or advo-cate of the highest moral principles; instead, it was a champion of the racial superiority of the West and exploiter of those who lived beyond its borders.

The economy is a machine that cannot think for itself

All violence is an act of injustice. No one understood this better than Tagore and Gandhi, and on this basis they firmly rejected any form of violence. Although they saw people in India being abused and exploited by the British colonial rulers, they didn't recognise a distinction between 'the Europeans' and 'the Asians'. Neither did they see 'women' and 'men', or 'good people' versus 'bad people'. They understood that everywhere in the world people could do wonderful things, but they could also sink to cruel and unjust behaviour.

Tagore and Gandhi admired the Europeans but criticised them at the same time. They saw that they had developed technical possibilities that were previously unimaginable, giving them the capacity to end hunger and improve nutrition, to cure and eradicate diseases and to understand the natural world better. Tagore and Gandhi recognised that economics and trade were the foundation stones of this progress. But it could not be ignored that the European drive for new conquests in the fields of science and technology also drove them to subjugate and control other countries.

It seemed that the Europeans' trading economy functioned according to its own rules, like a machine that cannot think and has no conscience. Tagore and Gandhi were concerned that this machine was dangerous if allowed to operate independently, without control – after all, it could not answer the questions that philosophers had posed since time immemorial: how does a good society work? What is right and what is wrong?

FASTER!

Around the world in less than eighty days

Since the beginning of modernity, the world had been in constant acceleration. How much faster and more comfortable it is to take the train compared to riding in a horse-drawn carriage over bumpy cobble stones! In the seventeenth century it had taken three weeks to travel the 190 miles from Plymouth to London. The introduction of the railway shortened this journey to little over a day, and by 1883 to just six hours.

Time and space was shrinking. Suddenly, you could travel around the entire planet in less than three months – at least that's what Jules Verne claimed in his novel *Around the World in Eighty Days*. Nellie Bly, a journalist for a New York newspaper, wanted to give it a try and aimed to complete the trip in even less time. Her employer, Joseph Pulitzer, gave her the funding. It took a year to prepare for the adventure, giving a rival newspaper enough time to send their own reporter and have a race. The plan was that Elizabeth Bisland would set off around the world the other way, hoping to beat Nellie Bly to the finish line.

The two covered most of their routes by steamboat and railway. Bly set sail for England in November 1889 and from there she travelled via France, Italy, the Suez Canal, Ceylon (now Sri Lanka), Hong Kong, China, Japan and America. Meanwhile, Bisland headed in the opposite direction. Every day, excited readers caught up on the latest news of the race. In France Bly made a detour to go and meet Jules Verne. When bad weather at sea meant a delay to Bly's arrival in San Francisco, Pulitzer sent a private train to help her make up the lost time. Seventy-two days after setting off, she arrived in New York.

Bisland reached her destination four and a half days later; she had lost the race.

The victory made Nellie Bly famous, and for a long time no one dwelled on the fact that the acclaimed journalist turned out to be a rather unpleasant tourist in her write-up of the trip. Instead of exploring the world with an open mind, she was often irritated by trivial things. Although she always travelled first class, she complained about uncomfortable trains and expressed disdain about her fellow passengers. The further she travelled from Europe, the more condescending she was in her reports: she displayed only contempt for the Egyptians and the Chinese – an intolerance that was not untypical for Europeans.

But despite this, the fact remains that Bly and Bisland demonstrated just how much the Industrial Revolution had accelerated life. They could race around the world in record time because railways and steamboats had created a dense network of passenger and trade routes spanning the globe. Another invention also allowed news to circulate around the world at high speed: the telegram. The first submarine cable was laid beneath the English Channel from Dover to Calais. The second crossed the Atlantic, connecting the USA and Europe – two powerful allies that formed a unit that came to be known as 'the West'.

Telegraphy allowed the newspapers' readers to follow the race between Nellie Bly and Elizabeth Bisland in near real time. And the two women's faces were well known, too: the invention of photography meant that, for the first time, portraits could be reproduced and printed all over the world. These days we see thousands of images, but in the late nineteenth century this was revolutionary.

1889–90: Journalist Nellie Bly travels the world in seventy-two days – faster than the hero in Jules Verne's novel *Around the World in Eighty Days*.

1858: The first transatlantic telegraph cable is laid under the Atlantic Ocean, connecting Europe and the United States.

FROM THE WEST TO ASIA

RESISTANCE

The mood in the colonies turns against the Europeans

The pace of change was breathtaking, and the West's advantage left the rest of the world little chance of catching up. In China, Japan, India, South East Asia and the Middle East, many felt that their pride was wounded. Not only because their states were politically weak, but also because they saw their own culture being devalued and suppressed by the Europeans.

The leaders in Istanbul and Cairo, and to an extent Tehran, initially tried to boost their countries' stature and strength in comparison with Europe through political reform and restructuring. The Ottoman sultan in Istanbul introduced a series of reforms called the Tanzimat Reforms. Tanzimat meant 'reorganisation'; this was an attempt to change almost every aspect of the state, from finance, the military and the legal system to education and administration. Everything was to be structured according to the Western model.

But implementing all of this was an extremely complicated process, hampered further by the fact that the rulers in Istanbul and Cairo casually squandered so much money that both states went bankrupt at about the same time. It quickly became apparent that these reforms weren't improving the situation in the Ottoman Empire, Egypt or Persia. Instead, their governments had become completely dependent on hand-outs from European backers.

A prime example was the fate of the Suez Canal. It was the French who first had the idea of connecting the Mediterranean to the Red Sea through the construction of a canal; it would avoid the need to sail around Africa, therefore considerably shortening the journey from Europe to the Arabian Peninsula and East Africa, and would take over a large part of trade. The Viceroy of Egypt, who was subordinate to the Ottoman sultan, seized upon the idea. He wanted to improve the economic situation in his country by building the canal as quickly as possible. Since the Americans were distracted by civil war and were no longer supplying cotton, Egyptian cotton was in high demand, meaning that the viceroy had money to invest in roads and railways, in building schools and in modernising the country on the European model.

The viceroy's plans were ambitious: about ten years later, when the Suez Canal was about to be opened, he had an entire new city built alongside the old Cairo. He didn't care that cotton prices had fallen, he simply borrowed the money from the Europeans. The opera *Aida*, which he had commissioned the composer Giuseppe Verdi to compose for the grand opening of the canal, wasn't finished, but that didn't detract from the extravagant celebrations. These were just a drop in the ocean compared to the astronomical debts the viceroy had accumulated. He had got Egypt into so much debt it couldn't possibly repay it, so the government could hardly refuse when British lenders offered to buy the Suez Canal at a discount price. Thirteen years later, financial dependence turned Egypt into yet another British colony.

The British and other European colonial powers acted in a similar vein in many other countries. The sultan in Istanbul had gone bankrupt a few years earlier and the Ottoman Empire was falling apart, and in Persia, British speculators were buying up huge quantities of land in the hope of finding oil.

This tendency of the Europeans to ruthlessly pursue their own interests played into the hands of those in the Muslim world who had resisted change from the outset. Gradually, the opponents of modernity began to prevail. For many, it seemed easier to stand up against the West in the name of religion, to reject not only the injustice inflicted by the European occupiers, but also their values and way of life – in short, to reject everything European.

The travelling political activist al-Afghani, who was initially open-minded about the West and had dreamed of a Muslim Enlightenment, changed his mind and was now dead against the colonial powers. Since imitating the European way of life had been so catastrophic and had turned Muslims into Europe's slaves, he came to the conclusion that the only means of defending themselves against the overwhelming might of the Europeans was armed resistance. He called on Muslims to join forces and form a unified Islamic state: only then would they be able to push back the invaders and survive.

For the first time, al-Afghani used the term 'holy war' – *jihad* in Arabic – for a political struggle. He responded to the brutality and condescension shown by the imperialists across Asia. Meanwhile, 100 years later, a small group of Islamic extremists have used al-Afghani's terms 'Islamic state' and 'jihad' to carry out a programme of violence and terror – to the horror of the whole world, including many Muslims; after all, by far the largest number of victims of Daesh (the contemporary group that calls itself Islamic State) are Muslims themselves.

Al-Afghani's dream of a vast, unified state for all Muslims had little to do with reality. The Turkish sultan, the Arab rulers, the Persian shah and the tribal leaders in Afghanistan and India had nothing to gain from the idea of all Muslims suddenly uniting into a new nation. Who would have the overall authority in this Islamic state? Between Constantinople and Kabul were huge populations with little in common apart from their overarching religion – besides being Muslim, they were also Turks, Persians, Pashtuns, Indians and Arabs, all with different languages and cultural identities. It wouldn't be easy to unify them. Instead, they each took a different path.

The Turks didn't dream of a religious state for all Muslims, but of Turkish nationalism. They wanted a secular Turkish nation with a constitution, where religion and state were separate, just as the West had done. Many Turks who fought for this goal were not opposed to the Western way of life. They maintained good relations with German and French politicians and thinkers, exchanging ideas with them and seeking advice. They valued education and cosmopolitanism, and provided schools for their daughters as well as their sons.

This benefitted women like Halide Edib, who attended an American school in Istanbul and became a mathematician and writer. She was one of the first Muslim women to give political speeches in public. In one of her novels, Edib described her notion of a modern Turkey where women were equal to men and all the ethnic groups within the

From about 1909: The writer Halide Edib considers what a modern Turkish state would look like. Later she fights alongside Mustafa Kemal in the Turkish War of Independence.

Ottoman Empire coexisted peacefully. The themes of Edib's writing would become existential questions for the Turks. What would come after the collapse of the Ottoman Empire? Would Armenians, Greeks and Arabs also find a home in a new Turkish state? What values and traditions should the new state draw on? This was a central issue for women in particular: if the Turks were to turn away from modernity and return to the anti-technology and misogynist politics of the past, women would struggle to determine their own future.

Because of her language skills, Edib was invited to represent the government in negotiations with foreign ambassadors. Like others before her, she also saw how the Europeans betrayed their own values and crushed the ambitions of anyone who hoped to participate in the modern age – the British and French pursued their own agenda in negotiations with the Turks. Disappointed and concerned for the future of her country, Edib teamed up with a young officer named Mustafa Kemal and joined his struggle for the liberation of the Turkish nation.

China and Japan

In Japan, the politicians and thinkers who prevailed were the ones who wanted to emulate the Europeans. They initiated reforms aimed at catching up with Europe in education, technology and science, and set about transforming the old Japan into a new empire, which gave itself a constitution and became a modern state on the Western model.

It was clear just how well they had managed to catch up when the Japanese developed the same imperialist craving for their neighbours' territory as the West. They invaded Korea after a quarrel with China over it, and eventually declared war on China itself. Little Japan had moved up a league and was able to inflict defeat on its big brother China and annex Chinese territories, including the island of Taiwan.

For the Chinese, the Japanese victory – following so swiftly after Chinese defeat at the hands of the British – was a new humiliation. In her desperation, Empress Dowager Cixi, who had assumed power

1900: Empress
Dowager Cixi
supports the
Boxer Rebellion
against
foreigners in
China. Eight
imperialist
nations join
forces and
crush the
uprising.

after the death of her husband, decided to take an unusual step. Although governments usually did everything they could to suppress uprisings, she supported a group of thugs called the 'Fists of Harmony and Justice', known as the 'Boxers' in the West. These rebels mutinied not against Cixi's family, the Qing dynasty, but against everything that came from abroad. They shouted the slogan 'Revive the Qing! Destroy the foreigners!' and persecuted Christians in the country. Although encouraging these thugs meant she was violating all diplomatic rules of hospitality, Empress Cixi went ahead and endorsed their attacks on foreign ambassadors. The situation came to a head when the Boxers shot a German diplomat and the government officially declared that all foreigners would have to leave Beijing. That wasn't an option the imperialists were willing to consider; instead, an alliance of eight nations – Britain, the USA, Russia, Germany, France, Italy, Austria and even Japan – retaliated by sending in troops.

By supporting the Boxers, Empress Dowager Cixi had brought defeat upon her own ruling Qing court. Now she tried, rather belatedly, to introduce the necessary reforms and abolished the examinations – based on the writings of Confucius – that Chinese officials had to pass. The government even considered whether the imperial administration would benefit from a modern constitution.

1912: The
last emperor
abdicates and
China becomes
a republic.

But the Qing didn't last long when a revolution broke out, ending the 2,000-year history of the empire. China became a republic based on the teachings of Karl Marx, with a communist party in charge. China continued to suffer under pressure from the foreign imperialists, because the trade regulations still applied with their 'unequal treaties'. Meanwhile there were countless power struggles and a civil war within the country – all of which eventually brought a strong leader to power.

His name was Mao Zedong and, although he was the Chairman of the Communist Party of China, he was a good match for his imperial predecessors. He was every bit as cruel.

THE MARCH OF IMPERIALISM: THE EUROPEANS CONQUER AFRICA

The lowest race

In around 1810, Londoners had the chance to admire a young African woman on stage. Sarah Baartman wore tight-fitting dresses that mimicked the dark hues of her skin, was adorned with pearls and feathers, and smoked a pipe. If you had money, you could rent her for a private show where you could even touch her. The audience was particularly impressed by her full and shapely behind; since fleshy buttocks represented the pinnacle of beauty at the time, she was given the nickname 'the Hottentot Venus'.

It wasn't a compliment. 'Hottentot' was a derogatory term used by Europeans to refer to South African people who had been colonised and enslaved by the Dutch. It was in South Africa that an English businessman, in the service of a Dutch gentleman, had become aware of Sarah Baartman; he bought her from her owner and took her to London, where he paraded her on stage as a curiosity. Abolitionists were outraged at the show and accused the management of treating her like a slave. The scandal resulted in a court case where Sarah in fact stood by her master – although no one knows whether she was loyal to him voluntarily or out of fear.

A short while later she was sold to a showman in Paris who earned a living exhibiting exotic wild animals. Sarah agreed to let artists paint her and scientists study her. Racism in science was persistent, and researchers still believed that the 'Hottentots' were the lowest race of humanity, just one step above the orangutan. In the early nineteenth century, the first scientific research into racial theory was made using

1810: Sarah Baartman is brought from Africa to Europe, where she is paraded as the 'Hottentot Venus'.

her body; these findings were turned into propaganda to justify the colonial rule of Europeans over other continents.

But Sarah clearly suffered psychologically: she smoked, drank a lot and died two years later at a young age, on her own in a strange and hostile land. After her death, the interest in her body persisted, and her skeleton, brain and genitals were carefully preserved and exhibited in a museum in France. Horrifyingly, they could be viewed until 1974.

When Nelson Mandela became President of South Africa in 1994, one of his first activities was to petition the French government for Sarah's remains to be returned home. The negotiations between the two countries continued for years. The ultimate tipping point came in 1998, when Diana Ferrus – a South African poet – wrote the poem 'I've Come to Take You Home' about Sarah. A French senator came across the poem in 2001 and restarted the campaign. This time, it was a success.

The highest race

Although the Portuguese had gained a foothold in Africa some time ago, in the nineteenth century the continent was still largely 'un-owned' territory as far as the European colonial powers were concerned. That is to say, the native Africans had no industry or modern civilisation and were easy to subjugate, like the Asians.

Around 1880: Europeans start a race for Africa.

The Europeans embarked on a race for Africa, to seize land and resources as they had done in Asia. Again, Britain was particularly successful, which prompted entrepreneur Cecil Rhodes to claim that the British were the 'first race in the world'. However, there were two new players in the scramble for Africa whose self-esteem could rival that of the British. The German Reich had emerged by now, encompassing the smaller German states and principalities, with the former Prussian king at the helm as Kaiser Wilhelm I, followed by Kaiser Wilhelm II. Around the same time, the small Italian states united under King Victor Emmanuel II to form the Kingdom of Italy.

Germany and Italy were finally nation states, and they were keen to catch up with the Dutch, the British, the French and the

Portuguese in the hunt for colonies, although these countries already had a head start by several centuries. Germany and Italy hadn't featured at all in the colonisation of Asia, but they were determined to secure themselves a 'place in the sun' in Africa. It was just a few decades before the entire African continent became a patchwork of European colonies.

For the mining of raw materials you needed workers, and you needed roads and canals, houses and food. Therefore, the colonial rulers came not only with weapons, but also with Christian missionaries; while entrepreneurs and soldiers plundered the country, the Church tended to the souls of the poor sinners and converted the people of Africa to Christianity. A poignant African proverb describes the outcome: 'When the missionaries came to Africa they had the Bible and we had the land. They said, "Let us pray." We closed our eyes. When we opened them, we had the Bible and they had the land.'

BRITAIN AGAINST GERMANY

A deadly race

In India and Afghanistan, the south of Russia and Africa, the Europeans were waging wars for the sake of land. It was only a matter of time before the fighting would come back to Europe itself. Not least because, here too, conflict was brewing. Czechs, Poles, Hungarians, Slovaks, Slovenes, Croats and many others all lived in the Austro-Hungarian Empire, Europe's last multi-ethnic state and a remnant of the Holy Roman Empire. Some were fighting to become independent nations, while others felt threatened by their neighbours, especially the all-powerful Britain and Russia.

Many German politicians and military commanders were convinced that the superiority of the British Empire was based on its fleet of large, fast ships. In order to compete they set about upgrading their own naval fleet with an almost obsessive zeal. Kaiser Wilhelm II personally called on the people to support the effort; suddenly, everywhere you looked, you saw little girls and boys dressed in sailor's clothes. Britain realised it had a competitor, and before long Germany and Britain were head to head in a spiralling arms race for the strongest navy. Every ship built had to be bigger and faster than any before. A rumour went around that the fastest ocean liner to cross the Atlantic would be awarded a Blue Ribband as a mark of victory. In fact, this medal was never really awarded.

At that time, a certain Lady Duff-Gordon was designer and tailor to the well-dressed ladies of London high society. This was another Lady Duff-Gordon, not the same one who had travelled through Egypt a few decades earlier. Inventor of the fashion show, she was the first to have her latest designs modelled on a catwalk and soon opened fashion houses in New York, Paris and Chicago.

Lady Duff-Gordon was due to sail to the United States on a transatlantic liner which was getting a lot of attention in the press. Many believed that the *Titanic*, the latest cruiser from shipbuilders Harland and Wolff, had a good chance of winning the coveted Blue Ribband. The *Titanic* was the most impressive ship they had ever built, and some people called it unsinkable. On 10 April 1912, the *Titanic* set sail from Southampton – five days later, on 15 April 1912, it hit an iceberg and sank in the Atlantic Ocean.

Lady Duff-Gordon was lucky to have survived, along with around 700 others who escaped on the lifeboats, but around 1,500 passengers perished. The shock reverberated around the world, including in the German press. However, some in Germany rejoiced at the demise of the British luxury liner because the *Imperator,* an even larger and faster ship, was under construction in a German shipyard.

The sinking of the *Titanic* was the topic on everyone's lips. Its manufacturers had been confident of victory in the race for speed, and the whole world had been following the news, excited to witness another triumph of technology. The media hype made the disaster all the more shocking. For the first time, people realised what could happen when we lose control of technology. Some were reminded of the Roman god Janus, who looked in two different directions at once: technology brought constant progress, but it could also cause great harm.

1912: The *Titanic* hits an iceberg and sinks while Britain and Germany compete in a naval arms race.

THE SUFFRAGETTES

Votes for Women

1911: Marie Curie becomes becomes the first person to win a Nobel Prize in two different disciplines when she wins the prize for chemistry. She was already the first woman to win a Nobel Prize after being awarded one for physics in 1903.

Doubts about technology didn't stand in the way of progress. A year before the *Titanic* sank into the Atlantic Ocean, a bright new star had risen: the scientist Marie Curie received her second Nobel Prize, for chemistry, after winning one for physics in 1903.

Marie Curie was born Marie Skłodowska and came from the Kingdom of Poland, which was ruled by Russia. As girls were not allowed to study there, she went to Paris. Together with her husband Pierre Curie, she carried out experiments focusing on the smallest particles, investigating matter at the atomic level. They coined the term 'radioactivity' to describe the radiation that emanates from the nucleus of an atom as it decays. Marie Curie also discovered the element polonium, which she named after her homeland Poland.

More and more women were becoming scientists, writers or businesswomen, like Marie Curie, Nellie Bly, Halide Edib or Lady Duff-Gordon. Although these were still rare exceptions, the number of exceptions was on the rise. The upheavals of modernity had shattered the old order of things, making it easier for women to get out and forge a new path for themselves.

On the one hand, things were looking up for women. And yet, in the long term, it was not enough for women who pursued a professional life or an education to be rare exceptions. When Marie Curie applied to join the French Academy of Sciences, not only was she rejected but she was also the subject of abusive jokes; she was nicknamed 'Radium Circe' after the sorceress Circe of Greek mythology. The University of Paris at that time had roughly one female student for every 100 male students, which was too few. And as for the right to vote, society remained deaf to women's demands.

What were women to do if nobody wanted to hear? They needed to shout louder.

And if shouting wasn't enough, what about throwing stones at a few windows?

Ironically, the first woman to throw stones as she campaigned for the right to vote was not a very good shot – Emmeline Pankhurst was known for missing her target whenever she threw a stone. But in the Women's Social and Political Union (WSPU), an organisation she founded in her living room in Manchester, she had enough suffragettes to do the stone-throwing for her.

Together, the suffragettes made their voices heard. They burst into political meetings, climbed up on chairs and unrolled posters with their slogan 'Votes for Women'. They etched the words with acid into the manicured lawns of golf courses, blew up postboxes, slashed seats on trains, set off bombs, committed arson and smashed windows. They even smashed the windows of 10 Downing Street, the official residence of the prime minister.

The composer Ethel Smyth tried to teach Miss Pankhurst how to throw stones, but without success. Smyth then composed 'The March of the Women', which was enthusiastically adopted as the suffragettes' campaign anthem. More and more women joined the protests; more and more British women applied for gun licences, chained themselves to the railings in front of 10 Downing Street, and found themselves getting into brawls and street fights with their opponents.

The British government arrested many of the protestors and put them in jail – but by now they had a groundswell of support across the country. Prominent figures such as James Murray MP stood up for Emmeline Pankhurst; Murray ordered an extravagant meal from the Savoy Hotel, consisting of several courses and fine wines, and had it delivered to Pankhurst in prison, even sending waiters to serve her. The director of the Savoy didn't want to miss out on the good publicity, so he insisted that the meal was on the house. The conductor Thomas Beecham also visited the suffragettes in prison. He reported later how the 'noble group of martyrs marched up and

Around 1900–14: In Britain, the suffragettes aren't afraid to resort to criminal damage in their fight for women's suffrage.

down ... and sang "The March of the Women" like a war march, while the composer [Ethel Smyth] looked on kindly from the gallery above and tapped along to the beat with a toothbrush'.

The suffragettes continued their protest in prison by going on hunger strike. The government ordered them to be force-fed through a tube inserted into the nose; it was extremely painful and distressing. It's no wonder that some described their treatment in prison as torture.

But the suffragettes didn't give up. Some of Pankhurst's followers learned the martial art jiu-jitsu so they could defend their leader against the police when they tried to arrest her again. Emmeline's daughter Christabel stood up and defended herself and her mother in court when they were both arrested. As a barrister and leading activist within the WSPU, Christabel was such a celebrity that a wax figure was made of her at Madame Tussauds.

A lot of noise and a wax statue – for the time being, these were the only tangible results of the fight for women's right to vote. The First World War broke out, and in times of war different rules prevail. Some suffragettes organised peace demonstrations and called on British mothers not to let their sons go to the front, but the majority of British people – and a majority of suffragettes themselves – rallied together to fight the enemies abroad.

WOMEN ARE NOT UNITED

'Proletarians of all countries, unite!'

Women were fighting for liberation on the continent, too. However, suffrage – the right to vote – was not their only goal, which made things more complicated. Women were united by not being allowed to vote or participate in public life, but there was just as much that separated them. The wives of the well-to-do resented having to sit at home and sew or play music, surrounded by servants, while their husbands went out to pursue politics or business. Meanwhile working-class women, who worked long hours in factories or as cooks and maids in wealthy households, had very different worries. And because of this the women's movement split in different directions.

Some women became teachers like Helene Lange, and they fought for the right to education and for women's right to work. But others, such as Clara Zetkin and Rosa Luxemburg, believed that, if you took the situation of all women seriously, you needed to fight not just for women's rights but for socialism. The socialists further developed the ideas of Karl Marx. They wanted an entire new structure for society: a state where power lay not in the hands of the rich few, but in the hands of the everyone.

From 1888: In Germany, Helene Lange campaigns for the right to education, while Rosa Luxemburg and Clara Zetkin become famous socialists.

The socialists did what had never been done before – they planned a revolution that finally included women too. August Bebel, a German Social Democrat, put it this way: 'It is the common lot of woman and worker to be oppressed.'

Communists and socialists called on the workers to overthrow the old powers that be and take government into their own hands. For this revolution to succeed, the workers of all countries needed to form an alliance, following the slogan Marx and Engels had expressed in the Communist Manifesto: 'Workers of the world, unite! You have nothing to lose but your chains!' And indeed, socialists of many countries joined together to form the 'International Workingmen's Association', later known as the 'First International'. At their meetings, they sang, 'So comrades, come rally, and the last fight let us face. The Internationale unites the human race.'

Clara Zetkin and Rosa Luxemburg were leading members of the Social Democrats, the first party in Germany to campaign for women's suffrage. They helped set up international organisations, published journals for women, gave political speeches, were among the first women elected to parliament, and became internationally renowned politicians. However, many in the women's movement disapproved of the two socialists, and the Federation of German Women's Associations excluded them from its ranks, feeling that Zetkin and Luxemburg went too far when they argued that the sexes should be absolutely equal. Neither did they identify with the cause of the workers. Many people – not just women – rejected socialism, because they feared that rule by the working class would lead to injustice of a new variety.

WARFARE GETS HARSHER

The lady with the lamp

With the help of science and research, the Europeans were able to constantly upgrade and improve their military technology. Essentially this meant that more people could be killed more cheaply and efficiently – not exactly an improvement. It was especially disastrous if the opponent's military technology was just as sophisticated.

The British were the first to feel the impact of this in a war in the Crimea (a peninsula on the northern coast of Russia) between the Ottoman Empire and Russia. England and France rushed to side with the Ottomans in an attempt hold back the Russians, who were militarily stronger. Shortly after the outbreak of the Crimean War, entire shiploads full of wounded casualties began to return from the battlefields.

The military had never seen anything like it. The field hospitals were woefully unprepared to treat so many injured soldiers and conditions were so catastrophically unhygienic that one English newspaper reported that far more soldiers were dying in the field hospitals than on the battlefield. The British public were horrified. In response, the Secretary of State for War sent a nurse called Florence Nightingale to lead a team of thirty-eight nurses to treat the wounded soldiers.

Florence Nightingale had learned her nursing skills as a young woman. Her parents had sent her off on travels through the British colonies, but instead of visiting ancient ruins like other tourists, Nightingale visited hospitals. This was dangerous as, in those days, little was understood about hygiene or measures to take to prevent infections – and that was precisely what she wanted to change.

1854–65: Florence Nightingale revolutionises nursing. Clara Barton founds the American Red Cross, inspired by Henry Dunant's International Red Cross.

The Crimean War gave her ample opportunity to change the approach to nursing. She reorganised everything in the military hospital, where, besides caring for the wounded soldiers, she also raised money to pay for materials that they urgently needed to have shipped out from the UK: bandages, blankets, medicines and operating tables. She was pictured in the media as a nurse who walked about the hospital wards at night, tirelessly tending to the sick and wounded. Later, people started calling her 'The Lady with the Lamp'.

One day, Nightingale met a military doctor who reprimanded her for how she was dressed. Despite the hot Crimean sun, women in the Victorian era were expected to be modestly dressed. Like Nightingale, Dr James Barry had travelled throughout the British Empire, working hard to improve the standard of medical care. But Barry, who was one of the UK's top military doctors, was very unconventional for the time, as a vegetarian who didn't drink alcohol. What nobody knew was that Barry and Nightingale had something in common: the highly respected Dr Barry had been born female. It was completely impossible for a woman to study medicine, but Barry spent his entire adult life living as a man, having been born Margaret Ann Bulkley. It was only after death that Barry's origins were revealed to the university, the British military and the public. James Barry was the first doctor in Britain to have been born female.

Nightingale wasn't the only nurse to become famous for her deeds at that time. In Jamaica, a nurse called Mary Seacole had also made a name for herself. She travelled to London and offered help to Florence Nightingale's team in the Crimea. However, her offer was refused, possibly because nobody back then would have dreamed of employing a black person. So, she decided to make the journey to the Crimea herself, along with a relative, where she opened a hotel and started treating soldiers at the front. After the war, back in London, she found support with the royal family and the British Army, who paid off her debts as a sign of their gratitude. Her biography, *Wonderful Adventures of Mrs Seacole in Many Lands*, became a bestseller.

Twenty years later, a nurse called Clara Barton founded the American Red Cross, a charitable organisation that was created to help the wounded in war and disaster, no matter whether they were friend or foe. The roots of this came from Clara's own work in the American Civil War, where, horrified by the brutality she was seeing, she took to the battlefield, nursing soldiers and providing supplies. After the war she visited Europe for a break, where she came to learn of Henry Dunant's International Red Cross and found herself taking part in their missions. She returned home determined to set up an American Red Cross – not only did she do this, but she then led it for twenty-three years.

Florence Nightingale, Mary Seacole, Clara Barton and Henry Dunant created a modern approach to nursing just in time to treat an unprecedented population of war casualties. As warfare became ever harsher, the number of wounded would rocket.

SOLDIERS MARCH, WOMEN BUILD BOMBS

Peace!

1889: Bertha von Suttner publishes her anti-war novel *Lay Down Your Arms!* whilst campaigning for pacifism and the idea of worldwide peace.

Once again, the public was shaken up by a work of fiction. It was a novel called *Lay Down Your Arms!* by the Austrian writer Bertha von Suttner. She had come to know the grim face of the war in Russia, where the conflict between the Ottomans and Russians simmered on even after the Crimean War had ended.

Bertha von Suttner declared that wars were 'human insanity'. With the tactics and technology of warfare becoming ever more sophisticated, she believed people needed to rethink and to learn how to prevent war. Since this could only be achieved by countries working together, she founded several peace organisations and formed networks with pacifists at home and abroad.

The pacifists took up an idea formulated by the philosopher Immanuel Kant, who had argued the need for an international law that could declare any attack on another country to be unjust. Of course, such an international legal framework could only work if it was recognised by as many countries as possible. The pacifists therefore lobbied their governments to establish an international arbitration tribunal; those who didn't comply with international law would face trial and sanctions imposed by the world community. Bertha von Suttner helped to draft the proposed international law and personally presented the proposal to the Austrian Emperor Franz Joseph I.

Bertha von Suttner made the most of her growing fame to promote the idea of a worldwide peace. She travelled to the USA, where she met President Theodore Roosevelt. She enthusiastically supported the American peace movement, which had its roots in the anti-slavery movement and the Quaker and other Christian communities. It was von Suttner who proposed the idea of creating the Nobel Peace Prize to the Swedish inventor Alfred Nobel. In 1905 she herself received the award – the first woman ever to do so.

... or war?

In Europe, people weren't ready to accept the idea of countries collaborating for the sake of world peace. They had only just started to see themselves as part of a nation that could compete with other nations. Suddenly science, technology and philosophy were no longer seen as the achievements of humanity generally, but of specific nations. Even the arts were seen through this nationalist prism: the French claimed their music was more elegant than the Germans', while the Germans felt their music was serious and substantial compared to Italy's shallow and superficial offering.

People everywhere became obsessed with 'purifying' their language of foreign words that had migrated from one language to another over centuries of existing side by side. Poles and Czechs rejected German words, while Germans threw out French and Italian ones. Occasionally, Czechs would reject a word for being 'too German', while at the same time Germans refused to use precisely the same word because it was 'too French'. As with people, so it is with words – it's not always easy to tell where they come from. But the patriots didn't care, for loyalty to their nation was more a matter of the heart than of the mind: nationalist feelings were so strong that many were ready to sacrifice their lives for their motherland.

Loyalty to your motherland meant being proud not only of your country's language and culture, but also of its military. For the strength or weakness of a nation was nowhere more evident than during a war from which it emerged as either winner or loser.

The idea of enduring peace was an alien concept to most governments in Europe, who were used to seeing war as a vehicle for politics.

They weren't ready to place their trust in international peace agreements and international law, instead preferring to rely on military alliances. When two countries signed a pact against a third, the two allies strengthened their position while weakening their opponent. And as nobody wanted to be left behind without an ally, it wasn't long before the world was a dense web of military alliances, which were sometimes public and sometimes secret. These pacts offered benefits and security, but at the same time everyone remained suspicious, because promises and contracts could be broken at any time.

Bertha von Suttner pointed out that arms dealers, manufacturers and military leaders were inciting the people to crave conflict, because warfare was their business and they stood to gain financially. She foresaw great danger in the politics of drawing up alliances and warned of a global war of annihilation. The mood was extremely tense. Nationalists' thoughts were focused on war – many even longed for it.

The First World War

As Bertha von Suttner and many others had feared, the politics of alliances set the stage for a single war to spiral into a world war.

The conflict that sparked it all off was started by Gavrilo Princip, a Serbian nationalist in the city of Sarajevo, who was angry that his country was still part of the multi-ethnic state of Austria–Hungary. He was a member of Young Bosnia, a resistance group that was fighting for a Serbian nation state. On 28 June 1914, he shot and killed Archduke Franz Ferdinand, the heir to the Austro-Hungarian throne, and his wife Sophie on the street. Chaos broke out. Four weeks after the assassination, Austria–Hungary and Germany declared war on the Serbs, the Russians and the French. Like a line of falling dominoes, one country after another followed with further declarations of war – some allying with Austria, but others against.

Zealous patriots marched to the front, ready to defend their homeland and become heroes on the battlefield. The war enthusiasts had no idea what horrors awaited them. They didn't know the scale of

Summer 1914: The assassination of Archduke Franz Ferdinand in Sarajevo leads to the outbreak of the First World War.

the damage that modern, industrially manufactured weapons could inflict – many had never seen modern machine guns in use. Twenty thousand soldiers were killed in a single day of intense battle.

The soldiers who marched to the front had no experience of shells that could hit targets 30 miles away. They knew nothing about tanks or planes (the latter of which still couldn't fly very far but were already being used to drop bombs). All of a sudden there were submarines which sank ships, regardless of whether they were warships or passenger ships. When the British ocean liner *Lusitania* was hit by a German submarine on its way from New York to England, 1,200 passengers drowned – almost as many as on the *Titanic*.

Instead of earning glory as heroes, the soldiers fell in staggering numbers and were buried in anonymous mass graves. By the time the war had been raging for a year, the race was on to come up with a solution that would put the enemy out of action once and for all, causing a conflict of conscience for many scientists. They knew full well that their research would be used to develop ever mightier weapons. However, it was one thing to accurately calculate the trajectory of a bullet, but quite another to produce a poison gas that would rip enemy soldiers' lungs to shreds and cause an agonising death.

When chemist Clara Immerwahr spoke out publicly about the devastating effects of the chemical weapons they were developing, her own husband accused her of betraying the German nation. Immerwahr had married Fritz Haber in the belief that their passion for chemistry was something that brought them together, but when she became pregnant, her husband locked her out of the lab. She wasn't even allowed onto the university campus. Something similar happened to nuclear physicist Lise Meitner, who was only allowed into the institute where she worked if she used a hidden side entrance.

To Clara's horror, Fritz Haber gave his skills and knowledge to the service of the defence industry. He helped the military to produce poison gas, which would soon be used in the first major gas attack by the Germans, killing 5,000 British and French soldiers. Haber received an imperial honour for his work. During the festivities held to celebrate the success of that operation, Immerwahr took her husband's pistol, went out into the garden and shot herself. She left

1915: The chemist Clara Immerwahr takes her own life – possibly because of the first German use of chemical weapons in an attack which killed 5,000 soldiers.

behind several farewell letters, which all mysteriously disappeared shortly after her death.

It's possible that even Immerwahr didn't realise the full extent of the harm that the poison gas would cause. Its gruesome effect would not be limited to the battlefield. Since the men were called to the front to fight, the women took their places in the weapons factories, manufacturing bombs and chemical agents. Many fell ill and their faces turned yellow from the poison gas.

Initially, the war was perceived as a continuation of the Great Game, especially by the Germans: it was a race for colonies, for raw materials, sea routes and fast ships. But even they were soon forced to recognise that the weapons of the modern age had turned the war into an absolute catastrophe. The chemical weapons attacks were one of the cruellest horrors of the First World War – a global conflict which spread from Europe to involve those from the Middle East, East Asia, Africa and the United States. By the end, almost 70 million people, from more than forty countries, had fought in the battles: 17 million were killed, while many millions came home wounded and traumatised.

Attempts to end the war

Modern weaponry had turned the First World War into a hell of senseless annihilation. But once it had started, how could it be stopped?

1915: Over 1,000 participants attend a International Congress of Women conference in The Hague.

Shortly after the outbreak of war, Jane Addams from the USA and Aletta Jacobs from the Netherlands hosted an International Congress of Women conference in The Hague. After only two days, the participants – over 1,000 women – had adopted a concrete proposal for a solution to end the fighting. They then sent representatives to the world's leaders to mediate the peace, but without success. It was not until three years later that US President Woodrow Wilson gave a speech in which he called on all combatants to make peace without victory. He had taken on many of the points covered by the women in The Hague. After receiving Jane Addams's proposal, he said, in admiration, 'I consider it by far the best that has been formulated to this day.'

But it was easier said than done. Among other things, Wilson's fourteen-point peace plan included the dissolution of the multi-ethnic state of Austria, which was rejected outright by Germany and Austria. The USA had entered the war a year earlier as an opponent of Germany and Austria. When the American president decided to lead his country into the war, his compatriots stood by him – and so Jane Addams, who had spoken out against the USA joining the war, was publicly condemned as a traitor. Some even called her the 'most dangerous woman in America'.

Such hostility didn't deter Addams and the women of her peace network from seeking to end the war. They continued to campaign to bring the international community together to find a common solution, but to no avail.

1918: US President Woodrow Wilson presents a fourteen-point plan aimed at ending the First World War, establishing lasting peace and making the world 'safe for democracy'.

The October Revolution

Socialists were campaigning in many countries of the world for a new structure for society, and in Russia they were persecuted and severely punished by the tsar and his secret police. When the country was ravaged by war and people were starving, the wives of soldiers and workers gathered for mass demonstrations. It was similar to the French Revolution: famine and starvation drove people onto the streets, the protests spread, and eventually Russia experienced a revolution.

The socialists seized the opportunity and took the lead in the revolution. They formed local councils – called 'soviets' in Russia – and, wherever there were particularly strong protests, these soviets took control of local government. Eventually they overthrew the tsar and ended centuries of imperial rule of the Russian Empire. The emperor, Tsar Nicholas II, was forced to abdicate and was murdered with his entire family.

The new rulers called themselves the Bolsheviks and, under the leadership of Vladimir Ilyich Lenin, they founded the Union of Soviet Socialist Republics (the USSR, also known as the Soviet Union). It was the first time in history that a country experimented with social-ism as the basis for restructuring society.

1917: Lenin and the Bolsheviks assume power in Russia after the October Revolution and found the Soviet Union. The tsar and his family are murdered.

Since the people's longing for peace was a strong driving force behind the revolution, the new Bolshevik government was keen to negotiate with Germany, Austria and their allies. Half a year after the Russian Revolution, they had agreed a peace treaty at Brest-Litovsk. This ended the war on one front, at least.

The Weimar Republic

Socialists in Germany had close ties with Russia. As members of 'the Socialist International', the leaders were in touch with each other – Lenin, the leader of the Russian Revolution, had corresponded with Clara Zetkin for years. Members of the Social Democratic Party of Germany (the SPD) were split over the war: many backed the government, while a small group led by Rosa Luxemburg, Karl Liebknecht and Clara Zetkin were vocal in their criticism. They founded the 'Spartacus Alliance' and the Communist Party of Germany. Zetkin distributed leaflets calling for an end to the war. For this, she was arrested as a traitor and sent to jail. But Zetkin was very popular and her arrest prompted protests; this public pressure led to her release soon after.

Over time, the German public also became sick of the war and desperate for it to end. Many had turned against the Kaiser and the military and were calling for a truce to end the fighting. The socialists saw their chance to seize power: there was a revolution and the socialist insurgents formed councils following the Soviet model. They tried to establish a socialist republic like the USSR, but they failed after just a few weeks. Instead of a purely socialist state, the Weimar Republic was born in Germany: a parliamentary democracy with several different parties.

1918: The First World War ends with the defeat of Germany and Austria. In Germany, the Weimar Republic is born.

The USA, UK and France had proven themselves to be unbeatable; Germany and Austria had to concede defeat and agreed to a ceasefire and eventual peace. Kaiser Wilhelm II abdicated, bringing an end to empire and the monarchy in Germany.

From international law to global injustice

Germany and Austria had started the First World War. This gave their opponents – the British, French and Italians – the moral upper hand and made it easier for them to present themselves as the defenders of freedom and democracy. When the war ended, they met at the Palace of Versailles, near Paris, to finally negotiate the terms of world peace. In Versailles, however, it became apparent that it wasn't going to be easy to divide the world into simplistic camps of 'good' and 'bad'.

1919: The Versailles Peace Conference is held after the end of the First World War.

US President Wilson did travel to Paris with noble intentions. With his fourteen-point plan, he hoped to make the world 'safe for democracy' and the first steps were to create a League of Nations and the basis of a common international law. This won Wilson tremendous popularity throughout Asia, initially at least. Chinese students were full of praise for the American president; people in Korea and Vietnam looked eagerly to Paris for news of this new world order; the Indian anti-colonialist campaigner Tagore planned to dedicate a book to him. Everyone hoped that the 'right to self-determination' would liberate them from colonial rule by the Europeans.

But things did not turn out as they hoped. The talks at Versailles did indeed lead to the foundation of a League of Nations and they did manage to draft the basis of international law – but it soon became clear that the 'good' side just meant the strongest countries, who did not feel the need to be bound by international law. They intended to pursue their own interests, just as before. This was obvious when a proposal put forward by the Japanese came to a vote. Japan wanted the written statutes of the League of Nations to include a racial equality clause. This boiled down to a clear statement that all races were equal, which some people still refused to accept. In the vote, the majority accepted the Japanese proposal, but President Wilson argued that the decision was invalid. He cited the questionable justification that there had been 'strong opposition' from certain parties: the USA, Australia and the UK. They didn't respect the principle of racial equality, and they feared losing their colonies and mandates if they agreed with the wording.

So, the Americans simply annulled the result of the vote, undermining international law at the very moment of its birth. International law was reduced to a tool of global injustice. Once again, a minority of particularly powerful states were content to disregard everyone else and pursue their own interests. The Japanese had been lucky to be represented at the negotiations at all – many countries hadn't even been allowed to attend. When Wilson returned to America, Congress also rejected his proposal and refused to join the new League of Nations. The idea seemed to have failed for now.

Fuel for further wars

1919: The Treaty of Versailles inflicts harsh punishments on the losing side that serve as fuel for new conflicts.

At the conference of Versailles, the allies negotiated a peace agreement with Germany and Austria. They dictated tough conditions. Germany had to relinquish its colonies to Britain and France; it was forced to disarm, relinquish territories on its borders and pay huge sums of compensation over the following years. To top it all off, the Germans were excluded from the League of Nations.

The multi-ethnic state of the Austro-Hungarian Empire was broken up and new nations were created from its regions: Czechoslovakia, Poland, Hungary, Yugoslavia and Austria. However, the new country of Austria wasn't truly a distinct nation because many of its inhabitants saw themselves as German; many of those who remained in the territory of Austria after the First World War preferred to belong to the German republic.

Austria wasn't the only place where it was obvious that the idea of nation states didn't work in practice. The Hungarians felt humiliated because they had to give up vast territories after the war. Czech, Slovak and German speakers lived side by side in Czechoslovakia while Yugoslavia had a population made up of Croats, Serbs and Bosnians.

Thus, the Versailles Peace Conference ended with treaties that, in one way or another, disappointed, humiliated or alienated almost the entire world. The women of the international peace movement recognised this. When they met for the second time, in Zurich, they protested vehemently against the Treaty of Versailles. They, like many others around the world, feared that the agreement would not bring about peace, but only provide the 'fuel for further wars'.

THE BRITISH CARVE UP THE MIDDLE EAST

Freshly drawn lines

Before the war had even ended, when the Ottoman Empire was on the brink of collapse, British politicians were looking at the map of the Middle East and thinking about how to carve it up. They drew a line through the former Ottoman Empire and agreed with the French that the area north of the line would be French and the area to the south would be British. The Sykes–Picot Agreement, as this became known, was top secret, because selling off parts of the Middle East didn't exactly fit the idea of a just world where every nation had the right to determine its own future.

The Sykes–Picot Agreement and the line through the Middle East are linked to the fate of a woman: Gertrude Bell, a British historian and archaeologist. She was an exceptional student of history at Oxford, but that didn't give her any professional recognition as, although women were allowed to study at that time, they were still not officially awarded a degree. Their education was considered to be just for fun or for ornament. However, at society balls, proof of female intelligence wasn't the kind of ornamentation men were after, and an intelligent woman was not considered good marriage material. At least, that's how it seemed to Gertrude Bell. After trying in vain to find a husband, she is said to have left England in frustration. She went to Tehran and then travelled through Persia and the Arab lands, making friends with locals and learning Persian and Arabic. The Arabs admired Bell and called her 'Daughter of the Desert' and 'Desert Queen'.

1916: The French and the British divide up the Middle East in the secretive Sykes–Picot Agreement.

In 1917 Gertrude Bell was called up to help the British in Baghdad, as she was a noted expert on the Arab world. The army refused to work with her initially, but when her language skills and knowledge of the local people proved invaluable, the British military commander eventually appointed her as an intelligence officer, or spy. Some said she was respected like a man, which Bell may have liked; after the humiliation she had experienced at the balls of fine English society, she looked down on the women in her homeland.

In Mesopotamia (modern-day Iraq), Bell had the chance to contribute to world history. 'I had a well spent morning at the office making out the Southern desert frontier of the Iraq,' she wrote to her father in December 1921. With her pen and paper, she had the power to decide how the state the British were founding in ancient Mesopotamia would look.

1920–22: With the consent of the League of Nations, Britain and France establish new states in the territory of the former Ottoman Empire, creating Syria, Palestine, Lebanon and Iraq.

After dividing the region up with their secret line on the map, the British played a duplicitous game. The area known in ancient times as Mesopotamia was then still part of the Ottoman Empire. Britain planned to share the territory with the French, but at the same time they promised it to the Arabs, as a way of encouraging them to overthrow the Ottomans. Meanwhile, Bell was urging British military leaders to give Iraq and Jordan a large degree of independence, and called for Arabs to be made Kings of Iraq and Jordan. Was she trying to help her friends, the Arabs? Her colleague T.E. Lawrence, also known as 'Lawrence of Arabia', played a similar role to Bell in Egypt. He was deeply ashamed when the secret Sykes–Picot Agreement and the British deceit became public.

Lawrence and Bell were admired for their knowledge of the Arab world, but even they didn't understand the conflicts among the local Muslims. They underestimated the divide between Sunnis and Shi'ites and didn't recognise that you can't just draw up arbitrary borders and declare a region to be a 'nation state'. Most people were Kurds or Arabs, Sunnis or Shi'ites, and yet all of a sudden they were expected to see themselves as 'Syrians', 'Iraqis', 'Jordanians' or 'Palestinians', because that's what was decided in London and Paris. In the long run, this would inevitably lead to new conflicts.

The Sykes–Picot Agreement was inflammatory for other reasons too. The Jews, who had lived scattered throughout the world for around 2,000 years, were constantly subject to pogroms. This persecution gave rise to a new movement, Zionism – the dream of founding a separate Jewish state, a place of sanctuary for all Jews. As part of the Sykes–Picot Agreement, the British promised the Zionists land for this purpose. The only problem was that they'd promised parts of the region to the Arabs as well because they hoped that both the Jews and the Arabs would support them against the Ottomans. However, after the First World War, it became clear that the same piece of land couldn't be divided among several groups. Nevertheless, the League of Nations mandated that the Jews should be given an area of Palestine for their new Jewish state. As a consequence, the Palestinians in the region were resettled and robbed of their land – an injustice that pitched both sides into an increasingly complex conflict.

ONE WORLD, TWO IDEAS

Free democracy and socialism

In 1917, the United States entered the First World War on the grounds of needing to defend democracy. In the same year, Lenin and the Bolsheviks overthrew the tsarist regime in Russia and founded the Soviet Union. When the whole world – with the exception of Germany and Austria, the war's losers – met two years later in Versailles, the USA and the Soviet Union represented opposing ideals. Both tried to win as many countries as possible over to their side: the USA emphasised the importance of democracy and the greatest possible freedom for citizens, while the Soviet Union focused on socialism and the equality of citizens. This ideological split created two political regions, which would come to be known as the Eastern and Western blocs.

Many in Asia still placed their hopes in President Wilson and international law, so Lenin tried to make them see that the USA was as greedy for natural resources and territory as the European imperialists. The Americans were every bit as exploitative and oppressive as the British and French, the socialists argued. Imperialism was the product of the West's economic system, capitalism.

In Russia, the revolution had just brought a new government to power. The Bolsheviks claimed that only socialism could create a fair and peaceful world, and they were determined to practise what they preached. First, the Russians made the secret Sykes–Picot Agreement public, exposing the UK and France's plans to control and influence the Middle East. Then the Soviet Union ended the unequal treaties the Russian Empire had signed with China (or, rather, *forced* China to sign). The Soviet Union supported liberation movements in China, India, Indonesia and Vietnam, and helped organise revolutions and set up communist committees. The West found itself under pressure. They now had to prove their liberal democracy was no less fair than socialism. It became increasingly difficult for the United States, the UK and France to justify their rule over their colonies.

The Turkish nationalists didn't trust either side, doubting good would come of supporting either the Western powers or the Soviet Union. Mustafa Kemal, who had campaigned with Halide Edib, therefore led the Turks into a war of liberation against Britain, France and Italy, and their neighbours Greece and Armenia. His fight to liberate his people was a success and Mustafa Kemal founded the Turkish state, a modern, independent state that was intended to console the Turks for the end of their great Ottoman past. Mustafa Kemal was given the name 'Atatürk' – the father of Turkey.

1923: Mustafa Kemal Atatürk builds the state of Turkey from the remnants of the Ottoman Empire.

THE WORLD FALLS INTO AN ABYSS

The advance of the fascists

'Freedom is always the freedom of dissenters,' wrote Rosa Luxemburg. Like Clara Zetkin, she was an independent thinker. Although the two admired Lenin and dreamed of a revolution in Germany, they were critical of the abuses they saw in the newly founded Soviet Union. The new Russian leadership didn't want to allow people the freedom to think differently: they feared critics could jeopardise the fledgling experiment of socialism and undermine the power of the new state.

In Germany too, arguments about the future of the country became more violent. The two socialist leaders Rosa Luxemburg and Karl Liebknecht were murdered by a militia in the middle of Berlin; their bodies were found in the Landwehr Canal the next morning. It is still unclear who exactly was behind the assassination.

Suddenly, militia groups of armed activists were a regular sight in many cities of Europe. Dressed in heavy boots and military uniforms, they marched through the streets intimidating the public, until soon very few people dared to oppose them. It started with militia groups in Italy that called themselves 'fascists'. They formed their own political party – the National Fascist Party – and helped their leader, Benito Mussolini, become Italy's prime minister. Everywhere there was talk of this new movement, 'fascism'.

1922: Benito Mussolini is appointed Italian Prime Minister. Fascism begins to spread throughout Europe.

The irritating thing about fascism is that it wasn't actually based on an idea. The fascists didn't dream of justice and equality, of humanity and peace. For them there was only 'us', the people – a community which felt bound together by blood and soil. Instead of discussing things democratically, the fascists followed a strong leader.

The fascists also thought that in Italy everything should be Italian, and likewise in Germany everything should be German, Polish in Poland and Hungarian in Hungary. In short, everyone should be ethnically pure or 'nationalist'. Unlike in the nineteenth century, when the idea of nationalism was limited to aspects such as culture and language, the fascists now combined their demand for purity with racial theory. The 'nation' should not just be pure culturally, but also ethnically – people should be 'of pure blood' and not have other races in their genetic heritage.

This idea had already surfaced 500 years earlier during the reign of Queen Isabella of Castile, when the Jews were forced to leave Spain in droves. Since then, anti-Semitism had never really gone away. Now, with the rise of fascism, anti-Semitism was given full rein. It was the same in the UK, France, Holland, Poland and the Soviet Union: everywhere there was a violent wave of hatred against Jews.

But nowhere did it become as extreme as in Germany and no one carried the cult of a strong leader, nationalism and hatred of Jews as far as Adolf Hitler, the leader of the National Socialist Party of Germany, the NSDAP.

Hitler takes power

Ten years after the First World War, the Great Depression shook the entire Western world. It was a severe financial crisis: many people across the world lost their jobs and faced hunger and fear.

The consequences hit Germany particularly hard. As the loser in the war, the country was suffering under the burden of high compensation payments as demanded by the Treaty of Versailles – something that the German population perceived as severe humiliation. Many see this as the reason that the Germans were so enthusiastic about the National Socialists, the party widely known as the Nazis. Their message offered people a simple explanation for their hardship. People needed someone to blame – and Hitler focused on the Jews.

The Nazis employed cheap slogans. Lacking any real ideas or arguments, the fascist militias – the SS (*Schutzstaffel*) and the

SA (*Sturmabteilung*) – won the public's attention through brute force. They attacked Jews on the street and beat up 'political dissidents', which was code for anyone who thought differently. They looted Jews' shops and businesses, condemning journalists as 'liars' and the media as 'the lying press'. They branded artists and writers as 'degenerate', confiscating artworks and burning books. The Nazi Party gave its followers the vocabulary to humiliate others in the worst possible way: anyone who didn't belong to their German 'master race' was condemned as 'filthy', 'unclean', 'vermin' or 'subhuman'. They painted the Nazi symbol, the swastika, on the walls of Jewish shops, smashed their windows and set fire to synagogues.

A large proportion of Germans sympathised with the Nazis and elected the NSDAP to the national parliament, the Reichstag. Now Hitler could take a decisive step and seize power: he deposed parliament, putting an end to the democracy of the Weimar Republic and declaring himself the Führer – leader – of all Germans.

1933: Hitler seizes power in Germany.

As soon as the Nazis came to power, the attacks on Jewish people intensified. They issued laws that placed more and more restrictions on Jews' lives. People who had never been anything other than German were marginalised from society and were suddenly perceived as enemies in their own country. Jewish people were expelled from schools and universities, public institutions, orchestras and museums; their property was seized and businesses looted. Jews were forced to live in ghettos or taken to concentration camps, where thousands were subjected to forced labour or murdered. It wasn't only Jews who were denied the right to life by the Nazis. They also arrested and persecuted groups whose lives were considered 'unworthy': political opponents, Sinti and Roma travellers, gay people and people with physical or mental disabilities.

After 1933: The National Socialists transform Germany into a dictatorship. Jews are excluded from public life and persecuted, as are other minorities such as gay, Sinti and Roma people.

Meanwhile the Nazis focused on boosting the German 'master race'. This task fell to women, who were pushed back into their age-old role as mothers and housewives. It was their job to produce a 'pure-bred' or 'Aryan' population of strong, blond and blue-eyed children.

To this day, historians puzzle over why so many people followed Hitler and his National Socialists. Why were they so keen to march in goose step and to wave the swastika flag? Why was it that so many men blindly followed their leader and women volunteered their services to the state as part of a selective breeding programme to give birth to 'pure Aryan' children? And why did those who didn't agree with him stand by in silence as Hitler seized power and turned a democratic country into a dictatorship?

One of the first to raise these questions was the Jewish philosopher Hannah Arendt. She was deeply disappointed to see how even highly educated individuals in her circle of friends – including the philosopher Martin Heidegger – fell for the National Socialists' empty rabble-rousing. Was it really down to the defeat in the First World War, the humiliation of the Versailles Treaty, the hunger and misery resulting from the financial crisis? Or did it come down to the power of the sophisticated Nazi propaganda?

The first 'talking movies' – films with sound – were being shown in the cinemas when Hitler met the young film director Leni Riefenstahl and commissioned her to make a series of full-length feature films of the NSDAP conference. Riefenstahl captured iconic images of huge crowds cheering for their leader, amidst a sea of swastika flags and flaming torches. Politics aside, her films set the standard for cinematography and even abroad her work won her great acclaim. She received a cinematic award for *The Triumph of the Will*, and forty years later the film inspired a large crowd scene in *Star Wars: A New Hope*.

Leni Riefenstahl was given lavish support by the National Socialists and there were other artists, scientists and entrepreneurs who, like her, made a pact with the devil. But for anyone who didn't toe the Nazi Party line, life became increasingly dangerous. Many artists, film directors, scientists and writers were arrested by Hitler's secret police, the Gestapo, or dispossessed, or banned from practising their profession. The more this happened, the more people decided to flee Germany and Austria. Many refugees from Nazi Germany and Austria later became British or American citizens, such as the philosopher Hannah Arendt or the actress Marlene Dietrich, who made a career in Hollywood after fleeing Germany and later entertained American soldiers on the front line in an effort to raise morale.

The Second World War

Hitler wanted to establish an empire to last a millennium – the 'thousand-year Reich', as he called it. He had long been preparing for this goal. He shifted the economy into gear for preparing for war, and poured money into building tanks and roads to move them around.

When the National Socialists felt ready for combat, they invaded Czechoslovakia and Austria. They justified this with a policy called *Heim ins Reich* ('back home to the Reich'), claiming they were defending the rights of the many German speakers in those territories after the collapse of Austria–Hungary. The British and French governments looked on helplessly and tried from afar to calm the situation. The last thing they wanted was to slide into another devastating war – but Hitler wanted 'total war'.

1939: Germany invades Poland on 1 September, prompting the outbreak of the Second World War.

Hitler believed he was invincible. His troops invaded Poland and France, and for many months the Luftwaffe inflicted heavy air strikes on British cities, in short, sharp and powerful attacks. The Germans called this *blitzkrieg*, which means 'lightning war'. This gave the English language the word 'Blitz' – an era still imprinted in British memory.

1941–45: The Germans carry out the mass murder of European Jews. In this genocide, known as the Holocaust, around 6 million Jews are murdered.

At the same time, the Nazi leadership began systematically preparing for their greatest crime against humanity: their plan to assassinate all Jews. This was referred to as 'the Final Solution'. They wanted to annihilate the entire Jewish population of Europe. The Nazis built extermination camps with gas chambers, where thousands of people could be killed in mere seconds. Then they rounded up Jews in Germany and the territories they had occupied, crammed them in railway carriages and transported them on the purpose-built railway network, which carried them directly to the gas chambers in concentration camps such as Auschwitz, Treblinka and Sobibór.

It was Fritz Haber, the husband of Clara Immerwahr, himself a Jew, who had helped develop the pesticide that was used to produce Zyklon B, the lethal chemical that was pumped from shower heads into the gas chambers, killing millions of Jews. It was beyond what most people could even imagine. They saw how the Nazis condemned other people as 'pests' and 'vermin', but few could imagine that they would also annihilate them as though they were insects.

The poet Paul Celan, whose parents were murdered by the Nazis, wrote that death was 'a master from Germany'. After the war, the world discovered from the diary of Anne Frank just how hard it had been to escape arrest and death at the hands of the Nazis. Anne was 13 years old when she began her diary, and she detailed how her family hid in the loft of a house in Amsterdam for two years, being brought food and news by former employees from her father's company. But eventually their hiding place was discovered and Anne and her family were split up and deported to various concentration camps, where most died; Anne is believed to have died from hunger and typhus at Bergen-Belsen concentration camp. Her father was the sole survivor from the family. After the war he ensured that her diary was published.

Resistance

It was dangerous to resist the Nazis. Most who tried failed and paid for their courage with life. When the Jewish ghetto of Warsaw, the capital of Poland, rebelled against Nazi occupation, the Nazis burnt the ghetto to the ground, killed thousands in the streets and sent the rest to concentration camps.

There were failed attempts to resist by individuals, such as Georg Elser or Claus Schenk Graf von Stauffenberg who tried to assassinate Hitler with a bomb attack. Their plots were thwarted and the would-be assassins were executed.

Among the courageous individuals who tried to bring down the Nazis were Hans and Sophie Scholl, students in Munich who were members of the White Rose Alliance, an underground resistance group. They printed thousands of flyers calling on Germans to rebel against Hitler. Some were smuggled to England and passed on to the Royal Air Force, who then flew over German cities and dropped the leaflets from the skies. But as with so many members of the resistance, Sophie and Hans Scholl were discovered and executed a few days later.

Others managed to save lives, such as the Polish woman Irena Sendler, who saved the lives of 2,500 Jewish children from the

Warsaw Ghetto after joining a Polish resistance group that helped Jews. When the Nazis arrested her, despite being subjected to severe torture, she refused to reveal the names of the hidden Jewish children.

Another 'great dictator'

The Germans were not the only criminals of that time. While the Nazis plunged Europe from the heights of the Enlightenment to the deepest barbarism, the dream of the Russian socialists was also fast becoming a nightmare. Joseph Stalin, the new leader of the Communist Party, turned the Soviet Union (the USSR) into a socialist dictatorship. His rule hinged on spreading fear and terror. Stalin feared nothing more than the loss of his power, so he carried out a series of 'purges' that targeted anyone who seemed at all suspicious. Many writers, artists and intellectuals were arrested and subjected to show trials – sham criminal trials where the judgement was clear from the outset.

1936–38: The Soviet dictator Joseph Stalin's 'purges' reach their peak. Every day, up to 1,000 people are murdered or deported to forced labour camps, known as the Gulag.

Above all, these measures served to scare the population into submission. Millions of people were executed after being arrested or were sent to a labour camp in Siberia, where they faced forced labour, dreadful sanitary conditions and food shortages. Many didn't survive the prison camps.

Stalin wanted to transform the Soviet Union from a land of peasants into a land of industry. This violence-enforced change triggered severe famine in some parts of the country, where staggering numbers of people starved to death. When resistance stirred in the Caucasus, Stalin had entire ethnic groups deported to the Siberian labour camps as punishment. Many people from Kalmuck, Ingush, Chechen, Crimean Tartar and other communities died in those camps.

The catastrophe

As they had similar ideologies, Mussolini and Hitler had met before the war and formed an alliance. Hitler and Stalin also signed a non-aggression pact before the war, agreeing to divide up the areas of Poland and the Baltic states between them. During the war, however, Hitler changed his mind; ignoring his agreement with Stalin, he sent his troops to invade the Soviet Union. The former allies Hitler and Stalin became opponents at war.

1941: Hitler breaks his pact with Stalin and invades the Soviet Union.

The Germans had driven Europe into another all-out war, but it was only when Hitler's allies in Asia got involved that this conflict become a world war. The Japanese emperor and his generals dreamed of becoming colonial rulers across Asia. In pursuit of this ambitious goal, they came into conflict with the USA: the Americans condemned Japan's brutal treatment of China, but they were also motivated by their own interest in gaining influence in Asia. The majority of the American population were against getting involved in the war, but this changed overnight, when the Japanese attacked the US naval base Pearl Harbor in Hawaii. The very next day, the United States entered the war against Germany and Japan.

1941: Japan attacks the US fleet in Pearl Harbor, which prompts the United States to enter the Second World War.

The United States' entry into the war turned the tide against Germany and its allies. With the support of the Americans, the Allied forces of France, Great Britain and the Soviet Union succeeded in defeating Germany and putting an end to the barbaric slaughter. One week before the German Wehrmacht (armed forces) signed their defeat, Hitler took his own life. Half of Europe lay in ruins.

1945: On 8 May, Germany surrenders, ending the Second World War in Europe.

In a way, the Germans were lucky, because it was only after the country was already defeated that the Americans tested out their atomic bomb. Japan refused to follow Germany in capitulating; as far as they were concerned, the war was not over. That was enough for the Americans to justify the use of their new super weapon. The first atomic bomb, named Little Boy, was dropped on Hiroshima, a second – Fat Man – fell on Nagasaki; more than 200,000 Japanese people were killed.

August 1945: The Americans drop nuclear bombs on the Japanese cities of Hiroshima and Nagasaki.

At the end of the Second World War, military technology had once again reached unprecedented murderous dimensions.

THE COLD WAR

After the two world wars

1945: The Potsdam Conference: the victorious Allied leaders divide Germany into four occupation zones. The borders of Germany, Poland and Ukraine are shifted by several hundred miles, forcibly displacing millions of people.

During the First World War, the last German emperor built Cecilienhof Palace in Potsdam for his son. Just thirty years later, at the end of the Second World War, Russian soldiers occupied the town. The Russians liked the little castle, and so Stalin personally invited the US president and British prime minister to Cecilienhof to negotiate the aftermath of the war. They decided to divide Germany into four occupation zones, which each of the four victorious powers – the three were joined by France – was to control.

The Potsdam Conference was their second meeting; they had previously met in Yalta in the Crimea, where it had become apparent that there were many points on which the victors didn't agree. They argued over how to divide up the regions between Germany, Poland and Ukraine. In the end, they simply moved the borders by several hundred miles, which resulted in millions of Poles and Germans being displaced many miles to the west. Above all, Britain and the USA disapproved of Soviet moves to establish communist regimes in the countries east of Germany. Two political camps emerged, allying themselves with either the Soviet Union or the United States, and these became consolidated as the Eastern and Western blocs. When the Western states came together to form the NATO military alliance, the East responded by founding the Warsaw Pact. This was the start of the Cold War.

1949: The Cold War pits the USA against the Soviet Union, and the Western bloc against the Eastern bloc. Germany is divided into the Federal Republic in the West and the German Democratic Republic in the East.

Europe was an important theatre of the Cold War, where the two superpowers faced each other in bitter enmity. The Soviet Union called on the Americans to declare Germany neutral territory, but the USA planned to rebuild Germany and make it a member of NATO.

The dispute escalated and eventually led to the division of Germany. In the Russian occupied zone, a socialist state was founded under Moscow's leadership: the German Democratic Republic (the GDR), often called East Germany. The other three zones were combined to form the Federal Republic of Germany, or West Germany.

Russia and the USA both developed nuclear weapons. They didn't build them with the intention of destroying the other side, but as a form of deterrence. It was about demonstrating to the other side that any attack would be immediately responded to with a devastating counterattack – a risky strategy that resulted in constant fear of a stand-off spiralling into a third world war.

The fear of impending war was mounting. When NATO relocated medium-range missiles to Turkey, the Russians felt threatened. To counter this move, they planned to station the equivalent weapons in Cuba, where the leader Fidel Castro was a socialist and a friend of the Soviet leadership. The situation deteriorated into the Cuban Missile Crisis – for a moment, the outbreak of a third world war seemed imminent. But it seemed that the principle of nuclear deterrence worked when the Cuban crisis was resolved at the last moment.

1962: The Cuban Missile Crisis: the USA and the Soviet Union are on the verge of nuclear war, placing missiles on each other's borders.

Equality ...

The Cold War was more than just a military conflict. On both sides, people believed they had created the better political system – the just social order that they had dreamt of for so long.

The socialist countries gave themselves titles like Workers' and Peasants' State or People's Republic, asserting the idea that the ordinary working population had risen to the ruling class. In these states, the same party remained in government: the Workers' Party. They formed the heart of the state apparatus, which regulated everything and ensured living conditions were as equal as possible for everyone.

The socialists had broken with the old society; they wanted a fresh start. So that nobody would get the idea that they were better than anyone else, titles were abolished and people addressed each other simply as 'comrade'. Companies were state-owned enterprises that belonged to everyone and were called co-operatives.

Socialist governments drew up five- or ten-year plans for what would be produced and in what quantities. Because of these plans, this way of running a country was called a 'planned economy'. The state only produced the essentials to meet people's needs, and only traded with socialist brother states.

But these 'brotherly' relations between socialist states weren't entirely voluntary. After the Second World War, the Soviet government installed communists in power in Czechoslovakia, the Baltic states, Poland, Hungary and Yugoslavia, which were all ruled as puppet states from Moscow. When the populations of Hungary and the GDR rose up in protest, the Soviet Union sent tanks to crush the uprisings.

The socialist governments restricted the freedom of the individual. That was the price they paid for a social order where there were as few differences as possible between comrades. As more and more people fled to the West, the Eastern bloc secured its borders with fences and barbed wire. Berlin also had a wall built through it, because part of the capital belonged to the victorious Western powers. The Berlin Wall became the symbol of the so-called Iron Curtain – a line running through Europe that would separate the Eastern and Western blocs from now on.

... or freedom?

In the West, the emphasis was on the very thing that most people lacked in socialism: freedom. The West celebrated liberalism: everyone living as they pleased, with as few restrictions as possible. It's no coincidence that ship passengers pass by the Statue of Liberty as they arrive into New York Harbor; she is perhaps the most famous woman in the United States.

In Western democracies, people were free to travel and to express their opinions. Questions of lifestyle, political views, diet, sexual orientation or religion were all left to the individual. A fair society wasn't based merely on equality, but on diversity. This became the epitome of freedom.

The means of guaranteeing this diversity was the market economy – the rule is that companies can produce whatever they like, as long as they find customers for their goods. This means companies have to compete and advertise their products to consumers. Competition between businesses is thought to spur them to be as creative as possible in the hope of creating products that are better and more desirable than their competitors'. Advocates of the free market economy argue that in this way the laws of the market regulate everything for the benefit of the people.

Since a functioning market economy was considered their highest political goal, the governments of the USA and Western Europe were above all responsible for enabling free trade. They endeavoured to remove any obstacles that slowed or hindered the flow of goods. To achieve this they signed international trade agreements.

In Europe, the European Economic Community was founded by France, Italy, Germany, Belgium, the Netherlands and Luxembourg. With time, they were joined by more and more European countries, and the European Economic Community eventually became the European Union (EU), the community of European states. However, the EU was intended as more than just a large trading area. It was intended to guarantee peace and to prevent future wars.

1957: In Europe, six states found the European Economic Community (EEC). Later, it evolves into the European Union (EU).

But even liberalism had its disadvantages. The international trade agreements and treaties promoted by the West have tended to provide trade benefits only to the rich industrial nations, while penalising poor countries in Asia and Africa. After the Second World War, some criticised global free trade as being simply a new means to continue exploiting countries that were formerly colonies.

Between East and West

In Asia, some countries gained independence and began to grow into strong industrial nations. China and India didn't join either the Eastern or Western bloc, but sought their own way to catch up with the West's economic advantage. Brazil and South Africa tried to do the same. The majority of countries were denied this success, however. To this day, people in many countries are living in poverty – from Indonesia to Haiti and almost the entire African continent.

1947: Mahatma Gandhi and Jawaharlal Nehru lead India to independence from the British through non-violent resistance.

In India, Gandhi led the resistance against the British. He remained true to his pacifist stance and rejected any form of violence. Instead, he encouraged resistance by way of hunger strikes, blockades and spectacular protests. In the end, the British colonialists were forced to leave the country and India became a democracy. When Prime Minister Jawaharlal Nehru died, his daughter Indira Gandhi became one of the first female prime ministers in the world.

In China, the Communist Party established a Communist People's Republic. After the end of the Second World War, the Communist Party's leader Mao Zedong rose to become the third 'great dictator' of the twentieth century (after Hitler and Stalin). Mao launched a reform programme called 'the big leap forward', intending to strengthen China's economy. However, those responsible in his administration made such alarming mistakes that what was intended as a major advance instead caused a terrible famine, which killed as many as 40 million Chinese people. It was one of the worst catastrophes in human history.

1949: Mao Zedong declares the foundation of the People's Republic of China.

The programme had to be terminated, but Chairman Mao clung to power all the same. Five years later, he announced a new programme, the Cultural Revolution, which was to destroy every single aspect of bourgeois culture. Literature, music, theatre, fine arts – everything was to give way to a new, communist culture. Many believe that, above all, the Cultural Revolution was a means for Mao to eliminate his opponents. Hundreds of thousands, if not millions, of Chinese people died; many were tortured, persecuted or exiled.

Chairman Mao's wife Jiang Qing, known as 'Madame Mao', was no less cruel and ambitious than her husband. She played an active role in the Cultural Revolution and was the first woman in the Chinese government, hoping to take the top spot after her husband's death. She didn't succeed. Instead, Mao's successor had Jiang Qing tried in court for her crimes during the Cultural Revolution and she was sentenced to death. This was subsequently changed to life imprisonment, which she served for eight years before being released to a hospital on medical grounds at the age of 77. Shortly afterwards, she took her own life.

Women in socialism

Since the beginning of the twentieth century, the suffragettes had been gaining support in their struggle for the right to vote. It was only a matter of time before many countries changed their laws: New Zealand and Australia led the way, followed by most of Europe, the Soviet Union and the USA. At last, all the barriers started to fall away and women finally had full access to schools and universities; they could take up positions in court, in medicine, in the world of business, in museums and orchestras, and in politics.

In the socialist countries, equality between women and men came about very quickly. Women were able to pursue all professions; indeed, they were expected to pursue a higher education or professional training and to work as their contribution to socialism. It now became apparent, however, that Marx hadn't thought to count housework as 'work'. This meant that many women, especially mothers, suffered from the double burden of doing the housework while also maintaining a job.

When Mao Zedong and the Communist Party founded the Chinese People's Republic, they also claimed that women and men would be equal. The Communist Party is still in power, seventy years later, but women have been pushed back into their old roles. The Chinese government has described unmarried women over the age of 27 as 'leftover women'. By dismissing them with this derogatory term, China's leadership seeks to discourage women from choosing an independent life outside of marriage and family.

The peace movement

In Western democracies, the situation of women did change – just slowly. There were still many who looked after the household and the children, leaving politics to the men. However, when the Soviet Union and the United States repeatedly tested atomic bombs, housewives and mothers in the USA decided to do something about it. The children's book illustrator Dagmar Wilson brought together a group of friends who shared her belief that only a strong protest by women could push their country's leaders to end the nuclear arms race.

Dagmar Wilson and her comrades called for a strike by women across the United States. For weeks they sent letters calling on friends and colleagues to join them, which resulted in 50,000 women gathering in Washington and other cities to demonstrate against nuclear weapons testing. This was the birth of the organisation 'Women Strike for Peace'.

Participants in Women Strike for Peace wrote to Jacqueline Kennedy and Nina Khrushchev, the wives of the USA and USSR's heads of government, asking them to persuade their husbands to adopt a new strategy. They also linked up with other civil rights movements, and were soon joined by women like Coretta Scott King. Coretta was the wife of Martin Luther King, who gave his famous 'I Have a Dream' speech during the 1963 March on Washington.

The Women Strike for Peace campaign was surprisingly successful, and the USA and Russian leaders genuinely began to negotiate disarmament treaties in a long series of conferences. In the end, both countries pledged to dismantle their expensive nuclear weapons.

Some believed that, as they had reached their goal, these women should now step out of politics and head back home to their children and housework. But the women who campaigned with Dagmar Wilson knew that the much sought-after peace was far from guaranteed. On the contrary, the US government was now embroiled in war in Vietnam, and Women Strike for Peace launched themselves into the next campaign.

The Americans saw themselves as the guardians of peace and human rights; President Wilson's post-First World War desire to make the world 'safe for democracy' still rang in their ears. But now

1961: The organisation Women Strike for Peace – one of the first American grassroots peace movements – starts protesting against nuclear testing.

1963: Martin Luther King gives his famous 'I have a dream' speech during the March on Washington. In 1968 he is murdered.

they had got involved in a conflict in Vietnam solely for the sake of asserting their own interests. When US planes dropped napalm on their opponents in North Vietnam, a photo of 9-year-old Phan Thi Kim Phúc went viral around the world. She had ripped off her burning clothes and was running from her village, naked and severely injured. The photograph, entitled 'The Terror of War', shook the American public.

1961–75: In the Vietnam War, the USA squanders its reputation as guardian of peace and democracy.

Women Strike for Peace called on the government to withdraw from Vietnam. They became the forerunners of a much larger civic movement – a wave of protest, led by students, swept from the USA to Europe and grew into a rebellion that echoed throughout the world.

Everywhere, even outside of the USA, people came together to protest against the war in Vietnam, and other topics. They condemned the economic world order where rich countries exploited poor countries. They protested against the white men who still ruled the world and maintained racial segregation; against women being tied to the kitchen sink; and against the unjust treatment of gay people who were still ostracised and punished. Protest was directed against every form of violence, oppression and exclusion, whether in Asia, the Americas, Europe or Africa.

1968: The summer of rebellion: there are worldwide protests against war and injustice.

The protestors sympathised with Czechoslovakia, where people were trying to break away from the rigid communist regime. There was talk of a thaw, of the 'Prague Spring' where socialism would soften to become 'socialism with a human face'. But the Russian leadership was not comfortable with such changes. They sent in tanks and put an end to the Prague Spring.

The civil rights and peace movements revealed liberalism to have the upper hand over socialism. In the free world, people were not prevented from interfering in politics. They were able to create new forms of civic participation, for example, by founding non-government organisations (NGOs) such as Amnesty International, which campaigns for freedom and human rights.

1968: The Prague Spring uprising in Czechoslovakia; the Russians invade with tanks to crush the rebellion.

The prime ministers and presidents of the world also sought to build an international community based on co-operation rather than wars and military threats. The United States and Britain seized on the earlier pacifist idea of the League of Nations and re-founded it, this time as the United Nations (UN). The first to join them were the Soviet Union and China, and by the time the founding treaties were signed, the UN already had fifty member states. Their most important task was – and remains – establishing and maintaining peace throughout the whole world, and upholding international law and human rights.

The UN is far from having achieved its mission of peace. Nevertheless, the UN does regularly bring its member states together for dialogue. Citizen movements have contributed much to this global discussion since the Women Strike for Peace movement first protested in the major cities of the USA.

CATCHING UP WITH THE PRESENT

Old conflicts and new

In 1989, the border crossings in Berlin opened. This was the start of the reunification of divided Germany. The Berlin Wall fell because the Eastern bloc states were failing: the planned economy hadn't worked and the Warsaw Pact countries couldn't keep up with the West. They literally ran out of money, causing the Eastern bloc to crumble and the Iron Curtain to fall away.

The world experienced a tumult of freedom; suddenly the long-awaited peace between East and West seemed within reach. Many believed that it was only a question of extending the West's economic model to the whole world, just as the EU states had come together to form a peaceful common economic area. Political soothsayers foresaw an end to all wars; there was even talk of the 'end of history'.

Since those heady days, disillusionment has spread. New conflicts have flared up, initially on the fringes of Europe, with Yugoslavia collapsing into civil war, then in the Middle East. Throughout the Cold War, the Russians and the Americans both meddled in a civil war in Afghanistabn – a conflict that is still raging to this day. In Rwanda, disputes between ethnic groups descended into a barbaric genocide waged by the Hutu people against the Tutsis. In South Africa, a minority of European settlers ruled over the majority black population for decades. This system, which was known as apartheid, was finally brought to an end by Nelson Mandela and the Anti-Apartheid Movement. For decades, the Jewish state of Isracl has been engaged in a bitter struggle for land with the Palestinians. Shortly after the fall of the Berlin Wall, the USA began

1989: The Berlin Wall falls on 9 November. Soon after, the Soviet Union disintegrates. This is the end of the Cold War.

2001: On 11 September, members of the terrorist group al-Qaeda hijack two planes and steer them into the twin towers of the World Trade Centre in New York. Nearly 3,000 people are killed.

to intervene in Iraq, leaving behind a devastated and disintegrating state. At the dawn of the new millennium, on 11 September 2001, hijackers flew planes into the twin towers of the World Trade Centre in New York, and almost 3,000 people died. Ten years after the 9/11 attack, civil wars began in Ukraine and Syria. Now, even the European Union – the biggest peace project in history – is full of internal conflict after the people of Britain voted to leave in a closely contested referendum.

In place of the dream of global peace, which many felt was within reach after the fall of the Iron Curtain and the end of the Cold War, a new fear has emerged: fear for the long-won values of freedom, democracy and human rights. Suddenly, there is a growing realisation that they are fragile goods.

Meanwhile, China, Korea, Brazil and India are catching up economically. The power centres of the world are beginning to shift: instead of the two poles of East and West, there are now several. Some predict that America and Europe will become weaker and China will lead the way in future. Only time will tell.

Lady Lovelace's algorithm

Since the twentieth century, no technical innovation has changed our lives more than the digital revolution. Before industrialisation, it took months for news to travel around the world; today a message typed in Switzerland can be read almost simultaneously in Australia. The internet has transformed the world into a place of communication where time and space seem to be suspended.

A second reality has emerged, a virtual reality. Almost everything that happens in the physical world also happens in parallel online, from love affairs to wars in cyberspace. Meanwhile, the physical world becomes increasingly dependent on the virtual, as ever more devices and systems are controlled digitally, be it cars, fridges or our power supply.

For a long time people underestimated what computers could do if given the right commands. The mathematician Ada Lovelace thought about this question as early as the nineteenth century. She insisted to her friend, the English mathematician Charles Babbage, that in the future a computer would be able to do anything, except perhaps to think for itself. Lovelace made this remark at a time when computers didn't even exist.

Ada Lovelace was 17 when she met Babbage at one of the salons he hosted. He had designed a huge, steam-powered analytical engine, but he didn't have a financial backer, so the machine was never built. Lovelace realised that this machine could be given commands using a mathematical language. Babbage had come up with the idea of providing commands, and Ada Lovelace was the first to formulate the algorithm for a detailed computer program. She created the first software almost 100 years before anyone had developed the hardware – the computer – to run it.

1843: Ada Lovelace writes the first computer program – 100 years before the invention of the computer.

Technology in everyday life

The analytical engine, for which Lovelace wrote the software, would have been nearly 20 metres long, 3 metres high, and would have consisted of 55,000 parts. That's probably why it was never built. While they relied on steam power, machines were colossal beasts and were staggeringly expensive to manufacture.

1879: The light bulb is invented; this heralds the start of the widespread use of electricity.

All that changed with electrification. Suddenly, mechanically generated power could be conducted as a current through small copper wires and transported everywhere. Suddenly, every household could get energy from an electrical socket.

Since then, our lives have been transformed by washing machines, electric ovens and vacuum cleaners. We use electricity for our radios, which bring conversation and music into our homes, and for the television that gives us images of the outside world. When the first human, the American Neil Armstrong, set foot on the Moon, spectators around the world gathered around the TV set to watch it live. An ancient dream – one that people had cherished ever since the Babylonians tried to touch the stars with their Tower of Babylon over 5,000 years ago – had come true and people were able to watch with their own eyes as it happened.

1969: The Americans land on the Moon.

1957: The
Russians
launch 'Sputnik'
– the first
satellite in
space.

The Americans were not the first in space. During the Cold War they were in a space race with the Russians, and twice the Soviets succeeded in overtaking their competitors. They launched the first satellite, called Sputnik, into space. This shocked the West. Could it be that the Russians, with their planned economy, had better space technology? Just a few years later, Yuri Gagarin and Valentina Tereshkova were the first people to fly into space – and again, they were from the Soviet Union. Maybe that was why the Americans insisted on broadcasting the Moon landing live on television. They wanted everyone to see that Neil Armstrong, who was making his 'giant leap for mankind', was an American.

The mathematician Margaret Hamilton wrote the software that ensured the lunar module landed safely on the Moon. The code – an emergency escape code in case something went wrong – was called 'Forget it', because it was hoped that it wouldn't be needed. However, as it turned out, it wasn't the code that was forgotten, but its creator. Over thirty years would pass before Hamilton was honoured for her contribution to the Moon landing mission.

Since space exploration began, countless satellites have been launched into space. Nowadays, we all have a smartphone or some kind of device that receives signals sent via satellites in space. From PCs, laptops, tablets and ever shrinking smartphones, we send data around the globe to vast servers that fill entire warehouses.

Most of the technology we use today was developed through military research programmes and the US space agency NACA, which later became NASA. NACA had already started employing female mathematicians around twenty years before Margaret Hamilton, and these mathematicians made a significant contribution to America's success in the Space Race. They worked in a department made up almost exclusively of black women, including Dorothy Vaughan, Katherine Johnson, Mary Jackson and Christine Darden. They were known as 'human computers'; one of them even remarked, rather sarcastically, that they were 'computers in skirts'. At the time, racial segregation in America was so strict that many white staff knew nothing about them or their work. Now, more than fifty years later, these female mathematicians have finally received their recognition: the story of these 'hidden figures' was told in a 2016 film of the same name.

It is difficult to say which of the many technical inventions that have emerged since the Industrial Revolution have changed our lives the most. Imagine, for example, trying to replace all the things around us that are made of plastic. How did things look before the existence of this material, a kind of 'artificial rubber'?

Life has been irreversibly changed by science and technology, and so too have the questions that philosophers ask themselves. They think about the internet, which has shrunk the world until it has become a 'global village'. They think about the non-stop acceleration that seems to be leading to a 'furious standstill'. They think about how the flood of images we see can change our perception and take the place of verbal communication. They think about the possibilities of genetic engineering, about how we can artificially fertilise egg cells and create life in a test tube. What does it all mean? Have we ourselves become creators of life, a kind of god?

Silent Spring

The two world wars showed the world how destructive technology can be when we lose control of it, but it was still hard to shake the enduring faith in the possibilities of technology. People's confidence in progress remained unbroken. That is, until American biologist Rachel Carson published her book *Silent Spring*.

At that time, the 1960s, farmers were spraying particularly aggressive weed killers and pesticides onto their fields to protect their crops from insects. Carson warned that if we continued this unrestrained contamination of farmland and groundwater, one day there would be no more birds to herald the arrival of spring.

For the first time, a scientist warned a broad readership that wars were not the only negative side effect of technology. The 'pests' that were killed by agricultural pesticides were also an essential part of a food chain, she argued. Soil, flowers, shrubs and trees, insects, vertebrates, birds and fish – all nature on the planet coexists in a complex ecosystem where everything is connected. Rachel Carson told her readers that any interference with this ecosystem had consequences – consequences

1962: Rachel Carson's book *Silent Spring* appears, shocking readers into action and inspiring the start of a global movement to protect the environment.

so grave that they could eventually adversely impact human life itself. After all, we too can only survive in a healthy ecosystem.

Silent Spring had a huge impact. Around the world, people began to campaign for environmental protection, founding conservation groups and organisations like Greenpeace. The environment became a topic on the curriculum in schools and universities, and green parties emerged to ensure the environment was on the agenda in politics. However, we are only slowly beginning to realise the extent to which we are destroying the Earth's ecosystem through our wasteful consumption of nature's resources – through the extraction of oil, gas, copper and other metals, and rare minerals; our consumption of water; deforestation and the destruction of rainforests; and our overfishing of seas and oceans. We're even starting to run out of sand.

Environmental problems were also made worse by the Industrial Revolution. Industry grew, and along with that grew a reliance on fossil fuels like coal, which polluted the atmosphere. It encouraged an increase in the consumption and use of non-essential goods, and the increase in living standards and life expectancy caused dramatic population growth. After the Second World War, one question rose in urgency: how would the rapidly increasing population be fed? The risk of famine was great in many regions. Fortunately, most catastrophes could be averted, again with the help of developments in science. Firstly, Fritz Haber – the same Fritz Haber who was involved in developing the poison gas during the First World War – succeeded in producing artificial fertiliser, which enabled farmers to vastly increase the yield of food crops. Then, after the Second World War, American scientists in Mexico cultivated wheat plants which could withstand harsher climatic conditions, eventually developing strains that yielded three times as much as the original wheat plant. This genetically modified wheat has been widely grown in Mexico, Pakistan and India, and many are convinced that this 'green revolution' has saved billions of people from starvation.

Since then we have found ourselves in a vicious circle: advances in medicine and agriculture have continually improved people's lives since the invention of the first industrial machines, but this has resulted in global population levels that are rising and a population that is getting older. This in turn makes it harder to feed everyone, so we again rely on science and technology to find solutions.

In the meantime, there are endless suggestions of what we can do, which generally look towards one of two directions. Some believe that, unless we humans drastically reduce our consumption and slow down population growth, the natural environment will eventually collapse. Humanity may not survive a catastrophe of this scale. Rachel Carson was not the first to recognise this, but her book helped to spread this way of thinking and was a catalyst for the environmental movement.

Others are convinced that people will always succeed in inventing new, better technology to protect life on this planet. In short, some see science and technology as the cause of the problem, while others see them as the solution.

Today climate change has come to the forefront of public consciousness worldwide. Time and again, the world's heads of state meet at climate summits to discuss and propose solutions, yet these are rarely embedded in policy and law. In response, the movement Fridays for Future was born, headed by the Swedish student Greta Thunberg. Now students from all over the world have joined her and are taking to the streets in protest against politicians' inaction. This action is promising, but we mustn't forget that species extinction, ocean acidification and the depletion of finite resources (such as sand) pose just as much of a threat to our planet as climate change.

Women can do anything

At the beginning of the modern era, Christine de Pizan opened up the debate about women with the words 'I, Christine'. She argued that women can do anything.

It was some 500 years before women finally had the chance to prove it. No sooner had the first aeroplanes taken off during the First World War than women were getting pilot's licences. They too were determined to cover ever greater distances in tiny vehicles with ever larger fuel tanks. Charles Lindbergh made the first flight across the Atlantic, but he was followed five years later by the pilot Amelia

Earhart. If she wasn't in the air, she was arguing passionately against the idea of 'male professions' for which women were unsuited.

Many others did the same. Early in the pioneering days of flying, there was an air race for female pilots in the USA, which was dismissively referred to in the press as the 'Powder Puff Derby'. When one pilot crashed and died in the course of the race, the media seized on it as proof that women couldn't fly. This was nonsense, of course, because in those days plane crashes were common: many planes and their pilots were lost in the great oceans, in the icy Arctic or in the jungles of Central America. Amelia Earhart's plane *Electra* disappeared one day over the Pacific, together with the pilot and co-pilot. They were never found.

At around the same time, Clärenore Stinnes took part in her first motor-car race. A little later, she drove around the world, even though there were no passable roads in many remote areas. This was a mere forty years after Bertha Benz had set out on the first cross-country jaunt in her motor car, covering a distance of over 100 kilometres. She had to fix the engine with her hat pin and a garter to successfully complete the planned route.

In the twentieth century, women like Marie Curie made groundbreaking discoveries in physics and chemistry. Women orchestrated major peace movements; think of the difference the pacifists Bertha von Suttner and Jane Addams made, or Dagmar Wilson with her organisation Women Strike for Peace. Women kickstarted social and political debate – like Rachel Carson, whose book changed the way people thought about the environment. Or they set philosophical discussions in motion, such as Hannah Arendt, whose thinking shaped public debate about the crimes perpetrated by the Nazis.

Women became prime ministers and presidents, such as Indira Gandhi in India, Benazir Bhutto in Pakistan or Corazón Aquino in the Philippines – or Margaret Thatcher, the 'iron lady' of British politics, and Angela Merkel in Germany. There's nothing stopping women becoming astronauts or footballers. In many countries of the world, girls and women can do anything and achieve anything. So why do we still argue about sexism and gender equality?

The Second Sex

The debate about women was by no means over when women won the vote. On the contrary, after the Second World War, women were pushed back into their roles as housewives and mothers, and once again it was time to think about the true nature of women. The debate had opened up during the French Revolution, with Olympe de Gouges and Mary Wollstonecraft questioning assumptions about the role of women. But it was not until the mid-twentieth century that the French philosopher Simone de Beauvoir added a theoretical dimension to the age-old debate. What was once referred to as the *querelle des femmes* had evolved into feminism.

'One is not born a woman, she becomes one,' wrote de Beauvoir. She explained that what we interpret as feminine is in fact an ideal that people have subconsciously formed over the course of centuries. It is not in the biological nature of women to be weak, sweet and shy; if they are, that's the result of how they're raised.

1949: The *querelle des femmes* becomes feminism, and Simone de Beauvoir's book *The Second Sex* becomes a pivotal text.

Girls grow up learning that they should be charming, modest and unambitious, argued de Beauvoir. They watch and learn from their mothers. When they go out into the world, they are constantly confronted by men. Everywhere they go, they see the names of famous men on the street signs and statues of important men. At school, all girls hear about is men who made history and wrote history, male painters and composers, male poets and thinkers, male mathematicians and inventors. That was how things were for a very long time.

Simone de Beauvoir wrote in French, where *l'homme* means both 'human' and 'man'. Similarly, in English, we spoke of 'mankind'. The default term for human or person was always 'man', while the separate word for women marked their otherness: *la femme*. Women, wrote Simone de Beauvoir, were 'the second sex'.

Women were something 'else', something abnormal. Aristotle had already described them as imperfect, less capable, of lesser worth than their male counterparts. For 2,000 years, people repeated the words ascribed to St Paul: 'Women should remain silent in the churches.' Even more frequently called on to justify women's treatment was the story of humanity's fall from grace, the story of Eve, who fell for the snake's trick and bit into the forbidden apple from the tree of knowledge. From this people concluded that men were strong and women were weak, and so these ideas settled in people's minds over thousands of years of being repeated. These ideas entered their bodies and coursed through their blood, shaping women's behaviour, the way they spoke, thought and moved.

Feminist theory found the term 'gender' to express this. Gender is what we *consider* female or male, because we are used to seeing it that way. When we talk about gender, we don't mean biological nature, but modes of behaviour that we interpret as masculine or feminine.

Women are not naturally housewives and mothers – this is clear from the fact that some women don't take on these roles at all. But centuries of social pressure have made most of them conform to this preconceived idea. At the same time, men are equally restricted by these preconceptions, such as when a man feels he can't be a stay-at-home dad without risking damage to his reputation or professional standing.

1990: In her book *Gender Trouble*, Judith Butler shows how our language shapes reality – including the way we see men and women.

The American philosopher Judith Butler opened the next major chapter in the gender debate. In her book *Gender Trouble*, she analysed how our preconceptions about women and men become reality through the way we speak and think. Language shapes our consciousness, as Karl Marx had already observed. That was why the socialists had done away with the language of the old social structures and addressed each other not as 'Mr' and 'Mrs' but as 'comrade'.

On the one hand, Butler wrote, the language we use can emphasise the common ground among people, while on the other hand it can overlook individual and cultural differences. It could be that in a group of two women and one man, one of the women has much more in common with the man than with her fellow woman. Since Butler's book came out in 1990, there has been much debate about how we should speak about men and women, as well as those who don't fit solely in either category. It's complicated, this gender trouble.

Female and male professions

In the nineteenth century, the post of secretary was a respected profession. Educated young men started their career as the right-hand man to the company director. A secretary had good prospects of promotion through the ranks: being responsible for written correspondence and accounts meant they got to know the company from the ground up, and would later rise to the top to become the director.

Then, in the twentieth century, women started to become secretaries. This didn't raise the status of women, but rather lowered the reputation of the profession. That was the end of the strong career prospects. The secretary became little more than a paper-pusher or typist.

The opposite has happened with programming – a profession that today carries considerable prestige and is a well-paid, typically male occupation. It wasn't always so. During the Second World War, the US military hired about 100 women to calculate the trajectories of various projectiles. To speed up the process, one of the first computers was built – the ENIAC – as part of a top-secret project ,and six women were employed to program it. This work was considered unmanly at the time, as little more than the menial work of a typist – even though the women needed a maths degree to be able to do it.

When the ENIAC was presented to the public as a technological innovation after the Second World War, the men who had built the computer were fêted and entered the history of science hall of fame. The women who had programmed it were forgotten, to the extent that later no one knew why they were even in the team photos from the time. Some suggested they had been invited along to pose for the sake of marketing.

These stories bring us to another question: why is that what women do is seen as less valuable than what men do? At the time of Copernicus, people came to terms relatively quickly with the idea that the Earth revolves around the Sun. But how is it that, even after 500 years, many still find it difficult to accept the simple idea proposed by Christine de Pizan that women and men have the same abilities?

1942: Women program the ENIAC, one of the first computers in the world.

Perhaps this contempt for women may also mean that as a society we show less respect for issues and aspects of life that were long considered 'female' or 'feminine'? The question has no easy answer; on the contrary, there is still much to argue about when it comes to the role and place of women in society.

Women in world history

When we sleep at night, things emerge in our dreams that we suppress from our consciousness during the day – things that seem dangerous, frightening or worrying. This was a theory expressed by the Austrian psychoanalyst Sigmund Freud in his book *The Interpretation of Dreams*, published at the beginning of the twentieth century. With it, Freud founded modern psychology.

1900: Sigmund Freud publishes *The Interpretation of Dreams* and establishes the field of psychoanalysis.

If world history is part of the consciousness of all humankind, then the dreams of humankind should be populated by an infinite number of women suppressed from our historical memory. There are far, far more than we could include in this one book. We've just made a start on this path, by bringing at least a few women from the realm of dreams back into the conscious memory of world history.

Many have followed this path already, and much progress has been made. Ada Lovelace was recently remembered for her work as the first to write a full computer program. Streets have been named after women in recent years. The Church has rediscovered forgotten saints like Thecla and Nino, who both helped to spread Christianity in its first three centuries. It's only been in recent years, after decades of debate, that the man St Paul had admiringly referred to as 'the apostle' was actually a woman. It's thought that the idea of a female apostle was so outlandish to medieval scholars that they changed 'Junia' to 'Junias' and called her male – even though Junias wasn't even a real name.

We are still unaware of the historical significance of the lives of many women. But this isn't the only reason we still have a long way to go in this debate: even today, far too much violence is still being committed by men against women. Women are still being oppressed and mistreated in too many regions of the world, and we see far too frequently that women are paid less than men for the same work.

Margaret Hamilton, the programmer who wrote the code for the Moon landing, was honoured in 2003 – thirty-four years after the historic event.

For many of the women mentioned in this book, the honours bestowed on them come too late; they're no longer alive, and in some cases have been dead for centuries or even millennia.

Who knows? Maybe there's somewhere – beyond space and time – where the Sumerian poet Enheduanna, high priestess of the Moon god Nanna; and Margaret Hamilton, instrumental in the moon landing, are celebrating their posthumous fame together.

BIBLIOGRAPHY

Abulafia, David. *The Great Sea: A Human History of the Mediterranean.* Oxford University Press, 2011.

Adıvar, Halide Edib. *House with Wisteria: Memoirs of Halide Edib.* Leopolis Press, 2003.

Anderson, Bonnie S., and Judith P. Zinsser. *A History of Their Own: Women in Europe from Prehistory to the Present.* Vol. 1. Oxford University Press on Demand, 2000.

Angela, Alberto. *A Day in the Life of Ancient Rome.* Europa Editions Incorporated, 2009.

Austen, Jane. *Northanger Abbey.* Wordsworth Editions, 1992.

Beard, Mary. *Women & Power: A Manifesto.* Profile Books, 2017.

Beecher Stowe, Harriet. *Uncle Tom's Cabin.* Wordsworth Editions, 1999.

de Beauvoir, Simone, and Howard Madison Parshley. *The Second Sex.* Vintage, 1953.

de Bellaigue, Christopher. *The Islamic Enlightenment: The Modern Struggle Between Faith and Reason, 1798 to Modern Times.* Liveright Publishing, 2017.

Black, Brian. *The Character of the Self in Ancient India: Priests, Kings, and Women in the Early Upanisads.* State University of New York Press, 2007.

Bock, Gisela, and Allison Brown. *Women in European History.* Blackwell Publishers, 2002.

de las Casas, Bartolome, and Nigel Griffin. *A Short Account of the Destruction of the Indies.* Penguin UK, 1992.

Charpin, Dominique. *Writing, Law, and Kingship in Old Babylonian Mesopotamia.* University of Chicago Press, 2010.

Chibnall, Marjorie. *The Empress Matilda: Queen Consort, Queen Mother and Lady of the English.* Blackwell, 1992.

Dawson, Jane E.A. *John Knox.* Yale University Press, 2015.

Dénes, Mirjam, and Fajcsák, Györgyi (eds). *In Search of Prince Genji: Japan in Words and Images.* Museum of Fine Arts (Budapest), 2015.

Dimitrova-Moeck, Svoboda. *Women Travel Abroad 1925–1932: Maria Leitner, Erika Mann, Marieluise Fleisser, and Elly Beinhorn: Women's Travel Writing from the Weimar Republic.* Vol. 168. Weidler, 2009.

Duby, Georges, Pauline Schmitt Pantel and Michelle Perrot. *A History of Women in the West: From Ancient Goddesses to Christian Saints.* Vol. 1. Harvard University Press, 1994.

Faroqhi, Suraiya. *The Ottoman Empire and the World Around It.* Bloomsbury Publishing, 2004.

Ferguson, Niall. *Civilization: The West and the Rest.* Penguin, 2012.

Foster, Benjamin R. *The Age of Agade: Inventing Empire in Ancient Mesopotamia.* Routledge, 2015.

Frize, Monique. *The Bold and the Brave: A History of Women in Science and Engineering.* University of Ottawa Press, 2010.

le Goff, Jacques. *The Birth of Europe.* John Wiley & Sons, 2009.

Gombrich, Ernst Hans. *A Little History of the World.* Yale University Press, 2005.

Gordon, Linda. *The Moral Property of Women: A History of Birth Control Politics in America.* University of Illinois Press, 2002.

Herrin, Judith. *Women in Purple: Rulers of Medieval Byzantium.* Princeton University Press, 2001.

Herrin, Judith. *Byzantium: The Surprising Life of a Medieval Empire.* Princeton University Press, 2009.

Herrin, Judith. *Unrivalled Influence: Women and Empire in Byzantium.* Princeton University Press, 2013.

Hobhouse, Henry. *Seeds of Change: Six Plants that Transformed Mankind.* Counterpoint Press, 2005.

Isaacson, Walter. *The Innovators: How a Group of Inventors, Hackers, Geniuses and Geeks Created the Digital Revolution.* Simon and Schuster, 2014.

Jaffé, Deborah. *Ingenious Women: From Tincture of Saffron to Flying Machines.* Sutton Publishing, 2004.

Jars de Gournay, Marie de, 'The Ladies' Complaint', in Clarke, Desmond M. (ed. and trans.). *The Equality of the Sexes: Three Feminist Texts of the Seventeenth Century.* Oxford University Press, 2013.

Lerner, Gerda. *The Majority Finds its Past: Placing Women in History.* UNC Press Books, 2005.

MacLachlan, Bonnie. *Women in Ancient Rome: A Sourcebook.* Vol. 19. A&C Black, 2013.

Malitz, Jurgen. *Nero.* John Wiley & Sons, 2008.

Man, John. *The Mongol Empire: Genghis Khan, his Heirs and the Founding of Modern China.* Random House, 2014.

Mernissi, Fatema. *The Veil and the Male Elite: A Feminist Interpretation of Women's Rights in Islam.* Basic Books, 1991.

Mishra, Pankaj. *From the Ruins of Empire: The Revolt Against the West and the Remaking of Asia.* London, 2012.

Mortimer, Ian. *Centuries of Change: Which Century Saw the Most Change?* Random House, 2014.

Neils, Jenifer. *Women in the Ancient World.* British Museum Press, 2011.

Obeyesekere, Ranjini (ed.). *Yasodharā, the Wife of the Bōdhisattva: The Sinhala Yasodharāvata (The Story of Yasodharā) and the Sinhala Yasodharāpadānaya (The Sacred Biography of Yasodharā).* SUNY Press, 2009.

Osterhammel, Jürgen, and Shelley L. Frisch (trans.). *Colonialism: A Theoretical Overview.* Markus Weiner Publishers, 2010 (3rd edition).

Osterhammel, Jürgen, and Niels P. Petersson. *Globalization: A Short History.* Princeton University Press, 2009.

Ouředník, Patrik. *Europeana: A Brief History of the Twentieth Century.* Dalkey Archive Press, 2005.

Pelt, Lori van. *Amelia Earhart: The Sky's No Limit.* Macmillan, 2006.

Rayor, Diane J. (ed. and trans.), and André Lardinois (Introduction). *Sappho: A New Translation of the Complete Works.* Cambridge University Press, 2014.

Roberts, John Morris, and Odd Arne Westad. *The Penguin History of the World.* Penguin, 2013.

Schäfer, Peter. *Mirror of his Beauty: Feminine Images of God from the Bible to the Early Kabbalah.* Princeton University Press, 2004.

Schivelbusch, Wolfgang. *Tastes of Paradise: A Social History of Spices, Stimulants, and Intoxicants.* Vintage Books, 1992.

Scholz, Piotr O. *Ancient Egypt: An Illustrated Historical Overview.* Barron's Educational Series, 1997.

Standage, Tom. *A History of the World in 6 Glasses.* Bloomsbury Publishing, 2006.

Swerdlow, Amy. *Women Strike for Peace: Traditional Motherhood and Radical Politics in the 1960s.* University of Chicago Press, 1993.

Turner, Denice. *Writing the Heavenly Frontier: Metaphor, Geography, and Flight Autobiography in America 1927–1954.* Rodopi, 2011

Turner, Ralph V. *Eleanor of Aquitaine: Queen of France, Queen of England.* Yale University Press, 2009.

Watkins, Sarah-Beth. *Catherine of Braganza: Charles II's Restoration Queen.* John Hunt Publishing, 2017.

Weatherford, Jack. *The Secret History of the Mongol Queens: How the Daughters of Genghis Khan Rescued his Empire.* Crown, 2010.

Wells, Bruce, and F. Rachel Magdalene (eds). *Law from the Tigris to the Tiber: The Writings of Raymond Westbrook. Cuneiform and Biblical Sources.* Eisenbrauns, 2009.

Wells, H.G. *A Short History of the World.* Penguin, 2006.

Windsor, Laura Lynn. *Women in Medicine: An Encyclopedia.* ABC-CLIO, 2002.

INDEX

Women are indexed in *blue*.

ABOUT THE AUTHORS, TRANSLATORS AND ILLUSTRATOR

The authors

Kerstin Lücker and Ute Daenschel studied musicology, philosophy, history, German, and Slavic studies, and met in Berlin as doctorate students. Week in, week out, they sat together, side by side, as they wrote up their PhD theses; occasionally, they swapped laptops and discovered that what they were trying to say sounded better in the other's words. That's when they had the idea of working on a book together: Ute came up with the concept of a history of the world for young female readers and, thanks to Kerstin, that concept became a reality. *A History of the World With the Women Put Back In* involved considerable research, as relatively little had been written about women in world history and, in the process of writing, the book went back and forth between the two authors, one writing and the other reviewing, until together they had woven the text of this book.

The translators

Ruth Ahmedzai Kemp and Jessica West are both freelance translators of German and Russian, with a shared love of history. Between them, the two have also studied Arabic, Norwegian, classical civilisations, Norse mythology, museum communication, environment and ecology, Enlightenment philosophy, Middle Eastern history, Slavic linguistics and modern European politics. This is the third book they have co-translated from German, the others reflecting their other shared passions of nature, crafts and writing for children. As with Kerstin and Ute's writing process, the translation process involved the manuscript going back and forth between them, as the two translators revised and reviewed each other's work.

The illustrator

Natsko Seki studied illustration at the University of Brighton and now lives and works in London. She draws inspiration from architecture and people from different ages and cultures to create vibrant illustrations that are worked up digitally from layers of sketches, research materials and textures. She has illustrated *Travel Book London* (Louis Vuitton, 2013) and *Architecture According to Pigeons* (Phaidon Press, 2013), and is the author of *Let's Go on the London Bus* (Fukuinkan Shoten Publishers Inc., 2017). Natsko's portfolio can be seen at www.natsko.com.

More inspiring books for women and girls

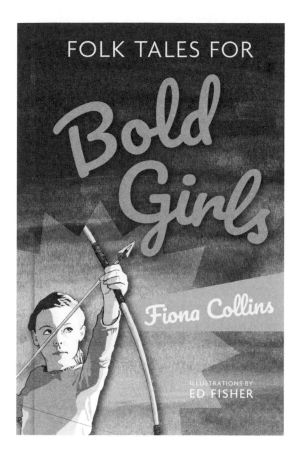

FOLK TALES FOR

Bold Girls

Fiona Collins

ILLUSTRATIONS BY
ED FISHER

9780750990493   £9.99

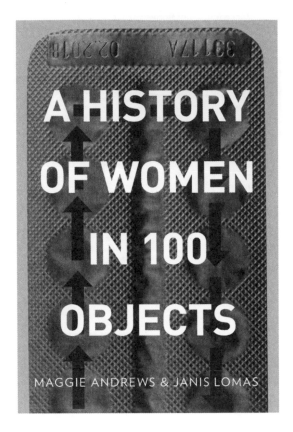

A HISTORY OF WOMEN IN 100 OBJECTS

MAGGIE ANDREWS & JANIS LOMAS

9780750967143 £20.00

The History Press

The destination for history
www.thehistorypress.co.uk